Publications of the Milman Parry Collection
of Oral Literature No. 3

OLD NORSE MYTHOLOGY —
COMPARATIVE PERSPECTIVES

OLD NORSE MYTHOLOGY—
COMPARATIVE PERSPECTIVES

Edited by Pernille Hermann,
Stephen A. Mitchell, and Jens Peter Schjødt
with Amber J. Rose

Published by
THE MILMAN PARRY COLLECTION OF ORAL LITERATURE
Harvard University

Distributed by
HARVARD UNIVERSITY PRESS
Cambridge, Massachusetts & London, England
2017

Old Norse Mythology—Comparative Perspectives

Published by The Milman Parry Collection of Oral Literature, Harvard University
Distributed by Harvard University Press, Cambridge, Massachusetts & London, England

The Ilex Foundation (ilexfoundation.org) and the Center for Hellenic Studies
(chs.harvard.edu) provided generous financial and production support for the
publication of this book.

EDITORIAL TEAM OF THE MILMAN PARRY COLLECTION

Managing Editors: Stephen Mitchell and Gregory Nagy
Executive Editors: Casey Dué and David Elmer

PRODUCTION TEAM OF THE CENTER FOR HELLENIC STUDIES

Production Manager for Publications: Jill Curry Robbins
Web Producer: Noel Spencer
Cover Design: Joni Godlove
Production: Kristin Murphy Romano

Library of Congress Cataloging-in-Publication Data

Names: Hermann, Pernille, editor.
Title: Old Norse mythology--comparative perspectives / edited by Pernille
  Hermann, Stephen A. Mitchell, Jens Peter Schjødt, with Amber J. Rose.
Description: Cambridge, MA : Milman Parry Collection of Oral Literature,
  2017. | Series: Publications of the Milman Parry collection of oral
  literature ; no. 3 | Includes bibliographical references and index.
Identifiers: LCCN 2017030125 | ISBN 9780674975699 (alk. paper)
Subjects: LCSH: Mythology, Norse. | Scandinavia--Religion--History.
Classification: LCC BL860 .O55 2017 | DDC 293/.13--dc23
LC record available at https://lccn.loc.gov/2017030125

Table of Contents

Table of Contents

Part Three. GLOBAL TRADITIONS

Series Foreword

As he planned his famous study of the living tradition of oral epic singing in the Balkans in the 1930s, the prominent Harvard Classicist, Milman Parry, signaled the significance that the Old Norse field held in his mind when he noted that the results of his investigations would be of importance, not only for the study of Greek and South Slavic epic, but also for such early poetries as Anglo-Saxon, French, and Norse.[1] Thus, key to Parry's approach to the study of Homeric Greek tradition—as both that comment and, of course, the entirety of his Yugoslavian fieldwork indicate—was comparativism, or as he knew it, the *méthode comparative*.[2] That the present collection of essays specifically focusing on Old Norse mythology in a comparative perspective should appear in a publication series of the Milman Parry Collection of Oral Literature might then be deemed especially appropriate.

Furthermore, Harvard's engagement with the study of Scandinavian history, culture, and literature has deep roots, a fact one can infer from its acquisition on January 14, 1766, soon after the destructive fire of the college library in 1764, of *A Compendious History of the Goths, Svvedes & Vandals, and Other Northern Nations*, the 1658 English translation of Olaus Magnus' 1555 ethnography of the Nordic world. And Harvard was one of the first, if not the first, institution in the New World to offer instruction in Old Norse—it is said that Henry Wadsworth Longfellow taught it in University Hall shortly after his 1835–1836 stay in Copenhagen and Stockholm. Of her visit to the Harvard College library in December of 1849, the famous Swedish writer, and feminist activist, Fredrika Bremer commented,

> I one day lately visited the several buildings of the university and the library. In the latter I was surprised to find one portion of the Swedish literature not badly represented here. This is owing to the

---

[1] See the complete text in Stephen A. Mitchell and Gregory Nagy, "Introduction to the Second Edition," in Albert B. Lord, *The Singer of Tales*, 2nd ed. Harvard Studies in Comparative Literature, 24. Cambridge, MA, 2000, p. ix. On the relevance of Parry's prediction for Old Norse studies, see, for example, the essay by Hermann in the current volume.

[2] Cf. Mitchell and Nagy, "Introduction to the Second Edition," xvii–xviii.

poet, Professor Longfellow, who having himself traveled in Sweden, sent hither these books. He has also written about Sweden, and has translated several of Tegnér's poems. I found also the Eddas among the Swedish books.

To which she adds—wryly and much bemused by the intensity of the young men's interest, one senses—speaking about her childhood friend and visiting legal scholar, Professor Pehr Bergfalk,

> Bergfalk laid his hands on the Westgötha laws, which he treated as an old friend, and in which he showed some of the gentlemen who accompanied us an example of that alliteration which was so much in vogue in the writings of our forefathers, and about which the gentlemen found much to say.[3]

A half-century later, massively supplementing Harvard's growing Nordic collection, the perspicacious acquisition of the personal library of the German scholar, Konrad von Maurer, took place, a purchase that brought some 10,000 titles to the library, as well as, to paraphrase the bill of lading, a trunkful of Icelandic manuscripts.[4] The university's continuing commitment to Scandinavian as a vital area of humanities research has not wavered greatly over the decades; indeed, the essays in the current volume, *Comparative Perspectives on Old Norse Mythology*, are an indication of this ongoing dedication, as most of them were presented at the Aarhus Old Norse Mythology Conference held at Harvard University in the autumn of 2013.

—David Elmer, Casey Dué, Gregory Nagy
and Stephen Mitchell

---

[3] Fredrika Bremer, *The Homes of the New World: Impressions of America.* Transl. by Mary Howitt of *Hemmen i den Nya verlden.* New York: 1853. I: 134.

[4] Some of these manuscripts formed part of the exhibit of Icelandic manuscripts at Harvard's Houghton Library, curated by Jóhanna Katrín Friðriksdóttir, Marie Curie Research Fellow at Harvard University and The Árni Magnússon Institute for Icelandic Studies, Reykjavík, held in conjunction with the conference, Old Norse Mythology—Comparative Perspectives, in 2013.

Foreword

Joseph Harris
Harvard University

INTEREST IN THE INDIVIDUAL MYTHS and the mythic systems of the pre-Christian North has traveled a varied way through highs and lows since the seventeenth century. The twenty-first continues a period of intense scholarly interest since, perhaps, the 1960s and in this volume renews and modernizes the comparative (and reconstructive) view that has been one of the main approaches for many decades. In fact, although the volume has nothing of the textbook about it, its fifteen particular studies of very high intellectual and scholarly quality, along with its usefully contextualizing introductions, embody and illuminate practically all the possibilities for comparative approaches. In Folklore 101 our students learn a framework for explaining cultural similarities generally as "descent, diffusion, and polygenesis". And there the topic ends in 101. This volume foregoes any such simple schema while potentially teaching subtle variations, combinations, and mediating forms of this very fundamental meme. Even as each scholar pursues his or her specific interests beyond theories of comparison and reconstruction, the meme remains a subtext well below the direct attention of most of the contributors.

The bookends of the volume, the volume's first and last two contributions, are constituted by essays that elevate typology, on the one hand, and the genetic (specifically, descent), on the other, to prime importance. Jens Peter Schjødt argues for the application of comparison between appropriately analogous but unrelated mythologies through a specific idea of the "model", a relatively complete mental map derived from one reality and hypothetically applied to the fragments of another to be reconstructed. He does not need to use the textbook term *polygenesis*, but the native Hawaiian mythology on which his model is based does share with Old Norse certain social facts, its relationship to Scandinavia being purely "typological". Schjødt's is the volume's most explicit in respect to theories of comparative mythology, including comments on the other bookend, the essay by Michael Witzel and on genetic comparison in general. But one might take up genetic comparison and its result in reconstruction less controversially with the volume's penultimate essay by Emily Lyle, who works here within the traditional framework of the Indo-European community, as represented by Iranian myth, but employs a model in a manner similar to Schjødt. And just as Schjødt is able to fill in some spaces between fragments of our knowledge of Odin, so Lyle—operating on one of the most fascinating myths in Old Norse, that of Baldr—is able virtually to augment that individual myth's relation to a whole. Witzel's comparativism in this essay is less explicitly concerned with theory and method, having previously written comprehensively in that vein. What makes his procedure startlingly new and controversial is his expansion of the historical field for comparison; it now stretches vastly farther into the human past than the Indo-European and presupposes genetic relations and evidences of population movements only recently introduced to historical studies.

Diffusion is most directly represented—and problematized—in Tom DuBois's "areal" study of conceptions of the sun in the Finnic and Baltic mythologies in comparison with Nordic, plotting the varied solar myths from the Sámi in the North right through the Lativian *dainas* in the South and examining the resulting pattern. DuBois does not directly invoke the "hard" concepts of the older historical-geographic school, but his analysis gives us evidence of the intercultural relations within the areal scheme. Incidentally, his analysis reminds us indirectly and without jargon that cultural patterns seeming to imply vague impersonal forces (the "superorganic") have to be complemented by focused and purposive diffusion in the form of "borrowing". The volume includes a second valuable study of Finnish and Old Norse myth, John Lindow's survey of many similarities between Nordic and Finnish mythologies; he tends to be skeptical of specific loans, even while giving a good account of the relevant cultural relations and making use of the model idea. Diffusion as specific borrowings comes into other papers as well. Joseph Nagy analyses a Nordic form of a strange tale with a history, presumably oral, extending back through Irish and Iranian. Contemporary, i.e., thirteenth-century, influences on Snorri's mythology from European learning, especially about the Jews, is Richard Cole's subject; Jonas Wellendorf shows, among other things, learned influences on conceptions of idols and other representations; and Mattias Nordvig posits influences from nature (in the specifically Icelandic form of volcanic eruptions) on the preserved cosmological passages and, reciprocally, mythic influence on the language used for such eruptions. Stephen Mitchell, Harvard's resident thaumaturge of this collection, gives a comprehensive survey of the background of Odin's communication with the dead, including possible source-representing analogues from the learned South.

While comparison and reconstruction in the senses just adumbrated do constitute themes through much of the volume, a core of excellent articles draw their comparisons more traditionally between segments of the greater field. The archeologist Torun Zachrisson and the history-of-religions scholar Olof Sundqvist, in their different ways, draw together evidence from both archeology and texts, two too often estranged disciplines. On the occasion of a striking new figural find from Southwest Sweden, Zachrisson gives an exhaustive account of Völund the Smith, especially in art and artifact. Sundqvist discusses the historical and archeological evidence for "the tree, the well, and the temple" at Uppsala, according to Adam of Bremen; but his article also has a strong theoretical component (favoring Eliade) and a valuable method that requires a broad survey of similar symbol-laden landscapes and of archival evidence. These two essays will be of great value to the mainly philological/literary readers of the volume. A voice from that literary side, that of Kate Heslop, also and very adroitly works with art-historical concepts around the "frame" in epigraphic and artistic contexts in comparison with eddic poetry. Heslop's essay will be seized upon by literary critics as theoretically rich and suggestive. Heslop and most of these contributors, when they deal with verbal art and content, assume oral contexts, but two papers deal principally with this vital theme of orality and literacy. Pernille Hermann's chapter embodies the more theoretical discussion, excellent of its kind; and Terry Gunnell applies oral tradition practically in a wide-ranging survey and defense of the Vanir gods.

At one point Lindow compares with Snorri's age the relatively sophisticated and thorough Finnish collecting of oral tradition in the nineteenth century; thousands of notebooks of the latter are neatly arranged in archives while loss of a few (more) medieval manuscripts would have left us with precious little knowledge of Nordic mythology. One point is the vastness of oral tradition vs. the limits of technology: the oral is fleeting by nature, and medieval writing gave only a fragile permanence to its accidental preservations. Another might be the reconstructive nature of any knowledge of fragmentary myths and their systems and the value of the comparative method in that enterprise. This book assembles an impressive and variegated team of senior and younger scholars with wide international distribution. Their contributions will be admired and built upon as an important phase in the evolving field.

Preface
Situating Old Norse Mythology in Comparative Contexts

Pernille Hermann, Stephen Mitchell, and Jens Peter Schjødt

THE ESSAYS IN THIS VOLUME are centrally concerned with an all-too-apparent reality about the study of pagan religions in Europe, namely, that the study of any mythology, especially archaic and only haphazardly recorded mythologies, requires careful assessment of sources and the attempt to reconstruct the "system" which is understood to be at its heart. For the mythology of pre-Christian Scandinavia, this perspective has long been understood to be not only highly desirable but also, importantly, highly available, more so than for many other European pagan traditions, mainly due to the substantial corpus of extraordinary texts from the Icelandic Middle Ages, above all, its *eddas*, sagas and skaldic poetry.

That we are in this fortunate situation has naturally had an overwhelmingly salubrious effect on the study of the pre-Christian era in Northern Europe. Yet at the same time, the study of Old Norse mythology has also, paradoxically, been in a position to pursue its materials in "splendid isolation", to poach George Foster's elegant political locution, to a greater degree than have many other comparable traditions despite some notable exceptions to this trend.[1] In partial response to this situation, the essays in this collection look to address the issue of Old Norse mythology as an area of inquiry that can benefit substantially from comparative scholarly inquiry, comparativisms of different sorts, that is, comparative with respect to theories as well as to tradition areas.

---

[1] Works like Georges Dumézil's 1959 *Les Dieux des Germains. Essai sur la formation de la religion scandinave* and Matthias Egeler's recent *Walküren, Bodbs, Sirenen. Gedanken zur religionsgeschichtlichen Anbindung Nordwesteuropas an den mediterranen Raum* are more exceptions than the rule in the field.

Comparativism and Old Norse Mythology

Comparativism has played a changeable role within the study of Old Norse mythology. Not surprisingly, the changes have largely followed the overall tendencies within the Humanities. Thus, in the History of Religions in the first part of the nineteenth century, the so-called nature-myth school flourished, in which the idea was that in order to understand mythology as such, one should compare mythologies from all over the world. The romanticism of the nature-myth school was towards the end of the century replaced by different theories based on evolutionism which were by necessity still moving within a comparative paradigm. In the beginning of the twentieth century, this view changed, and particularism became the ruling paradigm, with the idea that each individual culture is unique and can only be grasped as a universe of its own.

Although many of the results concerning the "essence" of mythology, as proposed by the older generation of comparativists, are not accepted today, the very idea that in order to understand a certain phenomenon, we should compare various expressions of this phenomenon at different times and places, seems quite rational. This procedure, however, involves a significant number of problems, perhaps the most conspicuous one being the very identification of similar phenomena within different cultures, and thus decisions involving categorization and classification. So, for instance, one is faced with questions as fundamental as "what is a myth"? Is the story of Adam and Eve in Genesis to be categorized together with the story of Þórr fishing for the World Serpent in *Gylfaginning*? And if so, what is it that bind these two narratives together, i.e., what do they have in common? No matter what answers are suggested, it must be clear that there are huge differences between them—in content, in transmission, in style, in the attitudes towards the narratives from contemporary audiences, and so on.

A similarly difficult issue arises regarding the relation between "similarities" and "differences" when a comparative method is applied. "Anti-comparativists" have often maintained that in applying this method, only the similarities are focused upon, whereas there may be huge differences, too, between the cultures being analyzed. Although it is very often true that the similarities are the focus of comparative analyses, it is, however, not the rule that the differences are rejected or denied. Mostly, this focus is due to the questions raised: what is similar between religion X and religion Y, or, conversely what is different between religion X and religion Y? Both types of questions are, of course, perfectly legitimate, but they require different perspectives and analyses.

These problems, and many more that have to do with comparativism, have been discussed at great length by scholars in the Study of Religion, taking into consideration most of the theoretical issues involved. A similar debate, however, does not seem to be the case within the study of pre-Christian religions of the North. The early proponents of the comparative method, exemplified by Jacob Grimm (1835) and Wilhelm Mannhardt (1858), were influenced by the romanticism of their day, and source criticism, as we know it today, had not really begun.

A debate of this sort within early Northern European studies happened towards the end of the nineteenth century, when the main opponent of comparativism within the study of Old Norse mythology was the Norwegian Sophus Bugge, especially in his *Studier over de nordiske Gude-og Heltesagns Oprindelse* (1881–1889). Bugge had an immense impact on the scholarship within the field for a very long time. The idea was—and is—that almost all our sources for Old Norse mythology are subject to Christian influence in one way or another. The opposite view—i.e., maintaining that the content and structures in Snorri's *Edda*, for instance, should be seen as anything truly pagan because of "superficial" similarities with indigenous or Indo-European mythologies—was rejected as pure romanticism and fantasy, and, in any event, not a "scientific" perspective. This position was the dominant one up to the 1950s or 60s, and has continued to play an important role to the present.

The "re-emergence" of comparative studies in scholarship on Old Norse mythology was mainly due to the analyses carried out by the great French linguist and historian of religion, Georges Dumézil (e.g., 1959). His idea that there were certain structural parallels between the various Indo-European mythologies, including that of Scandinavia, soon became rather popular among many students of religion, such as Jan de Vries (1955–1956) and E.O. Gabriel Turville-Petre (e.g., 1964), to mention only the most important. But many were very hesitant and just as many were very critical towards Dumézil, such as Folke Ström (e.g., 1961), Ray I. Page (1978-79) and a number of others. And one of the main criticisms was the very use of comparisons to reconstruct a pre-Christian mythology from the sources that are transmitted to us, reflecting specifically for Old Norse the ongoing discussions between advocates of comparativism and particularism in many of the human sciences.

Since the 1960s, however, this picture has been somewhat blurred, and it is far more difficult to pinpoint the various positions. Many scholars have accepted that there is a need for comparative perspectives in attempting to reconstruct the mythology of pre-Christian Scandinavia, combined, of course with traditional source criticism. The basic need for analogies when we try to create the lines of an entire mythology from scattered evidence in the sources—especially with all the source critical problems we face in applying the information we get from the medieval sources, such as Snorri's works—is the main reason. Just as analogies have been used by archaeologists in placing individual finds correctly within the culture in question, there appears to be a growing awareness that without using analogies from other mythologies (mythologies from cultures where we are often better informed than is the case with pre-Christian Scandinavia), we would be equally incapable of correctly placing the individual pieces of information in the written sources into their correct positions. Even if there is still a debate between the historical source critics and those scholars who are more inclined to bring in anthropological parallels, the hard lines of this opposition have "softened" during the last three or four decades.

"Comparison" should, however, also be viewed in a broader perspective. First and foremost it is obvious that even within the Old Norse area itself there were differences in the religious and mythical worldviews. That means that myths told in one part of Scandinavia were not necessarily told in the same way in other parts, and thus even comparing two versions of a myth would constitute a comparative enterprise. Secondly, comparing various written versions of a myth with what may have constituted oral versions, or myths related in different literary genres or in different media should also be seen as comparative analyses. In this sense, the articles in this book are all working with different aspects of "comparativism", some of which are not traditionally seen as such.

Accordingly, this collection is divided into several sections, organized by the individual essay's distinguishing comparative feature, although these categorizations are far from absolute: there are articles that deal more or less exclusively with theoretical problems, such as the significance of the oral character of the sources, the problems with analogies, and so on, here gathered together under the label, *Theoretical and Conceptual Comparisons*. A different category of essays are those that are more concerned with specific texts and other empirical data, a category we have here divided into sub-groups, one of which is concerned with mainly "local" comparisons to cultures located geographically close to the Scandinavians, or even within the Scandinavian area itself, where such problems as "loans", parallel developments, common "proto types", and so on are discussed, what we have here labeled, *Local and Neighboring Traditions*. And then there are additional examples of comparisons going far beyond the immediate neighbors of Scandinavia, occasionally expanding well beyond them, what we here for the sake of convenience label *Global Traditions*.

Of course, no collection of essays, however diverse in their disciplinary orientations and however discursive in their treatments, could ever capture the full range of comparisons modern scholars would regard as necessary to locate Old Norse mythology properly within the study of archaic belief systems, but our hope is that these essays collectively move us closer to that goal, and individually suggest what is to be gained by such an approach.

Works Cited

Bugge, Sophus. 1881–89. *Studier over de nordiske Gude- og Heltesagns Oprindelse.* Christiania.

Dumézil, Georges. 1959. *Les dieux des Germains. Essai sur la formation de la religion scandinave.* Mythes et religions, 39. Paris.

Egeler, Matthias. 2011. *Walküren, Bodbs, Sirenen. Gedanken zur religionsgeschichtlichen Anbindung Nordwesteuropas an den mediterranen Raum.* Ergänzungsbände zum Reallexikon der germanischen Altertumskunde, 71. Berlin & New York.

Grimm, Jacob. 1835. *Deutsche Mythologie.* Göttingen.

Mannhardt, Wilhelm. 1858. *Germanische Mythen. Forschungen.* Berlin.

Page, Raymond I. 1978-79. "Dumézil Revisited." *Saga-Book of the Viking Society* 20: 49-69.

Ström, Folke. 1961. *Nordisk hedendom. Tro och sed I förkristen tid.* Lund.

Turville-Petre, E.O. Gabriel. 1964. *Myth and Religion of the North: The Religion of Ancient Scandinavia.* History of Religion. London.

Vries, Jan de. 1956–1957. *Altgermanische Religionsgeschichte.* 2nd rev. ed. Grundriss der germanischen. Philologie, 12. Berlin.

Acknowledgements

Publication of this volume was made possible by the generous support of the Center for Hellenic Studies, Harvard University, and the Ilex Foundation. The essays in this volume largely derive from presentations at the Aarhus Old Norse Mythology Conference held at Harvard University, 30 October–1 November 2013. The funding for the conference itself was provided by The Royal Gustav Adolf Academy, Uppsala; The Provostial Fund at Harvard University; and the programs in Folklore and Mythology; Germanic Languages and Literatures; Medieval Studies; and the Study of Religion at Harvard University. Many individuals played key roles in bringing this volume to fruition: we especially thank Gregory Nagy, Jill Curry Robbins, and several senior Old Norse scholars who willingly served as peer reviewers.

PART ONE

THEORETICAL AND CONCEPTUAL
COMPARISONS

Pre-Christian Religions of the North and the Need For Comparativism
Reflections on Why, How, and with What We Can Compare

Jens Peter Schjødt
Aarhus University

Abstract: This article is concerned with some of the problems we have in attempting to reconstruct the pre-Christian religion of the North from extant sources which are for the most part much later than the beliefs and practices they describe. This situation, it is argued, necessitates the use of comparative material of various kinds. In discussing various theoretical considerations, the essay argues that models based on comparative evidence are always part of historical reconstructions and may even prove more important than traditional source criticism, but also that different kinds of comparative material create different kinds of models. Finally the paper argues that even material from cultures which are completely unrelated, historically, to the pre-Christian religion of the North may be of great value when it comes to formulating relevant questions about the Old Norse material.

Introduction

The aim of the following article is to discuss some of the problems involved in attempting to reconstruct the pre-Christian religion of the North. As will be argued in a moment, using comparisons, and thus a comparative method, is unavoidable in these attempts, and the emphasis, therefore, will be on the questions indicated in the title, namely: why is it necessary to compare; are there certain "rules" to observe when we compare if we are going to do so in a scholarly acceptable way; and are there some cultures or cultural phenomena with which it makes more sense to compare than others?

Before dealing with these questions, however, it will be necessary to make a distinction between two types of comparativism, a distinction which may have a heuristic value for the questions just raised, as they cannot be used in the same way or for the same purposes. These two comparativisms may be labeled "typological" and "genetic", the first category comparing cultures and religions which are not historically related—which have no political, economic, or linguistic relationship. The second category, on the other hand, compares cultures and cultural products that in some way *are* historically related at one of these levels, such as, for instance, the Scandinavians on the one hand and the Sámi, other Germanic peoples, or Indo-Europeans on the other. I have dealt with these issues in several recent articles (Schjødt 2012a, 2013, and forthcoming), and discussed (particularly in Schjødt forthcoming) some of the problems in using the second category of comparisons, arguing that such comparisons are of importance for the way we usually reconstruct Old Norse religion. In the following, I will in contrast deal primarily with the first category—the "typological" comparisons, i.e. the similarities not based on cultural historical relations. To make things more complicated, however, the distinctions between these two categories of comparisons are not necessarily absolute. What is thought by some to be typological may in fact turn out to be genetic. A good example of this can be seen in the so-called Laurasian mythologies recently analyzed by Michael Witzel. The term "Laurasian" designates, roughly, the mythologies of the northern hemisphere, the similarities of which, according to Witzel, are genetic, whereas the traditional view would clearly be that similarities between, say, Scandinavian and Chinese mythologies should be classified as typological (Witzel 2012).[1]

Typological comparisons have always played an important role within the history of religions. The founding father of the discipline, Friedrich Max Müller, pronounced in his famous statement back in 1873 that "he who knows one, knows none" (Müller 1873: 16), which, at least from a certain perspective, seems undoubtedly true: we would not even be able to recognize the very phenomenon of religion as a universal category if we knew only one religion. This is so because, as was pointed out by another of the great comparativists, Mircea Eliade, religion always manifests itself in a certain cultural form: religions are

---

[1] This raises the question of how far back in time it makes sense to distinguish between genetic and typological comparisons. It could be argued that all humans, and thus all human cultures, are fundamentally related; therefore all cultural similarities are due to genetic relations and comparisons between them would then be classified as genetic. On the other hand, if a kind of "common" culture existed 100,000 years ago, and two human groups have developed in different directions since then, one would need to consider whether certain similarities should rather be attributed to other factors, such as common societal structures, common brain structures, etc., and therefore should be studied with a typological comparative method.

different from each other because cultures are different from each other, but behind all the differences lies some common religious "essence" (e.g. Eliade 1969: 8–9). Eliade famously used this idea to reconstruct the "essence" of religion, with all the notions that are so well-known nowadays: "hierophany", the myth of eternal return, the sacred as the only true mode of existence, and so on. Eliade has been heavily criticized for his "quasi-religious" agenda, rightly so in my opinion, as often in his work there appears to be a total lack of methodological awareness in the way he carries out his comparisons. In this respect, Eliade may remind us strongly of a third of the great comparativists of the past, namely Sir James George Frazer. Of course, Frazer's and Eliade's projects were quite different. The idea, however, that religious phenomena that bear the slightest similarity, even when drawn from different cultures, should be seen as related to some sort of common "archetype"—although the notion was not explicitly expressed by Frazer—is to some extent implied throughout the latter's *The Golden Bough*, with its pivotal theme of the death and resurrection of the king. Having said this, however, I believe that we must also acknowledge that most religions, in some ways, *do* look alike. There are, beneath the surface, definitely similar elements that constitute prerequisites for recognizing religion as such in the first place. The reason for this being so is far beyond the scope of this essay, and concerns the reasons for the very origin of religion; and theories on this topic cannot be created through historical studies, but must occur in the context of psychological, cognitive, or sociological research.

Comparativism was long abandoned by the ruling elite of the history of religions and anthropology (Segal 2001), a point to which I will return; but, to put it briefly, there were several reasons for such a development, some of them having to do with the way comparativism was performed, others with its basis in the evolutionism of the second half of the nineteenth century and the beginning of the twentieth (see Kuper 1988). An additional factor derives from structural-functionalist views of how religions should be studied, namely as more or less closed universes in which all elements are parts of an "organism" that constitutes society. These issues will be dealt with briefly in the following.

Why?

In order to understand why it is particularly important to use a comparative method in order to reconstruct pre-Christian Scandinavian religion, we must examine some of the problems involved in such reconstructions, in relation to the source situation.

Although this situation will be known by everybody who has dealt with pre-Christian religion, it is nevertheless necessary to draw, however briefly, the main lines of the situation: on the one hand, we have sources that are what we may call "indigenous", that is, they are relics of the people who actually lived their lives within this pre-Christian world view.[2] These sources are of both an archaeological and a literary nature, although the second category is not very well represented, and consists mainly of some poems composed by "skalds" who would typically perform them with the purpose of praising a chieftain or king. The poems are often hard to interpret, but they frequently hint at various myths, and thus give us glimpses of the pre-Christian mythic world. The problems with interpreting the archaeological sources are not the same, but the individual artifact or site is just as difficult to put in the right place within the religious discourse (cf. Schjødt 2013).

On the other hand, we have those sources which we may term "foreign", although this term ought to be qualified. What is meant is that they are written by people who belong to another culture, whether geographically or historically, than that of the pre-Christian Scandinavians. Within this group it would be helpful to further divide the sources into two categories, namely the Nordic (mostly Icelandic) sources, on the one hand, and those written by people from abroad, mostly European Christians and Muslims, on the other. It may seem odd to classify Scandinavian sources as foreign, but in some sense, at least, they are, because their authors were medieval Christians, and thus foreign to the pagan religion they described. The main reason, however, for qualifying the term is that, even if these writers were formally Christian, their world view was at the same time doubtless heavily influenced by the pagan worldview of their ancestors, which has been shown to be the case by many scholars in history and folklore over the last two centuries.[3]

Put this way, scholarship faces a host of problems: on the one hand, we have a group of sources that are reliable but very hard to interpret with any certainty; besides, although the amount of archaeological source material is extremely high—and is growing very fast—the number of "indigenous" written sources is limited to not very many poems and a few relevant runic inscriptions. On the other hand, the foreign sources, whether we speak of the Scandinavian or the European, are, from a traditional source-critical perspective, doubtful in

---

[2]   There is another problem here, which, for reasons of space, cannot be dealt with in any exhaustive way: namely the distinction between "different" religions. What is aimed at here is the very notion of "pre-Christian Scandinavian religion" ("Old Norse religion", "the pre-Christian religion of the North", or whichever designation is preferred): are we dealing with one religion, or with several, more or less similar worldviews? The question is of great importance, but is not the focus of this article (cf. DuBois 1999; Schjødt 2009, and many other recent works).

[3]   The literature on the source situation is immense, and good accounts on various types of sources can be read in, for instance, Beck, Ellmers, and Schier 1992 and Clover and Lindow 1985; a brief but excellent overview is given by Margaret Clunies Ross (1994: 20–33).

many ways: they are often characterized by negative prejudice, both because of religious matters, but also because the Scandinavians were seen as enemies in most of Europe during the Viking Age, and just as the Scandinavians were seen as barbarians, so too were their gods and their cults. Among the Christian Scandinavians themselves, things are a bit more complicated, since, as mentioned, large parts of their pagan worldview continued to play a role in their daily lives. And besides, particularly in Iceland in the Middle Ages, much of the national identity was dependent on the period of settlement in the ninth and tenth centuries by their pagan predecessors, which is probably the reason why so much information about the pagan religion comes from this island in the North Atlantic. Regardless, by far the largest part of the information related in the sources is written by "foreigners", that is, by people who only knew the pagan tradition as something which was more or less in opposition to their own religion. And even if these, mostly Christian, authors did relate a good deal of information about various aspects of the pagan religion, we still have a lot of blind spots: thus we are pretty well informed about mythological matters, but know rather little about the ritual parts of the religion. This is not surprising, since other peoples' myths may take the shape of folktales, pseudohistory, or pure entertainment, while pagan rituals, at least in so far as they are recognized as such, cannot be performed among people who see themselves as Christians.

For these reasons our knowledge about pagan Scandinavian religion is far from exhaustive. What we have consists of bits and pieces that only constitute "the tips of the religious icebergs" (cf. Clunies Ross 1994: 25). In order to understand how these bits and pieces should be put together as a religious worldview, we therefore need to reconstruct the connecting lines between them, from sources which are not part of the pre-Christian religion itself. It is here that the comparative method finds its *raison d'être* in the specific context of this religion (and probably in all other religions that no longer exist), for without comparisons, we would not be able to create the models necessary in order to make sense of the various pieces of the information in the sources; without comparisons, this information would remain chaotic. "Model" should be understood here as a cognitive tool that can be characterized as a filter through which we perceive the world around us; thus all humans, scholars and religious people alike, in the course of their struggles with reality, use models that are often unconscious, in the same way as, for example, grammar is to native speakers of a given language. Such models are therefore part of the worldview of each individual.

Scholarly or scientific models, however, are both similar to, and different from, ordinary models. They are similar to the degree that whenever we approach a subject field, we necessarily see it through lenses that frame the way we can deal with a certain phenomenon at all, and these are surely time bound. To take a banal example, in explaining historical events, a modern historian would never recur to the intervention of God, which was, however, exactly how many medieval historians explained the events. One readily recalls, for instance, the Venerable Bede, who understood the Christianization process in England as one long line of divine intervention. In more recent times there seems to have been a shift away from viewing history as a process driven by the will of outstanding individuals to seeing it against the background of social and economic mechanisms. Yet scholarly models are also different in the sense that they are (or ought to be) based on reflective, critical, and rational thinking, meaning that they are construed in order to explain or understand certain aspects of reality in accordance with everything else we know about reality. As such, they have to be coherent, which is certainly not the case with many religious models. What is more, scientific models are always based on comparative thinking, such as, for instance, general social or economic models.

Therefore, as regards the study of religion, the applicable models will be generated partly from comparative religion itself, and partly from other branches within the human and social sciences, and even from the natural sciences. We do have expectations—even before we look at a certain culture— about what we will find in that culture, an issue that has been dealt with by, among others, the representatives of hermeneutics. In addition, models are, of course, closely related to classification systems, i.e., the way we organize the world around us into various categories. For instance, in order to analyze myths in a certain society we must have some sort of definition of "myth", explicit or implicit, based on comparisons between a vast number of narratives, in order to distinguish between different *kinds* of narratives. Therefore the question is not whether we should include comparative studies in our work, but rather for which reasons, and how it should be done.[4] For reasons of space, I cannot go into the use of "analogy"—which has been practiced within archaeology for a very long time—but essentially the problems and benefits of analogy correspond closely to those that are mentioned here in relation to comparisons.

It must be stated that models are, of course, man-made. The quality, therefore, is to a great extent dependent on the modeler's individual skills in relation to his or her purposes. These skills include his or her ability to perceive the important aspects of that part of the historical reality which it is the goal

---

[4] Benson Saler wrote back in 2001 that "Comparison is vital in certain of the activities of mind-brain. We regularly monitor the world and in doing so we creatively and selectively compare newly encountered phenomena to establish representational structures. Comparative processes are thus of crucial importance in cognition" (Saler 2001: 268), an assessment with which I fully agree (cf. also Lawson 2000 about universals in religious cognitive systems).

to reconstruct. From the outset there exist no such things as "right models" or "wrong models". Models are made in order to, on the one hand, make sense of, and thus to classify, the individual elements within a reality which would otherwise seem chaotic; and, on the other hand, when it comes to scientific models, to explain and interpret a chosen part of reality in accordance with our knowledge about the rest of reality. The quality of the model, then, depends on its usefulness for our purpose—in this case, the reconstruction of pre-Christian Scandinavian religion.

We may construe our models from various levels of comparisons. As was done by, for instance, Eliade, we can thus take into consideration religions from all over the world, in order to propose a general model for the "essence" of religion as a universal phenomenon. Notwithstanding some of the problems mentioned earlier, such a project may be quite legitimate. Likewise, in order to argue for some general mechanisms in the relationship between religion and society, we may take all manner of sociological theories and models into consideration; however, when it comes to the reconstruction of a certain historical religion from evidence which does not allow us to draw the whole picture of such a religion (partly because the sources do not tell us everything and partly because their reliability is often rather problematic) there are certain rules we ought to stick to in order to use comparisons in a reasonable way, a point to which I shall return in a moment.

Apart from helping us in creating models, however, comparisons may also assist us in posing relevant questions of the material.[5] I shall not deal with this in any detail here, but the switch of paradigms in scientific and scholarly discourse, theorized by Thomas Kuhn (Kuhn 1970) more than half a century ago, is probably at least as dependent on the questions posed by the scholars as on the answers they propose. The kind of questions that can meaningfully be posed within a certain scholarly field, *in casu* Old Norse religion, depend on many things, one of them being the source material and the content of the sources. It would not, for example, make much sense to ask questions about the psychological condition of the individual during ritual performances because this perspective is simply not related by the sources. More important than the sources, however, is the "climate" of the period in which the questions are asked: in order for us to address the changes that take place in the world around us, we need to pose new questions relating to the past concerning problems which may not have been seen as problems before.

---

[5] Good reasons for carrying our comparative studies in both general history and the history of religions have been discussed by Marcel Detienne (2008).

An example of such a paradigm shift would be the one that took place in the beginning of the twentieth century in the fields of anthropology and the history of religions, from evolutionism to functionalism.[6] In that situation, a whole new set of questions concerning social formation and religion were posed. In this process, therefore, there can be no doubt that comparisons in general play a large role: by being aware of certain problems, empirical as well as theoretical, in fields other than our own, we may become aware that these problems are actually relevant to our own field, too. Accordingly, questions that have never been thought of earlier may suddenly seem relevant.

How?

Comparativism, as noted in the introduction, is very old within the study of religion, although it played a less prominent role during most of the twentieth century than had previously been the case, and that I believe it will play again in the twenty-first century. Functionalism and certain (but by no means all) schools within structuralism were very hesitant regarding comparative enterprises, with scholars such as Bronislaw Malinowski, A. R. Radcliffe-Brown, Clifford Geertz, Edmund Leach, and many others insisting that in order to understand the worldview of a certain culture, it was necessary to view the individual elements as parts of the larger whole which constituted the culture under discussion. Thus the scholar dealing with religion would have to provide what Geertz calls "thick description", i.e., take notice of everything going on in the society, as far as possible, as the details will only make sense when they are viewed as parts of the whole. If we want to understand the full meaning of some symbolic expression, we have to be aware of the position of this expression within the overall symbolic structure. That means that even if we see apparently similar elements in two different cultures, their purposes and meanings will probably be different, because their contexts are different.

This perspective is, I believe, very sensible, at least regarding the encoding of details within certain myths and rituals in individual cultures, as has been shown, for instance, in the ritual analyses of Victor Turner (1969) and the myth analyses of Claude Lévi-Strauss (for example, his famous analysis of the Asdiwal story (1976: 146–96)): in order to understand the symbolism and meaning of a particular ritual or a particular myth, we must, as far as possible, take into consideration the whole ethnographic context. This program is definitely sound, and it is true that the comparisons carried out by some of the

---

[6] Evolutionism has also certainly been making a comeback from the end of the twentieth century, although not on the same theoretical basis as classical evolutionism, and certainly not at the expense of functional or structural perspectives.

comparativists mentioned above seem to transfer meanings from one culture to another without caring too much about the particularities of the individual culture.[7] Turner and Lévi-Strauss—and also some of the functionalists mentioned above—have however shown beyond doubt, as far as I can see, that at a certain level all rituals or all myths, and even all religions, circle around identical themes, such as the oppositions between liminal vs. non-liminal, or that between nature vs. culture, and many others. Therefore, at some level, we "know" what a certain religion is about, even without having looked at any primary sources for that religion. For example, we know that all religions imply communication between "this" world and the "other" world or worlds; we know that all religions need certain religious specialists in order to mediate between these worlds; we know that rituals, among other things, create social identity; and so forth. In this way a "rough" model is already at hand, although we can hardly hope, at this level, to be able to reconstruct many details. And we can certainly not use this "rough picture" to reconstruct the characteristics of individual religions in relation to each other.

As noted, one main reason why many of the older comparative studies of religion are not accepted as valid today is that the comparisons drawn often seem superfluous: just because things "looked" the same, they may very well have had very different meanings and functions within two different religions. Let us take an example from pre-Christian Scandinavian religion: because Óðinn, on certain occasions, seems to use magical techniques which remind us strongly of those performed by the shamans in neighboring cultures, he has by some been seen as a shaman. This interpretation is, for instance, the case in Eliade's great work on shamanism in general (Eliade 1972), but also in some more recent works dealing with pre-Christian Scandinavian religion in particular (Solli 2002; Price 2002; Hedeager 2011). It is of course necessary to be able to classify various phenomena, to put them in certain boxes, so to speak, which is one of the main tasks of the discipline usually called the phenomenology of religion; and it is certainly true that magical techniques such as soul travel and the infliction of pain upon oneself can be found among many genuine shamans from the arctic and subarctic area, and we can also see these in the case of Óðinn. The question is, however, whether this suffices to classify Óðinn as a shaman. We know that the Germanic-speaking Scandinavians, living in the northern part of the Scandinavian peninsula, had relatively close contacts with the Sámi, and that Sámi "magic" was therefore widely known, even famous,

---

[7] And this issue may be the main problem with many of the comparisons carried out by Frazer and Eliade: they did not concern themselves overly much about such contexts.

among these Scandinavians.[8] It is thus *à priori* likely that certain shamanistic rites were adopted into their own practices (of the sort we might term magical).

Shamanism, however, is constituted by a complex of beliefs and practices, in which many individual components can be found among ritual specialists in all sorts of religions (e.g., ecstasy, travel to other worlds, curing abilities, etc.); the existence of certain individual traits is therefore insufficient for classifying a religion as shamanistic, or a certain type of magician as a shaman. Without going into a discussion of all the individual traits associated with Óðinn that may or may not be shamanistic,[9] I believe that everybody can agree that the totality of shamanistic features, as analyzed by, for instance, Lazlo Vajda (Vajda 1964; cf. Fleck 1971) are absent, and many of those which may be present are heavily dependent on doubtful interpretations. Others, again, are very general, and can be applied to most magicians all over the world.

Thus, on the one hand, Óðinn's "shamanistic" traits cover only part of the constituent elements of shamanism. On the other hand, traits that are *not* typical for shamanism seem to be very important characteristics of Óðinn, such as his role as divine protector of kings and war bands, the existence of which cannot be found in typical shamanistic societies. What is more, several of the so-called shamanistic traits are strongly connected to his role as guardian god of the nobility, such as the acquisition of knowledge, which exists in order to be passed on to kings, and ecstasy, which is a prerequisite for the success of his warriors (see Schjødt 2008). Another rather important difference between Óðinn and what are traditionally seen as shamans is that Óðinn is a god, whereas shamans are, by definition, human beings (although there are, of course, also shamans in myth, just as there are also ordinary human beings).

Finally, mention should also be made of the differences between the societies which are usually classified as shamanistic and that of the Germanic-speaking Scandinavians. Whereas the former are typically hunting or nomadic societies, the Scandinavians were agriculturalists; the former generally live in very widespread, small groups of people, while the Scandinavians had, since the early Roman Iron Age, lived in larger groups in villages and eventually towns. So there are, not surprisingly, both similarities and differences between the typical

---

[8] This was most likely not the case with the Scandinavians living further south, and is thus not a part of the common heritage of the pagan Scandinavians. These southern Scandinavians would, on the other hand, probably have been much more strongly influenced by phenomena in the Germanic and the Slavonic worlds.

[9] See also Lindow 2003 for the view that Óðinn's shamanistic traits as they are found in *Ynglinga saga* ch. 7, which is the *locus classicus* when it comes to Óðinn's characteristics, are essentially modeled on medieval magicians.

shaman, as normally identified and characterized in the history of religions, and Óðinn. So is the figure of the shaman "the same" as the figure of Óðinn?

Of course, "sameness" is a tricky notion, since most people, including scholars, do not reflect very much on what it actually means; however, "the same" will always include differences too, because otherwise two entities would be exact copies, identical in every respect, and copies in that sense do not exist in the world of religions. Thus, when we do use the notion of "sameness" or "similarity", we are focusing on certain aspects of a certain phenomenon. For instance, "I have the same car as my neighbor" would normally mean that it is the same model, but not necessarily the same color or the same engine, and the two cars do not have to be of the same age. Thus, qualification of what we mean by "similar religious phenomena" is necessary, something which has not usually been done. "Similar" phenomena, or "sameness" of course has something to do with categories: "red" things are similar in relation to the category of color; bicycles and trains are similar because they both belong to the category of transportation, and so forth. For certain purposes, a model classifying bicycles and trains in the same category would certainly make sense (if, for example, we want to compare differences in health conditions among people who use different kinds of transportation), whereas it would make no sense if the purpose were to investigate the major sources of pollution created by various means of transportation (cars, aircrafts, and trains).

Returning to the Óðinn example, it is thus a matter of perspective whether we choose to see Óðinn as a shaman: there are similarities, but there are certainly also differences; and the question will then be which classificatory model we choose, and what we want to use it for. Even if we need to be aware that models are not reality, because we have no direct access to reality without the filter through which we perceive the world, we have to accept that some models are better than others for a given purpose, because they fit better with the evidence in the sources and with what we know about general social and psychological mechanisms. Or, rather: good models have a larger amount of explanatory power in relation to a certain problem than a bad model does. In applying these considerations to the Óðinn example, we may thus see that we are dealing with two different sets of methods, although both of a comparative nature, depending on whether we choose to characterize Óðinn as a shaman or not. The methods we use when we view Óðinn as a shaman are thus comparisons of individual elements: soul travel, ecstasy, and other traits that are characteristic of shamanism; since Óðinn certainly soul-travels, creates ecstasy, and so forth, accordingly, Óðinn should be seen as a shaman.

The problem with these kinds of comparisons, however, is that, as was suggested earlier, individual elements may occur in different contexts in various religions. Actually, in most religions, some sort of "soul traveling" can be found: for instance, mystics in many of the so-called "higher" religions are able to travel to the other world, and thus approach God in a way that is not possible for ordinary people, and myths from all over the world tell of people going to the land of the dead, or that of the gods—yet neither mystics or visitors of the dead are seen as shamans. Thus, similarities at the level of individual elements may be coincidental, in the sense that they can be found all over the world in quite different contexts. We can thus hardly use such similarities for reconstructions of any kind, although they may occasionally be used for establishing theories about influences.

Another, and in my opinion much more convincing, level of comparisons is that of structure, i.e., a whole group of elements which are related in similar ways in various cultures. That sort of comparativism has been carried out by such distinguished scholars as George Dumézil among genetically related cultures, and Claude Lévi-Strauss, sometimes using typological comparisons. Michael Witzel argued recently for another variant of the genetic comparisons in connection with his so-called Laurasian mythology, where he speaks of a common "story line" among a huge group of mythologies (Witzel 2012). A story line should, in this context, be understood as a syntagmatic structure, along the same lines as that Vladimir Propp utilized in his analyses of the Russian folk tale. It seems obvious that whether we are talking about paradigmatic (as with Lévi-Strauss) or syntagmatic structures (as with Dumézil[10] and Witzel), such structures would involve a sufficient number of elements, ordered in certain relations, such that we can use them in creating models that can be used for reconstructions, whether we are talking about reconstructions of "Laurasian mythology", "Indo-European mythology", or just "pre-Christian Scandinavian mythology". For as I have argued on other occasions, speaking about "pre-Christian Scandinavian mythology" certainly involves comparisons, which are, in principle, of the same nature as other genetic comparisons, since not many scholars would today subscribe to a view that only one "religion" existed in Scandinavia in the pre-Christian era (cf. Schjødt 2009, 2012a: 275–77).

These considerations mean that for our Óðinn example, in order for him to qualify as a shaman, I would suggest that we must be able to characterize the Óðinn figure in its entirety, or at least in its main components, as a shaman—that his "structure", so to speak, be isomorphic with that of the shaman. If this is not the case, as I do not believe it is, we may very well speak of shaman-like *traits*,

---

[10] Dumézil's famous "tripartite" structure should, however, be seen as an example of a paradigmatic structure, whereas his analysis of, for instance, the myth of the war between the Æsir and the Vanir in comparison with Indian and Roman material (Dumézil 1973) is clearly syntagmatic, as are probably the majority of his analyses.

most likely borrowed from the Sámi neighbors to the north. But the main traits of the Óðinn figure, which appear to be very old within Germanic religions, no doubt have parallels with figures such as the Vedic Varuna and the Germanic Mercury-Wodan from the beginning of the Common Era. These figures were probably influenced relatively little by shamanism, although also in these cases too, individual shamanic features may occur. Therefore it would, in my opinion, be methodologically incorrect to classify Óðinn as a shaman—he simply does not fulfill the condition of his individual characteristics forming a structure that is similar to that of a shaman.

Another point that should be briefly addressed here is the notion of "discourse", although I have dealt with that also in earlier publications (Schjødt 2012a, 2013). A discourse, as I use the term, should be seen as a space within which a certain notion, be it a god or some other social phenomenon, can be addressed and thought about by the members of a given culture. Thus we can speak of an Óðinn-discourse or a Þórr-discourse, etc., as well as of discourses connected to sexuality, war, ethics, nature, and all sorts of phenomena of some importance for the culture in question. Such discourses are constituted by everything that can be said about a certain phenomenon, not by what was actually said. Within the pre-Christian religions of pagan Scandinavia anyway, we would not know what was actually said about a certain god, for instance Óðinn, because what we *do* know is that only a tiny bit of what was said and formulated in the pre-Christian era has been passed down to us. Thus, all we can hope for is to reconstruct the discursive space within which every utterance about Óðinn took place.

As we saw earlier, it could be said that Óðinn was clever, that he knew about magic, that he could give advice about war strategy, and so on. What could *not* be said—what was outside the frames of the Óðinn discourse—would be, for instance, that he was unknowledgeable, or that he was a young brilliant warrior, or that he was reliable. In this sense we can say that the discourse is constituted by the sum of, and the relations between, the various pieces of information in the sources—and many more which are not in the sources, but which might be construed on the basis of structural comparisons. Yet more importantly, perhaps, are the relations that exist within a certain discourse, between the individual elements. Again, to give a rather banal example: when Saxo Grammaticus relates that Hadingus hanged himself in front of all his people (1, 8,27), we get no explanation for this spectacular behavior, beyond the fact that Hadingus did not want to survive his friend, the Swedish king; however, because we have a model, gained from the general study of religion, telling us that humans perform rituals which were often performed for the first time by the gods, we do not hesitate to see a relation between the self-sacrifice of Óðinn and Hadingus's suicide. This relation further becomes part of a larger structure involving the relationship between Óðinn and kings in general, so that we may use the Hadingus story (among other sources, of course) to reconstruct a discourse that involves the relationship between Óðinn and kings. It thus makes sense to maintain that a discourse is constituted by certain structural relations, be they social or purely mythological.

Parallels between two religions related through a common cultural-historical background can be used to fill in lacunae in one of these religions with the use of material from the other. They can also be used for evaluating pieces of information in doubtful sources from the religion we are about to reconstruct. This sort of comparison may prove much more convincing than traditional source criticism.[11] When it comes to typological comparisons things are a bit more complicated, since we cannot assume that details in one religion will also be part of the other. Still: if we see cultures that are, from a sociological point of view, comparable to that of the pre-Christian North, it would certainly be worthwhile to analyze whether a model, based on known structures from such a comparable culture, could be used as an organizing principle for the interpretation of the Old Norse sources, as we shall see shortly. We will never be sure if the result of such a procedure will bring us close to the historical reality, but it appears to be the only procedure available, if we want to avoid both wholly arbitrary comparisons and, as a consequence, wholly arbitrary reconstructions.

The next question that I believe natural to address would then be, which kind of cultures it would make sense to compare the pre-Christian of the North with.

With What?

In principle, as was discussed above, we can compare everything to everything else. It may not make much sense, but technically, there are almost no limits on what we can compare to, for instance, the pre-Christian Scandinavian religion. When, however, the purpose of the comparison is to reconstruct this religion, and to be able to pose new and relevant questions, some religions may be better suited than others for comparison. This situation is due to the fact that there are, of course, different types of religion, and that some are more similar to the pre-Christian religion than others. I omit here genetic comparisons because, as mentioned above, I have dealt with them in other publications. In general, however, I emphasize that there can be no doubt that genetic comparisons are

---

[11] This seems for instance to be the case with the theogony as related by Tacitus (*Germania* ch. 2) and Snorri Sturluson (*Gylfaginning* p. 11). See further the analysis in Schjødt forthcoming.

more helpful than typological ones when it comes to the reconstruction of details of myths and rituals (cf. Schjødt Forthcoming), but here I shall argue, nevertheless, that typological comparisons may also be of benefit to our reconstructions of Old Norse religion and to our construction of useful models if they are carried out properly.

In this connection, we must carefully reflect on the possibilities, as well as their limits. The main problem can be posed in a very simple way: is it possible to reconstruct some of the connecting lines between the individual pieces of information that were dealt with above, and might it even be possible to reconstruct elements of which we are not informed at all through the use of such typological comparisons? I think it is, although, again, we will never be sure that such reconstructions actually correspond to the pagan reality. Theories about, and thus models of, the past will never be in a 1-to-1 relationship with the past reality itself. Such comparisons may, however, inspire us to suggest new and fresh interpretations of the sources—to say nothing about posing new questions, as was also mentioned above.

I would like to draw attention to one, in my view, particularly interesting perspective, namely that recently suggested by Robert Bellah, the great American sociologist who died in 2013, and who, among many other things, had speculated on religious matters. In 1964 he wrote an interesting article on religious evolutionism, which was, as far as I can see, overlooked by most historians of religion, presumably because of the status of evolutionism in those years. His recently published book, *Religion in Human Evolution: From the Paleolithic to the Axial Age* (2011), seems, however, to have had a great impact already, and although I disagree with Bellah on many points, both in detail and on matters of principle,[12] I believe that there is much to be gained from his perspective. The book is large, and it is not at all possible to pay justice to all of his important observations, or for that matter to summarize Bellah's theoretical background or his methods in any detail.

Suffice it to say that, as regards theory, Bellah depends a great deal on cultural evolution, and particularly on the cognitive scientist Merlin Donald. Donald divides the evolution of the human mind into three stages, based on human communication strategies, namely the "mimetic", which can be seen as the "the missing link" between apes and humans (Donald 1991: 162–200), the "mythic", and the "theoretic" (Bellah 2011: 118). Likewise, Bellah divides

---

[12]   Thus, for instance, I agree with the criticism raised by Jan Assmann (2012) concerning the very status of the notion of "Axial Age": it should not be seen as a certain period in world history (800–200 BCE), but rather as a change that potentially could happen at all times and in all cultures, when certain social and cultural conditions are present (for instance, writing as a medium).

religious evolution into three types,[13] namely "tribal religions" (essentially the religions of hunter/gatherers), "archaic religions" (religions such as those of ancient Egypt, Mesopotamia, China, etc.), and "axial religions", the last term borrowed from the German philosopher Karl Jaspers.

In his book, Bellah deals with the evolution of human culture, and religion in particular, and with the relation between religion and society. I cannot, however, explore even these points in detail,[14] and will stick closely to what is immediately relevant to the topic here: the use we may make of parallels that can be found within an evolutionary scheme, creating a model of various religious types. I emphasize one programmatic sentence from Bellah, a line that underscores an extremely important point to remember when we talk about evolution in general, namely: *"nothing is ever lost"* (for instance 2011: 267), meaning, in our context, that even in the most "advanced" religions we can always find traits of tribal religions.

The relevant chapter in Bellah's book for our purposes is titled "From tribal to archaic religion", dealing with societies that have left the tribal stage, but have not yet reached the archaic stage (although there certainly are remarkable similarities among these transitional societies and the fully archaic ones). This stage is clearly also that of the pagan Germanic religions in the first millennium CE: even if we can speak of tribes, we are definitely not dealing with tribes in the sense that Bellah is talking about, namely societies up to about 150 persons. For instance, we know that the German leader Ariovistus could bring at least 30,000 warriors (and according to Caesar rather more than 80,000) from different tribes to his struggle against the Romans in the first century BCE; less than a century later, Arminius probably led an army of more than 20,000 warriors into battle against Varus. From the Roman Iron Age in Scandinavia, the weapon deposits in Illerup Ådal in eastern Jutland, for example, contain weapons from between 2,000 and 3,000 dead warriors (Andrén 2014: 44)—all of which takes us far away from the small tribal units that Bellah classifies as "tribes".

On the other hand, in the North, we cannot speak about "archaic societies" comparable with those of the Ancient Near East, Egypt, Greece or pre-Confucian China. The largest town in Scandinavia in the Viking Age was Haithabu, with

---

[13] Bellah actually operates with five stages, suggesting two after the Axial Age (Bellah 1964). These are, however, of no importance for the possibilities of reconstructing the pre-Christian religions of the North, and thus there is no reason to elaborate on them here. Interesting articles with further bibliographical information concerning Bellah can be read in *Religionsvidenskabeligt Tidsskrift* 60 (2013).

[14] Since this article was written, Simon Nygaard has published a very informative article in the Journal *Temenos*, analyzing the parallels between Hawaii and Scandinavia, using Bellah's theoretical framework in much more detail than is done here. This article is strongly recommended for those interested in this approach (Nygaard 2016).

approximately 1,000 inhabitants, or even fewer. So, all in all, if Bellah's evolutionary scheme resembles reality, the Germanic—including the Scandinavian (albeit with some delay)—societies had left the small-scale communities of earlier periods well before entering the Common Era, but had not reached the archaic phase before they were Christianized. In the chapter on the religion of such transitional cultures, Bellah analyses two societies in some detail, namely the Tikopian and the Hawaiian. In both cases, there seem to be many correspondences to Iron-Age Scandinavian culture, although the former were much smaller, and the latter considerably larger and more densely populated. As a sociologist, what interests Bellah is primarily the relationship between religion and social structure. Therefore, since the position of leaders is a focal point of his account, it would be natural to take this as the starting point for a discussion of whether we can use comparisons based on typological parallels to formulate relevant questions and propose relevant models for our reconstructions.

What distinguishes societies at this transitional stage from those of a tribal kind is that they tend towards a rather strong hierarchical structure with a powerful chief or king at the top, in contrast to tribal societies, which are characterized by egalitarianism. Of course, even in tribal cultures, we often see a kind of chief, but they are almost exclusively connected to religious duties, and play no role outside the ritual sphere (Bellah 2011: 181). However, as early populations grew, mainly because of the possibilities that agriculture offered, new land had to be conquered and greater planning—and much more discipline— was required, and things changed: to put it simply, more clearly institutionalized leadership was required. From then on, "leadership operates to intensify economic activity beyond what households alone would produce, but leaders gain in prestige rather than in enhanced material rewards: their gain is more from what they give than what they keep" (Bellah 2011: 194). Such land acquisition inevitably intensified warfare, and warfare created chiefs with warrior skills, although they might still be religiously legitimized (for "*nothing is ever lost*"); and thus "true" chiefdoms arose with hierarchical structures, including strong social and economic differences between chiefs and the circles around them (such as on Hawaii, for example, where a separate class of priests developed) on the one hand, and commoners on the other hand.

This development did not necessarily lead to large-scale social formations, but it could if there were cultural and geographical possibilities, that is, if the need for land became strong enough and if populations were dense enough. Thus the chief or leader's role changed dramatically in the transition from tribal to archaic society and religion: from being more concerned with rituals, he came to also deal with secular affairs, not least war, although not losing a strong and legitimizing role in ritual (Bellah 2011: 204). Thus, on Hawaii, from being a part of the community, and like the rest of the community a descendant of the gods, the chief and other members of the royal lineage became the *sole* descendants of the gods. Often the king was seen as a god himself (Valeri 1985: 142–44), not related to the common people at all, but rather holding an intermediate position between god and people, being seen as simultaneously divine and human and therefore the principal mediator between men and gods. For this reason, genealogies of the nobles came to play an important role (Valeri 1985: 157).

Let us take a closer look at the Hawaiian leader in relation to religion, according to Bellah.[15] The main function of the leader on Hawaii was to participate in rituals connected to agriculture and war, the two most important activities for society and the king. Thus, the year was divided into two main parts, those of the Makahiki and Luakini ritual cycles, lasting four and eight months respectively. The main god during the Makahiki was the male god Lono, a god of growth, horticulture, and rain. One of his bodies is the gourd, raising associations with pregnancy, and in general Lono is clearly associated with the feminine aspects of life. During the Makahiki, war and all forms of killing, including human sacrifice, were forbidden, and only pigs, which are connected to Lono (Valeri 1985: 59), are permissible sacrificial victims. The rituals carried out in this period often had a carnival-like status reversal, and generally follow Victor Turner's characterization of liminal rites and communitas rites, with a certain amount of sexual freedom during the dances. As Bellah writes: "It is as though, for a while at least, the old egalitarianism [that of the hunter/gatherer epoch] reappeared" (Bellah 2011: 201). One rite, in fact, included the chief more or less impersonating the god Lono in a circumambulation, collecting first fruit offerings from the various parts of the island (Valeri 1985: 200–26).

The other part of the year, during which wars were fought, was ritually centered around the Luakini temple, the temple for Ku, the greatest of the gods and a typical war deity. During these rituals, human sacrifices took place at every stage. Only the ruler, who also impersonated Ku, could authorize human sacrifice: "he was in a sense, sacrifier (the one on whose behalf the sacrifice is performed), sacrificer (the priestly officiant of the sacrifice) and, symbolically, the sacrifice, for the victim, through his sacrificial death, "becomes" the chief" (Bellah 2011: 202). Thus, the ruler impersonated the two gods who were of utmost importance for the Hawaiians, namely Lono and Ku, rulers over fertility and war, respectively.[16] In schematic form, we thus get the following:

---

[15] Bellah's main source is Valerio Valeri, *Kingship and Sacrifice: Ritual and Society in Ancient Hawaii* (1985).

[16] Valeri's analyses (1985) are extremely interesting and can be warmly recommended. The ritual cycle is mainly treated on pp. 191–339.

Makahiki	Luakini
Lono	Ku
Growth, fertility, femininity	War, masculinity
Sex	Death
No human sacrifices	Human sacrifices
Egalitarianism	Hierarchy
Circumambulation/first fruit	Authorizing human sacrifice
Ruler identifies with Lono	Ruler identifies with Ku

Admittedly this summary is somewhat selective, but, nevertheless, if we turn to the Old Scandinavian material, we find some remarkable parallels, although it is not possible here to present a detailed argument. We can, for instance, glimpse the same development in Scandinavia when it comes to descent: from Tacitus we learn that all the Germanic tribes were descended from the gods, whereas in Norse sources only chieftains and kings are believed to descend from gods, either Freyr or Óðinn. Only once—in the eddic poem *Rígsþula*, which is certainly a special case because it is a sociogony rather than an anthropogony— is it told that anyone other than the aristocrats are believed to be descendants of gods. There are also indications that the year was divided into two spheres, as has been argued by Terry Gunnell and more implicitly by John McKinnell, who wrote about the "winter king" and "summer king" (Gunnell 2000: 138–39; McKinnell 2005, esp. 78–79).

I have argued elsewhere that at some point during the pre-Roman and Roman Iron Ages it is possible to distinguish between "Freyr kings" and "Óðinn kings" as "peace kings" and "war kings", respectively, who eventually turn into a single ruler responsible for the two main areas for which a Scandinavian king was responsible, namely the well-being of the land and success in war (Schjødt 2012b: 73–79). The sources clearly indicate that human sacrifices were given mainly to Óðinn, the war god, whereas the ritual feasts for Freyr involved dancing and obscene songs. We are not told directly about sexual promiscuity, but in connection with the dances it could easily be imagined, as, for instance, during the sacrifices in Uppsala, as related by Saxo, concerning Starcatherus's stay there (*Gesta Danorum* 6, 5,10). We also know that circumambulation was connected to the fertility god, as is related by Tacitus concerning Nerthus (*Germania* ch. 40), and in *Ögmundar þáttr dytts ok Gunnars helmings*, concerning Freyr. Finally the description that Bellah gives of the king in his form of Ku reminds us strongly of what we know about Óðinn as he performs his famous "self-sacrifice" (*Hávamál* st. 138–41): Óðinn benefits from the sacrifice, since he is given the runes; it is he who performs the sacrifice, and should thus be seen as the sacrificer, and he is certainly also the victim.

More could be said, and more parallels found, but I believe the point is made. The first question we could therefore ask is how we can explain parallels of this sort? We cannot, of course, postulate any sort of influence between the two cultures. The Hawaiian society, as just described, probably developed between 1100 and 1500 CE, and it is not very likely that they met many Vikings in the Pacific. So we cannot speak of influence. Another explanation would be to maintain that we are dealing with some sort of "archetype", but in that case—apart from being unlikely, anyway—we should expect such parallels in many other societies, at different stages of their development, all over the world. That leaves us, as far as I can see, with only one potential solution: namely that, in accordance with Bellah's arguments, when it comes to the relations between ruler and people, between the ruler's participation in agricultural and warrior rituals, between gods of agriculture and gods of war, between kings and bloody sacrifices, and between kings and fertility rituals, parallel societal situations will tend to create similar religious phenomena on a structural level. Naturally, many differences exist as well—although we must remember that similarity is not identicality. This, however, is hardly surprising. The interesting thing here is the similarities. When the parallels are as clear as seems to be the case here, then, in my opinion, the situation strongly indicates that cultures which are more or less on the same technological and political levels will *tend* to develop parallel religious traits and structures, which is exactly what Bellah argues.

If Bellah is right—as I think he is—then the next question to be asked would be what use can we make of these parallels in dealing with the pre-Christian religion of the North? First and foremost, it is obvious that looking at such cultures will enable us to ask qualified and relevant questions of the material (e.g., to which gods was the king particularly connected?) as opposed to a different kind of question, such as those actually raised some fifty years ago, namely, "Was the king seen as sacral in pre-Christian Scandinavia?" which is simply not a qualified question, since in all comparable cultures, he certainly was sacred. With the Hawaiian and many other examples from pre-archaic and archaic cultures, we "know" that kings in such societies, as a means of legitimization, must, in all likelihood, have some divine qualities which were likely to be expressed in certain rituals. Thus, apart from suggesting relevant questions—and ruling out irrelevant ones—comparisons along the lines of this new social-evolutionary theory may also help us in reconstructing some basic traits in cultures which we, primarily because of the source situation, do not know as much about as we might wish. In this way, cultures with better source situations may help us construct relevant models, and therefore fill in some of the lacunae we face. In the case of pre-Christian Scandinavian religion, I therefore believe that this way of using a comparative method—to create basic religious models—will in most instances overrule traditional source criticism, as no source-critical method can reject this sort of model.

As mentioned earlier, these models, if they are good—i.e., well-argued—will be able to put, certainly not all, but some or perhaps even most of the individual pieces of information in the sources into their right places. In doing so, we will thus be able to reconstruct—not every discourse, and particularly not fine details—but quite a large part of some important discourses from the religion in question. The prerequisite for this is, of course, that the religions we choose for comparison are of the same socio-economic type as the one with which we are primarily dealing. It nonetheless bears reiterating, however, that we can never be certain that our reconstructions are "correct", but they may suggest a way of improving our understanding of what pre-Christian Scandinavian religion could have been like.

Conclusion

My aim here has been to show that without comparison it is almost impossible to reconstruct anything within pre-Christian Scandinavian religion. Even if some scholars are not aware that this is the case, comparisons, explicit or implicit, typological or genetic, have always played a major role for our understanding of this religion, or perhaps more correctly these religious traditions. Furthermore, it has been argued that although many details will remain enigmatic, we are, to a fairly high degree, able to reconstruct its basic structures on the basis of comparisons, against which we must view the information related in the source material. This has been acknowledged by many when it comes to genetic comparison, whereas typological comparisons have for a long time been discredited, partly because of the lack of methodological awareness among scholars such as Frazer and Eliade. Although also conducting typological comparisons, such scholars compared on the level of individual elements, whereas what we should compare are structures of various kinds, based on qualified models. We also have to acknowledge that religions used for genetic comparisons are often much more similar to the religion in question than are those of the typological kind. Nevertheless, accepting even partially Bellah's evolutionary theory, it seems that relations between societal types, and certain types of religion, may help us to connect the various pieces of information in the Old Norse sources in order to generate a clearer picture of pagan Scandinavian religion.

Works Cited

Primary Sources

Ecclesiastical History of the English People
Bede. *Bede's Ecclestical History of the English People*. Ed. Bertram Ciolgrave and R. A. B. Mynors. Oxford: 1979.

Flateyjarbók
Flateyjarbók. En samling af norske kongesagaer med indskudte mindre fortællinger om begivenheder i og udenfor Norge samt Annaler. 3 vols. Ed. Guðbrandur Vigfússon and Carl R. Unger. Christiania: 1860–1868.

Germania
Tacitus. *Tacitus: Agricola, Germania, Dialogus.* Transl. M. Hutton. Revised by E. H. Warmington. Loeb Classical Library 35. Cambridge: 1970.

Gesta Danorum
Saxo Grammaticus. *Saxo Grammaticus: Gesta Danorum: Danmarkshistorien.* Ed. Karsten Friis-Jensen and transl. Peter Zeeberg [into Danish]. Copenhagen: 2005.

TRANSLATION
Saxo Grammaticus: The History of the Danes: Books 1-9. Ed. Hilda Ellis Davidson and transl. Peter Fisher. Cambridge: 2008.

Gylfaginning
Snorri Sturluson. *Edda: Prologue and Gylfaginning.* Ed. Anthony Faulkes. 2nd ed. London: 2005.

TRANSLATION
Snorri Sturluson: Edda. Ed. and transl. Anthony Faulkes. London: 1995.

Hávamál: see *Poetic Edda*

Poetic Edda
Edda: Die Lieder des Codex Regius nebst verwandten Denkmälern. Ed. Gustav Neckel and Hans Kuhn. Germanische Bibliothek, Vierte Reihe. Heidelberg: 1962.

TRANSLATION
The Poetic Edda. Transl. Carolyne Larrington. Oxford: 1996.

Rígsþula: see *Poetic Edda*

Ögmundar þáttr dytts ok Gunnars helmings see Flateyjarbók

Secondary Sources

Andrén, Anders. 2014. *Tracing Old Norse Cosmology: The World Tree, Middle Earth, and the Sun from Archaeological Perspectives*. Lund.

Assmann, Jan. 2013. "Cultural Memory and the Myth of the Axial Age." In *The Axial Age and Its Consequences*. Ed. Robert Bellah and Hans Joas. Cambridge, MA. Pp. 366–407.

Beck, Heinrich, Detlev Ellmers, and Kurt Schier, eds. 1992. *Germanische Religionsgeschichte. Quellen und Quellenprobleme*. Berlin.

Bellah, Robert N. 1964. "Religious Evolution." *American Sociological Review* 29: 358–74.

———. 2011. *Religion in Human Evolution: From the Paleolithic to the Axial Age*. Cambridge, MA.

Clover, Carol J., and John Lindow, eds. 1985. *Old Norse-Icelandic Literature: A Critical Guide*. Ithaca.

Clunies Ross, Margaret. 1994. *Prolonged Echoes: Old Norse Myths in Medieval Northern Society. Vol. 1: The Myths*. Odense.

Detienne, Marcel. 2008. *Comparing the Incomparable*. Transl. Janet Lloyd. Stanford.

Donald, Merlin. 1991. *Origins of the Modern Mind: Three Stages in the Evolution of Culture and Cognition*. Cambridge, MA.

DuBois, Thomas A. 1999. *Nordic Religions in the Viking Age*. Philadelphia.

Dumézil, Georges. 1973. *Gods of the Ancient Northmen*. Ed. and transl. Einar Haugen et al. Publications of the UCLA Center for the Study of Comparative Folklore and Mythology, 3. Berkeley.

Eliade, Mircea. 1969. *The Quest: History and Meaning in Religion*. Chicago.

———. 1972. *Shamanism: Archaic Techniques of Ecstasy*. Transl. Willard R. Trask. Princeton.

Frazer, James George. 1911–1915. *The Golden Bough: A Study in Magic and Religion*. 3rd ed. London.

Fleck, Jere. 1971. "The Knowledge-Criterion in the Grímnismál: The Case against Shamanism." *Arkiv för nordisk filologi* 86: 49–65.

Gunnell, Terry. 2000. "The Season of the Dísir: The Winter Nights and the Disablót in Early Medieval Scandinavian Belief." *Cosmos* 16: 117–49.

Hedeager, Lotte. 2011. *Iron Age Myth and Materiality: An Archaeology of Scandinavia AD 400–1000*. London.

Kuhn, Thomas. 1970. *The Structure of Scientific Revolutions*. 2nd ed. Chicago.

Kuper, Adam. 1988. *The Invention of Primitive Society: Transformations of an Illusion.* London.

Lawson, E. Thomas. 2000. "Cognition." In *Guide to the Study of Religion.* Ed. Willi Braun and Russell T. McCutcheon. London. Pp. 75–84.

Lévi-Strauss, Claude. 1976. *Structural Anthropology.* Vol. 2. Transl. Monique Layton. New York.

Lindow, John. 2003. "Cultures in Contact." In *Old Norse Myths, Literature and Society.* Ed. Margaret Clunies Ross. Odense. Pp. 89–109.

McKinnell, John. 2005. *Meeting the Other in Norse Myth and Legend.* Cambridge.

Müller, Friedrich Max. 1873. *Introduction to the Science of Religion.* London.

Nygaard, Simon. 2016. "Sacral Rulers in Pre-Christian Scandinavia: The Possibilities of Typological Comparisons within the Paradigm of Cultural Evolution." *Temenos* 52: 9-35.

Price, Neil. 2002. *The Viking Way: Religion and War in Late Iron Age Scandinavia.* PhD diss., Uppsala University.

Saler, Benson. 2001. "Comparison: Some Suggestions for Improving the Inevitable." *Numen: International Review for the History of Religions* 48: 267–75.

Schjødt, Jens Peter. 2008. *Initiation between Two Worlds: Structure and Symbolism in Pre-Christian Scandinavian Religion.* Transl. Victor Hansen. Odense.

———. 2009. "Diversity and its Consequences for the Study of Old Norse Religion. What Is It We Are Trying to Reconstruct?" In *Between Paganism and Christianity in the North.* Ed. Leszek P. Slupecki and Jakub Morawiec. Rzeszow. Pp. 9–22.

———. 2012a. "Reflections on Aims and Methods in the Study of Old Norse Religion." In *More than Mythology: Narratives, Ritual Practices and Regional Distribution in Pre-Christian Scandinavian Religions.* Ed. Catharina Raudvere and Jens Peter Schjødt. Lund. Pp. 263–87.

———. 2012b. "Óðinn, Þórr and Freyr: Functions and Relations." In *News from Other Worlds: Studies in Nordic Folklore, Mythology and Culture: In Honor of John F. Lindow.* Ed. Merrill Kaplan and Timothy R. Tangherlini. Berkeley. Pp. 61–91.

———. 2013. "The Notions of Model, Discourse, and Semantic Center as Tools for the (Re)Construction of Old Norse Religion." *The Retrospective Methods Network Newsletter* 6: 6–15.

———. Forthcoming. "Reconstructing Old Norse Mythology: Source Criticism and Comparative Mythology." In *Myth and Theory in the Old Norse World.* Ed. Stefan Brink. Turnhout.

Segal, Robert A. 2001. "In Defense of the Comparative Method." *Numen: International Review for the History of Religions* 48: 339–73.

Solli, Brit. 2002. *Seid: Myter, sjamanisme og kjønn I vikingenes tid.* Oslo.

Turner, Victor W. 1969. *The Ritual Process: Structure and Anti-Structure*. Ithaca.

Vajda, Lazlo. 1964. "Zur phaseologischen Stellung des Shamanismus." In *Religionsethnologie*. Ed. Carl August Schmitz. Frankfurt. Pp. 265–95. Orig. pub. 1959.

Valeri, Valerio. 1985. *Kingship and Sacrifice: Ritual and Society in Ancient Hawaii*. Transl. Paula Wissing. Chicago.

Witzel, E. J. Michael. 2012. *The Origins of the World's Mythologies*. Oxford.

Methodological Challenges
to the Study of Old Norse Myths
The Orality and Literacy Debate Reframed

Pernille Hermann
Aarhus University

Abstract: In pointing to a theme of importance for source evaluation, this essay gives an overview of the study of Old Norse myths from the perspective of the orality/literacy debate. It seeks to provide a picture of emerging tendencies and directions in scholarship. Taking off from the now criticized book-prose/free-prose theory, it discusses the relevance of different types of orality, the relationship between text and context, and between word and image, modes of communication, and performance.

Most scholars would agree that dealing with Old Norse myths and related narratives from the medieval Norse world requires a double focus—on the one hand, a focus on the oral dimension, that is, on the presumed oral foundations of the surviving texts, and on the other hand, a focus on the written dimension of the preserved material, that is, on the codicological and other empirical or material aspects of the texts. Apart from its critical importance in evaluating textual sources, the concept pair orality/literacy is also crucial for understanding the nature of the transmission and dissemination of myths in pre-Christian Scandinavia, as well as in the centuries following the introduction of Christianity. Thus, if we are to retrieve the bygone Norse mythological world, a world neither easily nor immediately accessible, the ongoing refinement of our understanding of the implications of the dyad "orality and literacy" is an indisputably important tool. The present article addresses both orality and literacy; specifically, with reference to recent studies addressing such issues as performance and other orality-focused approaches, I want to underscore that Old Norse myths and other Old Norse narratives with roots in oral tradition are inadequately understood if they are viewed exclusively within a framework that focuses on the verbal dimension of the myths. I highlight that it is not merely these verbal components, that is the oral/aural aspects strictly construed, but also such cognate activities as the performance aspects and pictorial representations of the materials that should be recognized as integral to the study of Old Norse mythology. Although structured in the form of an overview, this essay looks not in the first instance to provide a comprehensive or fine-grained review of scholarship about mythology or orality and literacy, but rather seeks to identify emerging tendencies and directions in the scholarly debate.

Source Evaluation

Increasingly recognized as one of the ultimate source problems in our field, the relationship between orality and literacy is now understood to be much subtler than was once thought. Thus, John Lindow writes that challenges in the study of Old Norse mythology do not only relate to the fact that the myths were recorded in the Christian period by learned people, but also to "the problem of sources", which as he explains "is more than chronological, for written media and culture may be presumed to differ in important ways from their oral counterparts" (Lindow 2005: 22). Attempts to provide an exhaustive treatment of studies of Old Norse myths, and their relationships to discussions of orality and literacy, would be too wide-ranging for at least two reasons: firstly, the study of Old Norse mythology is multi-disciplinary, and the myths are being investigated by scholars from a large number of academic fields, such as philology, folklore, history of religion, literature, anthropology, and archaeology (see, e.g., Schjødt 1988; Mitchell 2000). In the quotation above, John Lindow refers to "written media and culture", and certainly media studies and cultural studies ought to be listed among those many other disciplines that can make a welcome contribution to the field (cf. Heslop forthcoming).

Secondly, debates about Old Norse myths, orality, and literacy overlap and converge with the study of genres. Old Norse myths and details about the mythology are transmitted to us by many avenues, most often as integral parts of the literary design of different genres, poetry as well as prose. The most important textual source material for Old Norse myths and mythology are the eddic poems, a group of mythological and legendary narratives that have been transmitted anonymously, and skaldic verses, which were mainly composed by Icelandic skalds. Of major importance among the prose texts is the *Prose Edda*, written ca. 1220 by the Icelandic chieftain and scholar Snorri Sturluson; also significant are the Icelandic sagas, among which the sub-class of the *fornaldarsǫgur* is most directly concerned with myth, and *Gesta Danorum*, written ca. 1200 by the Danish historian Saxo Grammaticus. Each of these literary genres has its own unique research history with a number of different interests attached to it, and within each the orality/literacy debate has been accentuated to different degrees and with different foci, spreading the study of myths in multiple directions (see, e.g., Clunies Ross 1994: 11–41; Quinn 2000).

The so-called book-prose/free-prose controversy, designated as such by the Swiss scholar Andreas Heusler as far back as 1913, grouped Old Norse scholars according to their opinions about the origin of the medieval Norse sagas, that is, roughly speaking, if they believed that these texts had their origins in oral tradition or in textual authorship.[1] In recent decades, the book-prose/free-prose controversy has been re-evaluated and criticized on a number of points (Mitchell 2003; Gísli Sigurðsson 2004, 2008), and partly due to more recent insights into the nature of oral art forms, the controversy as originally formulated is now considered old-fashioned on a number of points. The debate was not principally concerned with what are generally considered the core mythic texts, such as the eddic poems and the *Prose Edda*; however, the recent re-evaluation of the debate, which has targeted its understanding, or lack thereof, of the fluid character of oral tradition, has greatly influenced our way of looking not only at the sagas but also at the eddic material. The book-prose/free-prose controversy anticipated that the Great Divide (Foley 1991, with reference to Finnegan; Harris 2010: 119) would be echoed in Old Norse studies, and that, to a certain extent, Norse scholars too belonged to one of the two sides, focusing on either orality or written textuality, often to the active exclusion of what was on the other side.

It is difficult to give a single unified answer to the question of the status of the orality/literacy debate in the aftermath of the otherwise long-lived book-prose/free-prose controversy. For more than a century, dominant voices strongly emphasized the debt of Old Norse textually-transmitted material to written culture and literacy. This was the case not only concerning saga-texts (see, e.g., Sigurður Nordal 1920, 1940; Andersson 2008: 7–8), but also studies of myths (e.g., Bugge 1881–1889); studies treating the *Prose Edda* in particular tended to highlight its written aspects, including a specific interest in the impact of the ideological milieu of writing and the influence from Christian and classical literature on Snorri's representations of the myths (e.g., Holtsmark 1964; Dronke and Dronke 1977). Some scholars, of course, have insistently concerned themselves with the oral background of sagas and poems (e.g., Andersson 1964). Currently, as I will give examples of below, it would appear that there is an increased tendency to emphasize features connected to orality.

---

[1] Entries to thorough reviews of the book-prose/free-prose debate can be found in Andersson 1964 and Gísli Sigurðsson 2004: 17–50.

This change of focus obviously owes much to Milman Parry and Albert Lord's conclusions about oral composition (Lord 1960), and to the adoption of these results to the study of Norse material (see the overviews in Harris 2005; Gísli Sigurðsson 2003). Despite the fact that the notion of "composition-in-performance" (Lord 1960: 13–29) is not considered relevant for Old Norse oral genres by everyone (see e.g., Lönnroth 1981), it is beyond doubt that the principle of composition-in-performance has had a tremendous impact on how we understand typical features of oral genres, including oral genres of Norse provenance. Much recent scholarly literature, however, has absorbed and in varying degrees accepted Lord and Parry's results, and is now increasingly preoccupied with features of orality that go beyond a narrow interest in composition and the grammar of oral genres. Thus, such features as the relevance of non-verbal resources, the co-existence of various communicative levels, and the relevance of cultural conventions are increasingly emphasized as paramount for understanding oral genres in their oral contexts.[2]

Oral-Derived Texts

Since the myths and other mythological materials, represented in different genres, are transmitted primarily in medieval manuscripts, the fact that the mythic content has been transferred to writing in a cultural milieu of literacy cannot be ignored, an historical reality that prevents us from speaking of "pure orality". John M. Foley's term *oral-derived text* (Foley 1991a) is sometimes mentioned as suitable and appropriate for characterizing Old Norse texts (Gísli Sigurðsson 2003, 2004). The term implies that both the prose and poetry that transmit myths are written texts shaped by oral tradition. The term highlights the fact that although the mythic content is interwoven with, and mediated by, written textuality, we can assume that the texts recall their oral traditional character (Foley 1992). Features connected to the aesthetics of eddic poems, that is, the allusive nature of these forms of poetry, their often repetitive character, and the use of compositional units are just a few examples of their oral dimension (Harris 1979).

The study of oral-derived texts requires specific methodological consideration. One question traditionally subject to extensive debate is the dating and provenance of the eddic poems (see, e.g., Fidjestøl 1999). Before modern views of orality—with, for example, its emphasis on the lack of fixity of some oral narratives and poetic forms—began to influence seriously Old Norse studies, methodological concerns were not always adjusted to the material at hand,

---

[2] Such studies are inspired by, e.g., Finnegan 1992; Foley 1991a; and Bauman 1986.

something which also had consequences for the results. In "Recent Works and Views on the Poetic Edda" from 1963, Lee M. Hollander wrote:

> ...we have made little progress in understanding these [eddic] poems, in dating them, in attributing them to a certain country and to certain authors. It must also be admitted that, though some progress has been made, these problems still for the most part elude us, as did the luscious fruit hanging over Tantalos, just when we seem to have them within our grasp. (Hollander 1963: 101)

The resigned conclusion of this passage about the elusory character of eddic poems may very well be an implication of a lack of methodological concern and of a textually-biased view of the texts. Implicit to the questions of age and provenance are text-bound ideas of "works" as finalized textual units, and ideas about the possibility of exact dating and arranging the poems in chronological order are organizing principles that are not readily adaptable to oral texts nor, most likely, to oral-derived texts.

At this point, it seems relatively safe to view Norse mythological literature as oral-derived. Admittedly, as regards the prose genres, especially the sagas, the debate about the oral background has been heated, as evidenced by the book-prose/free-prose controversy, but the discussion of an oral background has been less polemical where poetry is concerned. As regards eddic poetry, the oral origin of the genre has been generally accepted, even if the specific character of its oral background has not always been clarified, or dealt with explicitly. As late as 1985, Joseph Harris wrote that "In a sense eddic scholars have always 'known' that eddic poetry was oral poetry, but that knowledge was mostly an unspoken assumption based on the age of the verse and the introduction of writing in the North" (Harris 2005: 112, 1983).

If not with regard to their oral backgrounds then, disputes have nevertheless arisen concerning eddic poems and their *types of orality*, and whether these poems are best understood from notions of improvisation, composition-in-performance, or memorization, topics which continue to be debated (see Acker 1998).[3] This discussion has not been considered relevant to skaldic poetry, since the consensus view has been that this kind of poetry runs counter to the assumption that orally mediated texts could not have a fixed form. Not least the skaldic meter, *dróttkvætt*, prevented distortion of this type of poetry, which was likely to remain non-flexible (e.g. Gade 2000: 65). A matter of much discussion

---

[3]   As summarized by Paul Acker, this debate is inextricably connected with, and highly relevant for, source evaluation, but unfortunately the biased points of view of scholars and their occasionally nationalistic tendencies have sometimes overshadowed fair source criticism (Acker 1998).

among modern scholars is whether complex and tightly composed skaldic poetry would have been understood directly by hearers, but the narrated world of, for instance, *Gísla saga Súrssonar* provides us with an example of how a fixed oral text could exist and of how exact repetition was possible in an oral context. In the saga, the protagonist's sister Þórdís remembers and repeats a skaldic verse, a verse which is crucial for the narrative, since it initiates Gísli's outlawry (*Gísla saga Súrssonar* ch. 18). Skaldic verse may demonstrate that more than one type of orality existed, that a stable text can be mediated orally (Jesch 2005, Harris 2010), and that, when dealing with literary genres that carry the mythic material, we must be careful not to establish distinctions too absolute between so-called oral and written features respectively.

But is it possible to penetrate beyond or behind the level of written textuality, that is, can we come to a better understanding of the oral dimension of the texts? In emphasizing how radically oral material is transformed during the process which transfers it to writing, one opinion is that the extant written texts actually do not allow us any access to the oral literature of the past. From this perspective, because of differences in media, the gap between the written text and oral material simply cannot be bridged. It is indeed a complicated matter, since the texts do not carry with them the extra-textual context to which any oral utterance is metonymically related. Accordingly, in this view, the challenge consists of two problems: we have neither access to the oral forms nor to their contexts.

It would seem, however, as though there are alternative perspectives, which are not quite so despondent, for some studies have convincingly shown that it is possible to picture the material's oral dimensions and contexts (Danielsson 2002). Lars Lönnroth (1971, 1978, and 2009) has consistently pointed to performance aspects of poetry and saga, and given examples of the fact that poems and narratives are not comprised solely of verbal expressions or simply as silent letters on the page. Stephen Mitchell (1991, 2001, and 2003) has turned our attention to performance aspects of the literary forms and has thus enhanced our understanding of saga and poetry in oral contexts. With a focus on performance and inspired by notions such as "thick description", "grammar of context", and "ethnopoetics", Mitchell has shown that the Norse textual materials actually provide us with possibilities of reaching a deeper contextual understanding of poetry and narrative in Norse culture (2001; see also Tangherlini 2003: 143–49). Terry Gunnell's contribution to the study of dialogical eddic poems composed in the *ljóðaháttr* meter is another investigation of major importance that elucidates the performance-dimension of eddic poetry (Gunnell 1995a, 1995b, 2013). In focusing on the theatrical and dramatic aspects of these poems, his studies essentially move the poems under discussion from the genre of poetry to the genre of drama, seriously calling for a re-evaluation of our methodological concerns. More recently, Stefanie Würth has dealt with the highly complicated question of performance in connection with skaldic poetry, both performance as recitation on stage and performance as a material act of writing (Würth 2007). Listing questions of performance among the approaches relevant for the study of myths means that the poems' extra-textual dimensions become foci of interest, as do their status as multi-dimensional and multi-sensory experiences.

Another tendency in current scholarship that opposes the book-prose position and its narrow focus on literary loans is a renewed interest in folklore and the importance of "living tradition" across time and space (cf. Heide and Bek-Pedersen 2014; Sävborg and Bek-Pedersen 2014). Scholars representing this tendency focus on the "all important issue of continuity of tradition through extended periods of time" (Bek-Pedersen 2014: 85; cf. Mitchell 2014). They argue that not only contemporary or near-contemporary material, such as the sources from the High Middle Ages, but also material from much later periods can reveal information about, for instance, the attributes and functions of Norse deities, such as Loki, Heimdallr, and Óðinn (e.g., Mitchell 2009; Heide 2011; Bek-Pedersen 2014). Confirming that late sources can be highly relevant for our attempts to reconstruct Old Norse mythology, these studies seriously extend the scale of sources.[4]

Text-Context

One of the major tasks of scholarship has been the reconstruction of this past Norse world's myths and mythology from representations in the form of lettered expressions in primarily medieval manuscripts. Concerning the texts as doorways to orality and underscoring the aspect of reconstruction, Joseph Harris and Karl Reichl write in their treatment of the topic:

> The medievalist is in any case necessarily bound first to the text, and only from that platform can he or she attempt to ascend to any oral milieu or specifically to informed speculation on the performances from which, logically, all our oral-derived texts originate. Medieval texts themselves vary greatly in their immanent power to reveal performance origins, but for us context, performance, and audience are always more or less reconstructions and the texts on which they are based, more or less, contested sites. (Harris and Reichl 2012: 144)

---

[4] See also The Retrospective Methods Network newsletters (RMN) edited by Frog et al. and published by the Folklore Studies/Department of Philosophy, History, Culture and Art Studies at the University of Helsinki (e.g. Lukin, Frog, and Katajamäki 2013).

Parallel with an increased awareness of "performance" and "living orality", it becomes relevant not merely to reconstruct the myths themselves, but also to recontextualize them. Thus, in acknowledging that in an oral situation, meaning emerges as much from the context as from the text itself, it becomes increasingly important to scrutinize in which ways it is possible to recontextualize the myths.

Here, when dealing with a past culture, we meet what has been one of the major methodological challenges in the study of Old Norse myth, namely that the same textual corpus that transmits and in various ways incorporates the myths is also among our very best entries to their context. In emphasizing the potential of the sagas for the anthropologist and the social historian, Victor Turner proposed new possibilities for understanding Old Norse texts and culture (Turner 1971). Yet in spite of the intriguing appeal of such a literary anthropology, the merging of text and context poses a major stumbling block for attempts to access a past reality, since the texts themselves constitute the context. Therefore debate must necessarily remain at a textual level. Consequently, the complex questions of genre and referentiality, i.e., the relationship between text and reality, are among the most vexed questions in relation to the advantages and the limitations of a literary anthropology (see Clover 2005: 253).[5]

The need for recontextualization confirms that the study of Old Norse mythology cannot be isolated from the study of Old Norse literature more generally. Since all the corners of the medieval Norse textual corpus—and, as is increasingly recognized, also post-medieval sources—offer highly relevant information for coming to grips with the myth-in-context, the study of myth can hardly be limited to include only poems and narratives that deal directly with gods and a sacred world. That the textual source material goes far beyond a restricted pool of mythic texts understood in a narrow sense implies that new results from the discipline of literature and philology are highly relevant for studies in Old Norse mythology.

New openings to the study of Norse myths partly come from study of folklore. But it seems to be the case that new approaches and heuristic engagement with methods and theories within other core disciplines, such as literature and philology, can also provide new insights that are relevant for our encounters with myth and its context. In this regard, Stephen Mitchell has suggested that a balanced view, where different methodologies and disciplines such as folklore

---

[5]   W. I. Miller's 1990 study that includes the Norse legal texts is one example, outside of the study of myths, where texts are invoked as context (1990).

and philology can meet, is preferable: "how do we take advantage of these advances while at the same time resisting the temptation to ignore what can be gained by old-fashioned philology and the study of mythology?" (Mitchell 2000, 2001: 169).

Literary and philological studies have not settled how the highly ambiguous saga-texts should be read and how the past world they describe should be accessed. The great complexity of this kind of medieval manuscript-based literature, and the many temporal and ideological layers it implies, was recognized by Preben Meulengracht Sørensen when he wrote:

> The debate about how the texts should be read has exhausted itself without any new consensus having emerged. The gap that historical investigation left when it gave up on the sagas as useable sources, literary scholarship has as yet been unable to fill, apparently because the available hermeneutic strategies are inadequate. (Meulengracht Sørensen 1993: 149)

However, some new pathways have been laid out (see Jochens 1993), implying that dichotomizing tendencies that have otherwise been dominant, say, between genres like history and fiction (Clunies Ross 1998; Hermann 2010) or between pagan traits and Christian influence (Lönnroth 1969; Vésteinn Ólason 1998), are not as firm as they may appear. For instance, Jürg Glauser has proposed that less focus on genre distinctions, that is, on textual classification and chronology, as well as an increased focus on alternative "concepts of text" (Glauser 2000a, 2007) may break down classifications that otherwise have guided our understanding of the source value of the texts. Studies in saga-texts increasingly turn attention to the number of ways in which these texts are discursively indebted to cultural, historical, and ideological forces at the time of each text witness, as well as to the reception of texts (Quinn and Lethbridge 2010). In having other foci than those literary approaches that emphasize author, literary borrowings, and the question of origins, future studies that follow up on such pathways may very likely bring to light new aspects of the textual material, aspects that will also inspire the study of myths in context.

It should be noted as well that similar to those scholars whose prevailing interest concerns orality (e.g. Gísli Sigurðsson 2004), textually-orientated scholars also work with new concepts of text, speaking not of the fluid character of oral narratives but of "mouvance" and of the "mobility of the medieval text" (see Glauser 2000a: 138, 2007: 16; and Driscoll 2010: 92). Thus, on both sides, there is an awareness of what is key to our understanding of the myths and their transmission, as well as of what is highly relevant for source evaluation, namely the instability of the text, both oral and written, over time. Such concepts of text indeed lay the ground for perceiving myths and other narratives as processes rather than as finalized units, that is, as context-dependent and changeable rather than as fixed and autonomous forms.

One of the areas of study that has the potential to pose new light on Norse mythology is the investigation of the function of memory in oral as well as in written cultures (Glauser 2000b, 2007; Mitchell 2013). In transitional cultures between orality and writing, memory functions as a vital storage room for knowledge of the past, making memory an important context for the mythology. Studies in memory can show, firstly, how personal and collective memories function and, secondly, how they were in dialogue with and had an impact on narratives and poems, in terms of both content and structure. One relevant question concerns the extent to which methods of memory and images of memory influenced the myths. It is commonly recognized that memory is structured, for example, by spatial and visual means; both spaces and visually striking images are conspicuously present in the mythology and may function as points of intersection between myths and memory (Bergsveinn Birgisson 2010; Hermann 2014, 2015).

Myth Performance

The tendency to focus on issues of performance and thus on the multidimensionality of orality has encouraged some scholars, whether implicitly or explicitly, to juxtapose the oral and the written, i.e., to conclude that writing is what the oral performance is not: that it communicates solely with the written word on the page and therefore offers a one-dimensional experience (see e.g. Gunnell 2006: 238). Such opinions support a non-neutral dichotomy between the oral and the written, a dichotomy that reinforces a difference between, on the one hand (and negatively), dead letters on the page and, on the other hand (and positively), living performances.

In accordance with such a valorizing tendency and with regard to the transfer of oral forms to writing, Ruth Finnegan maintains: "Transferring a multi-faceted en-staged enactment into the simplex medium of writing may make a stab at capturing one dimension—writable words—but passes by those other elements in which it lives" (Finnegan 2005: 173). Finnegan, however, modifies and nuances this widespread view, which reduces writing to a one-dimensional form of communication. She writes that "a growing number of crosscultural [*sic*] studies of literacy have been challenging this ethnocentric myth to bring out the multi-modality and materiality of writing" (2005: 173).

It is indeed relevant and important to investigate and come to a better understanding of the performance of mythic poems and narratives in oral contexts; that is, to emphasize all the nonverbal features as well as the social and cultural codes implied in oral performances, which is in fact the direction that scholarship takes. Only when doing that can we do justice to oral myths. But when investigating the transmission of myths in pre-Christian Scandinavia, as well as in the centuries after Christianity was formally introduced in that region, it becomes equally relevant to shed light on the performance of mythic poems and narratives in their written contexts.

The transfer of myths to writing happened in the Christian period and such activity goes hand in hand with the deprivation of the myths of their sacredness; thus at one and the same time it removes the myths from the oral medium and from their standing in a pre-Christian worldview. But despite the fact that when committed to writing myths are, strictly speaking, moved into a sphere of reception rather than one of belief, what happens to the myths over time on a media-related and communicative level is highly important, not least for source evaluation. Here it is also relevant to emphasize that myths cannot be reduced to narratives that merely explain "religious usage" (Clunies Ross 1994: 14). Rather they should be understood in a broader sense as expressions "of social and cultural concerns" (Clunies Ross 1994: 15), implying also what has increasingly been argued, namely, that Norse myths most likely continued to exist as cognitive tools well into the Christian period (e.g. Clunies Ross 1998; Lindow 1995).

There are indeed considerable differences between writing and the spoken word, but writing does not simply imply reduction and narrowing down of communicative levels. In the medieval period written texts could be an integral part of oral performances (Coleman 1996), in the sense that texts were not read silently by the individual but read aloud for an audience, and thus communicated and received aurally in a living context (e.g. Hermann Pálsson 1962; Mundal 2010).

In the medieval Norse world, written texts were in the beginning closely connected to clerical milieus. The following passage from *Jóns saga ins helga* (composed in the beginning of the thirteenth century) relates how a teacher in the cathedral school at Hólar in Iceland followed common church practice in relying on the (religious) book when communicating orally to his audience:

> Ok ávallt er hann prédikaði fyrir fólkinu, þá lét hann liggja bók fyrir sér ok tók þar af slíkt er hann talaði fyrir fólkinu, ok gerði hann þetta mest af forsjá ok lítillæti, at þar hann var ungr at aldri þótti þeim meira um

vert er til hlýddu at þeir sæi þat at hann tók sínar kenningar af helgum bókum en eigi af einu saman brjóstviti. (*Jóns saga ins helga* pp. 205–06)

(And ever when he was preaching before the people, he had a book lying before him, and took therefrom what he spoke to the people, and he did this most out of prudence and humility, because as he was young in years those that listened might lay more store by it, when they saw that he took what he taught out of holy books and not out of his own natural knowledge *or* breast-wit. (p. 552))

Books with non-ecclesiastical content were also read aloud in front of audiences. It has long been emphasized, and it is generally accepted, that this was the case for saga-texts; and it has been argued as well that eddic poems were intended to be read out loud and possibly even to be acted dramatically (Lönnroth 1979; Mitchell 1991; Gunnell 1995a, 1995b; Mundal 2010). This argument shows that when transferred to written form, the narrative material was potentially realized and received in a context that retained dimensions that otherwise confine themselves to oral situations. This observation thus locates the written texts in multi-media and multidimensional situations, where books and visible signs on the page would have been accompanied by such features as voice and bodily orientation.

In Old Norse studies, the so-called "multi-modality" of writing referred to in the quotation above by Ruth Finnegan has mostly been emphasized by scholars inspired by New Philology (see e.g. Glauser 2000a; Driscoll 2010). Such studies, looking at texts in their materiality as books and manuscripts and investigating the relationship between text and nonverbal features displayed in the manuscript, reveal how manuscripts were arenas for communication (Glauser 2007). When included in manuscripts, myths are not limited to communication through the written word, but also through such nonverbal visual features as the layout of the page, typographic arrangement, and the graphic features of the manuscript page, all of which assist in the communication of the written word (Johansson 2005; Vésteinn Ólason 2010).

Words and Images

No medium exists in a vacuum. Before writing in alphabetic literacy was available, the spoken word, runic inscription, artifacts, pictures, and ritual and bodily performances existed as parallel media, equally responsible for the mediation and transmission of myths. Like poems and narratives, pictures on physical objects (for instance, stones and buildings) transmitted scenes from myths and legend. Skaldic verse, especially in the form of ekphrasis, reveals that pictorial and oral performance were engaged in dialogue, pointing to the fact that image and orally-delivered words constituted not only parallel media, but also inter-related media.

When mediated in medieval manuscripts, the myths were communicated by other media strategies than just the act of writing. In Codex Regius (ca. 1270), the manuscript that preserves the compilation of eddic poems known as the Poetic Edda, speaker indications are made in the margins of the text, a phenomenon which illustrates that the eddic poems were received in a

Figure 1. The dialogue between Gangleri and Hár, Jafnhár, and Þriði.
Uppsala University Library, MS DG 11.

manner that in one way or other was indebted to oral performance (Gunnell 1995b). Furthermore, in the manuscript of Codex Upsaliensis (1300–1325), which preserves a version of the *Prose Edda*, a number of drawings in the margin of the text supplement the written parts of the manuscript, pointing to the circumstance that both verbal and nonverbal modes of communication were invoked by those producing and receiving the manuscripts (Glauser 2009, 2013).[6] The most famous of the drawings in the manuscript illustrates the dialogue between the disguised *æsir* calling themselves Hár, Jafnhár, and Þriði and the Swedish king who calls himself Gangleri (Figure 1).

In the *Prose Edda*, this dialogue constitutes the frame within which the mythology is revealed in a question-answer format, a form that imitates oral communication. The image that visually depicts this situation captures an oral situation which is underscored by the figures' bodily orientation, open mouths, and gestures. The *æsir* are neatly drawn and are depicted in great detail as rich and exotic kings in correspondence with what is being told in the narrative of *Gylfaginning*, where they are euhemerized as (human) kings from Troy who have migrated to the North. The Gangleri figure, in contrast, is drawn more simply and correspondingly dressed in rustic clothing. But both dialogue partners, the set of king/gods and Gangleri, have carefully depicted hand gestures, frozen in different movements (Glauser 2009: 298). It is possible that the gestures correspond to rules of figuration, like those we see in Old Norse manuscripts containing vernacular translations of Christian literature, where gestures seem to be drawn according to standards of figurative meaning in medieval clerical culture. But it is certain that the gestures serve to emphasize that the picture has as its theme an oral situation, and in supporting the narrative's form and content, this image is in dialogue with the text of the manuscript.

In medieval culture, when orality and literacy came to exist side by side, media strategies required consideration. Jürg Glauser has emphasized that the text of the *Prose Edda* deals in a self-reflective way with its status as written text (Glauser 2009: 296). Such focus on the text as a concrete physical entity clearly contrasts with the less concrete nature of oral communication; and it reveals that in the medieval period, manuscript redactors considered *how* texts should be conceptualized to be an issue. But whereas the *Prose Edda* in some instances highlights the text's relation to written culture, at the same time we note that the image depicting the *æsir* in dialogue with Gangleri, strongly emphasizing an oral situation, seems to deconstruct its claim of written textuality. Thus, the picture can be seen as a reaction to the written text's claim of

---

[6]   See especially Jürg Glauser (2013) where Codex Upsaliensis' images and texts, and their interactions, are treated in great detail and with special attention to the theoretical implications of the text-image relationships.

Figure 2. Figures with hand gestures. Uppsala University Library, MS DG 11.

being self-contained. In that sense, the illustration, at one and the same time, speaks with the text (its form and content) and against it (its medium). In the instance of Codex Uppsaliensis, the verbal and visual representations on the manuscript page comment on each other, and the interplay between these two modes underscores the degree to which manuscript compilers and redactors were reflecting on media strategies.[7]

Hand gestures represent a means of expression alternative to writing (Schmitt 1991). More than once we find representations of gestures in the margin of Codex Upsaliensis (see e.g. Grape 1962), opposing the view that the written text was isolated from other media-related strategies. In the Upsaliensis manuscript, the text of the *Edda* is accompanied by a list of skalds (*Skáldatal*), a genealogy of the Icelandic Sturlunga family, and a list of law-speakers. These inserted texts all refer to experts of the Old Norse world, experts who were capable of transmitting oral myths and other oral information (skalds and law-speakers) and to lore and structural principles (genealogies and the principle of listing) deriving from orality. On the page where the list of skalds ends

---

[7] Michael Camille has stressed the value of investigating the interplay between and commenting of several different modes and media, i.e., image and verbal forms (Camille 1992).

(Figure 2), three figures are drawn, two of which display an emphasis on their hand gestures, indicating visually once again the role of orality.

We cannot take for granted that the drawings were made contemporaneously with the text—they may very well be later additions—nor can we be sure that they refer directly to the text's content (cf. Aðalheiður Guðmundsdóttir 2009); however, it seems as if the drawings not only support the text's content, but also react to it, and it should be noted that one figure is a woman, despite the fact that the listed skalds are all males.

Drawings like these imply the possibility that in the margin of the text, outside of the text itself, recipients found a place for commenting on the text, its content, and its media. As claimed by Walter Ong, amongst others, writing separates narrator and audience and establishes a situation where narratives are not created in the actual oral communication situation, having narrator and audience in their bodily presence as simultaneous participants (Ong 1982). Whereas the oral speaker experiences the audience in front of him, the writer's audience is farther away in time and space, or, laconically phrased: with writing, distance replaces proximity. However, speaker indications such as those in Codex Regius and the illustrations in the margin of the texts (as in Codex Upsaliensis) show that, despite time and distance, recipients acted towards the written texts, providing evidence that manuscripts, including those containing myths and referring to mythic experts, acted as arenas for communication.

Diachronic and Synchronic Approaches

Despite the fact that the interplay between orality and literacy is expressed in multiple ways, scholarly debates have often concentrated on the question of the oral background and the oral prehistory of the Norse texts, and as a consequence the orality/literacy pair has predominantly been conceived diachronically, i.e., first there was orality, then writing. This diachronically orientated perspective has been slowly changing, and it is now more frequently being questioned (Ranković, Melve, and Mundal 2010; Danielsson 2002). It seems appropriate that the diachronic perspective would have been paramount at a time when scholarly interest focused on the myths' origins and their oldest forms. One of the major recent achievements, a result of the renewed focus on orality and the nature of oral forms, has been an enhanced awareness of the problems that are connected with the search for so-called original and authentic myths in their oldest forms. Emphasizing the fact that multiple versions of an oral text can have existed, as well as underscoring the non-fixity and non-hierarchical organization of oral texts, Gísli Sigurðsson has written the following about the narrative materials that form the backbone of the myths in the *Prose Edda:*

> We need hardly be surprised if there is not always complete agree-
> ment between the versions of stories reflected in prose and verse [...]
> It would be closer to the mark to assume that at any given time there
> would have been various versions of the story in circulation, without
> any of them precluding any other. (Gísli Sigurðsson 2004: 16)

This comment points to the existence of myth multiforms. Obviously, prose
and poetry represented the myths differently. Not only would allusive poetry
have relied to a higher extent than prose on foreknowledge, that is, on actively
participating recipients who shared a collective memory of the mythic tradition, but also within each genre, differences would have existed. This is seen, for
instance, in comparing the two existing prose versions of Baldr's death, namely
Snorri's and Saxo's, in the *Edda* and the *Gesta Danorum* respectively. Whereas
the first represents the myth in the context of a mythography, the latter incor-
porated it in a historiography. The ideologies of the writers, as well as their
thematic and stylistic choices, actually resulted in two different literary treatments of the same myth (e.g., Clunies Ross 1992).

To that crucial fact, which is indeed relevant for our view on the myths,
we need to bear in mind that, at any given time, these myths would have been
transmitted and exchanged in multiple media, the oral and the pictorial as
well as—with the introduction of alphabetic literacy—the written. The added
media layer of literacy introduced a higher level of complexity to the myths and
their transmission and, as the image shows, they were debated and discussed.
Undoubtedly, the transfer of mythic content between genres and between media
shaped the material in each its own way, in principle resulting in a number of
equally "authentic" myths. Consequently, we are currently in a place where
tracing things like the original myth, its oldest form, and its original medium
prove highly problematic. This conclusion implies that we need to rethink the
very concept of text (oral as well as written), which has obvious and profound
consequences for the evaluation of these texts as sources. Furthermore, when
we shelve the search for original forms, we need not insert the orality/literacy
pair in a diachronic perspective, and attention can be drawn to alternative ways
for the pair to meet, paving the way for synchronically orientated studies that
investigate the implications of mythic content and its transmission in parallel
oral and literary media—and non-verbal media, as well.

To sum up the key points of these remarks very briefly: elements of the
orality/literacy debate that have a bearing on the study of Old Norse myths
are concerned with performance and myths' non-verbal aspects, as well as the

move away from a diachronic perspective on the orality/literacy pair. Other related questions, such as the textual editing and staging of the myths and of oral performances, are, of course, highly relevant as well. The orality/literacy pair interacts in a number of ways in the transitional world that created the myths, and only continued investigation of these different meetings across time and space and their implications can bring us to a position more fruitful and desirable than that of Tantalos.

Works Cited

Primary Sources

Gesta Danorum
Saxo Grammaticus. *Gesta Danorum: The History of the Danes*. Ed. Karsten Friis-Jensen and transl. Peter Fisher. Oxford: 2015.

Jóns saga ins helga
Íslenzk fornrit, 15 (I:2). Ed. Sigurgeir Steingrímsson, Ólafur Halldórsson, and Peter Foote. Reykjavík: 2003. Pp. 173-316.

TRANSLATION
Origines Islandicae. Vol. 1. Transl. Guðbrandur Vigfusson and F. York Powell. Oxford: 1905.

Gísla saga Súrssonar
Íslenzk fornrit, 6. Ed. Björn K. Þórólfsson and Guðni Jónsson. Reykjavík: 1943. Pp. 1-118.

Prose Edda
Snorri Sturluson. *Edda: Prologue and Gylfaginning*. 2nd ed. Ed. Anthony Faulkes. London: 2005.
Snorri Sturluson. *Edda. Skáldskaparmál 1: Introduction, Text and Notes*. Ed. Anthony Faulkes. London: 1998.

Secondary Sources

Acker, Paul. 1998. *Revising Oral Theory: Formulaic Composition in Old English and Old Icelandic Verse*. New York.
Andersson, Theodore M. 1964. *The Problem of Icelandic Saga Origins: A Historical Survey*. New Haven.
———. 2008. "From Tradition to Literature in the Sagas." In Mundal and Wellendorf 2008: 7–17. Copenhagen.

Aðalheiður Guðmundsdóttir. 2009. "Dancing Images from Medieval Iceland." In Ney, Williams, and Charpentier Ljungqvist 2009: 13–20.

Bauman, Richard. 1986. *Story, Performance, and Event: Contextual Studies of Oral Narrative.* Cambridge Studies in Oral and Literate Cultures, 10. Cambridge.

Bek-Pedersen, Karen. 2014. "Reconstruction: On Crabs, Folklore and the History of Religion." In Sävborg and Karen Bek-Pedersen 2014: 83–101.

Bergsveinn Birgisson. 2010. "The Old Norse Kenning as a Mnemonic Figure." In *The Making of Memory in the Middle Ages.* Ed. Lucie Dolezalová. Later Medieval Europe, 4. Leiden. Pp. 199–213.

Bugge, Sophus. 1881–1889. *Studier over de nordiske Gude- og Heltesagns Oprindelse.* Christiania.

Camille, Michael. 1992. *Image on the Edge: The Margins of Medieval Art.* London.

Clover, Carol. 2005. "Icelandic Family sagas (*Íslendingasogur*)." In Clover and Lindow 2005: 239–315.

Clover, Carol, and John Lindow, eds. 2005. *Old Norse Icelandic Literature: A Critical Guide.* Toronto. Orig. pub. Ithaca, 1985.

Clunies Ross, Margaret. 1992. "Mythic Narrative in Saxo Grammaticus and Snorri Sturluson." In *Saxo Grammaticus: Tra storiografia e letteratura.* Ed. Carlo Santit. Rome. Pp. 47–59

———. 1994. *Prolonged Echoes: Old Norse Myths in Medieval Northern Society: Vol. 1: The Myths.* Viking Collection, 7. Odense.

———. 1998. *Prolonged Echoes: Old Norse Myths in Medieval Northern Society: Vol. 2: The Reception of Norse Myths in Medieval Iceland.* Viking Collection, 10. Odense.

———, ed. 2000. *Old Icelandic Literature and Society.* Cambridge.

Coleman, Joyce. 1996. *Public Reading and the Reading Public in Late Medieval England and France.* Cambridge.

Danielsson, Tommy. 2002. *Hrafnkels saga eller Fallet med den undflyende traditionen.* Hedemora

Driscoll, Matthew. 2010. "The Words on the Page: Thoughts on Philology, Old and New." In Quinn and Lethbridge 2010: 87–104.

Dronke, Ursula, and Peter Dronke. 1977. "The Prologue of the Prose Edda: Explorations of a Latin Background." In *Sjötíu ritgerðir helgaðar Jakobi Benediktssyni 20. júlí 1977.* Vol. 1. Ed. Einar G. Pétursson and Jónas Kristjánsson. Reykjavík. Pp. 153–76.

Fidjestøl, Bjarne. 1999. *The Dating of Eddic Poetry: A Historical Survey and Methodological Investigation.* Ed. Odd Einar Haugen. Bibliotheca Arnamagnæana, 41. Copenhagen.

Finnegan, Ruth. 1992. *Oral Traditions and the Verbal Arts.* London & New York.

———. 2005. "The How of Literature." *Oral Tradition* 20(2): 164–87.

Foley, John Miles. 1991. "Orality, Textuality, and Interpretation." In *Vox intexta: Orality and Textuality in the Middle Ages*. Ed. A. N. Doane and Carol Braun Pasternack. Madison. Pp. 34–44

———. 1991a. *Immanent Art: From Structure to Meaning in Traditional Oral Epic*. Bloomington.

———. 1992. "Word-Power, Performance, and Tradition." *Journal of Folklore* 105: 275–301.

Gade, Kari Ellen. 2000. "Poetry and its Changing Importance in Medieval Icelandic Culture." In Clunies Ross 2000: 61–95. Cambridge.

Gísli Sigurðsson. 2003. "Medieval Icelandic Studies." *Oral Tradition* 18(2): 207–209.

———. 2004. *The Medieval Icelandic Saga and Oral Tradition*. The Milman Parry Collection of Oral Literature, 2. Cambridge, MA.

———. 2008. "How to Read Written Sagas from an Oral Culture?" In Mundal and Wellendorf 2008: 19–28.

Glauser, Jürg. 2000a. "Marginalien des Sagatextes: Zu der Rändern von Texten in der mittelalterlichen Literatur Islands." In *Den fornnordiska texten: I filologisk och litteraturvetenskaplig belysning*. Ed. Kristinn Jóhannesson, Karl G. Johansson, and Lars Lönnroth. Gothenburg. Pp. 136–157.

———. 2000b. "Sagas of Icelanders (*Íslendinga sögur*) and *þættir* as the literary representation of a new social space." In Clunies Ross 2000: 203–220.

———. 2007. "The Speaking Bodies of Saga Texts." In Quinn, Heslop, and Wills 2004: 13–36.

———. 2009. "Sensory Deceptions: Concepts of Mediality in the Prose Edda." In Ney, Williams, and Ljungqvist 2009: 296–302.

———. 2013. "Unheilige Bücher: Zur Implosion mythischen Erzählens in der 'Prosa-Edda.'" *Das Mittelalter* 18(1): 106–121.

Grape, Anders. 1962. *Snorre Sturlasons Edda: Uppsala-handskriften DG 11*. Stockholm.

Gunnell, Terry. 1995a. *The Origins of Drama in Scandinavia*. Cambridge.

———. 1995b. "The Play of Skírnir." *Nordic Theater Studies* 7: 21–35.

———. 2006. "'Til holts ek gekk...' The Performance demands of *Skírnismál*, *Fáfnismál* and *Sigrdrífumál* in Liminal Time and Sacred Space." In *Old Norse Religion in Long-term Perspectives*. Ed. Anders Andrén, Kristina Jennbert, and Catharina Raudvere. Lund. Pp. 238–242.

———. 2013. "*Vǫluspá* in Performance." In *The Nordic Apocalypse: Approaches to Vǫluspá and Nordic Days of Judgement*. Ed. Terry Gunnell and Annette Lassen. Turnhout. Pp. 63–77.

Harris, Joseph. 1979. "The *Senna*: From Description to Literary Theory." *Michigan Germanic Studies* 5(1): 65–74.

———. 1983. "Eddic Poetry as Oral Poetry: The Evidence of Parallel Passages in the Helgi Poems for Questions of Composition and Performance." In *Edda:*

A Collection of Essays. Ed. R. J. Glendinning and H. Bessason. Manitoba. Pp. 210–35.

———. 2005. "Eddic Poetry." In Clover and Lindow 2005: 68–156.

———. 2010. "Old Norse Memorial Discourse between Orality and Literacy." In Ranković, Melve, and Mundal 2010: 119–133.

Harris, Joseph, and Karl Reichl. 2012. "Performance and Performers." In *Medieval Oral Literature.* Ed. Karl Reichl. Göttingen. Pp. 141–202.

Heide, Eldar. 2011. "Loki, the Vätte, and the Ash Lad: A Study Combining Old Scandinavian and Late Material." *Viking and Medieval Scandinavia* 7: 63–106.

Heide, Eldar, and Karen Bek-Pedersen, eds. 2014. *New Focus on Retrospective Methods. Resuming Methodological Discussions: Case Studies from Northern Europe.* Folklore Fellows Communications, 307. Helsinki.

Hermann Pálsson. 1962. *Sagnaskemmtun Íslendinga.* Reykjavík.

Hermann, Pernille, ed. 2005. *Literacy in Medieval and Early Modern Scandinavian Culture.* Viking Collection, 16. Odense.

———. 2010. "Founding Narratives and the Representation of Memory in Saga Literature." *ARV: Nordic Yearbook of Folklore* 66: 69–87.

———. 2014. "Key aspects of Memory and Remembering in Old Norse-Icelandic Literature." In *Minni and Muninn: Memory in Medieval Nordic Culture.* Ed. Pernille Hermann, Stephen A. Mitchell, and Agnes Arnórsdóttir. Acta Scandinavica, 4. Turnhout. Pp. 13–39.

———. 2015. "Memory, Imagery and Visuality in Old Norse Literature." *Journal of English and Germanic Philology* 114: 317–340.

Heslop, Kate. Forthcoming. "The Mediality of Mímir." In *Medial perspectives on textual culture in the Icelandic Middle Ages.* Ed. Kate Heslop and Jürg Glauser. Zurich.

Hollander, Lee M. 1963. "Recent Works and Views on the Poetic Edda." *Scandinavian Studies* 35(2): 101–109.

Holtsmark, Anne. 1964. *Studier i Snorres mytologi.* Oslo.

Jesch, Judith. 2005. "Skaldic Verse, a Case of Literacy *Avant la Lettre*?" In Hermann 2005: 187–210.

Jochens, Jenny. 1993. "Marching to a Different Drummer: New Trends in Medieval Icelandic Scholarship: A Review Article." *Comparative Studies in Society and History* 35(1): 197–207.

Johansson, Karl G. 2005. "On Orality and the *Verschriftlichung* of *Skírnismál.*" In Hermann 2005: 167–186.

Lindow, John. 2005. "Mythology and Mythography." In Clover and Lindow 2005: 21–67.

———. 1995. "Bloodfeud and Scandinavian Mythology." *Alvíssmál* 4: 51–68.

Lord, Albert B. 1960. *The Singer of Tales*. Harvard Studies in Comparative Literature, 24. Cambridge.

Lukin, Karina, Frog, and Sakari Katajamäki, eds. 2013. "Limited Sources, Boundless Possibilities. Textual Scholarship and the Challenge of Oral and Written Texts." Special Issue of *RMN Newsletter*. http://www.helsinki.fi/folkloristiikka/English/RMN/RMN_7_Dec_2013_Limited_Sources_Boundless_Possibilities.pdf [accessed June 2016]

Lönnroth, Lars. 1969. "The Noble Heathen: A Theme in the Sagas." *Scandinavian Studies* 41(1): 1–29.

———. 1971. "Hjálmar's Death Song and the Delivery of Eddic Poetry." *Speculum* 46: 1–20.

———. 1978. *Den dubbla scenen: muntlig diktning från Eddan till Abba*. Stockholm.

———. 1979. "The Double Scene of Arrow-Odd's Drinking Contest." In *Medieval Narrative: A Symposium*. Ed. H. Bekker-Nielsen et al. Odense. Pp. 94–119.

———. 1981. "Iǫrð fannz æva né upphiminn: A Formula Analysis." In *Speculum Norroenum: Norse Studies in Memory of Gabriel Turville-Petre*. Ed. Ursula Dronke. Odense. Pp. 310–327.

———. 2009. "Old Norse Text as Performance." *Scripta Islandica* 60: 49–60.

Meulengracht Sørensen, Preben. 1993. *Saga and Society*. Odense.

Miller, William. 1990. *Blood-taking and Peacemaking: Feud, Law, and Society in Saga Iceland*. Chicago.

Mitchell, Stephen A. 1991. *Heroic Sagas and Ballads.* Ithaca.

———. 2000. "Folklore and Philology Revisited: Medieval Scandinavian Folklore?" In *Norden og Europa: Fagtradisjoner i nordisk etnologi og folkloristikk*. Ed. Bjarne Rogan and Bente Gullveig Alber. Oslo. Pp. 286–94.

———. 2001. "Performance and Norse Poetry: The Hydromel of Praise and the Effluvia of Scorn." *Oral Tradition* 16(1): 168–202.

———. 2003. "Reconstructing Old Norse Oral Tradition." *Oral Tradition* 18(2): 203–06.

———. 2009. "Odin, Magic and a Swedish Trial from 1484." *Scandinavian Studies* 81(1): 263–86.

———. 2013. "Memory, Mediality, and the 'Performative Turn': Recontextualizing Remembering in Medieval Scandinavia." *Scandinavian Studies* 85(3): 282–305.

———. 2014. "Continuity: Folklore's Problem Child?" In Sävborg and Bek-Pedersen 2014: 41–58.

Mundal, Else. 2010. "How Did the Arrival of Writing Influence Old Norse Oral Culture." In Ranković, Melve, and Mundal 2010: 163–81.

Mundal, Else, and Jonas Wellendorf, eds. 2008. *Oral Art Forms and their Passage into Writing*. Copenhagen.

Ney, Agneta, Henrik Williams, and Fredrik C. Ljungqvist, eds. 2009. *Á austrvega: Saga and East Scandinavia*. Preprint papers of the 14th International Saga Conference. Gävle.

Ong, Walter J. 1982. *Orality and Literacy: The Technologizing of the Word*. London.

Quinn, Judy. 2000. "From Orality to Literacy in Medieval Iceland." In Clunies Ross 2000: 30–60.

Quinn, Judy, Kate Heslop, and Tarrin Wills, eds. 2007. *Learning and Understanding in the Old Norse World: Essays in Honour of Margaret Clunies Ross*. Medieval Texts and Cultures of Northern Europe, 18. Turnhout.

Quinn, Judy, and Emily Lethbridge, eds. 2010. *Creating the Medieval Saga*. Viking Collection, 18. Odense.

Ranković, Slavica., Leidulf Melve, and Else Mundal, eds. 2010. *Along the Oral-Written Continuum: Types of Texts and their Implications*. Utrecht Studies in Medieval Literary, 20. Turnhout.

Schjødt, Jens Peter. 1988. "Recent Scholarship in Old Norse Mythology." *Religious Studies Review* 14(2): 104–10.

Schmitt, Jean-Claude. 1991. "The Rationale of Gestures in the West: Third to Thirteenth Centuries." In *A Cultural History of Gesture: From Antiquity to Present Day*. Ed. Jan Bremer and Herman Roodenberg. Oxford. Pp. 60–70.

Sigurður Nordal. 1920. *Snorri Sturluson*. Reykjavík.

———. 1940. *Hrafnkatla*. Studia Islandica, 7. Reykjavík.

Sävborg, Daniel, and Karen Bek-Pedersen, eds. 2014. *Folklore in Old Norse: Old Norse in Folklore*. Nordistica Tartuensia, 20. Tartu.

Tangherlini, Timothy R. 2003. "Performing thorough the Past: Ethnophilology and Oral Tradition." Afterword. *Western Folklore* 62: 143–49.

Turner, Victor W. 1971. "An Anthropological Approach to the Icelandic Saga." In *The Translation of Culture: Essays to E. E. Evans-Pritchard*. Ed. T. O. Beidelman. London. Pp. 349–74.

Vésteinn Ólason. 1998. *Dialogues with the Viking Age*. Reykjavík.

———. 2010. "The Poetic Edda: Literature or Folklore?" In Ranković, Melve, and Mundal 2010: 227–52.

Würth, Stefanie. 2007. "Skaldic Poetry and Performance." In Quinn, Heslop, and Wills 2007: 263–81.

Framing the Hero
Medium and Metalepsis in Old Norse Heroic Narrative[1]

Kate Heslop
University of California, Berkeley

Abstract: This essay argues for a medial perspective on heroic legend. Traditional iconographic approaches to this material are methodologically problematic and their potential for generating new readings seems limited. The essay proposes focusing instead on the primary sources' own discourse on their materiality and historicity—their "medium theory", in W. J. T. Mitchell's words. This new approach is exemplified by a close study of the frame, a formal device that guides and enables interpretation, in both manuscript codices and decorated runestones. Among the examples used are the Codex Regius manuscript of the Poetic Edda and the Ramsund and Gök runic inscriptions.

Old Norse heroic narratives are stories that know they are stories. They have always raised questions of medium and mediation: in what form tales were transmitted before the advent of writing, how images can be used to track developments in the narratives, and whether traces of earlier forms can be discerned in later works. The field seems to be gradually abandoning its preoccupation with lost origins. But medial reflection retains its importance and interest, in the form of a double commitment to understanding medieval uses, in a broad sense, of these texts, and to expanding our sense of what media can do. This is because the advent of writing in Scandinavia opened new possibilities for the transmission of narrative and maintenance of cultural memory, and generated

---

[1] I am grateful to Stephen Mitchell for the invitation to present an earlier version of the following remarks at the Old Norse Mythology in its Comparative Contexts conference, and to my audience for their comments. My thanks also go to Judy Quinn and Karin Sanders, who read draft versions and made a number of helpful suggestions.

interferences between text, image, inscription and performance, laying the groundwork for a vernacular theory of the medium. Rather than appearing as a theoretical meta-discourse, this takes the form of what Mitchell (2004) calls "medium theory", and is expressed within the narratives themselves. In heroic narrative, it is especially apparent in the texts' negotiation of their own historicity, a defining characteristic of heroic legends as compared to mythological narratives. How their subject-matter was preserved and transmitted from the past is a question of urgent, existential interest to these texts. In what follows I will argue that the ways heroic narrative is *framed* offer particularly rich insights into these texts' self-conception as historical. The word *frame* can mean many things: from a "non-physical boundary" (Duro 1996b: 1) such as the institutional or gendered frame, through the frame narratives ubiquitous in medieval texts, to the physical border around an image. Cop movies offer the "frame-up" with its implications, relevant here, of purposeful invention. The common denominator is that the frame "guides and enables interpretation" (Wolf 2006: 3). Its presence in the conceptual armory of several disciplines suits the frame well to comparative study. The present contribution will sketch a comparison between two self-conscious and sophisticated acts of framing in medieval Scandinavia, the visual framing of images on late Viking Age Swedish runestones, and textual framing in the Codex Regius of the Poetic Edda. In relation to the central figure of Sigurðr Fáfnisbani, I will investigate what it means to frame the hero, and what happens when that frame is broken.

Edgar Degas called the frame "the pimp of the painting" (qtd. in Lebensztejn 1988: 38): that which offers access to the autonomous work of art it encloses (Simmel 1902). In his writings from the mid-1970s on the parergon, Jacques Derrida deconstructs this conception of framing, noting how the frame "is distinguished from two grounds, but in relation to each of these, it disappears into the other" (Derrida 1979: 24). As Paul Duro puts it, for Derrida the frame "rhetoricizes the relationship between inside [and] outside" (Duro 1996b: 8). The frame, as *parergon*, is neither a part of the work (*ergon*), nor extrinsic to it, but rather is a structure by means of which a differentiation between work and notwork is generated: "while enclosing and protecting an interior, the frame also produces an outside with which it must communicate" (Rodowick 1994: 98–99). Study of the picture frame lingers "in a no-man's-land between the fine and the decorative arts" (Mitchell, Roberts and Adair 2010), and its history is obscure. In a seminal article from 1969, Meyer Schapiro explored the material conditions of possibility of artworks, the frame among them. Schapiro points out that the regular image field is itself "an advanced artifact" (1969: 223) in contrast to the rough unbounded surface the natural rock offered to cave painters. Field and boundary, he argues, come into being as concepts when artists have regular

Figure 1. Lärbro Stora Hammars I, Gotland, mid-Viking Age, 3.12 x 1.43 m.
Image courtesy of Stephen Mitchell.

smooth surfaces to work on, such as ceramic pots or masonry walls, yielding "a field with a distinct plane (or regular curvature) of the surface and a definite boundary which may be the smoothed edges of an artifact" (Schapiro 1969: 224). The shaped runestone thus provides a minimal frame in the form of its edges. This is confirmed by the fact that runic inscriptions on natural rockfaces, unlike those on shaped stones, invariably have carved frames (cf. Stern 2013: 22n60).

The earliest frames are found on Egyptian ceramics and tomb paintings of the second millennium BCE, and take the form of horizontal bands. Ground lines both link the figures together and emphasize the axes of the field, enabling contrasts to be established between stillness and movement (Mitchell, Roberts and Adair 2010; Schapiro 1969: 224–26). Scandinavian instances of composition in bands include the Gotland picture stones (for instance Lärbro Stora Hammars I, Figure 1), although even the earliest, Lindquist's Group A, also exhibit interlace borders that follow the edge of the stone (see Karnell 2012: 16–21 for images).

Ancient Greek vase painting and architectural reliefs mark the advent of the so-called "open frame" (Hurwit 1977: 6), in which "pictorial content and enframed field do not precisely coincide" (Hurwit 1977: 14). Truncation of the image by the frame gives a sense of depth, as "the frame seems to cross a represented field that extends behind it at the sides" (Schapiro 1969: 227). A handsome Scandinavian instance is the Style E sword-pommel from Stora Ihre, Hellvi, Gotland (Figure 2), where a single continuous animal body is glimpsed through three "windows". The image crossing the frame, on the other hand, intensifies the illusion of movement. The wood-carvings from the stave church at Hylestad in Norway (Figure 3) nicely illustrate this, with Sigurðr's body spilling over the borders of the medallion he is confined within as he gives Fáfnir his death-blow. A final Greek development relevant to the runestone material is what Hurwit calls the "pictorialization of the border" (1977: 2), whereby figures in the image *interact with* the frame, leaning objects against it, seizing it in their hands, and so on. This implies a shift in the role of the image from decorative and emblematic to narrative, associated in the Greek material with the growth of a corpus of myth and heroic legend at the end of the Geometric period, ca. 900–700 BCE— an idea with resonance for the late Viking Age runestones. Medieval framing practices in media such as illuminated books, stained glass, stone sculpture, and embroidery yield many examples of the open frame (cf. Broderick 1982),

Figure 2. Detail of sword-pommel from Stora Ihre grave 174, Gotland, second half of the eighth century. Length: 9.5 cm. Image courtesy of the Swedish National Heritage Board.

Figure 3. Detail of Hylestad church portal, Setesdal, first half of the thirteenth century. 2.2 x 0. 52 m. Image courtesy of the Museum of Cultural History, University of Oslo.

as well as bearing witness to a new tendency, "the manic compulsion to divide and subdivide" (Kemp 1996: 19). Particularly in stained glass, where narratives are divided up between "semicircles or quarter circles, blossom leaves, half or whole quatrefoils" (Kemp 1996: 20), the complex geometrical structures that mediated visual narrative in the Middle Ages gave rise to conventions such as fixed *mise-en-page*, which worked as "ontological and epistemological maps" for reading these images (Whatling 2010: 83). The existence of stable conventions in turn allowed their violation to be marked and meaning-bearing, especially in the case of metalepsis, a point to which I will return in the final part of this essay.

Framing in the Runestone Medium

Although the "unframed" image persists, and occurs in every time and place, from the early Upplandic stones from Möjbro (U 877, fifth–sixth centuries) and Krogsta (U 1125, sixth century, Figure 4), to the Late Viking Age stones at Ålum (Ålum 3, DR 96, reverse side) or Altuna (U 1161), runestones exhibit broad, geographically inflected (cf. e.g. Barnes 2012: 68–70) tendencies towards increasing explicitness and complexity of framing through time. In particular, the latest phase of runestone production, the Swedish Late Viking Age stones, trouble easy distinctions between frame, content and ground.

Traditionally, runestone studies have focused on the runic inscription and placed the ornament and the stone itself in the parergonal roles of frame and

Figure 4. Krogsta (U 1125), Uppland, sixth century. 1.7 x 0.85 m.
Image courtesy of the Swedish National Heritage Board.

ground respectively.[2] Mats Malm describes the traditional view: "Runstenarnas skrivtecken [...] inramas [...] an utstuderade ornament" (2011: 4) (runestones' written characters are framed by studied ornament). On these late ornamented stones, however, a reversal of the frame/content relationship takes place, at least as far as the visual impact of the stones is concerned. Here the rune band becomes a frame, demarcating a pictorial field. A similar reversal has taken place in runestone scholarship in recent years, with a number of interesting contributions, especially by younger scholars, paying close attention to figural decoration on the Swedish Late Viking Age stones (Oehrl 2006 and 2011; Helmbrecht 2011; Stern 2013; Zilmer 2011); the complex medial signature of the combination of stone, inscription and ornament is taken up by Bianchi 2010. Some of this work touches on the topic of framing (Stern 2013; Zilmer 2011; cf. also, somewhat controversially, Andrén 2000), but as yet there has been no thorough study of the relationship between the images and the decorative borders, rune bands, or rune-animals that frame them.[3] This is not that study. Instead the following, necessarily brief overview serves as a background for the discussion of the Ramsund and Gök stones in the following section, by exploring the conventions that these stones play on.

The Eggja stone (dated to 650–700; see Spurkland 2005: 54, 56, for a drawing and photograph), with its horse motif framed by lines of runes on three sides, is an early and rather isolated runic instance of band composition.[4] Of the six decorated Norwegian stones in the younger *fuþark* (*NIyR* I: 159), only the Alstad (ca. 1000), Vang (early eleventh century) and Dynna (first half of eleventh century) stones are complete enough to draw any conclusions about framing practices as they relate to images. Runic inscription and figural decoration are strictly separated from one another on these stones (cf. Spurkland 2005: 92). On all three the inscription is on the narrow edge of the stone, with the vegetal ornament and/or images on the broad side framed by a decorative ground-line and simple incised lines running perpendicular to the ground-line along the stone's long sides.

[2] Of course there has been a good deal of art-historical interest in runestone ornament, especially as it relates to dating (see e.g. Thompson 1975; Fuglesang 1998; Lager 2002; Gräslund 2006). The Sigurðr engravings have also long attracted attention; for bibliography see below.

[3] Stern's 2013 dissertation comes the closest, collecting a large amount of data highly relevant to several topics touched on below, for example the issue of the spatial relationships between elements, but its main interest is in the images rather than the frame.

[4] It is possible that the image and runic inscription on the Eggja stone were executed at different times (Williams 2013: 200).

Figure 5. Hunnestad 3 (DR 284), Scania, late tenth-early eleventh century. 1.79 x 1.06 m. Image courtesy of Stephen Mitchell.

A Danish innovation is for the inscription to follow the outline of the stone within a band consisting of two parallel lines.[5] A refinement of this is the "portal" layout (Fuglesang 2001: 178), in which the rune band forms a doorframe-like shape mimicking the shape of the stone's top half. The Hunnestad monument (DR 282–6, late tenth–early eleventh centuries) offers several instances of portal framing of images, one with two parallel rune bands in "portal" configuration framing a warrior figure (DR 282), and one where the portal consists not of a rune band, but of a serpent-like animal (the Hyrrokkin stone, DR 284, Figure 5).

---

[5] Cf. *Danmarks Runindskrifter: Saglexikon*, s.v. "Indskriftordning b. Konturordningen". Erik Moltke has a figure giving an overview of Danish runestone layouts (1985: 270). He suggests that the fragmentary Horne stone (DR 34, tenth century) is the oldest representative of *konturordning* (1985: 246).

Figure 6. Jelling 2 (DR 42), southern Denmark, late tenth century. 2.43 x 2.90 m (inscription side). Image courtesy of the National Museum of Denmark.

This combination of the portal type with another Danish development, the rune band with snake-head termination, produces a rune-animal following the contours of the stone (see further examples at Fuglesang 2001: 180). Signe Horn Fuglesang sees this type as the precursor of the Urnes rune-animal, and suggests that the Danish Jelling 2 stone, where the double lines that frame the runebands are furnished with tendrils which intertwine with a (now-destroyed) snake, was an important influence on the later Swedish development of the rune-animal (2001: 161). The Jelling 2 stone (DR 42, late tenth century, Figure 6) exerted a powerful influence on later runestone fashions (Wilson and Klindt-Jensen 1966; Fuglesang 2001; Graham-Campbell 2013). Among its many innovations (cf Roesdahl 2013) is a new kind of framing. Two of its three sides are dominated by large images, of a quadruped fighting a serpent and a crucifixion

Figure 7. Stora Runhällen (U 1164), Uppland, eleventh century. 1.67 x 1.6 m. Image courtesy of the Swedish National Heritage Board.

respectively, above a single horizontal line of runes. It has long been recognized that the left-to-right, horizontal orientation of the runic inscription shows the influence of manuscript layout. Else Roesdahl has recently taken this idea further, suggesting that the monument is a "bog af sten" (book in stone):

> Den første og bredeste side med sin særlig udformning er en tekstside, mens de følgende sider, som kunne ses under ét og som hver har et stort billede inden for ensdannede og sammenhængende rammer, svarer til et billedopslag i en fornemt illustreret bog. (Roesdahl 1999: 242)

> (The first and broadest side with its special form is a text side, while the following sides, each of which can be seen as a whole and has a large image within a matching, continuous frame, corresponds to an illustrated opening in a splendid illuminated book.)

The Continental, Christian milieu in which Harald Blátǫnn (Harald Bluetooth, r. ca. 958–987) moved makes it likely that he and his artists were exposed to Carolingian and Ottonian manuscript art, with gifts given at his baptism as one possible vector (Wamers 2000: 158). The Ringerike- and Urnes-style Swedish runestones of the late Viking Age explore the idea of inscription as frame most intensively, perhaps due to the prominence of the ground in the Urnes style, in the form of the spaces enclosed by the style's characteristic loops (Owen 2001: 204).

The Late Viking Age runestone frame is an open frame, to use Hurwit's terms. Images are usually placed so that they touch one another or the frame.[6] This seems to have been an important organizing principle. One possible reason could be that this is a reflex of the space-filling interlace types of composition ubiquitous in Scandinavian art. It could also have been encouraged by the grooved incision technique used to carve these stones. The Gotland rune stones (Lindquist's Type E) are carved in a relief technique and here the tendency for decorative elements to touch the rune band is less marked. Many late Viking Age stones exhibit mutual encroachment of frame and image: cropping of the image by the rune band, overlapping of the rune band by the image, or, often, both. The majority of stones with this feature are images of the so-called "Great Beast", e.g. U 1164 Stora Runhällen (Figure 7),[7] and frame/image encroachments may have become visual conventions for expressing the beast's dynamic movement and strength, ideologemes central to runestone iconography, as Fuglesang (2005) observes. It has been suggested that cropping in the Gotland picture stones results from re-use and resulting misalignment of templates (Åhfeldt 2012b: 190), and a similar explanation could perhaps be considered here, especially as recent research suggests that the rune band and the ornament were often not carved by the same person (Åhfeldt 2012). However, the frequent occurrence of frame-image encroachment on the Swedish late Viking Age runestones strongly suggests that it was not accidental, and may have been intended to enhance certain spatial effects, notably depth and dynamic movement. The final aspect of the open frame as described by Hurwit is the interaction of figures with the frame, for instance on the Aspö stone (Sö 175), where the rune-animals intertwine with the frontal human figure's elbows and knees, giving rise to a striking illusion of depth, and at Rångsta (U 1065), where a frontally presented human figure grasps the rune-animal with its hands and hauls its head and upper body above the frame. The most famous instance of

---

[6] Stern notes that 78% of the images in her corpus touch one or more of "the inscription, the (serpent) ornamentation, a cross, or the other figural decoration", or are fully enclosed by other carvings (2013: 103–104).

[7] Further examples are U 678 (reverse side), DR 271, Vg 181, U 696, U 719, U 742, U 759, U 692, U 742, Vs 29, U 791, U 751, U 753, U 763, Vs 19.

Figure 8. Prästgården (U 855), Uppland, eleventh century. 2.57 x 2.12 m.
Image courtesy of Stephen Mitchell.

a figure interacting with the frame is, of course, the Sigurðr stones, where the framing rune-animal becomes Fáfnir, transfixed by the hero's sword. Pictorial motifs only rarely appear outside the frame on Swedish late Viking Age stones.[8] Placement of motifs outside the frame is therefore a marked, deliberate choice. As well as indicating the development of the frame in late Viking Age rune-stone carving practice towards complete enclosure of the image field, these instances throw light on the way the frame organizes space. Birds, perching on or flying above the upper rune band, are the commonest motifs to occur outside the frame (cf. for instance U 746, U 753, U 920, U 1071). Instances such as the Prästgården stone (U 855, Figure 8), where a bird alights on the upper rune band, which in turn encloses a hunting scene, suggests that the area inside the frame was coming to be considered as an oriented representational space, with

---

[8] Stern (2013: 105) gives the proportion of images in her corpus that occur outside the frame as 12%.

Figure 9. Ramsund rock engraving (Sö 101), Södermanland, Sweden, eleventh century. 4.7 x 1.8 m. Image courtesy of the Swedish National Heritage Board.

the upper border representing the sky, and the lower providing a ground line.[9] Carl Säve, one of the earliest scholarly commentators on the Sigurðr image at Ramsund, already gestures at an interpretation of this kind:

> Man könnte fast sagen, dass die Fläche des umrahmten Bildes, auf welchem diese Begebenheiten dargestellt sind, die halbmythische Gnitaheide selbst veranschaulichen soll, wo nach der Aussage alter Lieder die Haupt- und Schlusshandlung stattgehabt! (Säve 1870: 28)

> (One could almost say that the surface of the framed image on which these events are shown is itself meant to be an illustration of the half-mythical Gnitaheide, where according to old poems the main and climactic action took place.)

Pictures of Sigurðr

Carved in the first half of the eleventh century into a massive boulder, the Ramsund inscription (Sö 101, Figure 9) commemorates the building of a bridge

---

[9]   DR 42, U 678, U 696, U 719, U 742, G 77, G 114 are instances of stones where images are placed on a horizontal ground line. The Alstad and Dynna stones, in which a bird and a star respectively are uppermost in the image field, suggest that this sense of oriented representational space was also present in Norway around the same time.

by a woman named Sigrid in memory of a male relative, Holmger, and is decorated with the best-known pictorial representation of the Sigurðr narrative. The inscription at Gök (Sö 327, eleventh century, Figure 10), only a few kilometers away, is usually scorned in the scholarly literature as a bungled copy (cf. however Liepe 1989; Ney 2013), due both to its willful combination of motifs familiar from Ramsund and its indecipherable inscription—the corpus edition notes indignantly that it uses *reisti* "raised", the usual verb for erecting a runestone, in an inscription which is unmistakably on a natural rock face.

The fateful burden on Sigurðr's horse Grani's back is the center of both compositions. At Ramsund this is also where Sigurðr's gaze is directed, while at Gök, Grani is further emphasized by being placed under the central cross. The moment of transformation, in which Sigurðr consumes Fáfnir's blood, is encapsulated in the image of Sigurðr sucking his thumb. On the Gök stone, hands multiply (although how much so depends on which of the painted versions of the stone you are looking at), attaching themselves to various other objects and forming links in the motif chains characteristic of this stone. The frame, which

Figure 10. Gök rock engraving (Sö 327), Södermanland, Sweden, eleventh century. 2.5 x 1.65 m. Image courtesy of the Swedish National Heritage Board.

at Ramsund only enters into the image field at the far right and which is only touched once, by Sigurðr's sword, is at Gök multiply invaginated and touches the motifs in the field at several points. Ramsund presents a narrative moment (the transformation of Sigurðr from *Dümmling* into hero via the ingestion of Fáfnir's blood) encircled by a frame that, apart from the crucial moment of Sigurðr's dragon-killing, is decisively isolated from its "content". Gök, in contrast, unites rune band and figural motifs into a space-filling, decorative schema, which for all its bizarreness is more traditional.[10]

Sigurðr's dragon-killing pose in both carvings is the *Knielauf* (kneeling-running) position known from many archaic sculpture traditions. He pierces the rune-animal's body from underneath with an upward thrust of his sword, which passes via a slit in the animal's body through to the enframed area (at Gök it comes dangerously close to the bird's tail feathers). As has often been pointed out, this is in accordance with the version of the story in *Vǫlsunga saga*, according to which Sigurðr kills Fáfnir from a pit dug on Óðinn's advice. Skewered on Sigurðr's sword, the precarious status of the rune band between representational image, written inscription and decoration becomes apparent. The horizontal stroke indicating the wound contrasts with both the runic staves that surround it and the decorative pattern on the body of the upper rune-animals on the Ramsund stone (unlike the lower one, the upper animals function purely as framing devices). Different orders of representation literally *intersect* on these stones, making any assumption of primacy—which part of the ensemble has interpretive privilege over the others—impossible. The rune-animal frame is simultaneously inside and outside the narrative. It is both Fáfnir's body, that is, part of the diegesis, and the bearer of an utterance, the runic inscription, whose relation to the depicted narrative is anything but self-evident.[11] By escaping the frame and entering our space—a rare phenomenon in the Swedish runic corpus, as we have seen—Sigurðr is what the narratologists would call an "antimetaleptic" (Genette 2004: 27) figure. His sword crosses the unstable border, made of writing, between the extra- and intradiegetic worlds.

Artistic enthusiasm for Sigurðr Fáfnisbani makes itself felt in three geographically, chronologically and medially distinct settings (Düwel 2005): tenth-century insular stone reliefs (Isle of Man, Lancashire, Yorkshire), eleventh-century runestones from eastern Sweden (Södermanland, Uppland) and thirteenth-century southern Norwegian church furnishings, mainly wooden

---

[10] Agneta Ney has recently compared the rune-animals on the two stones. She concludes that Gök's belongs to an older iconographic tradition (Ney 2013: 32).

[11] Interpretations linking the content of the inscription with the images are listed by Klaus Düwel (2003: 128). See also Andrén (2000: 19–21).

reliefs (Aust-Agder, Telemark, Vestfold).[12] Each of these historical moments of Sigurðr-related creativity gave rise to a small body of artifacts. Only the last of them could have coincided with the written transmission of narratives about Sigurðr, as thirteenth-century Norway is a plausible locale for the writing down of early versions of *Vǫlsunga saga* (von See 1999; Larrington 2012: 263–4). This makes the Sigurðr images valuable evidence for the transmission of heroic narrative in media other than writing (von See 1999b: 190). The individual motifs used to depict the Sigurðr story, as well as the basic plot these objects sketch, show astonishing similarities across large gulfs of time and space, right down to the number of pieces of Fáfnir's heart in the kebab Sigurðr roasts for Reginn (three slices in both Viking Age Man and high medieval Norway). The likeliest explanation for this is a combination of visual and oral mediation: images on now-lost portable objects such as textiles, decorated metal- or wood-work, accompanied by a performance, most likely poetic. These similarities of motif also raise a number of methodological questions, however.

For one, what constellation of Sigurðr-associated motifs must be present to indicate a Sigurðr image? No single object displays the entire Sigurðr repertoire, pithily defined by Klaus Düwel as "Otterbuße, Drachenstich, Herzbraten, Fingerprobe, Vogelrat, Regins Tötung und Granis Bürde" (2003: 127) (otter-payment, dragon-stabbing, heart-roasting, finger-test, birds' advice, killing of Reginn and Grani's burden).[13] But how low can you go? Will one central motif do, as Düwel implies (2005: 421), and if so, how to decide which motif is central? The sword thrusting through Fáfnir's body is the obvious candidate, and reduced forms (Vladimir-Susdal axe, Tansberg stone) may suggest it alone was enough to make the link. But we have no other evidence that these objects have anything to do with Sigurðr, and Grani with his burden has at least an equal claim to prominence. Not only is Grani at the center of the composition at Ramsund and Gök, he appears on all the Manx carvings (Fáfnir does not) and his name is slightly better attested in gold-kennings than the dragon's is (cf. Finnur Jónsson 1931: s.v. "Grani", "Fáfnir"). Agneta Ney, following Thomas Lindkvist (1997) has recently argued that the central placement of the treasure motif at Ramsund confirms the monument's status as "ett socialt och ekonomiskt styrkebesked" (Ney 2013: 31) (a social and economic show of strength) on Sigrid's part. She thus sees its significance exclusively in terms of the social

---

[12] It has been proposed that the Gotland picture stones include elements from the Sigurðr narrative. The more expansive interpretation of them is, however, rather controversial (Andrén 1989) while the more conservative one (Aðalheiður Guðmundsdóttir 2012b) identifies only single motifs, raising the question canvased below: how reduced can the presentation of the narrative be and still be identifiable as such?

[13] Aðalheiður Guðmundsdóttir (2012b: 73–74) suggests a much longer list, spanning 24 items, which in turn yields a much larger corpus of Vǫlsung-related images.

status of its commissioner. The fact that Sigrid chose as the decorative program for her monument a narrative that turns on heroic triumph and death suggests that a purely quotidian reading is too narrow, however, especially considering the Christian allegorical meanings borne by the Sigurðr figure everywhere he appears in the visual arts. Grani's burden represents the apex of the treasure motif in the Vǫlsung legend. Freshly won, the dragon's gold bathes Sigurðr in a divine glow, arousing the envy of all who see him. Gjúki's watchmen observe of the approaching hero, "þat hygg ek at hér fari einn af goðunum. Þessi maðr er allr við gull búinn" (*Vǫlsunga saga* p. 46) (I think one of the gods is approaching. This man is gold all over), and Brynhildr describes how she and Atli "í hǫll húnscrar þióðar / eld á iǫfri ormbeðs litom" (*Guðrúnarkviða I* v. 26: *Edda* p. 206) (in the Hunnish people's hall [...] saw the fire of the serpent's bed shine on the prince (Larrington p. 175)). The lavish grave goods of the Viking Age demonstrate a strong association of treasure with the divine realms of the afterlife. Later written sources suggest that riches eased the passage of the dead thence, whether to Valhǫll (cf. the passages cited in Wanner 2008: 397–403) or to the watery kingdom of Rán:

> "Nú þykkir mér ván," segir Friðþjófr, "at nǫkkurir várir menn muni til Ránar fara. Munu vér ekki sendligir þykkja, þá vér komum þar, nema vér búmz vaskliga. Þykki mér ráð, at hverr maðr hafi nǫkkut gull á sér." (*Friðþjófs saga* p. 24)

> ("Now it appears likely," said Fridthjof, "that some of our men will journey to Ran. We will not appear properly attired when we come there, unless we prepare ourselves bravely. I think it's advisable for every man to have some gold on him." (Waggoner pp. 67–68))

Similar echoes of a traditional association between treasure, the world of gods and heroes and the numinous realms of the afterlife may have persisted even into the Christian commemorative practices at Ramsund and Gök (cf. Zachrisson 1998, who proposes just such a rationale for buried deposits of gold in Viking Age Uppland).

Another source of difficulty in interpreting these images lies not in the relationship of single motifs to the ensemble, but rather in their multivalence. Can we always be sure whether images showing smiths' tools, decapitated bodies and birds, such as the Halton and Leeds crosses, should be read as Sigurðr narratives or Vǫlundr ones? Perhaps this ambiguity was a feature not a bug, a visual equivalent to the repeated motifs and foreshadowings that are so prominent in compilations such as *Vǫlsunga saga* and the Codex Regius of the Poetic Edda. And finally—a question with a long history—is the presence, or more daringly, the absence of motifs at certain times or places useful for reconstructing the evolution of the underlying narrative (cf. Aðalheiður Guðmundsdóttir 2012)? The persistence of such issues means that much of the massive secondary literature on the Sigurðr images is devoted not to interpreting them, but to arguing for a particular object's inclusion in or rejection from the corpus (Oehrl 2013 is a recent example).

These problems are characteristic of a particular kind of comparativism, namely Erwin Panofsky's iconographic method. The reductionist, logocentric tendencies of iconographic analysis have frequently been criticized by art historians (Cassidy 1993b; Camille 1993; Liepe 2003), and W. J. T. Mitchell attacks the comparative method for its emphasis on relations of "similarity, resemblance and analogy" (Mitchell 1994: 89). Such relations are understandably important when we wish to identify figures in images with those in texts, but he argues that they drive out more complex readings.[14] Iconographic analysis makes it hard, we might say, for the images to talk back, or tell us anything surprising. From a discipline-internal position, Anne-Sofie Gräslund faults recent work on runestone images for its focus on motif and tendency to read the motifs it discovers in a *biologiskt* (biological) manner, neglecting the stylization that is central to the runestone carvers' artistic heritage (Gräslund 2013: 202). This stylization must temper our amazement at the congruence of Sigurðr motifs across widely separated times and places. They draw on a highly conventional and conservative artistic language. Almost every episode in the Sigurðr repertoire is conveyed by stereotyped motifs that also occur in other contexts, and often have long histories. The "Fingerprobe", for instance, where Sigurðr sucks not his finger, as in the textual sources, but his thumb, has antecedents on Migration Age bracteates and *guldgubber* (Ellis Davidson 1989; Hauck 1993: 458–59, Figure 11), which themselves are influenced by Late Roman images on coins and medallions, depicting hands raised in acclamation to a victorious emperor (Wamers 2003). Sucking or biting the thumb also has ancient associations with prophecy (Ellis Davidson 1989), which the artists may have been referring to. The birds on Ramsund's tree, with their hooked beaks, look like the birds of prey which appear elsewhere in hunting or battle scenes, but in the context of Ramsund they must be *igður* (nuthatches) (Stern 2013: 66–67). The visual representation of Sigurðr's sword-thrust at Ramsund and Gök, as a horizontal stroke in the animal's body

---

[14] Marcel Detienne presents a defense of comparativism as an interdisciplinary practice linking anthropology and history. He comes to the opposite conclusion to Mitchell, namely that comparison enables the researcher to "discover cognitive dissonances [...] bring out some detail or feature that had escaped the notice of other interpreters and observers" (Detienne 2008: 23) and "set in perspective the values and choices of the society to which one belongs" (Detienne 2008: 38).

Figure 11. Lellinge Kohave B bracteate (IK 105), Seeland, fifth–sixth century. Diameter: 2.79 cm. Image courtesy of the National Museum of Denmark.

through which the weapon passes, also appears in Danish Romanesque stone sculpture (Belling 1984). Even something as basic as the rightwards direction of Grani's gaze in all but one of the Sigurðr objects[15] need not imply anything about their filiation, as this is the commonest orientation for runic quadrupeds (Oehrl 2011: 18). All this is, however, no counsel of despair for would-be interpreters. It makes for porous boundaries: no two interpreters of the Vǫlsung images agree which objects make up the corpus. But the massive, solid presence of convention bolsters interpretation of the central witnesses, by underlining just how striking the departures at Ramsund and Gök are.

Breaking the Frame:
Metalepsis in Textual and Visual Media

Metalepsis is a traditional rhetorical term, although from the beginning there was little agreement as to what it actually meant (Nauta 2013). It is used in narratology in the sense made popular by Gérard Genette in his *Discours du récit* (1972), for when figures in a narrative transgress its levels of representation, for instance when the extradiegetic narrator enters the storyworld, or a figure from the storyworld breaks out of the diegesis. Metalepsis has attracted much interest of late, and has been found in narratives ranging from comic books, to "akkadischer und ägyptischer Literatur [...] der hebräischen Bibel [...] rabbinischen Midraschim [...] paganer antiker Literatur aller Epochen und [...] frühchristlicher

---

[15] I am grateful to Jürg Glauser for drawing this feature to my attention. The sole example of leftwards orientation is on the Manx cross from Jurby, although it is by no means certain that the saddled horse in the bottom right field is in fact Grani. The horse on the Kirk Andreas cross is annotated with a runic graffito reading **kan**, presumably, "Grani" (Margeson 1983: 100).

Literatur" (Eisen and Möllendorf 2013: cover text) (Akkadian and Egyptian literature [...] the Hebrew Bible [...] rabbinic midrashim [...] pagan antique literature of all epochs and [...] early Christian literature). The canonical example of metalepsis in modern literature is a short story by the Argentinian novelist Julio Cortázar, "Continuidad de los parques" (1956), in which a reader is murdered by a character in the book he is reading. Such a "transgression délibérée du seuil d'enchâssement" (Genette 2004: 14) (intentional transgression of the threshold setting) points, according to Genette, to a "théorie de la fiction" (Genette 2004: 7) (theory of fiction). This transgression involves "a deviant referential operation, a violation of semantic thresholds of representation that involves the beholder in an ontological transgression of universes" (Pier 2009: 190). Cortázar's story is a radical instance of metalepsis. Eisen and Möllendorf propose that metalepsis in ancient texts and artworks is more restricted, operating not, as Cortázar's does, to destabilize the entire narrative, but rather in a local fashion, in the form of "weiche, gleitende metaleptische Ebenenübergänge" (Eisen and Möllendorf 2013b: 2) (smooth, gliding metaleptic level transitions) from one narrative level to another. Rather than disjunctively staging illusionistic aspects of the artwork, as modern metalepsis does (Kukkonnen and Klimek 2011), antique metalepsis is primarily a matter of mediality:

> Hier ist etwa in Erwägung zu ziehen, dass sich antike narrative Plots außerordentlich häufig auf eine (skriptural oder oral vorliegende) Erzähltradition beziehen, die einen historisch realen Hintergrund suggeriert und behauptet. Der metaleptische Kontakt, so ließe sich mithin formulieren, durchschlägt dann nur eine als solche schon ontologisch durchlässige Grenze und verlängert die reale Gültigkeit und Existenz etwa eines mythischen Geschehens oder einer mythischen Figur bis in die Lesegegenwart, ohne aber im Grunde einen wirklichen Paralogismus zu generieren. (Eisen and Möllendorf 2013b: 2)

> (Here, for instance, it should be considered that ancient narrative plots draw very often on a (written or oral) narrative tradition that implies and asserts a real, historical background. The metaleptic contact, we may thus say, then merely breaks through a boundary which is as such already ontologically permeable, and extends the real validity and existence of a mythical event or figure, for example, into the present of reading; without, however, in principle generating an actual logical fallacy.)

Antique metalepsis acts, then, as Eisen and Möllendorf see it, to enhance the authority, plausibility and effectiveness of textualised traditional materials in the setting of vocality (Schaefer 1992). It supports textual discourse rather than calling it into question, as its modern cousin does. Further:

> Gerade in späteren antiken Epochen zunehmend selbstverständlicher Schriftlichkeit von Texten [...] ist der Einsatz metaleptischer Verfahren des Öfteren auch an die Thematisierung von Medialität gebunden und soll offenbar helfen, die härtere Grenzziehung, die der Einsatz von Schrift gegenüber einem oral-auditiven Übermittlungsverfahren darstellt, aufzuweichen. (Eisen and Möllendorf 2013b: 3)

> (Precisely in later antiquity, as the writtenness of texts was becoming increasingly a matter of course [...] the use of metaleptic techniques is frequently linked to the thematizing of mediality and evidently is intended to help soften the hardness of the demarcation between writing and oral-auditive processes of transmission.)

The prose in the heroic part of the Codex Regius collection of eddic poetry (GKS 2365 4to, ca. 1270) has been described as *fornaldarsaga*-like (Lindblad 1980: 144, 166), insofar as it makes a frame for the poems out of causal and genealogical links. This is in stark contrast to the mythological part, whose frame is discontinuous.[16] Another systematic difference between the framing of the heroic and mythological parts of the Codex Regius collection has attracted less comment. This is the presence or absence of narrative level switching, or to use Eisen and Möllendorf's terms, metaleptic level transitions. Mythological poems in Codex Regius that begin with direct speech are introduced with an *inquit*, as for example in *Grímnismál*: "Þá var eldrinn svá kominn, at feldrinn brann af Grímni. Hann qvað Heitr ertu [...]" (*Edda* p. 57) (Then the fire had come so close that Grimnir's cloak burned. He said: "Hot you are [...]") (Larrington pp. 48–49). *Skírnismál*, *Hárbarðsljóð*, and *Lokasenna* are also framed in this manner, with a prose passage concluding in an *inquit* that introduces direct speech in the first line of the poem. In these cases, the framing prose and the poetic text are on the same narrative level: the narrator does not step out of character at the interface between the two, but merely switches mode from prose to poetry. When the first line of the poem is not direct speech, the prose introduction is simply absent, and the Codex Regius manuscript either has a title rubric above

---

[16] It is well-established that the Codex Regius draws on a number of smaller manuscript collections (Lindblad 1954, 1980), and that a now-unidentifiable quantum of its prose frame came into being at a lower stratigraphic level of the written transmission. As the prose is retained in Regius, it can nonetheless be assumed to reflect the decisions of its compiler, and be read as the collection's narrative voice.

the poem (as is the case for *Hávamál*, *Vafþrúðnismál*, *Hymiskviða*, and *Þrymskviða*), or the poem has no rubric at all and simply begins with the first line of the text (*Vǫluspá*). Here again, no change in the narrative level is implied, with the only signal of the beginning of the poetic text being the paratextual, non-narrative one of the rubric. The only exceptions to this pattern in the mythological part are the two poems in the "hinge" between the mythological and heroic parts: *Alvíssmal*, which although it begins with direct speech, has no prose introduction and, revealingly, *Vǫlundarkviða*.

The prose text "Frá Vǫlundi" precedes *Vǫlundarkviða* in the Codex Regius, and it concludes in a way characteristic not of the mythological, but rather of the heroic part of the collection: "Níðuðr konungr lét hann hǫndom taca, *svá sem hér er um qveðit*" (*Edda* p. 116; my emphasis) (King Nidud had him seized, *as is told of here*) (Larrington p. 98). It is often observed that *Vǫlundarkviða*, on Vǫlundr/Weland the smith, is out of place in the mythological section of Regius, and the nature of its prose frame supports this assessment. The frame also, however, offers an opening for rethinking the nature of the distinction between the two parts, and retreating from its anachronistic implication that medieval Scandinavians thought in terms of "heroic" versus "mythic". Rather, the framing in Regius suggests, it is a matter of a different attitude on the part of the tradition bearers to the narrative material in the two sections. The medial form of the heroic texts, but not of the mythological ones, matters to the narrator of Codex Regius. A striking characteristic of the prose frame of the heroic part is its insistent reference to the poems *as poems*, the use of deictic phrases to refer to the texts in the collection, and its mentions of other poems that have not been included. Prose-heavy sections of the collection, such as *Helgakviða Hundingsbana II*, are especially rich in such references, both to the poem itself and to other texts: "í Vǫlsungaqviðo inni forno" (in the old *Vǫlsungakviða*), "í Helgaqviðo" (in *Helgakviða*), "svá sem qveðit er í Károlióðom" (as is told in *Káruljóð*). The mythological texts, on the other hand, trigger no such medial self-reflection and are presented in a "transparent" mode of unbroken narrative continuity.[17]

---

[17] The question remains: why is *Vǫlundarkviða* not with the other heroic poems? A convincing explanation has been proposed for its position in relation to the other poems of the mythological section: as an elf, Vǫlundr is ghettoized with Alvíss the dwarf close to the end of the sequence. Its absence from the heroic section, on the other hand, is probably due to the strong emphasis on cyclical arrangement in the heroic poetry. All the protagonists from *Helgakviða Hundingsbana I* on are shoehorned into the matter of Sigurðr, no matter the main force this may require. The Vǫlundr narrative offers no links to Sigurðr, and the Old English material, as well as the early and abundant visual sources, suggest this narrative was very well-known. Perhaps manufacturing such links seemed like taking things too far. The mid-thirteenth century compiler/s of *Þiðreks saga* had no such compunctions, but were working in the rather different literary milieu of Hanseatic Bergen (cf. Kramarz-Bein 2005).

As in the mythological part, poems in the heroic part of Regius that begin with direct speech[18] are introduced by an *inquit*. Framelessness is not an option in the heroic part. *Hamðismál* is the only heroic poem that lacks a prose prelude, and even it has a "postlude" at the end: "Þetta ero kǫlluð Hamðismál in forno" (*Edda* p. 274) (That is called the old *Hamðismál*).[19] The remaining poems[20] all begin with narration, and almost all are framed by a reference to the poem, often including a deictic pronoun:

Helgakviða Hundingsbana I: "Hér hefr upp qvæði frá Helga Hundingsbana þeira oc Hǫðbrodds" (*Edda* p. 130) (Here begins the poem about Helgi Hundingsbani and Hǫðbroddr)

Guðrúnarkviða I: "Þetta er enn qveðit um Guðrúno" ("Frá dauða Sigurðar", *Edda* p. 201) (This is also said of Gudrun (Larrington p. 172))

Sigurðarkviða in skamma: "svá sem segir í Sigurðarqviðo inni scǫmmo" (*Edda* p. 206) (as is told in the "Short Poem about Sigurðr" (Larrington p. 176))

Oddrúnargrátr: "Um þessa sǫgo er hér qveðit" (*Edda* p. 234) (About this tale, this is told)

Atlakviða: "Um þetta er siá qviða ort" ("Dauði Atla", *Edda* p. 239) (This poem was composed about it (Larrington p. 204))

Atlamál: "Enn segir gleggra í Atlamálom inom grœnlenzcom" (*Edda* p. 247) (The "Greenlandic Lay of Atli" tells this story more clearly (Larrington p. 210))

Guðrúnarhvǫt: "Enn er þat spurði Guðrún, þá qvaddi *hon* sono sína" (*Edda* p. 263) (And when Gudrun heard this, she spoke to her sons (Larrington p. 226))

[18] *Helgakviða Hjǫrvarðssonar, Helgakviða Hundingsbana II, Grípisspá, Reginsmál-Fáfnismál-Sigrdrífumál, Helreið Brynhildar, Guðrúnarkviða II & III.*

[19] The collection of eddic poetry in AM 748 4to (*Fragments of the Elder and the Younger Edda*) makes a similar distinction to Regius in the framing of mythological and heroic material, with the mythological poems *Baldrs draumar, Skírnismál* and *Hymiskviða* all lacking a prose frame, and *Grímnismál* and *Vǫlundarkviða* framed, as far as we can tell (*Vǫlundarkviða*'s frame is fragmentary) as they are in Regius. AM 748 II 4to introduces its single stanza from the heroic poem *Grottasǫngr* as follows: "þat er sagt, at þær kvæði lióð þau, er kallat er Grottasǫngr ok er þetta upphaf at" (it is said that they performed the song which is called *Grottasǫngr* and this is the beginning of it (my translation)). In GKS 2367 4to (Regius manuscript of the *Prose Edda*) *Grottasǫngr* has no introduction.

[20] *Helgakviða Hundingsbana I, Guðrúnarkviða I, Sigurðarkviða in skamma, Oddrúnargrátr, Atlakviða, Atlamál* and *Guðrúnarhvǫt*. The opening of *Brot af Sigurðarkviðu* is lost in the lacuna.

The consistency with which this distinction is adhered to is striking. *Guðrúnarhvǫt* is the sole instance of a mixture of the two framing options, as it is introduced by an *inquit* but does not begin with direct speech from one of the poem's protagonists. Rather, the poem's narrator speaks:

> Þá frá ec senno slíðrfengligsta,
> trauð mál, talið af trega stórom,
> er harðhuguð hvatti at vígi
> grimmom orðom Guðrún sono. (*Edda* p. 264)
> (Then I heard quarrelling of the most ill-fated sort,
> faltering words uttered out of great grief,
> when the fierce-spirited Gudrun whetted for the fight,
> with grim words, her sons. (Larrington p. 226))

The opening stanza of *Guðrúnarhvǫt*, with its emphatic first-person pronoun and multiple verbs of speaking, seems to have triggered the *inquit* type of framing. This left the compiler no choice but to make Guðrún the subject of the *inquit*. The medial signature (or, if you prefer, controlling fiction) of the collection is that of authentic, anonymous oral transmission from ancient times. This forbids both the Regius' narrator from stepping into the limelight as the poem's originating instance (*þá kvað ec* "then I spoke" is thus not possible),[21] and the use of the kind of stereotyped introductory phrases ubiquitous in the skaldic corpus (*sem skáldit kvað*, "as the skald said"). The framing prose is, then, an important site of Codex Regius' "medium theory".[22] The frame is also the place where one of the main stumbling-blocks to the collection's "medieval cyclic impulse" (Clover 1982: 59) is negotiated, namely the existence of conflicting variants of heroic narratives such as the death of Sigurðr.[23] Variants become problematic— or even visible as such—as a consequence of the "remediation" (Grusin and Bolter 1999) of oral poetry in a medium, the written codex, which adds a lasting, material dimension to the oral poem's temporal, performance-bound mode

---

[21] I do not think that the compiler wrote *Guðrúnarhvǫt*. My point is merely that the conventions of the collection prohibit a claim of authorship on the part of the narrative voice.

[22] The narrative voice in the heroic part of Codex Regius does much more than this, of course, also making cross-referential: "svá sem fyrr er ritað" (*Edda* p. 154) (as is written above (p. 135)); explanatory: "hon var Sváva endrborin" (*Edda* p. 151) (she [Sigrún] was Sváva reincarnated (p. 133)); evaluative: "hann ... kalla allir menn í fornfrœðum um alla menn fram" (*Edda* p. 163) (in the old tradition everyone says he [Sigurðr] was the greatest of all men (p. 142)); and downright critical comments on the texts: "þat var trúa í fornescio, at menn væri endrbornir, enn þat er nú kǫlluð kerlingavilla" (*Edda* p. 161) (there was a belief in the pagan religion, which we now reckon an old wives' tale, that people could be reincarnated (p. 141)).

[23] In the mythological part, such incommensurabilities are largely avoided, although we know that contradictory narratives existed, for instance, about Þórr's fishing of Miðgarðsormr.

of existence. It is this process that yields an emphatic sense of *sjá kviða* (this poem), and the possibility (or necessity) of evaluative commentary (cf. note 22). Where previous researchers have seen in the inclusion of multiple versions of events witnesses to the compiler's completist or antiquarian tendencies, they become on a narratological reading reckonings with the poem's historicity. A good example is the text headed "Frá dauða Sigurðar":

> Hér er sagt í þessi qviðo frá dauða Sigurðar, oc vícr hér svá til, sem þeir dræpi hann úti. Enn sumir segia svá, at þeir dræpi hann inni í reccio sinni sofanda. Enn þýðverscir menn segia svá, at þeir dræpi hann úti í scógi. Oc svá segir í Guðrúnarqviðo inni forno, at Sigurðr oc Giúca synir hefði til þings riðit, þá er hann var drepinn. Enn þat segia allir einnig, at þeir svico hann í trygð oc vógo at hánom liggianda oc óbúnom. (*Edda* p. 201)

> (In this poem the death of Sigurd is related and here it sounds as if they killed him outside. But some say this, that they killed him inside, sleeping in his bed. And Germans say that they killed him out in the forest. And the "Old Poem of Gudrun" says that Sigurd and the sons of Giuki were riding to the Assembly when he was killed. But they all say that they treacherously betrayed him and attacked him when he was lying down and unarmed. (Larrington, p. 171))

As Andreas Heusler wrote, "Die Heldenfabeln *geben sich* als Geschichte" (the heroic narratives *purport to be* history) (1941: 162; my emphasis). Historicity is becoming hard for the Regius narrator to maintain in the face of the variability of the tradition, even though, paradoxically enough, a sense that the heroic poems were historical documents, transmitting genealogically relevant information, was probably a significant motivation for the preservation of the variants in the first place (Rowe 2006). And it is a small step from a conception of the traditional material as a body of meaningful variation, to an understanding of it as fictional, in the modern sense of "a representation portraying an imaginary/ invented universe or world" (Schaeffer 2013), whose events unfold in a manner determined by literary rather than referential patterns and constraints. Once the convention that the narrator is reporting events that have happened has been broken with, the heroic material can be developed in ways that exploit narrative contingency.

The visual material is more tantalizing, and its metalepses more radical. It seems that the remediation of oral traditions about Sigurðr in a new medium, that of the image-bearing runestone, was also leading to a reconsideration of the ontological status of those traditions in eleventh century Sweden, as remediation in written form did in high medieval Iceland.[24] Perhaps the impetus to commit these narratives to the more permanent medium of stone was also associated in Sweden with the advent of writing? A related point has already been made, in a metaphorical mode: "Lange bevor die Heldensage des Nordens auf das Pergament gelangt, fand sie ihren ersten "schriftlichen" Niederschlag in den Bildzeugnissen" (Ploss 1966: 78) (Long before the heroic legends of the north made it on to parchment, they experienced a first "scriptural" deposition in the visual witnesses). The shortcoming of such an account is its underestimation of the medial specificity of the "visual witnesses": in the case of the Swedish runestones, their combination of monumental form, text, ornament and image. Similar problems befall the popular but at times facile comparison of runes with skaldic poetry (see Beck 2001 for an instance of this very widespread scholarly topos). The question can also be approached from another perspective, however: that of the history of media technologies. Here two possibilities present themselves, a weak and a strong theory. The weak version takes its point of departure from the widely-accepted influence of codex layout on the Jelling 2 stone, and the profound effect that Danish models had on the Swedish tradition of decorated runestones (Fuglesang 1998: 199). An *indirect* influence of the new technology of writing on the overall conception of the engravings at Ramsund and Gök can thus be safely asserted. The strong version seeks a more immediate context in eleventh-century Sweden for possible influences of the advent of writing. It is unlikely that heroic legends were being committed to Latin letters in eleventh-century Sweden. At any rate, no trace of such activity has survived. However, there is ample evidence that Latin and runic scripts coexisted and influenced one another, as close to the time and place of our witnesses as eleventh century Sigtuna (Källström 2012; cf. on Swedish runic Latinity more generally Gustavson 1994; Öberg 1994), and that manuscripts were not only used, but in fact produced in Sweden at this time (Åhfeldt 2012: 90; Gullick 2005: 32). The survey of runestone framing presented above suggests a growing tendency to consider the enframed field as a closed illusionistic space, the precondition of the metaleptic play at Ramsund and Gök. Laila Kitzler Åhfeldt describes a general trend for Swedish stones in the course of the eleventh century in the direction of "more formalised inscriptions and more elaborated ornament" (2012: 77). Signe Horn Fuglesang also sees the eleventh century as a moment of innovation, now in visual narration. The juxtaposition of emblematic scenes from different narratives, as seen on the Franks' Casket and Ardre VII picture stone (Fuglesang 2005: 81), is succeeded by the representation of several stages of one narrative in a single image (Fuglesang 1986: 187).

---

[24] On *Verschriftlichung* (textualization) in Codex Regius, cf. Johansson 2005.

Such developments in the visual sources could be associated with the practices of collection, canonization and cyclification, fellow travelers of *Verschriftlichung* (textualization) cross-culturally, not only of heroic epic, but also of traditions ranging from biblical narrative, through chronicles and genealogies, to laws (Assmann 1992; for Scandinavia in particular, cf. Quinn 2000). Could it be that formal innovations in eleventh century Swedish runecarving were influenced by the presence there of the new medium of the manuscript codex? The current state of our knowledge of textual culture in eleventh century Sweden does not allow for a certain answer to this question, although Öberg (1994: 221) points to early medieval examples of artists who were literate in both Latin and the vernacular, and so exposed to book culture. A clerical commissioner of the runic monument is another obvious conduit for such influences. But the emergence of the rune band as frame of an illusionistic space, whose "rhetoriciz[ation of] the relationship between inside [and] outside" the antimetaleptic Sigurðr makes abundantly clear, has suggestive parallels with the presentation of heroic narratives in Codex Regius as *sjá kviða*, concrete realizations crystallized from the flux of orality. The Codex Regius manuscript of the Poetic Edda is exquisitely self-conscious, but these processes also took place, often unmarked, in other text corpora (Rohrbach 2014), and may have begun earlier than surviving texts bear witness (cf. Bianchi 2010: 22). In this connection it is worth remembering that the tenth-century cross fragments from Kirk Andreas on the Isle of Man include not only a Sigurðr image, but also one of a figure carrying a cross and a book (Figure 12). It is a commonplace that such juxtapositions indicate "the meeting of the two religions" (Wilson 2008: 80); they also imply the meeting of two medial regimes. Perhaps Ramsund's and Gök's Sigurðr is bookish, too, in other ways than hitherto realized.

Conclusion

The foregoing study has sketched a new comparative approach to the visual and verbal records of Old Norse heroic narrative, as an alternative to the Panofskyan iconographic analysis that currently dominates the field. By focusing on formal criteria such as composition and the relationship between narratological levels, new aspects of even well-explored primary sources come into view, and the besetting problem of iconographic analysis, namely the difficulty of matching visual motifs with narrative materials, can be circumvented. In the case of the Codex Regius, the multileveled character of what we might call the "Heroic Edda" is revealed, in contrast to the mythological part of the Edda, where the prose introductions are on the same diegetic level as the poems and position them as dramas taking place in an unspecified, non-historical chronological

Figure 12. Kirk Andreas cross fragments: left, Thorwald's cross (inventory nr. 128) and, right, Sigurd's cross (inventory nr. 121), Isle of Man, tenth century. Length: 35 cm (128), 68 cm (121). Images courtesy of Manx National Heritage.

setting (Mohr 1940). The poems presented by the narrator of the heroic section are not unframed poetic "events" like the mythological poems, but rather contingent instances—"not the other poems, stories, or legends about Sigurðr, but *this one*"—positioned as fictions within a larger frame that appears as real in relation to them. By reminding the reader of the "alternate universes" of heroic legend, the text calls the historicity of the tradition into question even as it meticulously records and documents it.[25]

The rock engravings at Ramsund and Gök show an analogous awareness of the narrative closure of the Sigurðr story. This is more apparent at Ramsund than at Gök, as on the latter stone the visual field's organization is less illusionistic

---

[25] Victor Millet observes that the heroic material's juxtaposition with myth in Codex Regius pushes heroic legend back into the past and "präsentiert sie als den schauderhaften Bericht dessen, was zu jener mythischen, definitiv vergangenen Zeit geschah" (2008: 309) (presents it as a gruesome report on what took place in that mythic, definitively past time). In Norse literary history we can trace the further ramifications of this process of fictionalization in the rise of the fantastical later *fornaldarsögur* and indigenous *riddarasögur*.

and more indebted to traditional space-filling compositional norms. The fore-going analysis suggests that the differences between the two stones should be put down not to the Gök carver's bungling, or his poor memory, but to his unfamiliarity with new, textually-inspired ways of organizing narrative information. The largely incomprehensible runic inscription on the Gök stone, usually assumed to indicate a carver not fully conversant with runic script and not at home in the literate milieu, supports this interpretation. Sigurðr's sword both pins together the monuments' multiple media, and destabilizes the relationship between their orders of representation. The line it cuts into the rune band interrupts the syntax of linguistic symbols with an iconic visual sign, and draws attention to the materiality of the runic letters as lines on the rockface. The antimetaleptic figure of Sigurðr inverts the figure/ground relationship by making the ground outside the frame part of the image, and foregrounds the conventions undergirding the illusionistic space of the framed area. As Eisen and Möllendorf argue, it is not necessary—and perhaps it is anachronistic—to interpret this as a sophisticated undermining of narrative norms. Such a destabilization would also be surprising if these developments were as recent as they have been argued here to be. Rather, they suggest the lack of transparency of the conventions for those to whom they were new. The "medium theory" of these engravings is, on this reading, a reckoning with the narrative potentialities of runestone carving at a moment of medial innovation.

Works Cited

Primary Sources

Friðþjófs saga ins frœkna
Friðþjófs saga ins frœkna. Ed. Ludvig Larsson. Halle: 1901.

<small>TRANSLATION</small>
The Saga of Fridthjof the Bold. Transl. Ben. Waggoner. New Haven: 2009.

Poetic Edda
Edda: Die Lieder des Codex regius nebst verwandten Denkmälern. Ed. Gustav Neckel and Hans Kuhn. Germanische Bibliothek, Vierte Reihe. Heidelberg: 1962.
Fragments of the Elder and the Younger Edda: AM 748 I and II 4:o. Ed. Elias Wessén. CCI 17. Copenhagen: 1945.

<small>TRANSLATIONS</small>
The Poetic Edda. Transl. Carolyne Larrington. 2nd rev. ed. Oxford World's Classics. Oxford: 2014.

Runestones

DR = *Danmarks Runeindskrifter*. Ed. Lis Jacobsen and Erik Moltke. 2 vols. Copenhagen: 1941–1942.

NIyR = *Norges Innskrifter med de yngre Runer*. Ed. Magnus Olsen et al. 6 vols. Oslo: 1941–1951.

Sveriges runinskrifter. Ed. Sven Söderberg et al. 15 vols. Stockholm: 1900–1981.

Vǫlsunga saga

Vǫlsunga saga. Ed. and transl. R. G. Finch. London: 1965.

Secondary Sources

Aðalheiður Guðmundsdóttir. 2012. "Gunnarr and the Snake Pit in Medieval Art and Legend." *Speculum* 87: 1015–1049.

———. 2012b. "The Origin and Development of the *fornaldarsögur* as Illustrated by *Völsunga saga*." In Lassen et. al. 2012: 59–82.

Åhfeldt, Laila Kitzler. 2012. "Carving Technique and Runic Literacy." In Zilmer 2012: 63–97.

———. 2012b. "Picture Stone Workshops and Handicraft Traditions." In Karnell 2012: 183–94.

Andrén, Anders. 1989. "Dörrar till förgångna myter: En tolkning av de gotländska bildstenarna." In *Medeltidens Födelse*. Ed. Klavs Randsborg, Dan Carlsson, and Anders Andrén. N.p. (Gyllenstiernska Krapperupsstiftelsen). Pp. 287–319.

———. 2000. "Re-reading Embodied Texts—An Interpretation of Rune-stones." *Current Swedish Archaeology* 8: 7–32.

Assmann, Jan. 1992. *Das kulturelle Gedächtnis: Schrift, Erinnerung und politische Identität in frühen Hochkulturen*. Munich.

Barnes, Michael P. 2012. *Runes: A Handbook*. Woodbridge.

Beck, Heinrich. 2001. "Runen und Schriftlichkeit." In *Von Thorsberg nach Schleswig. Sprache und Schriftlichkeit eines Grenzgebietes im Wandel eines Jahrtausend: internationales Kolloquium im Wikinger-Museum Haithabu vom 29. September–3. Oktober 1994*. Ed. Klaus Düwel. Reallexikon der germanischen Altertumskunde Ergänzungsbände, 25. Berlin. Pp. 1–23.

Beck, Heinrich, Dieter Geuenich, and Heiko Steuer, eds. 1972–2008. *Reallexikon der Germanischen Altertumskunde*. 2nd ed. 37 vols. Berlin.

Belling, Dorte Lorentzen. 1984. "Gennemstukne dyr." *Romanske Stenarbejder* 11: 155–76.

Bianchi, Marco. 2010. *Runor som resurs: vikingatida skriftkultur i Uppland och Södermanland*. Runrön, 20. Uppsala.

Broderick, Herbert R. 1982. "Some Attitudes toward the Frame in Anglo-Saxon Manuscripts of the Tenth and Eleventh Centuries." *Artibus et historiae* 3: 31–42.

Camille, Michael. 1993. "Mouths and Meanings: Towards an Anti-iconography of Medieval Art." In Cassidy 1993: 43–54.

Cassidy, Brendan, ed. 1993. *Iconography at the Crossroads: Papers from the Colloquium Sponsored by the Index of Christian Art, Princeton University, 23–24 March 1990.* Princeton.

———. 1993b. "Introduction: Iconography, Texts and Audiences." In Cassidy 1993: 3–16.

Clover, Carol J. 1982. *The Medieval Saga.* Ithaca.

Derrida, Jacques. 1979. "The Parergon." Transl. Craig Owens. *October* 9: 3–41.

Detienne, Marcel. 2008. *Comparing the Incomparable.* Transl. Janet Lloyd. Stanford, CA.

Duro, Paul, ed. 1996a. *The Rhetoric of the Frame: Essays on the Boundaries of the Artwork.* Cambridge.

———. 1996b. "Introduction." In Duro 1996a: 1–15.

Düwel, Klaus. 2003. "Ramsund §2: Runologisches." In Beck et al., 24: 124–28.

———. 2005. "Sigurddarstellung." In Beck et al., 28: 412–23.

———. 2008. *Runenkunde.* 4th rev. ed. Stuttgart.

Eisen, Ute E., and Peter von Möllendorff. 2013. *Über die Grenze: Metalepse in Text- und Bildmedien des Altertums.* Berlin.

———. 2013b. "Zur Einführung." In Eisen and Möllendorf 2013: 1–10.

Ellis Davidson, Hilda. 1989. "The Seer's Thumb." In *The Seer in Celtic and Other Traditions.* Ed. Hilda Ellis Davidson. Edinburgh. Pp 66–78.

Finnur Jónsson, ed. 1931. *Lexicon poeticum antiquæ linguæ septentrionalis: Ordbog over det norsk-islandske skjaldesprog oprindelig forfattet af Sveinbjörn Egilsson.* 2nd ed. Copenhagen.

Fuglesang, Signe Horn. 1986. "Ikonographie der Skandinavischen Runensteine der jüngeren Wikingerzeit." In *Zum Problem der Deutung frühmittelalterlicher Bildinhalte: Akten des 1. Internationalen Kolloquiums in Marburg a.d. Lahn, 15. bis 19. Februar 1983.* Ed. Helmut Roth and Dagmar von Reitzenstein. Sigmaringen. Pp. 183–210

———. 1998. "Swedish Runestones of the Eleventh Century: Ornament and Dating." In *Proceedings of the Fourth International Symposium on Runes and Runic Inscriptions in Göttingen, 4–9 August 1995.* Ed. Klaus Düwel and Sean Nowak. Berlin. Pp. 197–218.

———. 2001. "Animal Ornament: the Late Viking Period." In *Tiere, Menschen, Götter: Wikingerzeitliche Kunststile und ihre neuzeitliche Rezeption; Referate, gehalten auf einem von der Deutschen Forschungsgemeinschaft geförderten internationalen Kolloquium der Joachim Jungius-Gesellschaft der Wissenschaften.* Ed. Michael Müller-Wille und Lars Olof Larsson. Göttingen. Pp. 157–94.

———. 2005. "Runesteinenes ikonografi." In *Runesten, magt og mindesmærker: Tværfagligt symposium på Askov Højskole 3/5 oktober 2002.* Ed. Gunhild Øeby Nielsen. Hikuin, 32. Højbjerg. Pp. 75–94.

Genette, Gérard. 1972. *Discours du récit: essai de méthode.* Paris.

———. 2004. *Métalepse: De la figure à la fiction.* Paris.

Graham-Campbell, James. 2013. *Viking art.* New York.

Gräslund, Anne-Sofie. 2006. "Dating the Swedish Viking-Age Rune Stones on Stylistic Grounds." In *Runes and Their Secrets: Studies in Runology.* Ed. Marie Stoklund. Copenhagen. Pp. 117–31.

———. 2013. "Stil och motiv: Några tankar kring vikingatidens ikonografi och ornamentik." In *Institutionens historier: En vänbok till Gullög Nordquist.* Ed. Erika Weiberg, Susanne Carlsson, and Gunnel Ekroth. Uppsala. Pp. 195–207.

Grusin, Richard, and Jay David Bolter. 1999. *Remediation: Understanding New Media.* Cambridge, MA.

Gullick, Michael. 2005. "Preliminary Observations on Romanesque Manuscript Fragments of English, Norman and Swedish Origin in the Riksarkivet (Stockholm)." In *Medieval Book Fragments in Sweden: An International Symposium.* Ed. J. Brunius. Stockholm. Pp. 31–82.

Gustavson, Helmer. 1994. "Runsk latinitet." In *Medeltida skrift- och språkkultur: nio föreläsningar från ett symposium i Stockholm våren 1992.* Ed. Inger Lindell. Stockholm. Pp. 61–78.

Hauck, Karl. 1993. "Die bremische Überlieferung zur Götter-Dreiheit Altuppsalas und die bornholmische Goldfolien aus Sorte Muld." *Frühmittelalterliche Studien* 27: 409–79.

Helmbrecht, Michaela. 2011. *Wirkmächtige Kommunikationsmedien: Menschenbilder der Vendel-und Wikingerzeit und ihre Kontexte.* PhD diss., Lund University.

Heusler, Andreas. 1941. *Die altgermanische Dichtung.* 2nd rev. ed. Potsdam.

Hurwit, Jeffrey. 1977. "Image and Frame in Greek Art." *American Journal of Archaeology* 81: 1–30.

Johansson, Karl G. 2005. "On Orality and the *Verschriftlichung* of *Skírnismál*." In *Literacy in Medieval and Early Modern Scandinavian Culture.* Ed. Pernille Hermann. Odense. Pp. 167–86.

Källström, Magnus. 2012. "Clerical or Lay Literacy in Late Viking Age Uppland? The Evidence of Local Rune Carvers and Their Work." In Zilmer 2012: 27–62.

Karnell, Maria Herlin, ed. 2012. *Gotland's Picture Stones: Bearers of an Enigmatic Legacy.* Visby.

Kemp, Wolfgang. 1996. "The Narrativity of the Frame." In Duro 1996a: 11–23.

Kramarz-Bein, Susanne. 2005. "Þiðreks saga af Bern." In Beck et al., 30: 466–71.

Kukkonen, Karin, and Sonja Klimek, eds. 2011. *Metalepsis in Popular Culture*. Berlin.

Lager, Linn. 2002. *Den synliga tron: Runstenskors som en spegling av kristnandet i Sverige*. Occasional Papers in Archaeology, 31. Uppsala.

Larrington, Carolyne. 2012. "*Vǫlsunga saga*, *Ragnars saga* and Romance in Old Norse: Revisiting Relationships." In Lassen et al. 2012: 251–70.

Lassen, Annette. 2011. *Odin på kristent pergament*. Copenhagen.

Lassen, Annette, Agneta Ney, and Ármann Jakobsson, eds. 2012. *The Legendary Sagas: Origins and Development*. Reykjavík.

Lebensztejn, Jean-Claude. 1988. "Framing Classical Space." *Art Journal* 47: 37–41.

Liepe, Lena. 1989. "Sigurdssagan i bild." *Fornvännen* 84: 1–11.

———. 2003. *Den medeltida kroppen: kroppens och könets ikonografi i nordisk medeltid*. Lund.

Lindblad, Gustaf. 1954. *Studier in Codex regius av Äldre Eddan I–III*. Lundastudier i nordisk språkvetenskap, Serie A, 10. Lund.

———. 1980. "Poetiska Eddans förhistoria och skrivskicket i Codex regius." *Arkiv för nordisk filologi* 95: 142–67.

Lindkvist, Thomas. 1997. "Saga, arv och guld i 1000-talets Södermanland." In *Historiska etyder: En vänbok till Stellan Dahlgren*. Ed. Janne Backlund et al. Uppsala. Pp. 139–47.

Malm, Mats. 2011. "Runornas litteratur." In *Litteraturbanken*. http://litteraturbanken.se/#!/presentationer/specialomraden/RunornasLitteratur.html (accessed on August 27, 2014).

Margeson, Sue. 1983. "On the Iconography of the Manx Crosses." In *The Viking Age in the Isle of Man: Select Papers from the Ninth Viking Congress, Isle of Man, 4-14 July 1981*. Ed. C. Fell et al. London. Pp. 95–106.

Millet, V. 2008. *Germanische Heldendichtung im Mittelalter: Eine Einführung*. Berlin.

Mitchell, Paul, Lynn Roberts, and William B. Adair. 2010. "Frame." *Grove Art Online*. *Oxford Art Online*. http://www.oxfordartonline.com/subscriber/article/grove/art/T029196 (accessed on August 28, 2014).

Mitchell, W. J. T. 1994. *Picture Theory: Essays on Verbal and Visual Representation*. Chicago.

———. 2004. "Medium Theory." *Critical Inquiry* 30: 324–35.

Mohr, Wolfgang. 1940. "Thor im Fluss. Zur Form der altnordischen mythologischen Überlieferung." *Beiträge zur Geschichte der deutschen Sprache und Literatur (PBB)* 64: 209–29.

Moltke, Erik. 1985. *Runes and Their Origin: Denmark and Elsewhere*. Transl. Peter Godfrey Foote. Copenhagen.

Nauta, Ruurd. 2013. "The Concept of 'Metalepsis': From Rhetoric to the Theory of Allusion and to Narratology." In Eisen and Möllendorff 2013: 469–82.

Ney, Agneta. 2013. "Bland ormar och drakar: En jämförande studie av Ramsundsristningen och Gökstenen." *Scripta islandica* 64: 17–37.

Öberg, Jan. 1994. "Vem kunde latin i medeltidens Sverige?" In *Medeltida skrift- och språkkultyr: nio föreläsningar från ett symposium i Stockholm våren 1992.* Ed. Inger Lindell. Stockholm. Pp. 213–24.

Oehrl, Sigmund. 2006. *Zur Deutung anthropomorpher und theriomorpher Bilddarstellungen auf den spätwikingerzeitlichen Runensteinen Schwedens.* Vienna.

———. 2011. *Vierbeinerdarstellungen auf schwedischen Runensteinen: Studien zur nordgermanischen Tier-und Fesselungsikonografie.* Reallexikon der germanischen Altertumskunde Ergänzungsbände, 72. Berlin.

———. 2013. "Neue Überlegungen zu mutmaßlichen Sigurddarstellungen." In *Vindærinne wunderbærer mære: Gedenkschrift für Ute Schwab.* Ed. Monika Schulz. Vienna. Pp. 359–92.

Owen, Olwyn. 2001. "The Strange Beast that is the English Urnes Style." In *Vikings and the Danelaw: Select Papers from the Proceedings of the Thirteenth Viking Congress, Nottingham and York, 21-30 August 1997.* Ed. James Graham-Campbell et al. Oxford. Pp. 203–22.

Pier, John. 2009. "Metalepsis." In *Handbook of Narratology.* Ed. Peter Hühn et al. Berlin. Pp. 190–203.

Ploss, Emil. 1966. *Siegfried-Sigurd, der Drachenkämpfer: Untersuchungen zur germanisch-deutschen Heldensage.* Graz.

Quinn, Judy. 2000. "From Orality to Literacy in Medieval Iceland." In *Old Icelandic Literature and Society.* Ed. Margaret Clunies Ross. Cambridge. Pp. 30–60.

Rodowick, David N. 1994. "Impure Mimesis, or the Ends of the Aesthetic." In *Deconstruction and the Visual Arts: Art, Media, Architecture.* Ed. Peter Brunette and David Wills. Cambridge. Pp. 96–117.

Roesdahl, Else. 1999. "Jellingstenen—en bog af sten." In *Menneskelivets mang- foldighed: arkæologisk og antropologisk forskning på Moesgård.* Ed. Ole Høiris. Aarhus. Pp. 235–44.

———. 2013. "King Harald's Rune-stone in Jelling: Methods and Messages." In *Early Medieval Art and Archaeology in the Northern World: Studies in Honour of James Graham-Campbell.* Ed. A. Reynolds and L. Webster. Leiden. Pp. 859–75.

Rohrbach, Lena. 2014. *The Power of the Book: Medial Approaches to Medieval Nordic Legal Manuscripts.* Berlin.

Rowe, Elizabeth Ashman. 2006. "Quid Sigvardus cum Christo? Moral Interpretations of Sigurðr Fáfnisbani in Old Norse Literature." *Viking and Medieval Scandinavia* 2: 167–200.

Säve, Carl. 1870. *Zur Nibelungensage: Siegfriedbilder.* Transl. Johanna Mestorf. Hamburg.

Schaeffer, Jean-Marie. 2013. "Fictional vs. Factual Narration." In *The Living Handbook of Narratology.* Ed. Peter Hühn et al. http://www.lhn.uni-hamburg.de/ (accessed on August 28, 2014).

Schapiro, Meyer. 1969. "On Some Problems in the Semiotics of Visual Art: Field and Vehicle in Image Signs." *Semiotica* 1: 223–42.

von See, Klaus. 1999. "Die kulturideologische Stellung der Volsunga saga ok Ragnars saga." In *Europa und der Norden im Mittelalter.* Ed. Klaus von See. Heidelberg. Pp. 397–412.

———. 1999b. "Die Nibelungen auf skandinavischen Bilddenkmälern." In *Europa und der Norden im Mittelalter.* Ed. Klaus von See. Heidelberg. Pp. 183–92.

Simmel, Georg. 1902. "Der Bildrahmen—Ein ästhetischer Versuch." *Der Tag* 541 (18). Transl. as "The Picture Frame: An Aesthetic Study." *Theory, Culture & Society* 11 (1994): 11–17.

Spurkland, Terje. 2005. *Norwegian Runes and Runic Inscriptions.* Woodbridge.

Stern, Marjolein. 2013. *Runestone Images and Visual Communication in Viking Age Scandinavia.* PhD diss., University of Nottingham.

Thompson, Claiborne W. 1975. *Studies in Upplandic Runography.* Austin.

Wamers, Egon. 2000. "*... ok Dani gærði kristna ...*: Der große Jellingstein im Spiegel ottonischer Kunst." *Frühmittelalterliche Studien* 34: 132–58.

———. 2003. "Io triumphe! Die Gebärde der ausgestreckten Hand in der germanischen Kunst." In *Runica, Germanica, Mediaevalia.* Ed. Wilhelm Heizmann. Reallexikon der germanischen Altertumskunde Ergänzungsbände, 37. Berlin. Pp. 905–31.

Wanner, Kevin. 2008. "Adjusting Judgments of *Gauta Þáttr*'s Forest Family." *Scandinavian Studies* 80: 375–406.

Whatling, Stuart. 2010. *Narrative Art in Northern Europe, c. 1140-1300: A Narratological Re-appraisal.* PhD diss., Courtauld Institute, University of London.

Williams, Henrik. 2013. "*Zentrale Probleme bei der Erforschung der älteren Runen: Akten einer internationalen Tagung an der Norwegischen Akademie der Wissenschaften.* Ed. John Ole Askedal, Harald Bjorvand, James E. Knirk and Otto Erlend Nordgreen [review]." *Futhark* 4: 195–201.

Wilson, David Mackenzie, and Ole Klindt-Jensen. 1966. *Viking Art.* London.

Wolf, Werner. 2006. "Introduction: Frames, Framings and Framing Borders in Literature and Other Media." In *Framing Borders in Literature and Other Media.* Ed. Walter Bernhart and Werner Wolf. Amsterdam. Pp. 1–40

Zachrisson, Torun. 1998. *Gård, gräns, gravfält: sammanhang kring ädelmetalldepåer och runstenar från vikingatid och tidig medeltid i Uppland och Gästrikland.* Stockholm.

Zilmer, Kristel. 2011. "Crosses on Rune-stones: Functions and Interpretations." *Current Swedish Archaeology* 19: 87–112.

———, ed. 2012. *Epigraphic Literacy and Christian Identity: Modes of Written Discourse in the Newly Christian European North*. Turnhout.

The Æsir and Their Idols

Jonas Wellendorf
University of California, Berkeley

Abstract: Accounts of the destruction of cult figures are conventional narratives that present a standardized sequence of events, although details may vary from one text to the other. The multitude and longevity of such accounts show that they remained popular through millennia. The standard polemic against cult figures includes lines such as "They have feet, but they will not walk" (Ps. 113: 15). This article discusses accounts of confrontations with idols in the Norse world. Although these accounts adhere to the conventions of such narratives, cult figures in Old Norse literature have been granted an unusual degree of agency. With this agency in mind, the article moves to the mythic sphere and briefly discusses examples of animated creations of gods as well as giants.

Introduction

In the early eighteenth century, a vicar of Western Telemark in central Norway visited the farm Flatland. An evil plague had struck the farmer, his family, and all of his livestock. As if this were not enough, the farmer's harvest had failed. The vicar soon discovered that the farmer harbored an ancient idol that had survived through generations, and with a fervor proper to the pietistic spirit of his time, the clergyman smote the ulcerous member of his flock with the lightning of the godly word. The farmer reluctantly admitted giving shelter to the idol, but he denied ever having directed any worship towards it. As the vicar was shown to the place where the abominable object was kept, he was horrified to see a decaying piece of wood onto which a hoary chisel ignorant of heaven had sculpted something not quite resembling a human face. The wooden idol, it turned out, was known by the name of Gudmund. The vicar commanded that it be destroyed, but when no one reacted, he seized an axe, chopped the worm-eaten idol to pieces and burned it. The farmer afterwards mended his ways, and all were healed.

This lightly paraphrased account of the destruction of the idol Gudmund comes to us through *Everriculum fermenti veteris*, or "Broom for Cleaning out Old Sourdough", published by the Danish theologian Erik Pontoppidan in 1737 (pp. 12–14). Pontoppidan, who seven years later became bishop of Bergen, Norway, had heard the story from the son of the idol-shattering vicar. This dramatic sequence of events reflects a long and unbroken tradition. Although the extent to which backward peasants in inland Norway venerated cult figures in the early eighteenth century, some seven hundred years after the official conversion to Christianity, is difficult to determine with any certainty, this account of meeting with and destruction of a pagan idol is highly conventional, and numerous parallel accounts can be found in both early Christian and medieval texts from Europe and elsewhere.[1]

Most of the medieval Scandinavian texts that describe the veneration of cultic figures participate in and reflect a dominant discourse in which such images are idols or false gods. The original meaning of the Greek word εἴδωλον (idol) was simply "image" or "likeness", and Old Norse texts might use a similarly neutral term, such as *líkneski*, which means the exact same thing: "likeness". While the Greek term was adopted into Latin (*ydolum* or *ydolon*) and used alongside Latin *simulacrum* (image, effigy) as a negatively loaded term, Old Norse *líkneski* is unbiased and can be used of idols or pagan cult figures as well as of painted wooden sculptures of saints—a *líkneski* can be a representation of Þórr as well as of the Virgin Mary (though not both simultaneously). There is even an Icelandic text of the early fourteenth century that is known as *Líkneskjusmíð* (The Making of a Likeness). In this fragmentary text, one finds a somewhat detailed set of instructions for making a *líkneski*: "Fyrst skaltu gera af trénu sem þú vilt ok þurrka áðr sem bezt" (*Líkneskjusmíð* p. 7) (First you shall cut off a piece of the wood as you please, having dried it carefully).[2] The text goes on to explain how the graven image shall be decorated with silver, paint, and so on. It goes without saying that the *líkneski* that results from following these directions will be a sculpture rather than an idol.[3] But history has, I think, taught us that the classification of graven images as idols or sculptures is in many cases

---

[1] Olav Bø cites a number of similar but less elaborate accounts from eighteenth- and nineteenth-century Norway. In some accounts the idol is not called Gudmund but Torbjørn (Bø 1959).

[2] I have silently normalized the orthography of this quotation and all other quotations from unnormalized texts. *Líkneskjusmíð* appears to be related to *De diversis artibus* by Theophilus, as noted by Ólafur Halldórsson in *Líkneskjusmíð*: 9.

[3] Another medieval text describes a fundraising effort in northern Iceland, in which farmers donated shorn sheepskins to the local cathedral in order to fund the making of a *líkneski* of Saint Jón of Hólar (*Lárentíus saga biskups* p. 340).

a matter of perspective and, as we shall see later on, it can also depend on the subsequent use of the *líkneski*. Less ambivalent than *líkneski* are terms such as *trémaðr* (wooden man) and *skurðgoð* (carved god). These designations may safely be considered the Old Norse equivalents of our "idol", and the same goes for the truncated form *goð* ([pagan] god).

Doctrine

The polemic against idols in Old Norse literature is ultimately founded on biblical texts.[4] Biblical writings on the reprehensible cultic practices of pagans fixate upon idols. The making as well as the worship of images is forbidden in the Ten Commandments;[5] in Jeremiah (10: 1–16), (Deutero-)Isaiah (40: 18–20; 41: 6–7; 44: 9–20; 46: 1–7), Psalms (115: 1–8; 135: 15–18), and the entirety of the Letter of Jeremiah, worshippers of idols are rebuked and ridiculed.[6] Among Biblical writings, The Wisdom of Solomon contains one of the most comprehensive statements on the matter of the cult of false gods. In the course of a protracted excursus on the origin and consequences of idolatry, this deuterocanonical text states that "Infandorum enim idolorum cultura omnis mali causa est et initium et finis" (Wisd. of Sol. 14: 27) (the worship of the abominable idols is the cause, origin and end of all evil). Of the multifarious evils occasioned by idolatry, it will at this point suffice to mention pollution of the soul, treachery, adultery, inversion of sexual roles, and murder (Wisd. of Sol. 14: 2–31).

Cross-fertilization with the mainstream Greco-Roman philosophical traditions, which held that the worship of cultic figures was silly at best,[7] ensured that the biblical rhetoric against idols was amplified by the writings of the early Church fathers and resonated loudly throughout the Middle Ages and all the way into Enlightenment. This rhetoric against idolatry was so strong that

---

[4]   See Myrup Kristensen (2013) for a recent study focusing on late antiquity. On statues and cult figures in antiquity, see Bremmer (2013) who traces ideas about the agency of such statues.

[5]   Here in the Old Norse rendition of *Stjórn II*: "Eigi skulu þér yðr skurðgoð gera eptir líkingu þeiri sem á himnum er eða á jǫrðu eða í vǫtnum eða undir jǫrðu. Eigi skulu þér þá hluti vegsama ok fága" (p. 456) (You shall not make idols in the likeness of that which is in the heavens, or on the earth or under the earth. You shall not worship or venerate those things). Cf. Exod. 20: 3–5 and Deut. 5: 7–9 (biblical references are to *Biblia sacra vulgata*).

[6]   See the studies on idol parodies by Wolfgang Roth (1975) and Michael Dick (1999).

[7]   Horace even presents an example of the kind of idol-parody that is commonplace in the Bible when he begins one of his satires with the following words: "Olim truncus eram ficulnus, inutile lignum | cum faber, incertus scamnum faceretne Priapum, | maluit esse deum. deus inde ego ..." (*Sat* I, 8, 1–3) (I once was a fig-tree trunk, a useless piece of wood, when a workman, uncertain of whether he should make a stool or a [figure of the god] Priapus, decided to make a god. So I am a god).

paganism almost came to be identified as worship of statues, and descriptions of paganism often highlight idolatrous practices.

A famous passage in Psalms jeers at idols:

> Os habent et non loquentur | oculos habent et non videbunt | aures habent et non audient | nares habent et non odorabunt | manus habent et non palpabunt | pedes habent et non ambulabunt | non clamabunt in gutture suo | similes illis fiant qui faciunt ea | et omnis qui confidunt in eis. (Ps. 113: 13–16)

> (They have mouths but they will not speak, they have eyes but they will not see, they have ears but they will not hear, they have noses but they will not perceive scents, they have hands but they will not make use of them, they have feet but they will not walk and they will not proclaim from their throat. May those who make them become like them and likewise all who put their trust in them.)[8]

The makers of idols feebly seek to create gods in their own image, but the psalmist hopes that in doing so the makers themselves are deprived of the very facilities with which they are unable to imbue their gods/creations.[9] Although these idols are anthropomorphic, they do not, unlike humans, possess life, and, unlike God, they have no powers whatsoever. They can do "neither good nor ill" as Jeremiah says (*nec male possunt facere nec bene*, Jer. 10: 5), and innumerable hagiographic texts use this point to show how utterly foolish it is to put one's faith and trust in an idol.

Although the idols themselves were considered lifeless, idolatry would be catalyzed by another kind of life that might take up residence in the idols in the form of evil spirits or demons. According to the standard hagiographic narratives, demons usurped the veneration offered to idols. Being essentially empiricists, idolaters would be more likely to offer veneration to an idol if the veneration seemed to pay off in some way. Idolatry therefore had to be benefi-cent to the idolater, or at least appear to be beneficent in the short term. If not, it might be difficult to see the point of venerating any particular idol. The Old Norse saga of Bartholomew illustrates this point:

---

[8] An Old Norse rendition of this passage is found in *Barbǫru saga* (p. 155). See also Kirby (1976–80 I: 68–69).

[9] *Pétrs saga postola I* quotes the last part of the passage from Psalms but sees the wish of the psalmist as a prophecy that has already been fulfilled: "Kom þá þat fram er fyrir var spát með hinum helgustum orðum: Verði þeir sem skurðgoð gera, þeim líkir" (*Pétrs saga postula I* 117–18) (Then that was fulfilled which was foretold with the most holy of words: May those who make idols become like them).

Á því landi [*sc.* Indíalandi] var blótat skurðgoð þat er hét Astaroð. Í því skurðgoði var djǫfull sá er sagðisk grœða sjúka menn, en þá eina grœddi hann er hann meiddi ipse, þvíat landsmenninir kunnu non sannan goð, ok urðu þeir af því tældir af ósǫnnum goði. En inn lygni goð tælir svá þá er non kunnu inn sanna goð at hann kastar á þá sóttum ok meinum ok skǫðum ok gefr svǫr ór skurðgoðum at þeir blóti honum. En þá sýnisk heimskum mǫnnum sem hann grœði þá er hann lætr af at meiða þá. En hann bergr engum, sed grandar hann ok sýnisk þá bjarga er hann lætr af at meiða. (*Barthólómeus saga postula* pp. 99–100)

(In India sacrifices were made to the idol Astaroth. A devil who said that he could heal the sick was in that idol, but he only healed those whom he himself had made sick. The Indians were ignorant of the true God, and a false god therefore deceived them. The mendacious god deceives those who did not know the true God by casting onto them illnesses, diseases, and harms, and he speaks from idols in order that they may make sacrifices to him. And the foolish pagans think that he heals them when he stops harming them. In fact, he heals no one; he harms and appears to heal when ceases to harm.)

The demon who dwells in Astaroth has remarkable powers, but his demonic nature ensures that, strictly speaking, he can do no good: rather, he can do evil and stop doing evil. The demon residing in the idol is capable of making the idol speak or, at least, of speaking from the idol, but he seems unable to animate it further. In the end, according to the saga, the demon is forced to leave, and the empty wooden effigy is subsequently smashed.

In antiquity, pagan philosophers had objected that the cognitive framework used by Christians to understand the worship of statues was too shallow, and that "those who make a suitable object for divine worship do not think the god is in the wood or the stone or bronze from which the object is made. Nor do they think if any part of the statue is cut off that it detracts from the god's power" (Porphyry: 216–217).[10] But points of view like this are not reflected in the mainstream Christian tradition except when they are being refuted. However, they do alert us to the fact that there is more to the veneration of statues than one would immediately expect from reading Christian polemics against idolatry.

[10] These lines, which are from Makarios Magnes's *Apokritikos*, have traditionally been attributed to Porphyry (see Porphyry: 5n26).

Jonas Wellendorf

Among Scandinavians

During the mission to Scandinavia, the thousand-year-old discourse on idolatry was, as it had been elsewhere, confronted with vigorous and living cultic practices different from those it had aimed at originally. This discourse sought to impose its particular and, at this point in time, fairly rigid cognitive model onto these practices. As far as we can judge from the preserved Old Norse texts, the teachings received by medieval Scandinavians reflected less sophisticated reasoning about idols, such as those found in the saga of Bartholomew, quoted above. The idols in these hagiographic texts are of the empty lifeless kind, unable to help themselves, let alone their worshippers. They might be inhabited by demons, but in such cases the demons are rather weak and incapable of mounting an effective defense when confronted with hostile missionaries. The ubiquity of pagan idols in conversion episodes ensured that the intended audience of such texts knew what an idol was supposed to be, and authors writing about conversion efforts could therefore refrain from describing them in great detail. Thus, as a kind of shorthand, one often encounters statements to the effect that the missionary "destroyed idols". One example of this is found among Styrmir Kárason's *articuli* (no. 23):

> Óláfr konungr kristnaði þetta ríki allt. Ǫll blót braut hann niðr ok ǫll goð, sem Þór engilsmannagoð ok Óðin saxagoð ok Skjǫld skánungagoð ok Frey Svíagoð ok Goðorm danagoð ok mǫrg ǫnnur blótskaparskrímsl, bæði hamra ok hǫrga, skóga, vǫtn ok tré ok ǫll ǫnnur blót, bæði meiri ok minni. (*Separate Saga of St Óláfr* p. 694; cf. pp. 711–12)

> (King Óláfr Christianized this entire realm [i.e. Norway]. He destroyed all worshipped entities and all [statues of] gods, such as Þórr, god of the Englishmen, Óðinn, god of the Saxons, Skjǫld, god of the Scanians, Freyr, god of the Swedes, Goðormr, god of the Danes, and many other sacrificial abominations, crags as well as *hǫrgar*, woods, lakes, trees, and all other worshipped entities, big as well as small.)[11]

This passage is interesting, among other reasons, because Styrmir—if the *articuli* do indeed stem from his otherwise lost saga about St. Óláfr—idiosyncratically attributes particular cults to each of the Germanic-speaking peoples of northwestern Europe, except the Norwegians, who had embraced the cults of all of

---

[11] Styrmir (d. 1245) was prior of the Augustinian house of Viðey and may have written a life of Óláfr Haraldsson around 1220. This work is now lost, but short sections (the *articuli*) are preserved in *Flateyjarbók*.

these peoples, apparently without having their own particular brand of idolatry or their own supreme god.

Because of the idols' status as the primary signs of paganism, idols in the preserved texts are routinely overthrown, shattered to pieces, and burned, often by missionaries but occasionally also by the recent converts themselves. One famous narrative of this kind is the story of Dala-Guðbrandr's idol of Þórr, which St. Óláfr confronts in *The Legendary Saga of St Óláfr* (pp. 29–30) and other sagas.[12] Were it not for the big hammer—an emblem of Þórr—that this idol clutches in its hand, it would not be out of place in a translated hagiographic work set in the Mediterranean world. The apparent lack of detailed knowledge that writers of these early texts exhibit about the veneration of cult figures in pre-Christian Scandinavia, in combination with their deployment of the traditional polemic against idols, makes it difficult if not impossible to determine the historicity of such accounts.[13] Since archaeologists have not identified sizeable cult figures from this period, commentators with revisionist inclinations might go so far as to deny the existence of cult figures of the Norse gods of the kind and size described in the texts.[14] However, the identification of paganism with idolatry must have ensured that Christianizers devoted particular attention to the destruction of cult figures. This in combination with the organic materials of which the figures were made ensures a low survival rate.

In the account about the destruction of Dala-Guðbrandr's idol of Þórr, the traditional polemic has been seamlessly inserted into a more elaborate account that exhibits features we normally connect with generic saga form and style (see Andersson 1988). One can observe a similar tendency in other accounts of overturning idols in Old Norse literature, such as the *mǫrg skurðgoð* (many idols) destroyed by Finnr in *Sveins þáttr ok Finns* (p. 103).[15] In this tale, Sveinn is a devoted idolater and keeps a sanctuary full of idols where Þórr (or an idol of Þórr) occupies the place of pride. Sveinn's difficult son, Finnr, is characterized as a bit of a loner. He is meddlesome, garrulous, self-assertive, and generally unruly. Although he is pagan, he loathes idols, and he persistently overturns

---

[12] See Andersson 1988.

[13] See also Wellendorf 2010b.

[14] The textual and archaeological evidence for the existence of smaller, less spectacular figurines is much better. In *Hallfreðar saga* (pp. 162–63) and *Vatnsdœla saga* (pp. 29–30, 33–36, 42) mention is made of *hlutir* (sg. *hlutr*) of Þórr and Freyr (cf. also Einarr skálaglamm's two manshaped *hlutir* mentioned in *Jómsvíkinga saga* (pp. 188–89)). The term *hlutr* is cognate with English "lot", and on the basis of the saga accounts, it is reasonable to surmise that *hlutir* might have played an important divinatory role. The archaeological evidence for cultic figures is assembled by Wijnand A. B. van der Sanden and Torsten Capelle (2002).

[15] *Sveins þáttr ok Finns* and some of the other anecdotes mentioned here have recently been analyzed from a literary perspective in an excellent article by Sian Grønlie (2013). Her main point is that these accounts contribute to the polyphony of *Óláfs saga Tryggvasonar in mesta*.

and mocks the idols in his father's sanctuary, calling them cross-eyed, dusty, and unable to be of assistance to anyone, even themselves. At one point, Finnr swears an oath that he will find the highest king. He sets out, succeeds, and then returns to his father's sanctuary towards the end of the story. In the temple, Þórr senses that something is brewing. Distressed, he shows himself to one of the people of the farm in a dream and asks to be hidden away in a nearby forest, but he does so in vain. The next day, Finnr strides towards the temple:

> Tók hann í hǫnd sér rótakylfu mikla ok gekk til hofsins. Þar var þá allt fornligt, um gætti hurðajárn ryðug ok allt heldr ófáguligt. Hann gekk inn ok skýfði goðin af stǫllunum. En reytti ok ruplaði af þeim allt þat er fémætt var ok bar í belginn. Finnr sló Þór .iij. hǫgg með kylfunni sem mest mátti hann áðr hann fell. Síðan lagði hann band um hals honum ok dró hann eptir sér til strandar, ok lét hann koma á bát. Fór hann svá til fundar við Óláf konung at hann hafði Þór lǫngum á kafi útbyrðis. Stundum barði hann hann. En er konungr sá þetta sagði hann Finn eigi fara vegliga með Þór. Finnr svarar: "Þat sýnisk í því at mér hefir lengi illa líkat við hann, ok skal hann enn hafa verri ok verðugari viðfarar". Klauf hann þá Þór í skíður einar, lagði í eld ok brenndi at ǫsku. Síðan fekk hann sér laug nǫkkurn. Kastaði þar á ǫskunni ok gerði af graut. Þann graut gaf hann blauðum hundum ok mælti: "Þat er makligt at bikkjur eti Þór svá sem hann sjalfr sonu sína". (pp. 113–114)

(He grabbed a great club and went to the temple. Everything there looked worn out, rusty door hinges on the doorframe, and all was quite tarnished. He entered and pushed the gods off their pedestals. He stripped and robbed them of all valuables and put them in his skin bag. Finnr struck Þórr three times as hard as he could with the club before he fell. He then tied a rope around the neck of Þórr, dragged him down to the beach and had him put on a boat. On his way to meet King Óláfr, Finnr often keelhauled Þórr, and occasionally he gave him a battering. When the king saw this, he remarked that Finnr did not handle Þórr with care, to which Finnr replied: "From this one can see that I have long had a dislike for him, and he will be given an even worse and more warranted treatment". Then he clove Þórr into small pieces, cast them in the fire, and burned them to ashes. After this, he got hold of some water, into which he threw the ashes, and made a porridge that he fed to the bitches, saying: "It is only fitting that bitches devour Þórr, just as he devours his sons".)

Finnr acts aggressively throughout the narrative. He becomes an overzealous follower of King Óláfr, and when the king seeks to convert the Norwegians to Christianity, Finnr, who accompanies him, was often so "óðr ok ákaf at helt við váða þeim er eigi gerðu skjótt hans vilja" (p. 114) (furious and violent that he almost killed those who did not immediately do as he wished). Despite his generally bellicose nature, Finnr's rage towards the idol is so extraordinary that even King Óláfr Tryggvason himself, who is not otherwise known for his gentleness towards non-Christian practices, is astonished by Finnr's fury and comments on it. Given that the idol is lifeless, powerless, and empty, it would seem that Finnr goes to extreme lengths in order to destroy it as completely as he does.[16] However, the metaphysics of cultic figures is complicated. The tale begins by identifying the objects venerated by Sveinn as *skurðgoð* (idols), but it immediately slips into speaking of them as simply *goð* (god/gods). The individual idols are referred to as Þórr or Óðinn, the only gods mentioned by name in the text. The text thus illustrates the common slippage from the representation to the represented that is so amply attested throughout the traditional polemic against idols. Sign and signified are united: the god becomes the idol, and the idol becomes the god. In the eyes of the newly converted Finnr, the idol is much more than a powerless piece of wood. It is the god himself, but he is false and utterly impotent.[17] The standard doctrine held that demons took possession of idols and imbued them with a kind of partial life. But the tale about Sveinn and

---

[16] Although the ultimate consummation of the idol is unusual in an Old Norse context, it recalls Moses's treatment of the golden calf (Ex. 32: 20), cf. *Stjórn*: "Hann hlaup þá at blótkalfinum ok braut hann allan í sundr ok brenndi svá at hann varð at ǫsku einni. Þeirri ǫsku sneri hann í vatn ok gaf Gyðingum at drekka af því vatnit" (p. 312) (Then he ran at the idolized calf and broke it into small pieces and burned it to ashes. He poured the ashes into water and gave it to the Jews to drink).

[17] A similar slippage is also found in more neutral accounts of cultic figures, like the famous passage about Nerthus, or Mother Earth, described by Tacitus in *Germania*. He describes how the goddess herself is escorted around the countryside by a priest in a consecrated wagon covered with hangings (*Germania* ch. 40, 2–4). After this, the goddess is washed in a hidden lake and restored to her temple. Since Nerthus can be washed, we must assume that she is an actual object. Tacitus is careful never to refer to the goddess as an image or a representation of Nerthus. Simultaneously, however, he explains that the goddess is not always present in the temple. The object therefore oscillates ontologically between being a sign and a signifier; it is periodically identical with the goddess and periodically not. Also interesting in this context are Einarr skálaglamm's lines, "herþarfir hverfa [...] til blóta [...] ásmegir" (*Vellekla* st. 16 (BI, 119; cf. AI, 126)) (the sons of the gods, needy of people / useful for people go to the sacrifices). These lines, which belong to an episode in the kings' sagas that describe the reinvigoration of a pagan cult in Norway after Jarl Hákon has chased out Haraldr gráfelldr and his brothers (cf. *Óláfs saga Tryggvasonar* pp. 241–43), might be interpreted as meaning that the gods are returning to the sanctuaries.

his son Finnr does not mention demons. Þórr is not a demon. He is pagan god who is as real as the god of the Christians, but he is obviously much weaker.[18]

In narratives such as these, demons/pagan gods are normally able to speak from the idol and appear to worshippers in dreams, but they are generally unable to animate the idols further.[19] However, some Old Norse idols have greater powers, and they are so *mǫgnut* (imbued with strength/power) that they are capable of locomotion. One example of this is provided by the well-known *Ǫgmundar þáttr dytts*. In this tale, a certain Gunnarr helmingr, a Christian Norwegian, dresses up as the pagan god Freyr and accepts offerings of gold, silver, and fine clothing from the Swedes. First, however, he has to defeat the animated idol of Freyr: "Hafði Freyr þar verit mest blótaðr lengi ok svá var mjǫk magnat líkneski Freys at fjandinn mælti við menn ór skurðgoðinu" (p. 13) (Great sacrifices had for a long time been made to Freyr in that place, and the image of Freyr had grown so strong that the devil spoke to people from the idol). The idol, or the devil who resides in it, is able to cast sour looks in Gunnarr's direction. At one point, the idol even attacks Gunnarr, and a wrestling match follows. So, the vivacity of a particular effigy may increase in proportion to the degree to which it is *magnat* or imbued with strength/power through worship. A pious impulse saves Gunnarr, and as he brings down the idol, the devil takes flight. All that is left is an empty piece of wood.[20] It is at this point that Gunnarr dresses up as the idol. The Swedes rejoice when they see that their god is even more vigorous than before: he eats, drinks, talks, and is even able to impregnate his priestess—and they continue to venerate Freyr with sacrifices (p. 16). When the time is ripe, Gunnarr flees Sweden and returns to Norway with his priestess. She is baptized, and they live piously ever after.

The tale of Rǫgnvaldr and Rauðr presents us with an even further invigorated idol and tells how the resolute idolater Rauðr makes such great sacrifices to an idol of Þórr that "the devil spoke to Rauðr from the idol and moved it so that the idol was often seen walking outside with Rauðr during the days".[21] This liveliness almost evaporates when King Óláfr Tryggvason makes his way to

---

[18] At one point in the tale Finnr and his father discuss the merits of Þórr and Óðinn. The father says that Þórr has "traveled through mountains and destroyed crags" (pp. 103–4). The son is not impressed and retorts: "Þat er harla lítill máttr at brjóta steina eða gnípur ok starfa í slíku [...] mér þykkir hinn máttugr er sett hefir í fyrstunni bjǫrgin" (p. 104) (smashing stones or peaks and busying oneself with such things requires very little power [...] I consider that one powerful who in the beginning created the mountains). Despite such polemics, Þórr is still considered coterminous with the idol.

[19] In *Pétrs saga postula* (pp. 91, 174–75, 185) and *Tveggja postula saga Pétrs ok Páls* (p. 306), Simon Magus is able to make it appear as though idols are moving and speaking, but it is mere illusion.

[20] "var þá tréstokkr einn tómr eptir" (p. 16).

[21] "Hann magnaði með miklum blótskap líkneski Þórs þar í hofinu at fjandinn mælti við hann ór skurðgoðinu ok hrœrði þat svá at þat sýndisk ganga úti með honum um dǫgum" (p. 320).

Rauðr's island. The idol becomes rather despondent, and when faced with the king, it loses all its might. A central scene in this story depicts Óláfr Tryggvason's standoff with the idol. Rauðr arranges a wrestling match close to a fire between King Óláfr and the rather unenthusiastic, dispirited idol:

> Þórr gekk at eldinum, ok var þó tregr til. Tokusk þeir konungr í hendr ok sviptusk fast. Þórr lét fyrir. Drap hann fótum í eldstokkana ok steyptisk á eldinn framm. (p. 332)

> (Þórr walked towards the fire even though he was reluctant. He and the king grabbed each other's arms and wrestled hard. Þórr yielded, stumbled over the firebrands, and tumbled forward into the fire.)

This text once again illustrates the doctrine that the idols themselves are powerless and that when they do exhibit some kind of power, it is caused by a devil who moves in once the sacrifices reach an appropriate level.[22] When confronted with missionaries, the pagans expect their idols to act, but it lies at the very heart of such stories that the idols are destined to be unsuccessful; conversion tales deal after all with successful missionary efforts. Outside the context of mission and conversion, beings created by human hands can occasionally be more effective. One example is found near the conclusion of *Ragnars saga loðbrókar*. In this saga, a group of sailors lands on Sámsey in Denmark and finds a colossal old idol completely covered in moss as they explore the island. The sailors are discussing the origin of this *trémaðr* (wooden man) among themselves when they are interrupted by the effigy, which explains in poetic form that it had been erected long ago by the sons of King Ragnarr and that sacrifices were made to it "for the deaths of men in Sámsey in the South".[23] The idol in this anecdote is not, and has not been, confronted by a zealous missionary. Therefore it is not predetermined to suffer ridicule and destruction. It is simply presented as an ancient relic of times long past.[24] The fact that the idol is overgrown with moss, on the other hand, should be taken as a sign that the idol suffers from a lack of veneration.

Yet another *trémaðr* who avoids destruction at the hands of a missionary in the course of the narrative in which it appears is mentioned towards the conclusion of *Þorleifs þáttr jarlsskálds*. In this tale, Jarl Hákon fashions a wooden man out of a piece of driftwood, places the heart of a human in him, clothes him,

---

[22] Lýtir, mentioned in *Hauks þáttr habrókar*, is yet another example of an animated idol or perhaps a living god. The text does not explicitly mention demonic possession, but Lýtir does not show himself before sacrifices are made to him.

[23] The idol says: "þá vark blótin | til bana mönnum | í Sámseyju | sunnanverðri" (p. 285).

[24] Note also how, in the quotation from *Sveins þáttr ok Finns* (above), Sveinn's temple was described as run-down and derelict.

and names him Þorgarðr. The earl and his two goddesses, the sisters Þorgerðr Hǫrgabrúðr and Irpa, then *mǫgnuðu* (imbued with strength/power) the wooden man with the power of the Devil so that he came to life and was able to walk and talk like other men. They arm Þorgarðr with the halberd of Hǫrgi, the mythical bridegroom of Þorgerðr Hǫrgabrúðr, and they send him to Iceland in order to dispatch Þorleifr jarlsskáld. Having successfully completed his mission, Þorgarðr disappears down into the earth, never to be seen again (pp. 225–26).[25]

This story has nothing to say about veneration of Þorgarðr, and he is made for the explicit purpose of being sent to Iceland in order to fulfill a specific task. For these reasons, it is obvious that he should not be considered an idol. Nevertheless, we do find some of the same elements as in stories about idols: Þorgarðr is fashioned by human hands and in the image of his maker, he is *magnaðr* or imbued with strength/power, and the human agent is confident that the effigy will be successful. Jarl Hákon is generally portrayed as a reprehensible character in Old Norse literature, but in this particular anecdote he is successful in his undertaking and is able to exact what the earl must have considered a suitable revenge upon the Icelander Þorleifr jarlsskáld. Had the anecdote involved a confrontation with a Christian missionary rather than a pagan skald, the outcome would surely have been different, but in the pagan context in which the acts of the earl are portrayed, they cannot be considered immediately objectionable. We might even see the account about the how the long dead Saint Mercurius killed Julian the Apostate with his spear as a parallel (*Maríu saga* pp. 699–702).

Another textual passage that alerts us to the considerable size of the gray zone between idols and other kinds of effigies can be found in the Old Norwegian law of the Eiðsífaþing district. Chapter 24 of the longer version of this law, *Eiðsifaþingslǫg: Kristinn réttr hinn forni*, contains a series of uniquely interesting paragraphs on cult figures and other practices that are forbidden according to Christian law:

24.1. Engi maðr skal hafa í húsi sínu staf eða stalla, vit eða blót, eða þat er til heiðins siðar veit.

[...]

24.3. Nú ef blót er funnit í húsi láslausu, matblót eða leirblót gert í mannslíki af leiri eða af deigi, þá skal hann þaðan leysa brott með lýrittareiði, sekr .iij. mǫrkum ef eiðr fellsk.

---

[25] Þorgarðr was a quite common name in Norway in the Middle Ages, but in this case, the name appears to have been chosen because it can be seen as a masculine variant of the name of Þorgerðr Hǫrgabrúðr.

24.4 En ef funnit er í lásum, í kerum eða kistum, í byrðum eða í ǫrkum, þá er sá útlægr er þeim lykli varðveitir er at gengr. (p. 24)

(24.1 In his house, no man is allowed to have a *stafr* or a *stalli* or *vitt* or *blót* or that which belongs to pagan practice.

24.3. Now, if a *blót* is found in an unlocked house, a *matblót* or a *leirblót* formed out of clay or dough in the shape of a man, he [the owner] shall free himself from this with a *lýritt*-oath; he is fined three marks if the oath fails.

24.4 But if it is found under lock, in vats, or chests, in boxes or cases, then the one who keeps the proper key is an outlaw.

Although the paragraphs are difficult to translate, it is clear that they prohibit the possession of a *stafr* (a wooden staff with some kind of representation of a deity?), a *stalli* (altar?), *vitt* and *blót*, which might be designations for items used for sorcery and sacrifices or perhaps objects to which sacrifices are made. The following paragraph shows that the sacrifices/objects to which sacrifices are made (*blót*) might be made out of dough or clay and given an anthropomorphic shape. The import of the passage is plain: there is a clear interdiction against making effigies of dough or clay and perhaps of wood as well. The purpose of these various kinds of effigies might differ from one item to another, but not so much that the lawmaker could not treat them in the same paragraph.

Among Their Gods

We have now moved from hagiographic texts that present stories of idols and idolatry to texts that include animated figures made of trees and men made of dough or clay. The hagiographies are permeated by a traditional and stereotypical polemic that makes it difficult, perhaps even impossible, to discern an underlying layer of historically reliable information about actual cult figures. On the other hand, the hagiographic texts that were translated into Old Norse do not feature any kind of animated figures or effigies prominently. They are of course well known from other traditions—examples might include the gingerbread man and Adam, who was created out of the dust or clay of the earth, *af jarðarinnar leiri*, as it is expressed in *Stjórn I* (p. 47).[26] At this point, golem traditions, Prometheus's fashioning humans out of clay, Daedalus's statues that needed to

---

[26] A different angle on the same theme is provided in *Konungs skuggsjá*, where the Devil is given the following line: "Þetta er oss ofmikil skǫmm at maðr sá er gǫrr var af leiri eða sorgu jarðar dupti skal vera leiddr í þá eilífa sælu er vér várum frá reknir" (p. 80) (It is too great a shame for us that

be chained in order to prevent them from running away, and the Saami Stallo legends could also be invoked, but I will turn to Old Norse mythology in a more strict sense.

Among the many possible social functions of myth, we might focus on the exemplary one. Acts of the gods might be seen as model examples of acceptable or even commendable behavior. A convenient aspect of this function is that it facilitates the detachment of worship and cultic practices from the stories about pre-Christian deities. This detachment might have ensured that some pagan myths could live on and acquire new meanings after Christianity had banned pre-Christian cultic practices. As long as a particular story is presented in a mythic mode, characters and practices that might be considered reprehensible in stories presented in a historical mode can without great difficulty function as admirable examples of desired behavior. Ingólfr Arnarson, the first settler of Iceland, provides a clear illustration of this. He observes all the appropriate practices of his time, takes omens, performs sacrifices etc., and he is ultimately successful in his undertakings. Ingólfr's brother, Hjǫrleifr, on the other hand, fails to do all of these things and ends up being killed by his slaves. Ingólfr even pronounces an explicit verdict over Hjǫrleifr's actions: "Sé ek svá hverjum verða, ef eigi vill blóta" (p. 44) (I see that this is what happens to those who do not want to make sacrifices.)[27]

Within this archetypal sphere, the Æsir themselves both build and preside over temples and altars in the world of the gods.[28] In *Hymiskviða* st. 1 and else-where, the collective of the gods also performs acts of divination. In spite of this, the available sources do not appear to tell to whom these altars were dedicated, towards whom the Æsir direct their questions or from whom they might expect an answer. It might be that there are no gods of the second degree, gods of gods so to speak, and that the gods erect altars where they can sacrifice to themselves or perhaps perform some kind of autosacrifice, offering up themselves to themselves as Óðinn is said to have done (cf. *Hávamál* st. 138). Another possibility is that it is the inscrutable All-father, the one who according to Jafnhár in *Gylfaginning* created heaven, earth, the air, and everything there is in them. This might then in a second move lead to ideas of an original monotheism, of *prisca theologia*, or of some kind of influence from Christian theology. Other potential candidates for the gods of gods might be the Norns, since even the Æsir had to abide by their decrees. One is therefore not unjustified in thinking that the Æsir

---

that man who was created of clay or of the unclean dirt of the earth should be led to that eternal happiness from which we were expelled).

[27] Cf. Preben Meulengracht Sørensen (2001) and Jonas Wellendorf (2010a).

[28] See e.g. *Vǫluspá* (K) st. 7 (the gods as a collective), *Vafþrúðnismál* st. 38 (Njǫrðr), *Grímnismál* st. 13 and 16 (Heimdallr and Njǫrðr, respectively).

might try to appease them—or some other mythological power whom the gods are unable to control—through sacrifice. Xenophanes of Colophon famously criticized the cult of the gods and the myths about them for being projections of human conduct and characteristics onto a divine power that had no countenance and was far elevated over the petty concerns of humans. He claimed that if cattle and horses had hands they would depict their gods in the shape of cattle and horses. Xenophanes's line of thought could in this case lead to the conclusion that the gods, who are essentially anthropomorphic, have altars because humans have altars.

In the end, the available material is not sufficient to determine who the gods of the second degree were.[29] Nor, as far as I know, do we hear anything about cult figures of the gods. We do, however, learn that they fashioned the first two humans, Askr and Embla, out of two pieces of wood and imbued them with life.[30] Imitating this, humans can, to the best of their ability, strive to do the same. Like Ingólfr, they make sacrifices, perform acts of divination, and heed the answers of the gods. Like Ragnarr or his sons, they make wooden idols, and like the Norwegian earl, they may create a living being out of a wooden log and send it on a deadly mission to Iceland.

Conversely, an anti-paradigmatic example may be found in a myth that features a confrontation between the gods and their adversaries. We might see this as a case parallel with the saga accounts of standoffs between missionaries and (sometimes animated) idols. In one myth the giant Hrungnir challenges Þórr to single combat, and Þórr is very keen to go, "for", as *Skáldskaparmál* tells us, "no one has granted him this before".[31] The giants are looking forward to the encounter with less enthusiasm. Worried that Hrungnir might be incapable of defeating Þórr, they create a gigantic figure out of clay, equip him with the heart of a mare, and name him Mǫkkurkálfi. The champion of the gods, Þórr, fights and is ultimately victorious, but only because of the assistance offered to him by his servant Þjálfi, who, as *Gylfaginning* explains (p. 37), is a human rather than a god. As a human, Þjálfi must be counted among the creations of the Norse gods. The giants, on the other hand, try feebly to create a being that can support their champion. Even though their creation might look impressive—Mǫkkurkálfi is after all nine leagues high—he turns out to be of little help to the giants, and he falls, having won little acclaim. The only additional piece of information we

---

[29] Kimberley Patton treats this question, in a larger comparative context, in a fascinating study that draws mainly on Greek materials. Among other things, she argues that the gods should be seen as the source of cult rather than the objects of cult (2009: 13).

[30] *Gylfaginning* (p. 13); cf. *Vǫluspá* (K) st. 17–18.

[31] "þvíat engi hefir honum þat fyrr veitt" (*Skáldskaparmál* I p. 21).

have about Mǫkkurkálfi is that he wets himself when he sees Þórr approach Grjótúnagarðar, the site of the single combat.[32]

Mǫkkurkálfi is a relatively enigmatic figure, and interpretations of his origin and significance in the myth vary from one commentator to another.[33] Even the etymology of his name, customarily interpreted as "Mist-Calf", is uncertain.[34] A recent contribution to the scholarship on Mǫkkurkálfi suggests that Mǫkkurkálfi originally was "a mighty giant with a stout heart of a stallion [...] from the land of mist, perhaps Hrungnir's servant" (Liberman 2009: 97). Whatever Mǫkkurkálfi's origin,[35] his role in the preserved myth is clearly different. What I will briefly suggest here is that the audience of the myth who encountered it in some version of *Snorra Edda* might have understood it in the same frame of reference as they understood stories about inanimate and animated effigies. From the perspective of the giants there would have been nothing inherently wrong with Mǫkkurkálfi—except, perhaps, that they were unable to find him a suitable heart—while from the perspective of the gods Mǫkkurkálfi was about as efficient and successful as an idol faced with a hostile idoloclast. It is mainly a matter of perspective. The ontological status of creations or representations thereof, whether made by gods or giants, pagans or Christians, changes along with the perspective from which it is observed, and the god of one is the idol of another.

I wish to stress the importance of perspective by returning to Gudmund, the idol who might have been venerated by Norwegian peasants in the early eighteenth century. In 1959, the Norwegian folklorist Olav Bø devoted a long study to the traces of early modern Norwegian idolatry. He argued that the

[32] That the mare's heart partly is to blame for Mǫkkurkálfi's lack of bravery is clear from a passage in *Fóstbrœðra saga* where a certain Þordís yells to the protagonist Þormóðr, who has found it wisest to hide himself: "Nú ef hann er snjallari en geit eða hugprúðari en merr, ok megi hann heyra mál mitt, þá svari hann" (p. 254n4) (Now if he [Þormóðr] is wiser than a goat and braver than a mare and can hear what I say, then he would answer me). If Þormóðr had not been protected by some kind of magic, he would definitely have responded to this taunt, but doing so would probably have cost him his life.

[33] Mǫkkurkálfi is only known from *Skáldskaparmál*'s prose account. Although this text clearly drew on Þjóðólfr ór Hvíni's skaldic poem *Haustlǫng*, neither Þjálfi nor Mǫkkurkálfi is mentioned in the preserved parts of the poem. George Dumézil's idea that Mǫkkurkálfi is somehow related to an initiation ritual in which the initiated fight a harmless but formidable-looking enemy held sway for some time, but it has now been rejected by Jens Peter Schjødt (2008: 233–41).

[34] His name would make more sense if interpreted as "dust-born" or "clay-calves". Scholars normally take -*mǫkkur* to mean "mist, fog", as Modern Icelandic *mökkur*, but this word is only attested in Old Norse prose as a part of a composite.

[35] Kurt Wais (1952) argued that the story about Þórr's encounter with Hrungnir is an old Indo-European myth that is also reflected in the Hittite myth about the weather god Tasmisu's fight with the Ullikummi, a giant of stone. The Hittite myth itself is translated from Hurrian. Even though this theory has found proponents (Stitt 1998 is one), it does not explain the function of Mǫkkurkálfi.

effigies mentioned by Pontoppidan and a number of other sources did not originate as images of pagan gods but were originally statues of saints or remains of supporting pillars of stave churches with humanoid faces carved onto them. In the wake of the Reformation, churches were purged of their old papist interiors, including figures of saints. Some of these effects fell into disuse and were repurposed. The status of the statues of the saints then was unstable, just like that of the Old Norse gods and their cult figures had been centuries before. The post-Reformation material allows us to follow the development of their ontological standing more closely and through additional reversals of fortune. Like the Old Norse gods and their statues, the statues of saints were degraded to idols and discarded, but some were salvaged and elevated to gods by peasants, only to be degraded once again to idols and smashed by zealous Lutheran vicars.

Accounts of the destruction of idols are conventional narratives that present a standardized sequence of events, although details may vary from one text to the other. The multitude and longevity of such accounts show that they remained popular through millennia. At the same time, these accounts are often stereotypical to such an extent that it is an insurmountable challenge to penetrate the layers of convention and uncover a historical reality in which representations of pagan gods lost their divine status and came to be identified as idols. The texts discussed in this article nevertheless demonstrate how the undoubtedly long and complex process of conversion to Christianity came to be remembered as a series of stand-offs between champions of the Church and of the pagans.

Works Cited

Primary Sources

Barbǫru saga
Heilagra mana søgur: Fortællinger og legender om hellige mænd og kvinder: efter gamle haands[k]rifter. Ed. C. R. Unger. Christiania: 1877. I: 153–57.

Barthólómeus saga postula
Isländska handskriften N° 645 4° i den arnamagnæanska samlingen. Ed. Ludvig Larsson. Lund: 1885. Pp. 99–108.

Biblia sacra vulgata
Biblia sacra: Iuxta vulgatam versionem. Ed. Roger Gryson, Bonifatius Fischer, and Robert Weber. Stuttgart: 1994.

Jonas Wellendorf

Eiðsifaþingslǫg: Kristinn réttr hinn forni
De eldste østlandske kristenrettene. Ed. Eyvind Fjell Halvorsen and Magnus Rindal. Norrøne tekster, 7. Oslo: 2008. Pp. 1–117.

Einarr skálaglamm: see *Vellekla*

Everriculum fermenti veteris
Erik Pontoppidan. *Everriculum fermenti veteris seu residuæ in Danico orbe cum paganismi tum papismi reliqviæ in apricum prolatæ, opusculum restituendo suæ, aliqva ex parte, integritati Christianismo velificaturum.* Hafniæ: 1737.

Fóstbrœðra saga
Íslenzk fornrit, 6. Ed. Björn K. Þórólfsson and Guðni Jónsson. Reykjavík: 1943. Pp. 119–276.

Grímnismál: see *Poetic Edda*

Gylfaginning
Snorri Sturluson. *Edda: Prologue and Gylfaginning.* Ed. Anthony Faulkes. London: 1988. Pp. 7–55.

Hallfreðar saga
Íslenzk fornrit, 8. Ed. Einar Ól. Sveinsson. Reykjavík: 1939. Pp. 133–200.

Hauks þáttr Hábrókar
Flateyjarbok: En samling af norske konge-sagaer med indskudte mindre fortællinger om begivenheder i og udenfor Norge samt annaler. Ed. Guðbrandur Vigfússon and C. R. Unger. Kristiania: 1860–1868. I: 577–83.

Hávamál: see *Poetic Edda*

Horace
Q. Horati Flacci. *Opera.* Ed. Edvardus C. Wickham. 2nd. ed. Ed. H. W. Garrod. Oxford: 1967.

Hymiskviða: see *Poetic Edda*

Jómsvíkinga saga
Flateyjarbok: En samling af norske konge-sagaer med indskudte mindre fortællinger om begivenheder i og udenfor Norge samt annaler. Ed. Guðbrandur Vigfússon and C. R. Unger. 3 vols. Kristiania: 1860–1868. III: 96–106, 153–205.

Konungs skuggsjá
Konungs skuggsiá. Ed. Ludvig Holm-Olsen. Norrøne tekster, 1. Oslo: 1983.

Landnámabók
Íslenzk fornrit, 1. Ed. Jakob Benediktsson. Reykjavík: 1968. Pp. 29–397.

Lárentíus saga biskups
Íslenzk fornrit, 17. Ed. Guðrún Ása Grímsdóttir. Reykjavík: 1998. Pp. 215–441.

Legendary Saga of St. Óláfr
Olafs saga hins helga: Efter pergamenthaandskrift i Uppsala Universitetsbibliotek, Delagardieske samling nr 8[II]. Ed. Oscar Albert Johnsen. Kristiania: 1922.

Líkneskjusmíð
"Líkneskjusmíð." Ed. Ólafur Halldórsson. *Árbók hins íslenzka fornleifafélag*. 1973. 70: 5–17.

Maríu saga
Maríu saga: Legender om Jomfru Maria og hender jertegn. Ed. C. R. Unger. Christiania: 1871.

Óláfs saga Tryggvasonar
Íslenzk fornrit, 26. Ed. Bjarni Aðalbjarnarson. Reykjavík: 1941–1951. Pp. 225–372.

Pétrs saga postula I
Postola sögur: Legendariske fortællinger om Apostlenes liv, deres kamp for kristendommens udbredelse samt deres martyrdød. Ed. C. R. Unger. Christiania: 1874. Pp. 1–151.

Poetic Edda
Eddukvæði I-II. Ed. Jónas Kristjánsson and Vésteinn Ólason. *Íslenzk fornrit*. Reykjavík: 2014.

Porphyry
Porphyry: Against the Christians. Ed. Robert A. Berchman. Ancient Mediterranean and Medieval Texts and Contexts, 1. Leiden: 2005.

Ragnars saga loðbrókar
Fornaldarsögur Norðurlanda I. Ed. Guðni Jónsson. Reykjavík: 1959. Pp. 219–85.

Rǫgnvalds þáttr ok Rauðs
Óláfs saga Tryggvasonar en mesta. Ed. Ólafur Halldórsson. Editiones Arnamagnæanæ, ser. A. 3 vols. 1958–2000. I: 313–33.

Separate Saga of St. Óláfr

Saga Óláfs konungs hins helga: Den store saga om Olav den Hellige efter pergament-shåndskrift i Kungliga biblioteket i Stockholm nr. 2 4to, med varianter efter andre håndskrifter. Ed. Oscar Albert Johnsen and Jón Helgason. 2 vols. Oslo: 1941.

Skáldskaparmál

Snorri Sturluson. *Edda: Skáldskaparmál.* Ed. Anthony Faulkes. 2 vols. London: 1998.

Stjórn

Stjórn. Ed. Reidar Astås. 2 vols. Norrøne tekster, 8. Oslo: 2009.

Sveins þáttr ok Finns

Óláfs saga Tryggvasonar en mesta. Ed. Ólafur Halldórsson. Editiones Arnamagnæanæ, ser. A. 3 vols. Copenhagen: 1958–2000. II: 102–14.

Tveggja postula saga Pétrs ok Páls

Postola sögur: Legendariske fortællinger om Apostlenes liv, deres kamp for kristendommens udbredelse samt deres martyrdød. Ed. C. R. Unger. Christiania: 1874. Pp. 283–318.

Vatnsdœla saga

Íslenzk fornrit, 8. Ed. Einar Ól. Sveinsson. Reykjavík: 1939. Pp. 1–131.

Vellekla

Einarr Helgason skálaglamm. Ed. Finnur Jónsson. In Den norsk-islandske skjaldedigtning. Copenhagen: 1912–1915. AI: 122–31, BI: 117–24.

Vafþrúðnismál: see *Poetic Edda*

Vǫluspá: see *Poetic Edda*

Þorleifs þáttr jarlsskálds

Íslenzk fornrit, 9. Ed. Jónas Kristjánsson. Reykjavík: 1956. Pp. 213–29.

Ǫgmundar þáttr dýtts

Óláfs saga Tryggvasonar en mesta. Ed. Ólafur Halldórsson. Editiones Arnamagnæanæ, ser. A. 3 vols. Copenhagen: 1958–2000. II: 1–18.

Secondary Sources

Andersson, Theodore M. 1988. "Lore and Literature in a Scandinavian Conversion Episode." In *Idee, Gestalt, Geschichte: Festschrift Klaus von See: Studien zur europäischen Kulturtradition.* Ed. Gerd Wolfgang Weber. Odense. Pp. 261–84.

Bremmer, Jan N. 2013. "The Agency of Greek and Roman Statues." *Opuscula: Annual of the Swedish Institutes at Athens and Rome* 6: 7–21.

Bø, Olav. 1959. "Faksar og kyrkjerestar." *By og bygd. Norsk folkemuseums årbok (1957–58)* 12: 43–76.

Dick, Michael B. 1999. "Prophetic Parodies of Making the Cult Image." In *Born in Heaven, Made on Earth: The Making of the Cult Image in the Ancient Near East*. Ed. Michael B. Dick. Winona Lake, Indiana. Pp. 1–53.

Grønlie, Sian. 2013. "Þáttr and Saga: The Long and the Short of Óláfr Tryggvason." *Viking and Medieval Scandinavia* 9: 19–36.

Kirby, Ian J. 1976–1980. *Biblical Quotations in Old Icelandic-Norwegian Religious Literature*. 2 vols. Rit, 9–10. Reykjavík.

Liberman, Anatoly. 2009. "Þjalfi." In *Approaching the Viking Age: Proceedings of the International Conference on Old Norse Literature, Mythology, Culture, Social Life and Language, 11–13 October, Vilnius, Lithuania*. Ed. Ērika Sausverde and Ieva Steponavičiūtė. Vilnius. Pp. 95–116.

Meulengracht Sørensen, Preben. 2001. "Sagan um Ingólf og Hjörleif: Athugasemðir um söguskoðun íslendinga á seinni hluta þjóðveldisaldar." In *At fortælle historien: Studier i den gamle nordiske litteratur*. Trieste. Pp. 11–25. First published in *Skírnir* (1974) 148: 20–40.

Myrup Kristensen, Troels. 2013. *Making and Breaking Gods: Christian Responses to Pagan Sculpture in Late Antiquity*. Aarhus Studies in Mediterranean Antiquity, 12. Århus.

Patton, Kimberly Christine. 2009. *Religion of the Gods: Ritual, Paradox and Reflexivity*. Oxford.

Roth, Wolfgang M. W. 1975. "For Life He Appeals to Death (Wis 13: 18): A Study of Old Testament Idol Parodies." *Catholic Biblical Quarterly* 37: 21–47.

van der Sanden, Wijnand A. B., and Torsten Capelle. 2002. *Götter, Götzen, Holzmenschen*. Archäologische Mitteilungen aus Nordwestdeutschland, 39. Oldenburg.

Schjødt, Jens Peter. 2008. *Initiation between Two Worlds: Structure and Symbolism in Pre-Christian Scandinavian Religion*. The Viking Collection, 17. Odense.

Stitt, Michael J. 1998. "Ambiguity in the Battle of Þórr and Hrungnir." In *Telling Tales: Medieval Narratives and the Folk Tradition*. Ed. Francesca Canadé Sautman, Diana Conchado, and Guiseppe Calo Di Scipio. New York. Pp. 121–36.

Wais, Kurt. 1952. "Ullikummi, Hrungnir, Armilus und Verwandte." In *Edda, Skalden, Saga: Festschrift zum 70. Geburtstag von Felix Genzmer*. Ed. Hermann Schneider. Heidelberg. Pp. 211–61.

Wellendorf, Jonas. 2010a. "The Interplay of Pagan and Christian Traditions in Icelandic Settlement Myths." *Journal of English and Germanic Philology* 109(1): 1–21.

———. 2010b. "The Attraction of the Earliest Old Norse Vernacular Hagiography." In *Saints and Their Lives on the Periphery: Veneration of Saints in Scandinavia and Eastern Europe (c. 1000–1200).* Ed. Haki Antonsson and Ildar Garipzanov. Turnhout. Pp. 241–58.

PART TWO

LOCAL AND NEIGHBORING TRADITIONS

Blótgyðjur, Goðar, Mimi, Incest, and Wagons
Oral Memories of the Religion(s) of the Vanir[1]

Terry Gunnell
University of Iceland

Abstract: This article focuses on the recurring motifs concerning the peculiarities of the religion of the gods referred to as the Vanir, drawing on a range of Old Norse accounts from different times including *Landnámabók, Gísla saga Súrssonar, Hrafnkels saga, Vatnsdæla saga, Ynglinga saga, Gunnars þáttr helmings, Gesta Danorum*, and more. Many of the aforementioned motifs (commonly concerning ritual activities, religious centers, female religious leaders, and particular types of animal) tend to be unexplained in the texts. Their recurring patterns in the narratives nonetheless imply that in the oral traditions of Norway and Iceland people seem to have viewed the religious activities connected with the "Vanir" (with their center in Sweden) as having been different in nature to those encountered elsewhere. They also seem to have envisaged closer connections between the Vanir and the landscape than existed between the Æsir and the natural environment. This evidence lends weight to the argument that, in spite of recent arguments to the contrary, the religions associated with the Vanir and the Æsir gods had a different nature and origin.

In 2010, Rudolf Simek wrote a now-famous "obituary" for the Vanir in which, among other things, he argued that "there is no inherent difference between the gods [the Vanir and the Æsir] ascribed to by Snorri" (Simek 2010: 13). His general argument, following the earlier ideas of Lotte Motz (Motz 1996: 123–24), is that the idea of a special family of gods called the Vanir was essentially "a figment of imagination from the thirteenth to the twentieth centuries" that began with

---

[1] I would like to express my gratitude to the editors for their careful reading over of the text of this article, and their suggestions for improvements.

Snorri Sturluson's *Prose Edda* (Snorri Sturluson 2005: 23, 30; 1998: 3). The aim of this article is to add some support to the ripostes given by Clive Tolley and Jens Peter Schjødt to Simek's article, which have pointed to methodological weaknesses in Simek's argument (Tolley 2011) and raised the suggestion that the Vanir definitely had a different "functional tendency" to the Æsir gods (Schjødt 2014: 22, esp. 25–30), an argument that the present author is less convinced of.[2] Here, the focus will not be on function (stressed by Schjødt) or the early use of the word "Vanir" for a group of gods (to which, like Tolley, the present author has no objection), but rather on the degree to which the early oral tradition of western Scandinavia[3] (reflected in Old Norse poetry and the sagas) seems to have viewed those gods classed as "Vanir" as having been different in background, origin, and geographical association from the so-called Æsir (contrary to Simek's argument). Among other things, it will be argued that the western Scandinavian view of Vanir "otherness" involved a strong sense that the religious practices of the so-called Vanir were somewhat different to those associated with the so-called Æsir.[4] This article will concentrate on evidence of those religious practices reflected in the saga and eddic materials.[5] In addition to this, attention will be paid to some interesting and revealing features concerning the beliefs and practices relating to other gods which are *not* mentioned in written medieval sources. While Tolley is right that in arguing that "absence of evidence

[2]   Among other things, Schjødt's suggestion that "the Vanir are not thematised as warriors" (Schjødt 2014: 30) seems to sidestep the fact that Freyr has a horse named Blóðughófi/Blóðhófr, (Blood-hoof); that he is described as being "bǫðfróðr" (battle-experienced); kennings like "as-Freyr", "es-Freyr", "él-Freyr" and "víg-Freyr" (for warrior) (*Skáldskaparmál*, pp. 19, 65, 89, 100, 265–66); and the archaeological and literary evidence of helmets crowned with images of boars (the animal most closely associated with the Vanir; see below, note 14), which are more likely to be related to the battle prowess of the boar than its relation to fertility (see Kovárová 2011). As I suggest here, like Þórr, the Vanir seem to have had a wide range of functions, ranging from sovereignty (not least through genealogical connection to the Ynglingar), to close associations with magic and ritual (not least through Freyja's connection with *seiðr*, discussed below), battle-prowess, and fertility. See also Olof Sundqvist (2000: 136–55) on the genealogical connections between the Vanir and the Ynglingar kings.

[3]   On the West Norse bias of the accounts in Old Norse belief in Old Norse literature, see further Andreas Nordberg's article, "Continuity, Change and Regional Variation in Old Norse Religion" (Nordberg 2012: 122–24).

[4]   It is also questionable whether the "Æsir" were commonly viewed as having existed as a united pantheon (see Gunnell 2015).

[5]   The question of the degree to which this material has roots in the oral tradition is one that has been argued for decades, and there is unfortunately too little space here to examine this point in detail. Nonetheless, it might be stated that while there is little question that the sagas, *Prose Edda* and eddic poems were recorded in a Christian environment, there is equally little doubt that much of the material they preserve has a background in the oral tradition (see Gunnell 2008, 2013a, 2014). If the apparently historical writing did not have a basis in recognized concepts and knowledge, it would not have been passed on or rewritten.

is not evidence of absence" (Tolley 2011: 20; also Schjødt 2014: 22), it must also be borne in mind that not all absences are "created equal". As will be explained in more detail below, in the field of the history of Old Norse myth and religion, absence can sometimes be as informative as presence.

To start with, a review will be given of the extant (essentially literary) "evidence" concerning the religious practices of the Vanir (said to include essentially Njǫrðr, Freyr, and Freyja), limited as it is, and the ways in which the Vanir are presented in the written sources in comparison to the other gods. Less attention will be given to the extant myths dealing with the Vanir, which are limited in number.

The paucity of Vanir myths in the extant literature certainly underlines the fact that Snorri apparently knew much less about the religious worldviews and practices associated with the Vanir than he did about about those related to Óðinn or Þórr. This is probably natural since, as many scholars have stressed (see, for example, Vikstrand 2001; Sundqvist 2000; and Brink 2007), a relatively high number of Vanir-related place names point to their association with the Uppland area of Sweden, an area probably unfamiliar to many Icelanders.[6] This association is, of course, backed up by *Ynglingatal*, Snorri's account in *Ynglingasaga* (ch. 9–10), and other saga accounts that also appear to have a background in the oral tradition, such as *Gunnars þáttr helmings* (*Ögmundar þáttr dytts* pp. 109–15; *Flateyjarbók* I, ch. 277–78).[7] It might be remembered that Snorri's personal associations with Sweden were limited to his visit to Skara in Västergötland in 1218 (see further *Sturlunga saga* p. 238), and the same probably applies to his personal knowledge of Swedish tradition. One should be careful about assuming the advantages of twenty-first century communications when considering the Nordic world of the thirteenth century. As Sighvatr Þórðarson's *Austrfararvísur* (Verses on an Eastern Journey) in *Ólafs saga helga* (ch. 61) effectively demonstrate, travel took time in this period. The Uppland area of Sweden was some distance from Norway, where Snorri spent most of his time abroad, the distance being further complicated by lakes and forests. It is thus likely that Snorri's personal knowledge of the mythology and pre-Christian religious activities of

---

[6]   Certainly, as Brink's maps show, Vanir-associated place names are also found here and there in western Norway (just as they are found in Iceland: see Svavar Sigmundsson 1992: 242–43), but they are much less widely distributed than those associated with Þórr. The Freyr and Njǫrðr place names in Sogn in Norway tend to be comparatively deep inland: see note 8 below. Their particular association with Sweden is stressed by the fact that they are hardly found at all in Denmark or the British Isles.

[7]   While there has been some discussion about the oral background of *Gunnars þáttr helmings* (see Brink 1990: 51–52, cf. 55–62), it should be remembered that no trustworthy literary foreign model has yet been suggested. Furthermore, as will be stressed below, almost all of the motifs in the account echo ideas elsewhere closely associated with Vanir cult activities.

the people of Uppland was essentially limited to Norwegian oral accounts (and those of a few Swedes). As the *Prose Edda* demonstrates, his knowledge of the eddic poem *Skírnismál* was also limited, as was his knowledge of the now-lost *ljóðaháttr* poem about Njǫrðr and Skaði (*Gylfaginning* ch. 36 and 23). It seems logical to assume that Sweden and Swedish traditions were "other" to him, and somewhat more "other" than Danish traditions. The question is exactly how "other" they were seen as being?

That Vanir worshippers were seen as "other" in Iceland would appear to be immediately apparent in the use of the name "Freysgoði" for Hrafnkell Hallfreðarson and Þórðr Ǫzurarson "Freysgoðar",[8] mentioned in *Hrafnkels saga Freysgoða* (ch. 2), *Víga-Glúms saga* (ch. 5) and *Landnámabók* (ch. S 316/H 276; S 325/H 286; S330/H 289–90; S 335; H 354; S 398/H 355), both of whom lived in eastern and north-eastern Iceland.[9] The expression immediately raises the question of intriguing absences, and not least why the extant written sources never refer to a "Þórsgoði" or "Óðinsgoði". This in turn encourages questions of why these particular men should specifically be referred to as "Freysgoðar". One logical reason is that they were different from the norm, and, of course, it tends to be those people and things that are out of the ordinary that attract attention and get into oral legends (like those connected with *Hrafnkels saga*, *Vatnsdæla saga*, *Gísla saga*, and *Víga-Glúms saga* which contain most information about Icelandic settlers who were worshippers of Freyr: see below).[10] The impression is that those original settlers who worshipped Freyr were seen as "different" or "foreign", comparable perhaps to Catholics in a Protestant nation, or even Muslims, Hindus or Buddhists in a mainly Christian society.

Freyr, however, is not only associated with *male goðar* in the Icelandic sources about the settlement. The *Hauksbók* version of *Landnámabók* (ch. H 276) adds that Þórðr's half-sister, Þuríðr, was referred to as Þuríðr "hofgyðja", or the

---

[8] According to *Landnámabók* (ch. S 316/H 276 [S refers to chapters in Sturlubók; H to chapters in Hauksbók]), Þórðr's forefathers came from Høyanger ("Heyangr") on Sognefjord, an area which contains a number of place names that would appear to be associated with Vanir worship including Fretland, Fresvik and Nærøyfjord. It might also be noted that according to *Víga-Glúms saga* (ch. 5), Þórðr's wife was called Ingunn (a name with potential Vanir connotations).

[9] One might also include in this list the *goði* Þorgrímr Þorsteinsson in *Gísla saga Súrssonar* (ch. 15 and 18), who appears to have focused his worship on Freyr in spite of being the grandson of Þórólfr Mostra(r)skegg, a famous believer in Þórr (see *Landnámabók* ch. S 85 and H 73 and *Eyrbyggja saga* ch. 4).

[10] The expression would make sense if only two or three gods were worshipped in Iceland, and if Þórr were the most common of these, as is argued in Gunnell forthcoming a. Naturally, as time went on, and more interaction between settlers took place (not least in the form of intermarriage between families with different religious backgrounds), one can expect the differences between religious practices to have become less prominent, and some degree of blending to have taken place.

hof (temple?)[11] priestess. It also states that the name of Þórðr and Þuriðr's shared mother was Álfheiðr, a name which has added interest considering Freyr's alleged connection to *Álfheimr* according to the fifth stanza of *Grímnismál*.[12] (On the close connections between the *álfar* and the Vanir, see further Gunnell 2007.)

While Þuriðr "hofgyðja" herself is never directly referred to as a "Freysgyðja", her role as priestess and her close association to a "Freysgoði" remind us that in the extant written sources, the Vanir are the *only* northern gods (in the later Iron Age) whose worship is said to involve females serving in important religious roles (see below). Þuriðr's association with Freyr also seems logical considering her family, local Icelandic place names (Freysnes; Freyshólar; and Njarðvík: Svavar Sigmundsson 1992: 242–43), and the other oral traditions about the religious practices of the area that seem to be reflected in both the sagas and *Landnámabók* (see above). Among other things, it seems logical to place her alongside another "hofgyðja" from the same general area who is mentioned in *Vápnfirðinga saga* (ch. 5), that is, Steinvör "hofgyðja", who apparently "varðveitti hǫfuðhofit" (protected the *hof*). Both figures can in turn be placed alongside the "ung ok fríð" (young and beautiful) priestess in *Gunnars þáttr helmings* who was "fengin til þjónostu" (brought into service) with Freyr and who should "mest ráða með Frey fyrir hofstaðnum ok ǫllu því, er þar lá til" (have most control over the *hof* site and everything that belonged to it along with Freyr) (*Ögmundar þáttr dytts* p. 112; see also Flateyjarbók I, ch. 277). In this context, one might also bear in mind the statement in *Ynglinga saga* (ch. 4) that Freyja served as the "blótgyðja" (sacrificial priestess) of the gods in Sweden (see further below).

Another recurring idea that seems to have lived on in the family oral traditions of the Icelanders with regard to the practices of Vanir worshippers is their connection with sacred horses, something which is mentioned in both *Hrafnkels saga* (see ch. 3, in which half of Hrafnkell's stallion Freyfaxi is said to belong to Freyr); and *Vatnsdæla saga*, where we encounter a horse called Freysfaxi (ch. 34).[13] In this context, it might also be borne in mind that *Ólafs saga Tryggvasonar en mesta* (in Flateyjarbók I, ch. 322) similarly mentions a herd of stallions belonging to Freyr which were kept near his *hof* in Þrándheimr (on these materials and others, see also Sundqvist 2000: 206–21). The idea of horses having had special religious importance for the Germanic tribes receives earlier

---

[11] On the nature of the *hof* (which is still disputed), see further Gunnell 2001 and the references contained there. From here on, the word *hof* will be used in its original form in translations rather than "temple", which has a range of questionable associations.

[12] For all references to the eddic poems in this article, see the versions of the poems contained in *Eddadigte* 1961, 1964, and 1971, see Poetic Edda.

[13] On Freyfaxi (and Freysfaxi), see further Elmevik 2003 and 2011: 352.

support from Tacitus (*Germania* ch. 10) and perhaps also Bede's account of Coifi's destruction of the temple in Northumbria (*Historiæ Ecclesiastica* Book II, ch. 13). More directly relevant to the current discussion, however, are the ritual depositions found at Skedemosse in Öland, Sweden, from the pre-Roman to the late-Viking period, which also seem to have placed emphasis on horses which appear to have been eaten in ritual meals (see further Monikander 2010).

In the present context, it is again worth bearing absence in mind. It is noteworthy that in the extant historical sources, no Nordic gods seem to have as many associations with "sacred" animals directly connected with ritual activities as the Vanir.[14] To the horses one can add the boar (*sónargǫltr*) on which the Swedish king Heiðrekr was supposed to have sworn an oath at Christmas time, according to the legendary *Hervarar saga ok Heiðreks* (*Saga Heiðreks konungs ins vitra* ch. 8), a similar account being contained in the prose of *Helgakviða Hjörvarðssonar* (Poetic Edda p. 26). Considering that Freyr and Freyja alone are directly associated with boars in Nordic mythology (*Skáldskaparmál* ch. 35; *Gylfaginning* ch. 49; *Hyndluljóð* st. 7), there would seem to be little question that these Swedish "sónargöltr" oaths should also be associated with them.

Alongside the idea of animals being dedicated to the Vanir gods, or used as symbols for them, one can place the account in *Víga-Glúms saga* (ch. 7) of an area of ever-fertile land in north-east Iceland called "Vitazgjafi" (sure-giver) which seems to have been closely associated with Freyr.[15] The idea of land being dedicated to the gods in this way is, of course, given support by numerous place names in Scandinavia (see, for example, Olsen 1926; Vikstrand 2001; and Brink 2007), and also the account in *Eyrbyggja saga* (ch. 4) and *Landnámabók* (ch. S 85/H 73) of Þórólfr Mostra(r)skegg directly dedicating land to Þórr "ástvin sin" (his loving friend). Worth bearing in mind in this context is that no similar saga accounts ever tell of land being dedicated to Óðinn (see further Gunnell forthcoming a). While the account in *Víga-Glúms saga*, like that in *Hrafnkels saga* (ch.

---

[14] The only exception is the description of the image of Þórr's wagon in the *hof* in Þrándheimr which is said to be pulled by goats in *Ólafs saga Tryggvasonar en mesta* in Flateyjarbók (I, ch. 268). Nonetheless, nothing is actually done with the goats in this account and there are no accounts of special flocks of goats being dedicated to Þórr (like the horses apparently dedicated to Freyr). The same applies to Óðinn's wolves, whose real-world representatives would naturally be more difficult to keep in fields. The fact that the mythical boar belonging to Freyr is said to be made of gold (see Snorri Sturluson, *Skáldskaparmál* ch. 35) may also contain a faint memory of other boar images—perhaps like those adorning the Benty Grange and Pioneer helmets, and also those mentioned in connection with helmets in *Beowulf*. In addition to the horse and boar, one might perhaps add the bull sacrificed to Freyr in *Brandkrossa þáttr* (ch. 1) and the bull sacrificed at the *vetrnætur* in *Þiðranda þáttr ok Þórhalls* (ch. 2) (here seemingly associated with the arrival of the *dísir*), bearing in mind that in *Gísla saga* (ch. 15) the *vetrnætr* are directly associated with Freyr.

[15] A parallel idea might be reflected in the account of the snow never settling on the grave mound of Þorgrímr Þorsteinsson in *Gísla saga Súrssonar* (ch. 18).

5) telling of Hrafnkell's luck with the breeding of livestock and fishing, supports the idea of Freyr being efficacious with regard to fertility, it also adds weight to the idea of the god's close connections with particular spaces in the local living environment, a pattern that will be discussed further below.

Other remnants that appear to point to the enduring key role of the Vanir in ritual activities apparently practiced in both Iceland and Norway after the settlement period can be seen in the wording of the so-called "hofeiðr" (*hof-oath*) that was supposed to have formed part of early Icelandic law, *Úlfljótslög*,[16] and the sacrificial toasts from Þrándheimr described in *Hákonar saga góða* (ch. 14). In the case of the former, one notes that two of the three gods called on to witness the oath are Vanir (Freyr and Njǫrðr), who are accompanied by "hinn almáttki áss" (the mightiest god [*áss*]).[17] Njǫrðr's presence here is particularly intriguing if only because he is so rarely mentioned in other Icelandic sources, in spite of appearing in two Icelandic place names (both called Njarðvík: see Svavar Sigmundsson 1992: 242–43). Interestingly enough, both gods reappear together in the sacred *full* (toasts) closely associated with sacrificial activities in *Hákonar saga góða* (ch. 14), made by Sigurðr Hlaðajarl "til árs ok friðar" (for good harvests and peace).[18] The account runs as follows:

Þat var forn siðr, þá er blót skyldi vera, at allir bændr skyldu þar koma, sem hof var, ok flytja þannug fǫng sín, þau er þeir skyldu hafa, meðan veizlan stóð. At veizlu þeiri skyldu allir menn ǫl eiga. Þar var ok drepinn alls konar smali ok svá hross, en blóð þat allt, er þar kom af, þá var kallat hlaut, ok hlautbollar þat, er blóð þat stóð í, ok hlautteinar, þat var svá gǫrt sem stǫkklar, með því skyldi rjóða stallana ǫllu saman ok svá veggi hofsins útan ok innan ok svá støkkva á mennina, en slátr skyldi sjóða til mannfagnaðar. Eldar skyldu vera á miðju gólfi í hofinu, ok þar katlar yfir. Skyldi full um eld bera, en sá, er gerði veisluna ok

---

[16] See *Landnámabók* (ch. H 268); and also *Hauksbók* (Tillæg, ch. IX). *Úlfljótslög*, believed by many to be the earliest Icelandic law (possibly going back, in part, to around 930) is also contained in *Þorsteins þáttr uxafóts* (in Flateyjarbók I, ch. 201) and *Brot af Þórðar sögu hreðu* (ch. 1). On the dating and trustworthiness of *Úlfljótslög*, see further Jón Hnefill Aðalsteinsson 1998: 44–50.

[17] There is some dispute about who "hinn almáttki áss" was, but the likelihood must be that it was Þórr, since Óðinn seems to have been little known in Iceland (see Gunnell forthcoming a). The appearance of two Vanir gods in a *hof* oath apparently practiced by all Icelanders naturally raises questions about the argument made in this article with regard to the Vanir worshippers being "other" in Iceland. Nonetheless, the formula may also have been meant to cover all the relevant gods worshipped in Iceland (Þórr, Freyr, and Njörðr being the names most prominent in extant place names).

[18] It might be noted that later in in the same saga (*Hákonar saga góða* ch. 16–17), other sacrificial toasts are also made "til árs ok friðar", but then only to Óðinn (rather strangely) and Þórr. On the formula "til árs ok friðar", see further Hultgård 1993: 224–54 and Sundqvist 2000: 176–79.

hǫfðingi var, þá skyldi hann signa fullit ok allan blótmatinn, skyldi fyrst Óðins full—skyldi þat drekka til sigrs ok ríkis konungi sínum—en síðan Njarðar full ok Freys full til árs ok friðar. Þá var mǫrgum mǫnnum títt at drekka þar næst bragafull. Menn drukku ok full frænda sinna, þeira er heygðir hǫfðu verit, ok váru það minni kǫlluð.

(It was an ancient custom that a *blót* (sacrifice) should take place in which all farmers should come to the site of the *hof* and bring those goods that they would need while the feasting was taking place. Every man should have ale for this feast. Many cattle, sheep and horses were killed there and all the blood that came from them was called *hlaut*, while the containers in which the blood was caught were called *hlaut-bollar* (hlaut-cups), and *hlautteinar* (hlaut-sticks), which were made like *aspergillum* and were used to redden the altar completely and then the walls of the *hof* inside and out, and then to splatter the people, the sacrificial meat then being boiled for the gathering. There should be a fire in the center of the floor and over this should be cauldrons. The *full* (toast) should be carried around the fire by the chieftain who had organized the feast, after which he should *signa* (mark/sign/bless) the toast and all the sacrificial meal. First should be Óðinn's *full*, which should be drunk to the victory and state of his king; and then a *full* to Njǫrðr and a *full* to Freyr for "ár ok friðr". Then it was common for many men to drink a *bragafull* (to Bragi?). They also drank a *full* to their relations who had been buried. This was called a *minni* (memory toast).)

The wording of the passage implies a possible textual relationship with the detailed descriptions of *hof* buildings and activities given in *Úlfljótslög* (see above), *Eyrbyggja saga* (ch. 4), and *Kjalnesinga saga* (ch. 2). The formulaic wording of both the *full* and the oath in *Úlfljótslög* suggest they have roots in a pre-Christian oral formula that had ritual associations and connections to religious buildings.

Further, more direct connections between the Vanir gods and religious buildings appear in other types of text that appear to have lived for some time in the oral tradition in western Scandinavia before being recorded on parchment, namely the eddic poems which have a better claim to antiquity than the Icelandic family sagas. The texts in question are *Grímnismál* (st. 16) and *Vafþrúðnismál* (st. 38), both of which concern Njǫrðr. The former states:

Nóatún ero en ellipto,	Nóatún is the eleventh,
en þar Niǫrðr hefir	where Njörðr has
sér um gǫrva sali,	made himself a hall,
manna þengill	prince of men

enn meins vani	lacking in harm,
hátimbroðom	the high-timbered
hǫrg <i ræðr>.	hǫrgr (altar) rules.

The latter runs:

Segðu þat it tíunda,	Answer a tenth,
allz þú tíva røk	since about the fate of the gods
ǫll, Vafþruðnir, vitir,	you know everything, Vafþrúðnir:
hvaðan Niǫrðr um kom,	where did Njörðr come from
með ása sonom,	to join the sons of the Æsir,
hofom og hǫrgom	hof and hǫrgar
hann ræðr hunnmǫrgom,	countless, he rules over,
ok varðat hann ásom alinn.	and was not raised among the æsir.

While there is reason to take an odd expression like "hátimbroðum hǫrgi" with a pinch of salt, bearing in mind that "hátrimbroðo" also appears after the reversed formula "hǫrg ok hof" in the seventh stanza of *Vǫluspá*, the striking features here are not only the connection the poems make between Njǫrðr and sites of religious practice, but also that Njǫrðr is the *only* god to be directly associated with religious practices in these two poems. (It might be noted that even though the Æsir gods build the *hof* and *hörgr* mentioned in *Vǫluspá* st. 7, it is not stated who functions in them.) In both of the stanzas cited above, one also notes that Njörðr is said to actively "ráða" (control/rule) the *hof*.[19]

It seems natural to place these stanzas (and the other passages about ritual practice noted above) alongside the famous words of *Hyndluljóð* st. 10, in which Freyja, referring to Óttarr ungi, states:

Hǫrg hann mér gerði	He made me a hǫrgr
hlaðinn steinum,	piled with stones;
nú er griót þat	now that rock
at gleri orðit,	has become [like] glass,
rauð hann í nýiu	he reddened it in new
nauta blóði,	bull's blood;
æ trúði Óttarr	Óttarr has always believed
á ásyniur.	in goddesses.

---

[19] In this context, it is worth bearing in mind st. 51 of *Lokasenna*, where Skaði, Njǫrðr's wife, refers to *her* "véom ok vǫngum" (shrines and sacred fields), something that is arguably backed up by place-name evidence of numerous sites called "Skedevi"/ "Skedvi", especially in the east of Sweden: see de Vries 1956–57: II, 161–62 and 335–40.

While one can expect some degree of variation and reconstruction to have taken place in the wording of accounts that were passed on in the oral tradition over centuries, prior to eventually being recorded, it would seem questionable whether the stanzas noted above were composed by Christians—or even by Icelanders, since no specially-constructed *hof*, *hǫrgar*, or so-called *kulthus* (cult-houses) of the kind described in the sagas and eddic poems and later found in archaeological excavations in mainland Scandinavia have ever been found in Iceland (see further Gunnell 2001 and the references noted there). The above stanzas would thus appear to have roots in earlier Nordic tradition, and a Nordic tradition that had some reason for connecting Njǫrðr and Freyja (Njǫrðr above all and Freyja secondarily) to sacred spaces: once again, no mention is ever made of a *hǫrgr* being dedicated to any other god. As noted above, the same ideas of Vanir connections with religious practice, ritual, and *hof* are reflected in Snorri's comments in chapters 4 and 10 of *Ynglingasaga*, in which Njǫrðr and Freyr are called "blótgoðar", and Freyja a "blótgyðja". In terms of absence, it should be borne in mind that Snorri makes no similar statements about either Óðinn or Þórr (or even Frigg). Furthermore, while *hof* and *hofgoðar* are mentioned elsewhere in *Ynglinga saga* in connection with the Æsir (ch. 2 and 5; cf. *Vǫluspá* st. 7), Snorri stresses that "Freyr reisti at Uppsǫlum hof mikit" (Freyr raised a large *hof* at Uppsala), underlining once again the direct connections he saw as existing between the Vanir (and especially Freyr), Uppland, and the religious activities he describes elsewhere as taking place at Gamla Uppsala (*Ynglinga saga* ch. 15, 34 and 38; and *Ólafs saga helga* ch. 67). No similar statements are made about Þórr (who is strangely near absent from *Ynglinga saga*).

Finally, it is worth considering Snorri's words about Freyja, which underline that she, a woman, not only ruled after Freyr's death, but also personally "hélt þá upp blótum, því at hon ein lifði þá eptir goðanna" (kept up the sacrifices because she was the only surviving member of the gods) (*Ynglinga saga* ch. 10). Freyja is also said to have been the one who introduced the Æsir to *seiðr*[20] which "Vǫnum var títt" (was common amongst the Vanir) in *Ynglinga saga* (ch. 4), an idea which suggests yet further close associations between the Vanir and ritualistic activities. In both cases, as in *Hyndluljóð*, Freyja is said to play a particularly active role in these rituals, even though the nature of this role is never described in detail. One must assume that it was similar to that of the *hofgyðjur* noted above.

The Vanir, however, are not only shown to be more closely associated with religious *buildings* than other gods in the extant accounts. They are also depicted as being more directly bound up with particular *holy sites in the landscape*, and not

---

[20] On the nature of *seiðr*, see further Strömbäck 2000; and Price 2002: 91–232.

least sites where they are supposed to "live on" after their deaths: in contrast to Óðinn and Njǫrðr, who are cremated (*Ynglinga saga* ch. 8 and 9), Snorri, for example, tells how:

> er Freyr var dauðr, báru þeir hann leyniliga í hauginn ok sǫgðu Svíum, at hann lifði, ok varðveittu hann þar þrjá vetr. En skatt ǫllum helltu þeir í hauginn, í einn glugg gullinu, en í annan silfrinu, í inn þriðja eirpenningum. Þá hélzt ár ok friðr. (*Ynglinga saga* ch. 10)

> (when Freyr died, they carried him secretly into the grave mound and told the Swedes that he was still alive and preserved him for three winters. They poured the taxes into the mound, the gold going into one window, while the silver went into another, and the bronze into a third. Then the harvests and peace were maintained.)

As was noted above, the formulaic expression "ár ok friðr" seems to have been closely associated with the Vanir in oral tradition (and rarely with other gods).

Snorri's euhemeristic account is echoed in *Ólafs saga Tryggvasonar en mesta* (Flateyjarbók I ch. 323) which gives more detail about how Freyr had been a king in Uppsala, and, after his death, was placed in a grave mound with a door and windows, and called a "veralldar guð" (god of the world).[21] The Flateyjarbók account ends by stating that "gerdu Suiar tremenn .ij ok settu þa j haug hea honum þuiat þeir hugdu at honum mundi gaman þikia at læika ser at þeim" (the Swedes made two wooden figures and put them in the mound with him, because they thought he would like to entertain himself with them), describing how these objects were later taken by grave robbers. The account then adds that both figures were later called "Freyr", and went on to receive sacrifices in their own right, one in Sweden and the other in Þrándheimr, as mentioned above.

Whatever the background of these accounts was, the idea of Freyr being directly associated with a particular mound in the landscape known by the local inhabitants (wherever it was) finds very close parallels in the account in *Ólafs þáttr Geirstaðaálfs* of the grave of King Ólafr Geirstaðaálfr, who, after his death, was said to have had a grave mound made for him in which he was:

> fliotliga j lagidr hea sinum monnum með myklu fe ok eftir þat haugrinn aftr byrgdr. þa tók ok at letta manndaudnum. sidan gerde uaran mikit

---

[21] This expression naturally raises further questions with regard to Óðinn's supposed function as ruler-god and "alföðr". In addition to the meaning of the word Freyr (generally associated with the meaning of "lord", but see also Elmevik 2003 on possible links to fertility), this expression underlines that for some people, Freyr was seen as the highest god.

ok hallære. var þa þat rad tekit at þeir blotudu Olaf konung til árs ser ok kolludu hann Geirstada alf. (Flateyjarbók II, ch. 6)

(quickly placed alongside his men with a great many riches and after that the mound was closed. After that the number of deaths began to reduce. Then commenced many bad harvests and poverty. The decision was then taken to give sacrifices to King Ólafr for good harvests, and he was called the Álfr[22] of Geirstaðir.)[23]

Both narratives would seem to offer an explanation as to why the *Gulaþingslög* (c.1250) felt it necessary to state that "Blot er oss oc kviðiat at vér scolom eigi blota heiðit Guð. ne hauga. ne horga" (It is also stated regarding sacrifices that we should not make sacrifices to pagan gods, or grave mounds, or altars) (*Den Eldre Gulatingslova* 1994: 52). Similar ideas might also be reflected in the statement from the thirteenth century *Guta saga* that the Gotlanders "troþu [...] a hult ok a hauga, vi ok stafgarþa ok a haiþin guþ" (believed in groves, grave mounds, shrines, and fenced-off areas as well as the pagan gods) (*Guta saga* ch. 1). The parallels and probable associations between the buried and worshipped Ólafr, son of Álfhildr, daughter of Álfarinn of Álfheimar (Flateyjarbók II, ch. 5) and the buried and worshipped Freyr, ruler of Álfheimr (see above) are obvious. To this list of holy sites in the landscape connected with Vanir gods, however, one can perhaps add the island on which the fertility goddess Nerthus was supposed to have lived when she was not traveling, according to Tacitus (*Germania* ch. 40), which once again shows Vanir-associated gods being physically "anchored" to sites in the landscape. To the best of my knowledge, no Old Norse account tells of any natural places in the landscape in which the Æsir gods could physically be found.[24]

The same idea of direct connections between the Vanir and the land-scape might also be reflected in the earlier-mentioned account from *Ólafs saga Tryggvasonar en mesta* (Flateyjarbók I, ch. 322–23) about how one of the two wooden images of Freyr stolen from his mound was taken from Uppsala to Þrándheimr, where it went on to be worshipped until it was eventually destroyed by Ólafr Tryggvason. This unique account of people *transferring* a statue of an

---

[22] On the connections between the *álfar* and the Vanir, see above and also Gunnell 2007.

[23] Alongside this account one might place that concerning the ever-green nature of the grave mound of the Freyr-worshipper Þorgrímr *goði* noted above; and possibly also the account of the field of Vitazgjafi, also noted earlier.

[24] Here I am not talking of sacred buildings or landscape dedicated to the gods according to place names, but rather accounts of particular places in the landscape in which they were supposed to have lived. Of course, there are a range of other accounts telling of Icelanders "dying into" and living on the landscape (see further Gunnell 2014), but the same does not ever apply to the Æsir gods.

Old Nordic god from one place to another (rather than simply constructing a new one) would seem to contain a similar idea to that involved with the moving of high-seat pillars and sometimes sacred earth from Norway to Iceland as part of settlement practice, as for instance referred to in *Landnámabók* (ch. S 297/H 258; see further Gunnell 2009 and the references contained there). What seems to be taking place in both cases is the moving of environmental sacredness, an act which involves what James George Frazer and Arnold van Gennep referred to as "contagious magic" (Frazer 1957: 14–6; van Gennep 1960: 7–9, 14).

Continuing this line of investigation about the idea of physical connection between the Vanir gods and landscape, and the subsequent transference or spreading of the "goodness" of a god (or goddess) to other places permanently or temporarily, it is worth considering a little further the Latin and Norse narratives describing the seasonal ritual journeys made by wagons of Nerthus, Freyr, and Lytir described in *Germania* ch. 40; and *Hauks þáttr hábrókar* (in Flateyjarbók I, ch. 467). None of these accounts show direct literary borrowings from each other, and the writers had not seen the Dejbjerg wagon (from Jylland, Denmark, c. first century BCE) or the Oseberg wagon (c. 850 CE), now on display in museums in Copenhagen and Oslo, both of which are believed to have had a ritual purpose.[25] It is equally certain that the writers had never viewed the images of wagons shown as taking part in what appear to be ritual processions on the Oseberg tapestry (Krafft 1956). Nor would they have observed the processional road and sloping ramp leading into the huge hall recently discovered behind the church at Gamla Uppsala,[26] which one assumes might have allowed wheeled vehicles to be drawn in and out; or the straight processional road leading from what appears to be a building at Rösaring, in Uppland, Sweden, which might conceivably have accommodated a wagon like that from Oseberg (which cannot turn).[27] In short, it would appear that each of the accounts telling of sacred wagons noted above has an independent origin, and roots in local oral tradition of some kind (see further Brink 1990: 61). Whether the accounts in question are factually true is beside the point. What matters most here is that for some reason, people believed them to have had some foundation in reality. In short, they appear to have had firm roots in oral tradition, just like the numerous local legends recorded in Sweden and Denmark (including Dejbjerg) telling of golden wagons hidden in lakes that the Swedish folklorist Bengt af Klintberg (1998) has compiled. Each account of the journey of a god reflects the same idea that goodness, focused in a spatial center, could be brought to bear on

---

[25] For the Dejbjerg wagon, see "The Wagons at Dejbjerg". With regard to the Oseberg wagon, see Christensen et al. 1992: 119–23 and 248–49.

[26] For details on recent and ongoing finds at Gamla Uppsala, see Ljungkvist et al. 2015.

[27] See further Sandén n.d.; 2002.

other places, as occurred also with Christian processions around a settlement or the visitation of a bishop with a holy relic.

As I have noted elsewhere (Gunnell 1995: 54–57, 2006a, and 2011), the ritual journey of Freyr and his wife across the Swedish landscape in wintertime, as described in *Gunnars þáttr helmings* (*Ögmundar þáttr dytts*; Flateyjarbók I, ch. 278), contains not only the idea of a ritual procession but also strong elements of drama and performance which are said to have encouraged active belief on the part of those observing. Bearing this in mind, it is interesting to note that when dramatic activities are most obviously implied by the extant literary materials concerning Old Norse mythology or religion, they appear first and foremost in connection with one of the few works that directly concerns the Vanir. The work in question, the wholly dialogic eddic poem *Skírnismál*, with its outdoor (st. 10, 15 and 32), night time (st. 1 and 10), and apparently midwinter setting (st. 42), and its movement from a civilized, male, inside space to the wild, female, outside space on the periphery represented by a woman called Gerðr (lit. field/delineated space)—who is separated from the rest of the world by a ring of fire (st. 17 and 18)—also contains a strong element of the processional. Its action, which seems to link a central place (inhabited by gods) to a peripheral sacral spot, describes a movement which could well have had a basis in fifth- or sixth-century sacral reality. Indeed, this was a time when many sacrificial practices in Sweden seem to have been starting to move from outdoor spaces on the periphery with close connections to female goddesses (cf. *Grímnismál* st. 7 and *Völuspá* st. 33) to the indoor spaces of the male ruler, in other words from natural spaces to the man-made hall. In spite of this, it is probable that many of these later indoor activities still needed the validation of some form of connection with the earlier sacred outdoor sites (see further Gunnell 2001; Fabech and Näsman 2013; Jørgensen 2009; and Fredengren 2011).[28]

It is noteworthy that outdoor movement of the kind depicted in *Skírnismál* is not a central feature of either monologic or dialogic Óðinic-focused eddic dramatic poems, such as *Vafþrúðnismál*, *Grímnismál*, *Eiríksmál*, and *Hákonarmál*,[29] all of which are firmly situated in an internal hall environment. *Skírnismál* is very different, and, as noted above, seems to have been comparatively less well known to Snorri. In addition to its movement between spaces, which essentially involves one character (Skírnir, the "Shining One") moving from one static figure to another (from Njörðr to Freyr to the herdsman to the "ambátt" to Gerðr and

---

[28] I would like to express my gratitude to Torun Zachrisson and Olof Sundqvist for their assistance with finding recent sources concerning this subject.
[29] *Eiríksmál* and *Hákonarmál* both tend to be classed as skaldic poems rather than eddic works, but their meter and form (not least their use of the dialogic form) show close associations with eddic poetry. This subject is dealt with in more detail in Gunnell forthcoming b.

back to Freyr [possibly thence to the grove of Barri]), the poem also contains a number of very ritualistic features, ranging from the cutting of fresh wood for a "gambantein" (power wand), to a seeming call on supernatural powers related to different cardinal directions (st. 34), to the physical carving of runes which were evidently still seen as having magical power in the thirteenth century (st. 36: see further Gunnell 2006a and 2011). One also notes the near total absence of the Æsir gods in the poem, outside a strange reference to Skírnir offering Óðinn's ring Draupnir to Gerðr (st. 22). In the context of *Skírnismál*, this feature sounds almost as suspicious as the suggestion in the introductory prose (taken directly from Snorri's *Gylfaginning*; see Gunnell 1995: 229–32) that Freyr had usurped Óðinn's high seat when he first observed Gerðr from afar. Bearing in mind that Snorri suggests elsewhere that Óðinn owned Freyr's ship Skíðblaðnir (*Gylfaginning* ch. 43; see also *Grimnismál* st. 43, cf. *Ynglinga saga* ch. 7), and that Frigg owned Freyja's "fiaðrhamr"/"valfall"/"valshamr" (bird costume) (see *Þrymskviða* st. 3–5 and 9 and *Skáldskaparmál* ch. G56 and 20; cf. *Skáldskaparmál* ch. 18), there is good reason to consider whether both the ring and the high-seat were seen by some people as having originally been attributes of Freyr rather than of Óðinn.[30] Whatever the case, there is reason to believe that *Skírnismál* originated in a different environment than the Óðinic poems, even if its structure, form, and movement find certain parallels in the heroic *Fáfnismál* and *Sigrdrífumál* (see Gunnell 2006a and 2011).

It seems natural to place both *Gunnars þáttr helmings* and *Skírnismál* alongside various comments made by Saxo Grammaticus in his early thirteenth-century *Gesta Danorum* about the ritualistic activities involved in the worship of Freyr, which Saxo, like Snorri, associates directly with Uppsala. Naturally Saxo, like Snorri, was writing over a century after Sweden had formally adopted Christianity. Nonetheless, it is worth noting that Saxo (like Snorri) saw pre-Christian Uppsala (and Sweden in general) as having not only different beliefs to those of the Danes, but also quite different practices. According to Saxo, Starkatherus spent time with the "sons of Freyr" (Filiis Frø) in Sweden, where he was disgusted by the "womanish body movements, the clatter of actors on the stage and the soft tinkling of bells" (effeminatos corporum motus scenicosque mimorum plausus ac mollia nolarum crepitacula fastidiret) at the time of the sacrifices in Uppsala (see *Gesta Danorum*, Book 6; see further Gunnell

---

[30] Of course, it might be argued that Frigg was the original owner or that both women owned similar costumes. All the same, Snorri offers no poetic evidence to support Frigg being the owner of such garb. Furthermore, unlike Freyja, Frigg rarely moves anywhere. As regards the idea of Freyr's connection to the high-seat, it might be noted that a number of throned figures (and thrones/chairs) have now been found in archaeological finds both in Sweden and elsewhere (see further Price 2002: 163–67). One wonders whether all—or any—of these figures and thrones were originally related to Óðinn, or whether at least some might have represented Freyr.

1995: 76–79). While there is a faint possibility that Saxo is actually referring to activities at the markets later held at Uppsala, described in Snorri's *Ólafs saga helga* (ch. 77), his description closely reflects aspects of Adam of Bremen's earlier account of the same festivals contained in chapters 26 and 27 of his *Gesta Hammaburgensis ecclesiæ pontificum* (c. 1050).[31] Adam's description, purportedly based on the first-hand experience of an informant, and written when the festivals were still taking place, describes, among other things, the "multiplices et inhonestae" (manifold and unseemly) incantations that could be heard at the festival in a surrounding that, according to a later twelfth-century scholium, was like a "teatrum" (*Gesta Hammaburgensis ecclesiæ pontificum* ch. 26–27; see also scholia 139).

Adam's account differs slightly from that of Saxo in that he suggests that the festival, set in early spring, was also dedicated to the male Æsir gods, the statues of "Wotan" and "Frikko" apparently standing on either side of a statue of "Thor".[32] One wonders where the goddesses are, especially when other accounts, such as that by Snorri in *Ynglinga saga* (ch. 29), stress connections between the festival, a "Dísarsalr", and a "dísablót", an idea later supported by the Upplandslög and Swedish tradition which both talk of a central "Dísæþing" and market taking place at this time (*Upplandslagen* p. 169; see also Gunnell 2000). The discrepancies between these accounts are rarely discussed, but might perhaps be answered if one considers the timing and nature of the nine-year festivals, which took place at the beginning of the "male" time of the year (in which planting, military activities and trade took place, all of which needed "male" blessing: see further Gunnell 2006b). Like the Alþing in Iceland, they also

---

[31] While Saxo may have read Adam's account, his description contains no direct borrowings, and differs in several features.

[32] Naturally, there are questions why, in a place commonly associated in oral tradition with Freyr, Þórr is said to be the central god. One possibility (if the festival was not associated with the "male" part of the year as suggested above, and the central gods alternated) is that Þórr had a central role at this time because he was the god more associated with growth, as *Ynglinga saga* (ch. 8) suggests: "Þá skyldi blóta í móti vetri til árs, en at miðjum vetri blóta til gróðrar, it þriðja at sumri, þat var sigrblót" (Then sacrifices should be made at the start of winter for good years, in the middle of winter, sacrifices for growth, the third at the start of summer, that was a sacrifice for victory). According to this pattern (which is echoed in Adam's suggestion that the gods had particular functions), sacrifices more associated with Freyr would have taken place at the start of winter (as suggested by *Gísla saga*: see note 14), while the sacrifices at the start of the summer would have been more associated with Óðinn (usually associated with victory). Those closer to midwinter would then have centered on Þórr (although the Uppsala sacrifice seems to have taken place some time in February). As noted at the start (note 2), however, I am wary of such simple functional interpretations. As underlined in the other original references given in Gunnell forthcoming b, Þórr is regularly said to have a central role amongst the gods (not least in accounts describing statues). His central role in Adam's account might simply be based on expectation rather than memory.

involved the entire nation rather than a single local group, and thereby poten-tially needed to involve *all* the representative gods of *all* those present (in other words, all the groups represented). None of this detracts from the fact that the activities associated with the Uppsala festivals (traditionally associated with the Vanir by both Snorri and Saxo) were seen as being particularly visual and dramatic, and different from those known elsewhere (hence the attention that they receive). As noted above, the validity of Adam's and Saxo's accounts seems to be gaining ever more support from the wealth of archaeological evidence that has been coming to light at Gamla Uppsala over the last few years. The like-lihood must be that the format and nature of these festivals, situated in an area marked out by the grave mounds of forefathers and close to another royal burial area at Valsgärde, must have grown out of earlier Vanir rituals (considering the strong traditional connections between the Vanir and the area).

Naturally the textual evidence listed above cannot be trusted as histor-ical records concerning the state of things in Sweden during pre-Christian times. Nonetheless, it does suggest that those behind these accounts would have disagreed with Simek's statement quoted at the start about there having been "no inherent difference between the gods ascribed to both groups by Snorri". It also underlines that people in western Scandinavia, Denmark and Hamburg-Bremen seem to have viewed the people of Uppland as different, as "other" to themselves, especially concerning their religious practices, and those concerning the Vanir in general. In the very least, it seems clear that the oral tradition on which these accounts were based, which had been passed on through time, regularly undergoing minor changes, and later came to be recorded mainly in the thirteenth century, possibly influenced by Christianity, seems to have retained vague memories of the religious activities associated with those believing in the Vanir having been different from those known by most people "at home".

Of course, it is possible that these differences were exaggerated by all the authors in question as part of a "conspiracy" designed to suggest that the old religion of the Swedes (which endured longer than in the other Nordic coun-tries) was especially depraved. Perhaps the more prominent practical role of women in the religion and the interest in animals and ritual drama noted above were deliberately spotlighted alongside the incestuous activities of the Vanir[33] as a means of underlining the pagan depravity of the Swedes in particular (a

---

[33] These incestuous activities are only noted by Snorri in *Ynglinga saga* (ch.4): "Þá er Njǫrðr var með Vǫnum, þá hafði hann átta systur sína, því at þat váru þar lǫg. Váru þeira bǫrn Freyr ok Freyja. En þat var bannat með Ásum at byggva svo náit at frændsemi" (ch. 4) (When Njörður was with the Vanir, he had lived with his sister because that was the law there. Their children were Freyr and Freyja. Such close relations amongst relatives were banned amongst the Æsir).

view that Saxo Grammaticus seems to have held). Such an argument, however, must be viewed as somewhat questionable, not least because, as has been noted above, similar traits keep recurring in accounts that do not obviously borrow from each other. These accounts appear to have a background in cultural memories of tradition, among others those relating to early accounts that were rife with details about the nature of the festivals that were held at Gamla Uppsala from at least the mid Iron Age. As noted above, recent archaeological finds suggest that the accounts given by Adam, Snorri, and Saxo concerning the activities that took place around the large grave mounds in Gamla Uppsala had some basis in reality. They also indicate that the activities which took place on this site, reached by a kilometer-long processional avenue marked with tall pillars off which dead animals seem to have been hung, were more spectacular than those occurring at any other site so far discovered in Scandinavia, apart from perhaps the Oseberg burial (and the Oseberg tapestry, noted earlier, is believed to reflect the kind of activities that took place at funerals of this kind). The grand processional route and the recently-discovered large hall found at Gamla Uppsala towards which the route leads, with its three-meter wide doors and hinges in the form of spears, demonstrate that, whatever was going on at the festivals in Gamla Uppsala c. 800 CE, it was meant to attract attention. In short, it was intended that it burn itself into the memory of those present, and be passed on to those in foreign climes, in a somewhat similar fashion to a televised American presidential inauguration, or a prominent terrorist attack. The Icelandic evidence from *Landnámabók* and the sagas, along with the eddic poems, suggests that the close associations people saw as existing between ritual activities and the gods associated with the Vanir certainly seem to have continued in the minds of those who encountered Vanir worshippers elsewhere (in Norway and Iceland).

To sum up, both the oral tradition described in this article and the recent archaeological evidence suggest that the religious activities and belief of the Vanir (centered in Sweden) had a slightly different nature, and perhaps a different origin to those connected to Æsir gods like Þórr and Óðinn. If the essence of these accounts can be trusted, it seems that somewhat like the Catholic or Greek Orthodox churches in comparison to Lutheran churches, the "religion" associated with the Vanir was viewed as being more ritualistic. It was also seen as being less sexist and more connected to the local environment (and perhaps also the forefathers buried in the environment). Such differences, to my mind, were not solely related to function. The nuances of such Vanir ritual and how it was enacted and understood by the original believers and later Nordic peoples may never be fully accessible to us. Much will depend on what new discoveries the archaeologists may reveal in the years to come.

Works Cited

Primary Sources

Brandkrossar þáttr
Íslenzk fornrit, 11. Ed. Jón Jóhannesson. Reykjavik: 1950. Pp. 181–91.

Brot af þórðar sögu hreðu
Íslenzk fornrit, 14. Ed. Jóhannes Halldórsson. Reykjavik: 1959. Pp. 227–47.

Den Eldre Gulatingslova: see *Gulaþingslög*.

Eiríksmál
Eiríksmál. Ed. and transl. R.D. Fulk. In *Skaldic Poetry of the Scandinavian Middle Ages: Vol. 1: Poetry from the Kings' Sagas 1: From Mythical Times to c. 1035*. Ed. Diana Whaley. Turnhout: 2012. Pp. 1000–13.

Eyrbyggja saga
Íslenzk fornrit, 4. Ed. Einar Ólafur Sveinsson and Matthías Þórðarson. Reykjavik: 1935. Pp. 1–184.

Flateyjarbók
Flateyjarbók: En samling af norske konge-sagaer med indskudte mindre fortællinger om begivenheder i og udenfor Norge samt annaler. 3 vols. Ed. Guðbrandur Vigfússon and C. R. Unger. Christiania: 1860–1868.

Germania
Tacitus. *Germania*. In *Tacitus: Agricola, Germania, Dialogus*. Transl. M. Hutton and W. Peterson and rev. R.M. Ogilvie, E. H. Warmington, and M. Winterbottom. Loeb Classical Library. London & Cambridge Massachusetts: 1975. Pp. 127–215.

Gesta danorum
Saxo Grammaticus. *Saxonis Grammatici Gesta Danorum*. Ed. Alfred Holder. Strassburg: 1886.

TRANSLATION
Saxo Grammaticus. *The History of the Danes*. Vol. I: Text. Ed. Hilda Ellis Davidson and transl. Peter Fisher. Cambridge: 1979.

Gesta hammabergensis

Adam of Bremen. *Gesta Hammaburgensis ecclesiæ pontificum.* Ed. Bernhard Schmeidler. Scriptores rerum Germanicarum 2. 3rd edition. Hanover: 1917.

<small>TRANSLATION</small>

Adam of Bremen. *The History of the Archbishops of Hamburg-Bremen.* Ed. and transl. Francis J. Tschan. New York: 1959.

Gísla saga súrssonar

Íslenzk fornrit, 6. Ed. Björn K. Þórólfsson and Guðni Jónsson. Reykjavik: 1943. Pp. 1–118.

Gunnars þáttr helmings: see *Ögmundar þáttr dytts*

Grímnismál: see *Poetic Edda*

Gulaþingslög

<small>MANUSCRIPT</small>

Gulaþingslog hin eldri. MS DonVar 137 4to. Kongelige Bibliotek, Copenhagen.

<small>EDITION</small>

Den Eldre Gulatingslova. Ed. Bjørn Eithun, Magnus Rindal, and Tor Ulset. Norrønne tekster, 6. Oslo: 1994.

Guta saga

Guta Saga: The History of the Gotlanders. Ed. Christine Peel. Viking Society for Northern Research Text Series, 12. London: 1999.

Hákonar saga góða: see *Heimskringla I*

Hákonarmál

Eyvindr skáldaspillir Finnson. Ed. and transl. R.D. Fulk. In *Skaldic Poetry of the Scandinavian Middle Ages: Vol. 1: Poetry from the Kings' Sagas 1: From Mythical Times to c. 1035.* Ed. Diana Whaley. Turnhout: 2012. Pp. 171–94.

Hauks þáttr hábrókar: see Flateyjarbók

Hauksbók

Hauksbók, udgiven efter de Arnamagnæanske håndskrifter no. 371, 544 og 675, 4° samt forskellige papirshåndskrifter af Det Kongelige Nordiske Oldskrift-Selskab. Ed. Finnur Jónsson. København: 1892–96.

Heimskringla
Íslenzk fornrit, 26–28. 3 vols. Ed. Bjarni Aðalbjarnarson. Reykjavik: 1941–51.

Historiæ Ecclesiastica
Bede. *Ecclesiastical History of the English Nation*. 2 vols. Transl. John Edward King. Loeb Classical Library, 246 & 248. Cambridge: 1930.

Hrafnkels saga
Íslenzk fornrit, 11. Ed. Jón Jóhannesson. Reykjavik: 1950. Pp. 95–133.

Hyndluljóð: see *Poetic Edda*

Kjalnesinga saga
Íslenzk fornrit, 14. Ed. Jóhannes Halldórsson. Reykjavík: 1959. Pp. 1–44.

Landnámabók
Íslenzk fornrit, 1. Ed. Jakob Benediktsson. Reykjavík: 1968. Pp. 29–397.

Lokasenna: see *Poetic Edda*

Ólafs saga helga: see *Heimskringla II*

Poetic Edda
Eddadigte. 3 vols. Ed. Jón Helgason. Nordisk filologi. Serie A: tekster. I: *Völuspá*. *Hávamál*, 2nd edition (1964); II: *Gudedigte*, 2nd edition (1971); III: *Heltedigte*, første del (1961). Copenhagen.

Prose Edda
Snorri Sturluson. *Edda: Prologue and Gylfaginning*. 2nd ed. Ed. Anthony Faulkes. London: 2005.
Snorri Sturluson. *Edda: Skáldskaparmál 1: Introduction, Text and Notes*. Ed. Anthony Faulkes. London: 1998.

Saga Heiðreks konungs
Saga Heiðreks konungs ins vitra/The Saga of King Heiðrek the Wise. Ed. and transl. Christopher Tolkien. London, Edinburgh, Paris, Johannesburg, Toronto, & New York: 1960.

Skírnismál: see *Poetic Edda*

Sturlunga saga
Sturlunga saga including the Islendinga saga of Lawman Sturla Thordsson and Other Works. Vol. 1. Ed. Guðbrandur Vigfússon. Oxford: 1878.

Upplandslagen
Upplandslagen. Ed. O. F. Hultman. Helsinki: 1916.

Vafþrúðnismál: see *Poetic Edda*

Vatnsdœla saga
Íslenzk fornrit, 8. Ed. Einar Ólafur Sveinsson. Reykjavik: 1939. Pp. 1–131.

Vápnfirðinga saga
Íslenzk fornrit, 11. Ed. Jón Jóhannesson. Reykjavik: 1950. Pp. 21–65.

Víga-glúms saga
Íslenzk fornrit, 9. Ed. Jónas Kristjánsson. Reykjavik: 1956. Pp. 1–98.

Vǫluspá: see *Poetic Edda*

Ynglingasaga: see *Heimskringla*

Ögmundar þáttr dytts
Íslenzk fornrit, 9. Ed. Jónas Kristjánsson. Reykjavik: 1956. Pp. 99–115.

Þiðranda þáttr ok Þórhalls
Þiðranda þáttr ok Þórhalls. In *Íslendingasögur og þættir.* Ed. Bragi Halldórsson, Jón Torfason, Sverrir Tómasson, and Örnólfur Thorsson. Reykjavík: 1987. Pp. 2253–55.

Þrymskviða: see *Poetic Edda*

Secondary Sources

Brink, Stefan. 1990. *Sockenbildning och sockennamn: Studier i äldre territoriell indeling i Norden.* Acta Academiae Regiae Gustavi Adolphi, 57. Studier till en svensk ortnamsatlas utgivna av Thoersten Andersson. Uppsala.

———. 2007. "How Uniform was the Old Norse Religion?" In *Learning and Understanding in the Old Norse World: Essays in Honour of Margaret Clunies Ross.* Ed. Judy Quinn, Kate Heslop, and Tarrin Wells. Turnhout. Pp. 105–35.

Christensen, Arne Emil, Anne Stine Ingstad, and Bjørn Myhre. 1992. *Oseberg-dronningens grav: Vår arkeologiske nasjonalskatt i nytt lys.* Oslo.

Elmevik, Lennart. 2003. "Freyr, Freyja och Freyfaxi." *Studia anthroponymica Scandinavica* 21: 5–13.

———. 2011. "Yggdrasill: En etymologisk studie." In *Från rabbal till Yggdrasill: Valda uppsatser av Lennart Elmevik, återutgivna till hans 75-årsdag 2 februari*

2011. Ed. Maj Reinhammar. Medelanden från Sällskapet för svensk dialektologi, 2. Uppsala. Pp. 347–56.

Fabech, Charlotte, and Ulf Näsman. 2013. "Ritual Landscapes and Sacral Places in the First Millennium AD in South Scandinavia." In *Sacred Sites and Holy Places: Exploring the Sacralization of Landscape through Time and Space*. Ed. Sæbjørg Walaker Nordeide and Stefan Brink. Turnhout. Pp. 53–109.

Frazer, James George. 1957. *The Golden Bough: A Study in Magic and Religion*. Abridged edition. London & Basingstoke.

Fredengren, Christina. 2011. "Where Wandering Water Gushes: The Depositional Landscape of the Mälaren Valley in the Late Bronze Age and Earliest Iron Age of Scandinavia." *Journal of Wetland Archaeology* 10: 109–35.

van Gennep, Arnold. 1960. *Rites of Passage*. Transl. Monika B. Vizedom. London.

Gunnell, Terry. 1995. *The Origins of Drama in Scandinavia*. Cambridge.

———. 2000 "The Season of the *Dísir*: The Winter Nights and the *Dísarblót* in Early Scandinavian Belief." *Cosmos* 16: 117–49.

———. 2001. "Hof, Halls, Goðar and Dwarves: An Examination of the Ritual Space in the Pagan Icelandic Hall." *Cosmos* 17: 3–36.

———. 2006a. "'Til holts ek gekk': Spacial and Temporal Aspects of the Dramatic Poems of the Elder Edda." In *Old Norse Religion in Long Term Perspectives: Origins, Changes and Interactions: An International Conference in Lund, Sweden 3-7 June, 2004*. Ed. Anders Andrén, Kristina Jennbert, and Catharina Raudvere. Lund. Pp. 238–42.

———. 2006b. "Ritual Space, Ritual Year, Ritual Gender: A View of the Old Norse and New Icelandic Ritual Year." In *First International Conference of the SIEF Working Group on the Ritual Year (Malta, March 20-24, 2005): Proceedings*. Ed. George Mifsud-Chircop. Malta. Pp. 285–302.

———. 2007. "How Elvish Were the Álfar?" In *Constructing Nations, Reconstructing Myth: Essays in Honour of T. A. Shippey*. Ed. Andrew Wawn, Graham Johnson, and John Walter. Turnhout. Pp. 111–30.

———. 2008. "The Performance of the Poetic Edda." In *The Viking World*. Ed. Stefan Brink in collaboration with Neil Price. London. Pp. 299–303.

———. 2009. "Ansgar's Conversion of Iceland." *Scripta Islandica* 60: 105–18.

———. 2011. "The Drama of the Poetic Edda: Performance as a Means of Transformation." In *Progranicza teatralności: Poezja, poetyka, praktyka*. Ed. Andrzeja Dąbrówki. Studia Staropolskie, Series Nova. Warsaw. Pp. 13–40.

———. 2013a. "*Vǫluspá* in Performance." In *The Nordic Apocalypse Approaches to 'Vǫluspá' and Nordic Days of Judgement*. Ed. Terry Gunnell and Annette Lassen. Turnhout. Pp. 63–77.

———. 2013b. "From One High One to Another: The Acceptance of Óðinn as Preparation for the Acceptance of God." In *Conversions: Looking for*

Ideological Change in the Early Middle Ages. Ed. Leszek Słupecki and Rudolf Simek. Studia Medievalia Septentrionalia, 23. Vienna. Pp. 153–78.

———. 2014. "Nordic Folk Legends, Folk Traditions and Grave Mounds: The Value of Folkloristics for the Study of Old Nordic Religions." In *New Focus on Retrospective Methods: Resuming Methodological Discussions: Case Studies from Northern Europe.* Ed. Eldar Heide and Karen Bek-Pedersen. Helsinki. Pp. 17–41.

———. 2015. "Pantheon? What Pantheon? Concepts of a Family of Gods in Pre-Christian Scandinavian Religions." *Scripta Islandica* 66: 55–76.

———. Forthcoming a. "How High Was the High One? The Role of Oðinn in Pre-Christian Icelandic Society."

———. Forthcoming b. "Performance Archaeology, *Eiríksmál, Hákonarmál* and the Study of Old Nordic Religions."

Hultgård, Anders. 1993. "Altskandinavische Opferrituale und das Problem der Quellen." In *The Problem of Ritual: Based on Papers Read at the Symposium on Religious Rites Held at Åbo, Finland on the 13th–16th of August 1991.* Ed. Tore Ahlbäck. Åbo. Pp. 221–59.

Jón Hnefill Aðalsteinsson. 1998. *A Piece of Horse Liver: Myth, Ritual and Folklore in Old Icelandic Sources.* Reykjavík.

Jørgensen, Lars. 2009. "Pre-Christian Cult at Aristocratic Residences and Settlement Complexes in Southern Scandinavia in the 3rd–10th Centuries AD." In *Glaube, Kult und Herrschaft: Phänomene des Religiösen im 1. Jahrtausend n. Chr. In Mittel- und Nordeuropa: Akten des 59. Internationelen Sachsensymposions und der Grundprobleme der frühgeschichtlichen Entwicklung im Mitteldonauraum.* Ed. Uta von Freeden, Herwig Freisinger, and Egon Wamers. Römisch-Germanische Kommission, Frankfurt A. M. Eurasien-Abteilung, Berlin, des Deutschen Archäologischen Instituts: Kolloguien zur Vor- und Frühgeschichte, 12. Bonn. Pp. 329–54.

af Klintberg, Bengt. 1998. "Traditioner om guldvagnar." In *Kuttrasju: Folkloristika och kulturhistoriska essäer.* Stockholm. Pp. 7–38.

Kovárová, Lenka. 2011. "The Swine in Old Nordic Religion and Worldview." MA thesis, University of Iceland.

Krafft, Sophie. 1956. *Pictorial Weavings from the Viking Age: Drawings and Patterns of Textiles from the Oseberg Finds.* Oslo.

Ljungkvist, John, et al. 2015 etc. "Gamla Uppsala: The Emergence of a Mythical Centre." In *Gamla Uppsala: A Mythical Centre.* Blog. Uppsala University, Uppland Museum, National Heritage Board, and Societas Achaeologica Upsaliensis. http://glaup.blogspot.se/ (accessed on April 15, 2017).

Monikander, Anne. 2010. *Våld och vatten: Våtmarkskult vid Skedemosse under järnåldern.* Stockholm Studies in Archaeology, 52. Stockholm.

Motz, Lotte. 1996. *The King, The Champion and The Sorcerer: A Study of Germanic Myth.* Vienna.

Nordberg, Andreas. 2012. "Continuity, Change and Regional Variation in Old Norse Religion." In *More than Mythology: Narratives, Ritual Practices and Regional Distribution in Pre-Christian Scandinavian Religions.* Ed. Catharina Raudvere and Jens Peter Schjødt. Lund. Pp. 119–51.

Olsen, Magnus. 1926. *Ættegård og helligdom: Norsk stedsnavn sosialt og religionshistorisk belyst.* Oslo.

Price, Neil S. 2002. *The Viking Way: Religion and War in Iron Age Scandinavia.* Aun, 31. Uppsala.

Sandén, Börje. n.d. "Rösaring—Cult site." Upplands-Bro Research Institute for History of Culture. http://www.ukforsk.se/rosa-eng.htm (accessed on April 15, 2017).

Sandén, Börje. 2002. "Fifty Years with the Cult Site of Rösaring." Upplands-Bro Research Institute for History of Culture. http://www.ukforsk.se/nya/vhm.htm (accessed on April 15, 2017).

Schjødt, Jens Peter. 2014. "New Perspectives on the Vanir Gods in Pre-Christian Scandinavian Mythology and Religion." In *Nordic Mythologies: Interpretations, Intersections, and Institutions.* Ed. Timothy R. Tangherlini. The Wildcat Canyon Advanced Seminars: Mythology, 1. Berkeley & Los Angeles. Pp. 19–34.

Simek, Rudolf. 2010. "The Vanir: An Obituary." *Retrospective Network Methods Newsletter* 1 (Dec.): 10–19.

Svavar Sigmundsson. 1992. "Átrúnaður og örnefni." In *Snorrastefna, 25.-27. júlí 1990.* Ed. Úlfar Bragason. Rit Stofnunnar Sigurðar Nordals, 1. Reykjavík. Pp. 241–54.

Strömbäck, Dag. 2000. *Sejd och andra studier i nordisk själsuppfattning.* 2nd ed. Uppsala.

Sundqvist, Olof. 2000. *Freyr's Offspring: Rulers and Religion in Ancient Svea Society.* Uppsala.

Tolley, Clive. 2011. "In Defence of the Vanir." *Retrospective Methods Network Newsletter* 2 (May): 20–8.

Vikstrand, Per. 2001. *Gudarnas platser: Förkristna sakrala ortnamn i Mälarlandskapen.* Uppsala.

de Vries, Jan. 1956–57. *Altgermanische Religionsgeschichte.* 2 vols. 2nd ed. Ed. Hermann Paul. Grundriss der Germanischen Philologie, 12. Berlin.

"The Wagons from Dejbjerg." National Musueum of Denmark. Online exhibition. http://en.natmus.dk/historical-knowledge/denmark/prehistoric-period-until-1050-ad/the-early-iron-age/the-wagons-from-dejbjerg/ (accessed on April 15, 2017).

Volund Was Here

A Myth Archaeologically Anchored in Viking Age Scania

Torun Zachrisson
Stockholm University

Abstract: A recently discovered object from the Viking Age shows a winged human figure. It has been interpreted as a representation of Volund the smith, and, more specifically, the version of the legend found in *Þiðreks saga*. The context for the object, the center Uppåkra in Sweden, is compared with the context presented in *Þiðreks saga*. The article concludes that an audience in Viking Age Uppåkra would have felt at home with the winged man and the version in *Þiðreks saga*, but less familiar with the social setting for Volund presented in *Vǫlundarkviða* that represents a setting that would have been more easily understood further north in mid-Sweden.

Introduction

Archaeologists do not always find it easy to discuss myths; when we do it is usually based on pictorial evidence, such as rune stones and picture stones. In the world of the runic inscriptions from the late Viking Age (ca. 1000–1100 CE) in present-day Sweden, for instance, we meet Þórr fishing for the Midgard serpent on the Altuna-stone in Uppland (U 1161)[1] and Sigurðr the dragon slayer on the runic rock carving at Ramsund and on the Gök-stone in Södermanland (Sö 101 and 327), and on other rune stones from northern Uppland and Gästrikland: Drävle (U 1163), Vittinge (U 1175), Österfärnebo (Gs 2), Årsunda (Gs 9), and Ockelbo

---

[1] Modern names are used, after Faulkes' translation of the *Prose Edda* and Carolyne Larrington's translation of the Poetic Edda. When referring to Old Icelandic *Vǫlundr*, Low German *Welent*, High German *Wieland*, Old Norwegian *Velent* the modern English form Volund is used for all of them (the different names are discussed in Nedoma 2006; Insley 2006; Marold 2012: 236).

(Gs 19). Viðarr with his thick shoe is depicted on the rune stone from Ledberg in Östergötland (Ög 181) and, on the Västerljung stone from Södermanland, we see Gunnar in the snake pit (Sö 40).[2] The Gotlandic picture stones are famous for their rich pictorial world; here, among others, we meet Óðinn mounted on Sleipnir on stone I from Tjängvide in Alskog (G110, Lindqvist 1941–1942: fig. 137) and Volund in his bird's guise on stone VIII from Ardre (Lindqvist 1941–1942: fig. 139).

Various archaeological objects have also been interpreted as depicting gods, who have either been identified by their attributes or through a certain scene central to a myth. A gold bracteate from ca. 500 CE discovered at Trollhättan, Västergötland, Sweden shows Týr putting his hand in the wolf Fenrir's mouth (Öberg 1942; Oxenstierna 1956; Axboe and Källström 2013: 155) and another depicts the scene where Baldr is being killed by the twig of mistletoe (Hauck 1970: 184). Óðinn has been identified on the plates from the helmets in the boat burials at Vendel (Stolpe and Arne 1912: pl. 5, 6) and on the plates used for producing this type of helmet from the late sixth and early seventh centuries at Torslunda on Öland (Arrhenius and Freij 1992). The most renowned helmet with figural plates of this type was discovered in the Sutton Hoo boat burial from East Anglia. That helmet alludes to Óðinn: it was deliberately constructed so that one eyebrow had gold foils behind the red garnets, which made the brow reflect the light and glow, while the other brow, without gold foil, remained dark, giving the impression of a one-eyed god (cf. Price and Mortimer 2014).

The Viking Age pendant from Aska in Östergötland that shows a pregnant female with rich dress and jewelry has been interpreted as Freyja with her necklace Brísingamen (Arrhenius 1969), whereas the ithyphallic bronze statuette from Lunda in Södermanland has been interpreted as the god of fertility, Freyr (Salin 1913). Although these identifications have engendered discussion and critique (e.g., Price 2006), they are accepted by most scholars. As a whole, most of the material representations of divine figures that appear during the late Iron Age (550–1050 CE) can be identified from Old Norse written sources, but this is seldom the case for representations dated earlier than that (Andrén 2014: 187).

In this article, I will discuss a recently discovered object that shows a winged human figure. It has been interpreted as a representation of Volund the smith, and, more specifically, the version of the legend found in *Þiðreks saga*. I will compare the context—Uppåkra, Sweden, where the object was discovered— with the context presented in *Þiðreks saga*. My conclusion is that an audience in Viking Age Uppåkra would have felt at home with the winged man and the version in *Þiðreks saga*, whereas for an audience further north in Scandinavia,

---

[2] For the identification of the rune stones mentioned above, see Samnordisk runtextdatabas.

such as mid-Sweden, former Svíþjóð, the social setting for Volund presented in *Vǫlundarkviða* would have been more familiar.

The Object

In September 2011, a highly interesting object turned up during the research excavation of an Iron Age settlement in Uppåkra in southernmost Sweden. The find and the object were described and analyzed by Michaela Helmbrecht in an article in the antiquarian journal *Fornvännen* (2012). The object is 7.5 centimeters long, 4.5 centimeters wide, and weighs 52.6 grams. It is a piece of openwork in high relief made out of a gilded copper alloy. Three iron rivets on the backside show that it was going to be mounted onto something, but since the object shows no signs of wear, we can conclude that this never happened. It is gilded on all sides, including the reverse, which is unusual, and it is thus a costly piece of work. It is slightly bent in the middle, and it has been suggested that it might be a scabbard-chape or -fitting (Helmbrecht 2012: 171). This, however, seems unlikely since it is too heavy for that.

The object is shown in bird's eye view: we see a human intertwined with a pair of wings—a mix of a human body and a flying device. It portrays a winged man dressed in armor and boots, bearded and possibly wearing a helmet. His

Figure 1. The mount from Uppåkra, Sweden. Photo by Bengt Almgren, Lund University Historical Museum.

arms are connected to the wings and the feathered tail through a shield-like dotted structure in the middle. This type of ring-chain motif is common in the Borre style (Wilson 1995: 88–89); therefore the object likely dates to the mid-Viking Age, 950–1000 CE (Helmbrecht 2012: 175). The ring chain has by some scholars been associated with symbolical binding and border-crossing (Domeij Lundborg 2006; Oerhl 2011; Helmbrecht 2011: 134–38).

Already during the fieldwork, the male figure on the object was identified as Volund (after an idea by Iohannes Miaris Sundberg and Bengt Söderberg; see Helmbrecht 2012), the legendary master smith who was captured by a king and hamstrung to prevent him from fleeing. Thereafter, Volund had to make jewelry for the king's family. But he avenged himself by killing the king's two sons and making drinking bowls with silver fittings out of their skulls. Volund also violated the king's daughter and left her pregnant. Then he managed to flee from captivity.

Volund's story is told in the eddic poem *Vǫlundarkviða* and in *Þiðreks saga af Bern*, where he is called Velent. In other narrative sources known from Old Norse and Western European texts, Volund is also alluded to, as a master smith (Nedoma 1988: 40–43; see also Nedoma 2006: 608–18; Insley 2006).

Not every winged figure with a human head must be identified as Volund, as giants and gods may appear in a bird's guise. But this object is surely meant to depict Volund. It refers to the version of the myth where Volund/Velent is said to escape by using a flying device made of birds' feathers and thus illustrates perfectly the passage in *Þiðreks saga*: "nv em ec fvgl oc nv em ec maðr" (*Þiðreks saga* ch. 133) (now I am bird and now I am man).[3] Furthermore there are droplets of blood on the figure's left hand/wing (Figure 2), droplets that are completely missing on the right wing where there is only a double line (Helmbrecht 2012: 176), thus illustrating the saga almost as if it were a cartoon. In the saga, Velent/Volund says to his brother Egill: "oc neyðir hann þic til at skiota at mer. þa hœf þv vndir vinstrv hond mer þar hevi ec bvndit vndir eina blaðro þar er i bloð svna niðvngs konongs" (*Þiðreks saga* ch. 132) (and if he forces you to shoot at me, then hit under my left arm where I have bound a bladder with the blood of King Niðungr's sons). So "egill leggr or astreng oc skytr vndir hond velent hina vinstri oc fellr nv bloð a iorð" (*Þiðreks saga* ch. 135) (Egil places an arrow on the bowstring and shoots under Velent/Volund's left arm, and blood falls to the ground). The winged man from Uppåkra indicates that the version of the legend known from *Þiðreks saga* was known in Scania in the late tenth century.

---

[3]   Translations are my own unless otherwise indicated.

Figure 2. The mount from Uppåkra. Detail of the left wing, with the droplets of blood. Photo by Bengt Almgren, Lund University Historical Museum.

The Context

The object was found in Uppåkra in Scania, which during the Viking Age was a part of Denmark. Uppåkra is one of the nodal points of southern Scandinavia, being a dense settlement of long tradition, a so-called "central place" complex with roots that date to 100 BCE. The site has been subject to considerable metal detecting, as well as geophysical surveying and archaeological excavation, the results of which indicate that the whole settlement area covered some 40 hectares. The core of the settlement has been identified south of the parish church at Stora Uppåkra, and here an excellently preserved building dating to ca. 200–1000 CE has been excavated. Traces of large roof pillars indicate that it had been a very tall house. A large door ring found at the southwestern entrance suggests that this was the main gate. The house had been rebuilt on the same spot seven times. Inside, gold–foil figures (*guldgubbar*) were found, as well as two special objects used in ceremonial drinking, a unique beaker with gilded ornamented panels (Hårdh 2004) and a blue glass vessel (Stjernqvist 2004). These objects date to the Migration Period (400–550 CE), but had been deposited in a Viking Age floor-level, thus presumably having been used for several hundred years before being ritually buried. This building has been interpreted as a cult house (Larsson and Lenntorp 2004). That specific ritual houses were constructed must have been the result of interactions with the late Roman world: the Christianization of the Roman and Byzantine empire in the fourth and fifth centuries meant that rituals moved from the open air and altars next to

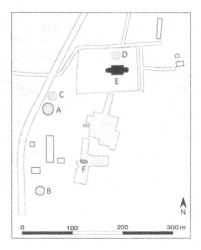

Figure 3. Uppåkra in Scania, Sweden. Excavation trenches and the cult house (F) marked south of the present Stora Uppåkra church (E); grave mounds Storehög (A), Lillehög (B), and two destroyed grave mounds (C, D). Map after Larsson and Söderberg 2012: 7.

temples into the interior of buildings (Andrén 2004: 12, 2007: 130–31). The cult house in Uppåkra has been perceived as an echo of an early Christian church, where a Roman/early Christian model was reinterpreted and creatively transformed in Scandinavia (Andrén 2007: 131).

Outside and around the ceremonial building, there were substantial deposits of animal bones, mostly of meat from cattle cut into portion-sized pieces, interpreted as traces of large feasts for many people (Magnell 2011). Numerous objects located in the surrounding courtyard are believed to have been ritually deposited (Larsson and Söderberg 2013: 239). A significant number of them are weapons: 300 spears and lances, mostly placed north of the house (Helgesson 2004).

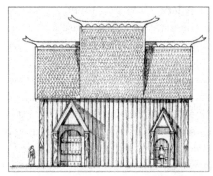

Figure 4. Reconstruction of the cult building. Drawing by Loïc Lecareux, Larsson and Söderberg 2012: 9, fig. 5.

Close by, large residence halls were found. These are at least as old as the cult house, thus first built in the third century or somewhat earlier. Northwest of the cult house, a house (A) had burnt down in the 400s with three persons inside. Afterwards, the remains of the burnt hall were evened out. Approximately a hundred years later, two gold bracteates and a gold pendant, half of a collier, were spread out over the area, on top of where the remains of the dead persons lay in the former house. The area continued to be used for the same type of activities as the area around the cult house and was covered with large numbers of animal bones. There were also un-cremated body parts from six humans, amongst them parts of a skull that had been hit by a severe but not fatal blow before the individual finally met his or her death (Larsson and Söderberg 2012: 10, 2013: 240). Southwest of the cult house, there was a residence hall that had stood on the same spot from the fifth through the tenth centuries. It had been repeatedly burnt down during the period 400–800 CE and rebuilt three times (B, C, D). Finds of human bones show that here too there were burnt humans inside. Among the body parts was the shoulder blade of a young person who had been run through from behind by a spear (Larsson and Söderberg 2013: 242). The Volund-object was found in the top layer of fire-cracked stones by the gable of the youngest hall (D), where it had been deliberately deposited. Fire-cracked stones are associated with late Iron Age elite settlements and have been related to preparation of large amounts of meat in cooking pits and the process of brewing ale (Söderberg 2005: 267–79, 465).

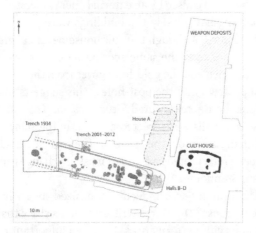

Figure 5. Excavated buildings (house A, halls B–D) west of the cult building. Illustration by Henrik Pihl. After Larsson 2015: 146.

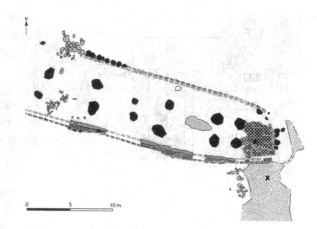

Figure 6. The Viking Age hall (D) and the layer of fire-cracked stones at the gable end of the building, where the Volund-object, marked with an X, was found. Illustration by Birgitta Piltz Williams. After Larsson and Söderberg 2012: 11.

Frands Herschend has suggested that the repeated destruction of the hall was a recurrent theme when rivals of the elite struggled for power in the Iron Age (Herschend 1996: 35). It is peculiar, however, that the cult house had no traces of fire whatsoever, although it stood less than 10 meters away from the residence hall and became even closer as the halls were enlarged over time. This shows that special respect must have been paid to this building. The excavators cautiously interpret this as if the hall-burning was more likely the result of internal feuds, rather than caused by an external enemy (Larsson and Söderberg 2013: 246). Considering how closely the buildings were placed, the fires must have been very controlled. Although the cult house never caught fire, it nevertheless was rebuilt on exactly the same spot perhaps as many as seven times: the postholes were reused and the gold-foil figures from the former house were, for instance, pushed down into the post-holes. This suggests that the repeated renewal of the cult house constituted ritual action. The excavated halls in Scandinavia show that halls were erected on exactly the same spot as the one where the earlier hall had stood, the space for the high seat and hearths being reused. This has been interpreted as a way of masking changes and emphasizing continuity (Hållans Stenholm 2012: 184).

At Uppåkra, continuity was indeed emphasized, but why the repeated renewals of the cult house? Old Norse written sources show that rulers played central roles in public cult performances. They had important ritual functions, especially in sacrificial rituals, and they served as guardians of the sacred places (Sundqvist 2002, 2003, 2007). In the research on the biographies of longhouses from the Iron Age, many scholars agree that a new longhouse was constructed when a new household was created (Gerritsen 1999). Considering this, it would seem logical that if the cult house had been rebuilt in accordance with the construction of a new residence hall presumably these re-buildings can be equated with the establishment of new ruling families. This means that a new ruling family used what was structurally the same ritual indoor arena for its "Old Norse temple", rebuilt on the same spot with the same placement of entrances, hearth, and high seat, but was able to put its own mark on the decoration of the temple.

Archaeologist Ny Björn Gustafsson has suggested that the winged man-object could be a nasal for a helmet (Gustafsson 2015). This would then have been part of a parade helmet with ornaments. As a nasal, the winged man would replace, for example, the bird on the helmet from the boat grave Vendel XIV or the man on the helmet from the boat grave Vendel I (Lindqvist 1925: 191, 193; Stolpe and Arne 1912: V–VI). Many of the human beings on such helmet plates have been interpreted as Óðinn, a primary war god. Normally this helmet type belongs to the Merovingian period (ca. 550–750 CE; Lindqvist 1925). Helmets dating to the Viking Age have rarely been found. A conical type of helmet without ornaments is, however, known from a burial in Gjermundbu in Norway, and this type is often referred to (Grieg 1947), being the same sort of helmet depicted on the Bayeux tapestry. A pair of helmet eyebrows with late Viking Age ornaments has been found on Gotland. Together, these finds serve to indicate that the traditional type of parade helmet with figural panels was still in use in the Viking Age (Lindqvist 1925: 194; "Ur främmande samlingar," 1907: 208).[4] Parade helmets were used in rituals in Uppåkra. A gilded eyebrow and the two gilded boars, parts of a Merovingian helmet from the late fifth or early sixth century, were deposited and placed south of the cult house (cf. L. Larsson 2007: 14).

The winged man-object was placed just south of and outside the gable in the central courtyard of Uppåkra, which as we have seen was a highly ritualized area with martial aspects. Unfinished precious objects that are ritually deposited, such as the one in question, have sometimes been interpreted as part of smiths' hoards (cf. Kristoffersen 2012). At least by the Merovingian period, bronze casters—and thus smiths—seem to have been permanently present in Uppåkra (Kresten et al. 2001: 163–64; Larsson and Lenntorp 2004: 7, 18, 31;

---

[4] Stray find from Lokrume, Gotlands fornsal B 1683, Thunmark-Nylén 2006: 317; see also Sune Lindqvist, who thinks that it was imported from the Continent during the Merovingian period (Lindqvist 1925: 193–94), while Lena Thunmark-Nylén shows that it is clearly from the Viking Age. This type of ornament also occurs on the Norwegian swords of Petersen's type S, as Thunmark-Nylén notes (2006: 317). It is a sword type that was introduced from the Continent in the tenth century and was imitated in Norway (Martens 2004: 127).

Axboe 2012: 129). Crucibles and slag were found inside the cult house, along with traces of gold from the manufacturing of gold-foil figures, all dating from the Merovingian period. Specialized craft of this type requires tradition and specific knowledge (Callmer 2002). Uppåkra and Helgö, "the holy island" in Lake Mälaren in mid-Sweden, were the only sites in modern Sweden where smiths were present on a permanent basis during the Iron Age. In large permanent workshops, smiths seem to have practiced many crafts: goldsmithing, casting of different metals, working wrought iron, and producing weapons. These workshops were linked to major political and economic centers (Lamm 2012: 143f.).

Uppåkra is rich in finds. From the second century onwards, the objects and buildings show extensive contacts with the world outside: different regions in northern Europe, the Roman Empire, the Rhein region, the Near East, Eastern Europe, the Balkans, northern Italy, the Arab world, and the British Isles (Larsson and Söderberg 2012: 28). Whether Uppåkra was a seat for a warlord or a king, we do not know. What we do know is that the history of Uppåkra can be connected with the old town of Lund, established ca. 980 CE (Hårdh and Larsson 2007; Hårdh 2010).

Volund/Velent in *Þiðreks Saga*

The winged-man object from Uppåkra accords well with the version of the myth recorded in *Þiðreks saga* (ch. 73–133), as we have already seen. In the saga, Velent, as Volund is called now, is said to be the son of a king from *Sioland* "Sea-Land" who is also a giant (*risi*). His mother is said to be one of the sea-maidens (*siokonar*) (*Þiðreks saga* ch. 84 [ch. 57]). Velent sets off to the court of the Jutish king, Niðungr, to become his follower. Velent is regarded as a hero, but presented as being dangerous and powerful—a liminal person. He had developed his smithing skills by being first taught by the smith Mímir for three winters in the land of the Huns, then by being a trainee of the dwarfs in the mountains across the sea. Later on, he is captured by king Niðungr, made lame, and forced to work at the royal court. Velent takes revenge by luring the king's two sons to the forge where he murders them. He hides the corpses in the pit under the bellows. With the help of a drink, he then rapes the king's daughter impregnating her, before declaring to the king what he had done. Finally, Velent flees with the help of a flying device made of birds' wings (*Þiðreks saga* ch. 73–136). The saga adds that Velent's brother, Egill, helps in the flight (cf. Marold 1996).

Þiðreks saga dates to the middle of the thirteenth century (Nedoma 2006: 615) and is a Norwegian compilation of heroic saga materials that likely have a Continental background (von See et al. 2000: 88; Nedoma 2006: 609; Insley 2006: 621; Marold 2012: 235). Velent mysteriously escapes with the help of a mechanical device called *flygil* "wing" or *fiaðrhamr* "feather-guise" (*Þiðreks saga* ch. 130; Nedoma 2006: 615). This probably shows influences from the antique Dædalus-myth, in which the Greek master smith Dædalus and his son Icarus escape from imprisonment by fashioning wings (Marold 2012: 235). Velent's numinosity has its roots in the Otherworld. He is the offspring of a giant of royal lineage and a sea-maiden. But he is placed in a royal court in the Danish realm. The legend must have been known in Uppåkra in the late tenth century. People there who saw the object and listened to the myth were familiar with ruling families in a Danish realm and the skills of master-smiths and might have been able to imagine one of them constructing a flying device.

The Social and Geographical Setting in *Vǫlundarkviða*

In the other main source for the myth—the eddic poem *Vǫlundarkviða*, possibly dating to the ninth or tenth century (Nedoma 2006: 613)—the master-smith Volund is set in another type of social environment that would not have been at all as familiar to the Uppåkra audience. In the poem, Volund is described with all the ethnic markers of a Sámi person (famous weapon smith, hunter, eating bear meat, skiing, living in the woods, foretelling weather); perhaps some of these traits were also the markers of a high-born Sámi of royal descent. In *Vǫlundarkviða*, "Hlæiandi Vǫlundr / hófz at lopti" (*Vǫlundarkviða* st. 29 (cf. st. 38)) (Laughing, Vǫlundr rose into the air) (*Vǫlundarkviða* pp. 106, 108) but the poem does not describe *how* he "rises" (Nedoma 1988: 155, 2006: 613; von See et al. 2000: 230–36; Marold 2012: 235). For an audience in the late Iron Age in northern Scandinavian, such a description would not have been necessary. Rising into the air would be logical—Volund was shape-shifting—and we may wonder whether the laughing played a part in his transformation. The setting in *Vǫlundarkviða* sketches a type of social landscape that would have been relevant and obvious in, for example, the seventh, eighth, and ninth centuries in the halls of the Ynglingar at the court in Old Uppsala, but it would also have been relevant for an audience in Norway, where the same type of close links existed between parts of "Norvegr" and the kingdoms of the Sámi.

Apparently the Sámi brothers in *Vǫlundarkviða* live close by the king of Svíþjóð, just as the Sámi did during the Iron Age (I. Zachrisson 1997; T. Zachrisson 2009: 69–70, 86, 94). The archaeological material from 550–1000 CE in mid-Sweden shows that Sámi objects are found in the core area of Svíþjóð, such as the Sámi boat parts on the sacrificial site at Rickebasta bog in Alsike (G. Larsson 2007: 240). At Tuna, close by, a man was buried in a boat. He had had a Sámi father and a Nordic mother, i.e. a woman from the South, as has been concluded from DNA analysis (Götherström 2001: 26). Furthermore, the dietary patterns deduced from skeletal material from the same cemetery indicate consumption of food rich in selenium, possibly reindeer meat (Lidén and Nelson 1994: 19).[5] Sámi birch-bark sails used as tent covers have been found in the famous boat-graves of Vendel VII and XII and Valsgärde 6 and 8 in Uppland, Sweden (Arwidsson 1942, 1954; I. Zachrisson 1997: 194; G. Larsson 2007: 95), and in the boat-grave Tuna 75 in Badelunda, Västmanland, a woman was buried in a boat that is sewn together with a technique typical of the Sámi, with the shape and construction of the boat being typical of the Sámi as well (Nylén and Schönbeck 1994). Probably another five boats from the cemetery were of the same type (G. Larsson 2007: 124).

In Viking Age Scandinavia, the Sámi were renowned as expert smiths. Early iron technology was characterized by iron production in the forest areas of the Sámi (I. Zachrisson 2006), and would thus be more in line with Volund's smithy in the wooded areas next to Svíþjóð. In Norse mythology, Lydia Carstens, referring to *Vǫluspá* st. 7 and *Gylfaginning* st. 14, states that smithies were located close to the halls and temples of the gods, in close proximity to the power and not in a remote forest (Carstens 2012: 246).

In the sixth century, Jordanes in *Getica* (Miller 1915: 56) and Procopius in *De Bello Gothico* book VI, ch. xv call the Sámi *skridfenni, scrithiphini* (Dewing 1979) a term that alludes to their habit of skiing (*skriða á skidum*; see I. Zachrisson 1997: 158). Skis were produced by Sámi and predominantly used by them; before the nineteenth century, skis are only found in the north of the Nordic countries (I. Zachrisson 1997: 215–16). It is an open question but quite probable that the gyrfalcons that were found in the cremation graves from the seventh and eighth centuries in Vårberg in Huddinge parish, Södermanland and Söderby in Danmark parish, Uppland, as well as in one of the famous boat graves in Uppland (Vendel III), were tamed—by the Sámi?—as chicks in the mountainous region in Northwestern Sweden and traded down to Svíþjóð (cf. Ericson and Tyrberg 2004: 113; T. Zachrisson 2010).

According to written sources, the kings of Svíþjóð intermarried with Sámi kings' daughters. In *Ynglinga saga*, the marriages of Drífa "snowdrift", daughter of King Snjár "snow", to King Vanlandi and that of Skjálf, daughter of king Frosti

---

[5]   Tuna in Alsike is a burial ground comprising twelve boat graves and five other graves that were excavated by Hjalmar Stolpe and T. J. Arne (Arne 1934; see also Arvidsson 1999). These include twelve Viking boat burials, two built over women, the rest over men. Two chambers, dated to 550–600 CE, were graves that preceded the boat graves (Arne 1934; Hjulström 2008: 11). One of the Viking Age men (grave VI) had had a male ancestor who was of Sámi descent, while his mother was of Nordic descent (Götherström 2001: 26). Therefore it is of great interest that the parts of the boat that were found in the sacrificial site the Rickebasta bog, on the grounds of the Tuna farm, were of late Iron Age Sámi type (G. Larsson 2007: 240). On their possible reindeer diets, see also I. Zachrisson 2012.

"frost", to Vísburr, whose sons are called Gísl and Ǫndurr (ski pole and ski) are described by Snorri Sturluson (*Ynglinga saga* ch. 13–14, 19; see also Lönnroth 1986; I. Zachrisson 1997: 169; on the use of "Finn" and "Finland" for Sámi see *Heimskringla* [Johansson] 2: 352n100). Elsewhere in *Heimskringla*, Snorri recounts the tale of the Norwegian king Haraldr hárfagri (Harald Fairhair) and his betrothal to Snæfríðr "snowpeace", the daughter of yet another Sámi king (*Heimskringla* ch. 26). These types of legendary marriages may have added to the numinosity of the future kings yet to be born, since their Sámi wives were perceived as possessing unusual powers (*Heimskringla* [Johansson] 1: 312n14). Volund in *Vǫlundarkviða* is the product of such a marriage in reverse. He is the son of a Sámi king who marries a girl from the south, Hervǫr (interestingly, the Viking Age man in a boat grave in Tuna in Alsike mentioned above mirrors this heritage).

Generally, we tend to think of the Sámi as living far up in the north. But future research may well alter that picture. In the seventeenth century, the woodland Sámi (*skogslappar*) living in Gästrikland, just north of Uppland—both regions in former Svíþjóð—had their own names for plants that do not grow north of the limes Norrlandicus, the geographical/biological borderline that divides Svealand and Norrland (Lars-Gunnar Larsson, University of Uppsala, emeritus; pers. comm., March 2015).

Mid-Sweden and Old Uppsala not only show contacts with the regions to the North; during the same period, the seventh to ninth centuries, there were also many other distant contacts. Almost all the imported objects were from Western Europe. Some types of objects stand out, such as elephant ivory objects, golden threads from woven silk garments, and amethyst beads, which probably traveled from the Byzantine Empire via the Anglo-Saxon area or Merovingian France (Ljungkvist 2008, 2009: 44–47, 2010). Helgö in Mälaren was a permanent workshop, and there was also a center of artisanship at the royal manor in Old Uppsala (Ljungkvist et al. 2011: 578–81). At such sites, there must have been close contacts between the ruler and his smiths.

Edith Marold points to the fact that Volund is depicted in the *Vǫlundarkviða* as a creature from the wilderness who is captured and who takes revenge. She compares the lay with structurally similar tales and shows that it can be read as a story circling around the theme of initiation (Marold 2012: 237–39). Volund is the mythical being that breaks into the world of an old king and denies the continuation of the royal lineage by killing the male offspring and violating the female offspring (cf. Callmer 2002: 357).[6] In the other tales, Marold notes that

---

[6] Johan Callmer discusses the Volund myth as a whole, combining details from *Vǫlundarkviða* and *Þiðreks saga* when discussing Volund's revenge (which leads to the downfall of the royal family of Nidud and perhaps the dominion of the Njarar). Callmer stresses the didactic nature of the Volund myth in the treatment of skilled craftsmen (Callmer 2002: 357–58).

the creature from the wilderness returns after his revenge as the future ruler (2012: 235–40). Volund, however, does not guarantee the continuation of the royal line but rather its destruction.

Some Other Representations of Volund

The Volund myth is presented in other pictorial sources. The earliest of those is a Volund-figure depicted on a gold solidus from Schweindorf in East Frisia (Figure 7). This coin had a solidus for emperor Theodosius II (r. 402–450 CE) as a model, but is dated to 575–650 CE. The runes read *volundu* in Anglo-Frisian. The figure is shown with a bow and a pair of tongs as well as a stick or perhaps an extra leg, illustrating that he is lame (Oehrl 2012). The limping smith is, as Edith Marold has shown, a concept with deep historical roots, already present in Asia Minor and among the Phoenicians, in the Greek god Hephaistos and many others places (Marold 1966: 480–483). Whether this can be understood to mean that smiths were recruited from among crippled persons, or if it was a result of mutilation to hinder a craftsman from escaping with valuables, or if it perhaps had to do with the dangerous substances and the conditions under which the smiths worked, has been debated. But it could also be interpreted as a visible sign and consequence of an initiation ritual (see overview in Marold 1966: 480–500, cf. Marold 2012: 237).

More famous is the so-called Franks casket (also known as the Clermont Runic casket; Becker 1973), a carved casket dated to the eight century CE adorned with Anglo-Saxon runes (Figure 8). It was probably made in a Northumbrian monastic context. The casket speaks of itself in Old English as being made from *hronæsban* "whalebone" from a stranded whale. It combines pictorial scenes

Figure 7. The solidus from Schweindorf. Photo: Hinrich Dirksen, Ostfriesisches Landesmuseum Emden.

Figure 8. Front panel of Franks casket, showing Volund in his smithy.
After Stephens 1867–1868: 145.

from the classical and Christian worlds: the adoration of the Magi, the destruction of Herod's temple in Jerusalem by the Roman general Titus, and the suckling of Romulus and Remus by the she-wolf of Roman mythology. Furthermore, there are three scenes from Germanic tradition with accompanying rune-texts showing Volund's revenge, his brother Egill defending himself with bow and arrows, and at last the suffering of a woman called Hos (Becker 2012). These are among the earliest scenes in Europe to have been articulated in this type of extended visual narrative and accompanied by a long text in the vernacular (Webster 2012).

As a whole, the pictorial program of the casket alludes to the perception or creation of a universal history. On the front to the left we see the hamstrung Volund (known in Anglo-Saxon tradition as Wēland) in his smithy receiving the daughter of King Niðungr (or Niðhad as he is called in Old English sources). In one hand he holds a cup of beer, which he offers to her. Once she drinks it, he will be able to violate her (cf. Oehrl 2012: 284). Volund has just killed one of her brothers, whose corpse is lying under the anvil. The boy's head is still in the pair of tongs that Volund holds in his other hand. Volund, having committed infanticide, can thus be regarded as a Germanic equivalent to Herod, murdering the male children of Bethlehem. This panel is placed to the left, while the panel to the right shows the adoration of the holy child, the gift of the magi motif (cf. Staecker 2004: 45–47). The lid shows the master archer Egill, whose name is written in runes above; he is Volund's brother, who defends himself against the attacking Niðungr. Leslie Webster suggests that the casket was intended to contain a sacred text, a psalter, and that it was made for a member of an Anglo-Saxon royal house (Webster 2012), whereas Alfred Becker argues that the casket may have been a royal one, from which the king handed out gifts to his

Figure 9. Detail of the picture stone from Ardre VIII, Gotland.
Photo courtesy of the Swedish History Museum.

companions in the hall (Becker 1973; 2012). Historian Barbara Yorke, however, thinks it can be compared with the late antique wedding caskets. The women in the carved pictures have a special position and this probably reflects the person who ordered the casket (pers. comm.). The Franks casket seems to refer to the same Volund tradition as the Uppåkra object and *Þiðreks saga*.

On the Gotlandic picture stone from the church of Ardre (Ardre VIII), dated to the same century as the winged man from Uppåkra, that is, the tenth (Imer 2001: 99, 105), Volund is depicted as a large bird escaping from an opening in a turf-roofed smithy (Figure 9). The large bird above the smithy has no anthropomorphic traits. This can be interpreted as meaning that it illustrates a metamorphosis of Volund himself, because it provides no mechanical explanation as to how Volund rises into the air. The bodies of the princes can be seen in the deep pit under the bellows and thereunder probably also the key to a chest, as argued by Louis Buisson and Sigmund Oehrl (Buisson 1976: 76; Oehrl 2012: 285). It is not shown directly, but the composition indicates that the smith quite likely beheaded the boys by using the chest lid (von See et al. 2000: 213). This has been compared with the lines in *Vǫlundarkviða*, "Kómo þeir til kisto, krǫfðo lucla, /opin var illúð, er þeir í sá" (*Vǫlundarkviða* st. 24) (They came to the chest, demanded the keys; the evil intention was patent when they looked inside (*Vǫlundarkviða* p. 105)). It is possible that this picture stone shows a Volund tradition similar to that found in the eddic poem. In northern Gotland, however, the picture stone from Stora Hammars III in Lärbro, dated to roughly the same period (ninth century; Lindqvist 1941–1942: II 87), shows an anthropomorphic bird in combination with a lady (Oerhl 2012: 298-300). It has been interpreted as Óðinn stealing the mead of poetry (Lindqvist 1941–1942), but comparisons with other pictorial representations of Volund show that it probably belongs to the smith's story instead (Oerhl 2012: 299). Could it mean that different versions of the Volund-myth were told on Gotland in the early Viking Age? Perhaps this is to go too far; a comparison can be drawn to the stone crosses and hogback-fragments from Yorkshire which show just how complex it can be to interpret the different smith-representations (Oehrl 2012: 294–98).[7]

To sum up: the Uppåkra mount from late tenth-century Sweden perfectly illustrates a version of the myth of the master-smith Volund known from *Þiðreks saga*, dated to mid-thirteenth-century Iceland. Uppåkra as an Iron Age central place of prime status was a site where rulers and smiths met. The theme of succession of the leadership must have been highly relevant and absolutely crucial for the rulers of Uppåkra. I argue here that the succession may have included the burning down of halls and rebuilding of the cult house. It is therefore highly plausible that the courtyard was an arena for inauguration rituals, where a new ruler was installed. The Volund figure could allude to the role of the smith as healer, as forging, creating humans—a role that the smith had in initiation tales where he "forged" the initiate. It is an open question whether the smith also could have had such a role involving a new ruler.[8]

Works Cited

Primary Sources

Ágrip
Ágrip af Noregs Konunga Sögur. Ed. V. Dahlerup. Copenhagen: 1880.

---

[7] For a comprehensive account for all the Volund representations, see Oerhl 2012.

[8] The saga of Harald Dofrafóstri in *Ágrip* and in *Halvdanar saga svarta* (*Heimskringla* ch. 9) tells of a Sámi, Dovre, who is skilled in magic and steals food from King Halfdan Svarti's Yule feast, but gets caught and is held as a captive. He is freed by young Haraldr hárfagri, who stays on with the Sámi until his father dies. Haraldr then returns and takes over the kingdom (Marold 2012: 236). This fostering might have had influence on the new ruler Haraldr and his numinosity and contact with the Otherworld.

Gylfaginning: see *Prose Edda*

De Bello Gothico

<small>TRANSLATION</small>

Procopius. *History of the wars. Book VI.* Transl. Henry B. Dewing. Cambridge, MA: 1979.

Getica

<small>TRANSLATION</small>

The Gothic History of Jordanes. Transl. Charles Chr. Mierow. Princeton: 2006.

Heimskringla

Íslenzk fornrit, 26–28. 3 vols. Ed. Bjarni Aðalbjarnarson. Reykjavik: 1941–1951.

<small>TRANSLATIONS</small>

Heimskringla: History of the Kings of Norway. Transl. Lee M. Hollander. Austin: 1964.
[Into Swedish]: *Nordiska kungasagor.* 3 vols. Transl. Karl G. Johansson. Stockholm: 1991.

Halvdanar saga svarta: see *Heimskringla*

Ynglinga saga: see *Heimskringla*

Poetic Edda

Edda: Die Lieder des Codex Regius nebst verwandten Denkmälern. Ed. Gustav Neckel and Hans Kuhn. 5th ed. Heidelberg: 1983.

<small>TRANSLATION</small>

The Poetic Edda. Transl. Carolyne Larrington. Oxford World's Classics. Oxford: 1996.

Vǫlundarkviða: see *Poetic Edda*

Prose Edda

<small>TRANSLATION</small>

Snorri Sturluson. *Edda.* Ed. and transl. Anthony Faulkes. London, Vermont: 1995.

Samnordisk Runtextdatabas
Online at http://www.runforum.nordiska.uu.se/samnord/

Þiðreks saga af Bern

Þiðreks saga af Bern. Ed. Henrik Bertelsen. Samfund til Udgivelse af Gammel Nordisk Litteratur, 34. Copenhagen: 1905–1911.

TRANSLATION

The Saga of Thidrek of Bern. Transl. Edward R. Haymes. New York: 1988.

Velents þáttr smiðs see *Þiðreks saga*

Vǫluspá: see *Poetic Edda*

Secondary Sources

Andrén, Anders. 2004. "Mission Impossible? The Archaeology of Norse Religion." In *Belief in the Past: The Proceedings of the 2002 Manchester Conference on Archaeology and Religion.* Ed. Timothy Insoll. BAR International Series, 1212. Oxford. Pp. 7–16.

———. 2007. "Behind *Heathendom*: Archaeological Studies of Old Norse Religion." *Scottish Archaeological Journal* 27: 105–38.

———. 2014. *Tracing Old Norse Cosmology: The World Tree, Middle Earth and the Sun in Archaeological Perspectives.* Vägar till Midgård, 16. Lund.

Andrén, Anders, Catharina Raudvere, and Kristina Jennbert, eds. *Old Norse Religion in Long-Term Perspectives: Origins, Changes and Interactions.* Vägar till Midgård, 8. Lund.

Arne, Ture Algot Johnsson. 1934. *Das Bootgräberfeld von Tuna in Alsike, Uppland.* Kungliga Vitterhets Historie och antikvitets akademien monografier, 20. Stockholm.

Arrhenius, Birgit. 1969. "Zum symbolischer Zinn des Almandin im frühen Mittelalter." *Frühmittelalterliche Studien* 3: 47–59.

Arrhenius, Birgit, and Henry Freij. 1992. "'Pressbleck' Fragments from the East Mound in Old Uppsala Analysed with a Laser Scanner." *Laborativ arkeologi* 6: 75–110.

Arvidsson, Maria. 1999. *Kön, Släktskap och Diet: Molekulära Analyser av Individerna på Båtgravfältet i Tuna i Alsike.* MA thesis, Stockholm University.

Arwidsson, Greta. 1942. *Valsgärde 6: Die Gräberfunde von Valsgärde 1.* Acta Musei antiquitatum septentrionalium Regiae Universitatis Upsaliensis, 1. Uppsala.

———. 1954. *Valsgärde 8: Die Gräberfunde von Valsgärde 2.* Acta Musei antiquitatum septentrionalium Regiae Universitatis Upsaliensis, 4. Uppsala.

Axboe, Morten. 2012. "Late Roman and Migration Period Sites in Southern Scandinavia with Archaeological Evidence of the Activity of Gold and Silver Smiths." In Pesch and Blankenfeld 2012: 123–42.

Axboe, Morten, and Magnus Källström. 2013. "Guldbrakteater fra Trollhättan— 1844 og 2009." *Fornvännen* 108: 153–71.

Becker, Alfred. 1973. *Franks Casket: Zum Runenkästchen von Auzon.* Regensburger Arbeiten zur Anglistik und Amerikanistik, 5. Regensburg.

———. 2012. *Franks casket.* http://www.franks-casket.de (accessed on May 5, 2014).

Buisson, Ludwig. 1976. *Der Bildstein Ardre VIII auf Gotland: Göttermythen, Heldensagen und Jenseitsglaube der Germanen im 8. Jahrhundert n. Chr.* Abhandlungen der Akademie der Wissenschaften in Göttingen. Philologisch-historische Klasse, F. 3, 102. Göttingen.

Callmer, Johan. 2002. "Wayland: An Essay on Craft Production in the Early and High Middle Ages in Scandinavia." In *Centrality and Regionality: The Social Structure of Southern Sweden during the Iron Age.* Ed. Lars Larsson and Birgitta Hårdh. Uppåkra studies, 7. Stockholm. Pp. 337–61.

Carstens, Lydia. 2012. "Might and Magic: The Smith in Old Norse Literature." In Pesch and Blankenfeld 2012: 243–69.

Danstrup, John, et al., eds. 1956–1978. *Kulturhistorisk lexikon för nordisk medeltid.* 22 vols. Copenhagen.

Domeij Lundborg, Maria. 2006. "Bound Animal Bodies: Ornamentation and Scaldic Poetry in the Process of Christianization." In Andrén, Raudvere, and Jennbert 2006: 39–44.

Ericson, Per G. P., and Tommy Tyrberg. 2004. *The Early History of the Swedish Avifauna: A Review of the Sub-fossil Record and Early Written Sources.* Kungliga Vitterhets Historie och Antikvitets Akademien handlingar, antikvariska serien, 45. Stockholm.

Gerritsen, Fokke. 1999. "To Build and to Abandon." *Archaeological dialogues* 6: 78–97.

Götherström, Anders. 2001. *Acquired or Inherited Prestige? Molecular Studies of Family Structures and Local Horses in Central Svealand during the Early Medieval Period.* Theses and Papers in Scientific Archaeology, 4. Stockholm.

Grieg, Sigurd. 1947. *Gjermundbufunnet: En hövdingegrav fra 900-årene fra Ringerike.* Norske oldfunn, 8. Oslo.

Gustafsson, Björn Ny. 2015. "Är Uppåkra-Völund näsbärgan till en hjälm?" *Fornvännen* 110: 286–88.

Hållans Stenholm, Ann-Marie. 2012. *Fornminnen: Det förflutnas roll i det förkristna och kristna Mälardalen.* Vägar till Midgård, 15. Lund.

Hårdh, Birgitta. 2004. "The Metal Beaker with Embossed Foil Bands." In Larsson 2004: 49–92.

———. 2010. "Case Study 2: Uppåkra – Lund. A Central Place and a Town? Western Scania in the Viking Age." In *Trade and Communication Networks of the First Millenium AD in the Northern Part of Central Europe: Central Places,*

Beach Markets, Landing Places and Trading Centers. Ed. Babette Ludowici et al. Neue Studien zur Sachsenforschung, 1. Hannover. Pp. 101–11.

Hårdh, Birgitta, and Lars Larsson. 2007. *Uppåkra—Lund före Lund.* Gamla Lunds årsskrift. Lund.

Hauck, Karl. 1970. *Goldbrakteatern aus Sievern: Spätantike Amulett-Bilder der 'Dania Saxonia' und Sachsen-'origo' bei Widukind von Corvey.* Münsterische Mittelalter-Schriften, 1. Munich.

Helgesson, Bertil. 2004. "Tributes to be Spoken of: Sacrifice and Warriors at Uppåkra." In Larsson 2004: 223–39.

Helmbrecht, Michaela. 2011. *Wirkmächtige Kommunikationsmedien—Menschenbilder det Vendel- und Wikingerzeit und ihre Kontexte.* Acta Archaeologica Lundensia, Series Prima in Quarto, 30. Lund.

———. 2012. "A Winged Figure from Uppåkra." *Fornvännen* 107: 171–78.

Herschend, Frands. 1996. *The Idea of the Good.* OPIA, 15. Uppsala.

Hjulström, Björn. 2008. *Patterns in Diversity.* Theses and Papers in Scientific Archaeology, 11. Stockholm.

Hoops, Johannes et al., eds. 2006. *Waagen und Gewichte—Wielandlied.* Vol. 33 of *Reallexikon der Germanischen Altertumskunde.* 2nd ed. Berlin.

Imer, Lisbeth. 2001. "Gotlandske billedsten—dateringen af Lindqvists gruppe C og D." *Aarbøger for nordisk oldkyndighed og historie* 2001 (published 2004): 47–111.

Insley, John. 2006. "Wieland § 3." In Hoops et al. 2006: 618–22.

Kresten, Peter, Eva Hjärtner-Holdar, and Hans Harryson. 2001. "Metallurgi i Uppåkra: Smältor och halvfabrikat." In *Uppåkra—centrum i analys och rapport.* Ed. Lars Larsson and Birgitta Hårdh. Acta Archaeologica Lundensia. Series in 8°, 36. Uppåkrastudier, 4. Lund. Pp. 149–66.

Kristoffersen, Siv. 2012. "Brooches, Bracteates and a Goldsmith's Grave." In Pesch and Blankenfeld 2012: 207–14.

Lamm, Kristina. 2012. "Helgö as a Gold Smiths' Workshop in Migration Period Sweden." In Pesch and Blankenfeld 2012: 123–42.

Larsson, Gunilla. 2007. *Ship and Society: Maritime ideology in Late Iron Age Sweden.* Aun, 37. Uppsala.

Larsson, Lars, ed. 2004. *Continuity for Centuries: A Ceremonial Building and Its Context at Uppåkra, Southern Sweden.* Uppåkrastudier, 10. Lund.

———. 2007. "Rum, rymd och areal, ett kulthus och dess närmiljö ur ett cere-moniellt perspektiv." *Bebyggelsehistorisk tidskrift* 52: 7–19.

Larsson, Lars. 2015. "Expressions of Cosmology at the Central Place of Uppåkra, Southern Sweden." In *Dying Gods. Religious Beliefs in Northern and Eastern Europe in the Time of Christianisation.* Ed. Christiane Ruhmann and Vera Brieske. Neue Studien zur Sachsenforschung 5. Hannover. Pp. 145–158.

Larsson, Lars, and Bengt Söderberg. 2012. *Vetenskapligt program för de arkeologiska undersökningarna av fornlämning raä 5, Stora Uppåkra socken, Staffanstorps kommun, Skåne.* Rapporter från Insitutionen för arkeologi och antikens kultur, Lunds universitet, 9. Lund.

———. 2013. "Brända hallar—diskontinuitet och kontinuitet." *Fornvännen* 108: 238–48.

Larsson, Lars, and Birgitta Hårdh. 1998. "Uppåkra ett hövdinga—eller kungasäte." *Fornvännen* 92: 139–54.

Larsson, Lars, and Karl-Magnus Lenntorp. 2004. "The Enigmatic House." In Larsson 2004: 3–48.

Lidén, Kerstin, and Erle. D. Nelson. 1994. "Stable Carbon Isotopes as Dietary Indicator, in the Baltic Area." *Fornvännen* 89: 13–21.

Lindqvist, Sune. 1925. "Vendelhjälmarnas ursprung." *Fornvännen* 20: 181–207.

———. 1941–1942. *Gotlands Bildsteine.* 2 vols. Kungliga Vitterhets Historie och Antikvitets Akademien Monografier, 28. Stockholm.

Ljungkvist, John. 2008. "Dating of the Two Royal Mounds of Old Uppsala: Evaluating the Elite of the 6th–7th century in Middle Sweden." *Archäologisches Korrespondenzblatt* 38: 263–82.

———. 2009. "Continental Imports in Scandinavia: Patterns and Changes between AD 400–800." In *Foreigners in Early Medieval Europe: Thirteen Studies International Studies on Early Medieval Mobility.* Ed. Dieter Quast. Monographien des Römisch-Germanischen Zentralmuseums, 78. Mainz. Pp. 27–50.

———. 2010. "Influences from the Empire Byzantine—Related Objects in Sweden and Scandinavia—560/70–750/800 AD." In *Byzanz—Das Römerreich im Mittelalter. Peripherie und Nachbarschaft* 3. Ed. Falko Daim and Jörg Drauschke. Monographien des Römisch-Germanischen Zentralmuseums, 84: 3. Mainz. Pp. 419–41.

Ljungkvist, John et al. 2011. "Gamla Uppsala: Structural Development of a Centre in Middle Sweden." *Archäologisches Korrespondenzblatt* 41: 571–85.

Lönnroth, Lars. 1986. "Dómaldi's Death and the Myth of the Sacral Kingship." In *Structure and Meaning in Old Norse Literature.* Ed. John Lindow, Lars Lönnroth, and Gerd W. Weber. Viking Collection, 3. Odense. Pp. 73–93.

Magnell, Ola. 2011. "Sacred Cows or Old Beasts? A Taphonomic Approach to Studying Ritual Killing with an Example from Iron Age Uppåkra, Sweden." In *The Ritual Killing and Burial of Animals: European Perspectives.* Ed. Aleksander Pluskowski. Oxford. Pp. 192–204.

Marold, Edith. 1966. *Der Schmied in germanischen Altertum.* Vienna.

————. 1996. "Die erzählstruktur des Velentsþáttr." In *Hansische Literaturbeziehungen: Das Beispiel der Þiðreks saga und verwandter Literatur. Ergänzungsband der Germanischen Altertumskunde.* Ed. Susanne Kramarz-Bein. Berlin. Pp. 53–73.

————. 2012. "Mytische Schmiede in deutcher und skandinavischer Sagentradition." In Pesch and Blankenfeld 2012: 279–332.

Martens, Irmelin. 2004. "Indigenous and Imported Viking Age Weapons in Norway—A Problem with European Implications." *Journal of Nordic Archaeological Science* 14: 125–37.

Nedoma, Robert. 1988. *Die bildlichen und schriftlichen Denkmäler der Wielandsage.* Göttingen.

————. 2006. "Wieland § 2." In Hoops et al. 2006: 608–18.

Nylén, Erik, and Bengt Schönbeck. 1994. *Tuna i Badelunda: guld, kvinnor, båtar.* Västerås kulturnämnds skriftserie. Västerås.

Öberg, Herje. 1942. *Guldbrakteaterna från Nordens folkvandringstid.* Kungliga Vitterhets- Historie- och Antikvitets Akademiens handlingar, 53. Stockholm.

Oerhl, Sigmund. 2011. *Vierbeinerdarstellungen auf schwedischen Runensteinen: Studien zur nordgermanischen Tier- und Fesselungsikonografie.* Berlin.

————. 2012. "Bildische darstellungen vom Schmied Wieland und ein unerwarteter Auftritt in Walhall." In Pesch and Blankenfeld 2012: 279–332.

Oxenstierna, Erik. 1956. *Die Goldhörner von Gallehus.* Lidingö.

Pesch, Alexandra, and Ruth Blankenfeld, eds. *Goldsmith Mysteries: Archaeological, Pictorial and Documentary Evidence from the 1st millennium AD in Northern Europe. Papers Presented at a Workshop Organized by the Centre for Baltic and Scandinavian Archaeology (ZBSA), Schleswig, October 20th and 21st, 2011.* Schriften des Archäologischen Landesmuseums. Ergänzungsreihe, 8. Neumünster.

Price, Neil. 2006. "What's in a Name?" In Andrén, Raudvere, and Jennbert 2006: 179–83.

Price, Neil, and Mortimer, Paul. 2014. "An Eye for Odinn? Divine Role-Playing in the Age of Sutton Hoo." *European Journal of Archaeology* 2014: 1–22.

Salin, Bernhard. 1913. "Några ord om en Fröbild." In *Opuscula Archaeologica Oscari Montelii.* Stockholm. Pp. 405–12.

von See, Klaus et al., eds. 2000. *Götterlieder.* Vol. 3 of *Kommentar zu den Liedern der Edda.* Heidelberg.

Söderberg, Bengt. 2005. *Aristokratiska rum och gränsöverskridande: Järrestad och sydöstra Skåne mellan region och rike 600-1100.* Arkeologiska undersökningar. Skrifter, 62. Riksantikvarieämbetet. Stockholm.

Staecker, Jørn. 2004. "Hjältar, kungar och gudar: Receptionen av bibliska element och av hjältediktning i en hednisk värld." In *Minne och myt: konsten att skapa det förflutna*. Ed. Anders Andrén, Catharina Raudvere, and Kristina Jennbert. Vägar till Midgård, 5. Lund. Pp. 39–78.

Stephens, George. 1867–1868. *The Old-Northern Runic Monuments of Scandinavia and England.* Vol. 2. London.

Stjernqvist, Berta. 2004. "A Glass Beaker with Cut Decoration, Found at Uppåkra." In Larsson 2004: 153–66.

Stolpe, Hjalmar, and Ture Johnsson Arne. 1912. *Graffältet vid Vendel.* Kungliga Vitterhets Historie och Antikvitets Akademien Monografier, 3. Stockholm.

Sundqvist, Olof. 2002. *Freyr's Offspring: Rulers and Religion in Ancient Svea Society.* Acta Universitatis Upsaliensis, 21. Historia Religionum, 21. Uppsala.

———. 2003. "The Problem of Religious Specialists and Cult Performers in Early Scandinavia." *Zeitschrift für Religionswissenschaft*: 107–31.

———. 2007. *Kultledare i fornskandinavisk religion.* OPIA, 41. Institutionen för arkeologi och antik historia. Uppsala.

Thunmark-Nylén, Lena. 2006. *Die Wikingerzeit Gotlands.* Vol. 3:1. Stockholm.

Stiftelsen Uppåkra Arkeologiska Center. 2012. *Uppåkra en järnåldersstad.* Säsongen 2012. Staffanstorp.

"Ur främmande samlingar." 1907. *Fornvännen* 2: 205–08.

Webster, Leslie. 2012. *The Franks Casket.* British Museum: Objects in focus. London.

Wilson, David. 1995. *Vikingatidens konst.* Lund.

Yorke, Barbara. Emeritus Professor of Early Medieval History at the University of Winchester. Personal communication, September 2013.

Zachrisson, Inger. 1997. "Skrivet och sagt." In *Möten i gränsland: Samer och germaner i Mellanskandinavien.* Ed. Inger Zachrisson et al. Statens Historiska Museum Monographs, 4. Stockholm. Pp. 158–75.

———. 2006. "Magiska pilar och mystiska tecken, något om samer och järn." *Med hammare och fackla* 39: 25–35.

———. 2012. "Samer i syd i gången tid—till Uppland och Oslotrakten i söder. Ny forskning från Norge och Sverige." In *Uppsala mitt i Sápmi: Rapport från ett symposium arrangerat av Föreningen för Sámiskrelaterad forskning i Uppsala, Upplandsmuseet 4-5 maj 2011.* Ed. Håkan Tunón et al. CBM:s skriftserie, 55. Uppsala. Pp. 8–12.

Zachrisson, Torun. 2009. "Vetenskapligt program." In *Stiftelsen Kulturmiljövård Mälardalen Vetenskapligt program 2009.* Ed. Anna Lihammer. Västerås. Pp. 23–143.

———. 2010. "Kungsämnen i Söderby och kungens Sigtuna: Om den materiella kulturen i och kring Söderby i Danmarks socken." *Situne dei*, 2010: 163–75.

The Temple, the Tree, and the Well

A *Topos* or Cosmic Symbolism at Cultic Sites in Pre-Christian Northern Europe?

Olof Sundqvist
Stockholm University

Abstract: Revisiting the sanctuary in Uppsala described by Adam of Bremen in the *Gesta Hammaburgensis Ecclesiae Pontificum*, this essay finds additional evidence from a comparison with West Slavic materials, and argues that the mythic elements rendered by the cultic site (Valhǫll, Yggdrasill and the well of Urðr) are based on a real cultic topography rather than literary sources. It further emphasizes that Uppsala was not solely a cultic center, but also a political and economic center and that the mythological-cosmological structures of the sanctuary were used to support the authority of rulers.

Introduction

Detailed, reliable Old Norse sources relating to sanctuaries in pre-Christian Northern Europe are rare.[1] Fortunately, an especially significant Latin text on this subject exists, namely, the description of the "Uppsala temple" in Adam of Bremen's famous chronicle, *Gesta Hammaburgensis Ecclesiae Pontificum*, written ca. 1075.[2] Even if Adam's information of the ninth and tenth centuries must be treated with some caution (cf. Reuter 2002: xi), this chronicle is regarded as the main historical source for eleventh-century Scandinavia, including the medieval region of Svetjud, a Swedish kingdom of somewhat uncertain geographical extent (cf. Sawyer 1991: 16–19). Adam's text was written in the genre called

---

[1] This essay synthesizes, builds on, and extends several previously published works in Swedish and English, including Sundqvist 2002, 2004, 2007, 2013, and 2016.

[2] On Adam and his work, see e.g. the (new) introduction to Francis J. Tschan's translation of Adam's work, *History of the Archbishops of Hamburg-Bremen* (2002).

gesta episcoporum "the deeds of bishops". Thus, it recorded the campaign made by the Hamburg-Bremen archbishopric to convert Slavic and Scandinavian peoples. This chronicle is preserved in several medieval manuscripts; however, the relationship between them is very complex (Nyberg 1984: 302–7). Bernhard Schmeidler divided them into three classes in *Monumenta Germaniae Historica*: class A, class B, and class C (*Gesta Hammaburgensis*). The oldest manuscript, dated to ca. 1100 CE, is commonly called A2, or the "Leiden manuscript" (Cod. Voss. Lat. 4º 123). Although the first three books in this manuscript are fragmentary, Book 4, where Adam's description of the Uppsala sanctuary appears, is complete. All additional notes (*scholia*) relating to the chapters about the sanctuary are present in this manuscript; however, the relationship between *scholia* and the main text is quite complicated (cf. Hultgård 1997a: 915; Sundqvist 2016: 110).

Book 4, *Descriptio insularum aquilonis*, consists of, as the title suggests, an ethno-geographical description of the Nordic world. Adam details the successes of the Hamburg-Bremen diocese's missionary activities in this region as well as the missionary work remaining to be done. In his estimation, the sanctuary at Uppsala is the final obstacle standing in the way of the victory of Christianity in the land of the Svear (Hallencreutz 1997; Sundqvist 2016). In 4, 26, we are thus told about Uppsala (or actually Ubsola[3]):

> Nobilissimum illa gens templum habet, quod Ubsola dicitur, non longe positum ab Sictona civitate. In hoc templo, quod totum ex auro paratum est, statuas trium deorum veneratur populus, ita ut potentissimus eorum Thor in medio solium habeat triclinio; hinc et inde locum possident Wodan et Fricco. Quorum significationes eiusmodi sunt "Thor", inquiunt, "presidet in aere, qui tonitrus et fulmina, ventos ymbresque, serena et fruges gubernat. Alter Wodan, id est furor, bella gerit hominique ministrat virtutem contra inimicos. Tercius est Fricco, pacem voluptatemque largiens mortalibus". Cuius etiam simulacrum fingunt cum ingenti priapo. Wodanem vero sculpunt armatum, sicut nostri Martem solent; Thor autem cum sceptro Iovem simulare videtur. Colunt et deos ex hominibus factos, quos pro ingentibus factis immortalitate donant, sicut in Vita sancti Ansgarii legitur Hericum regem fecisse. (*Gesta Hammaburgensis* 4, 26)

---

[3] Despite objections in previous research, few scholars hesitate today to relate Ubsola to the place called Old Uppsala (Gamla Uppsala) in the contemporary province of Uppland, Sweden. Sictona is usually related to Sigtuna, situated in the same province. This town was founded ca. 970 (Hultgård 1997a: 13).

(That folk [the Svear] has a very famous temple called Uppsala (Ubsola), situated not far from the city of Sigtuna (Sictona). In this temple, entirely decked out in gold, the people worship the statues of three gods in such wise that the mightiest of them, Thor (Þórr), occupies a throne in the middle of the chamber; Wodan (Óðinn) and Fricco (Freyr) have places on either side. The significance of these gods is as follows: Thor, they say, presides over the air, which governs the thunder and lightning, the winds and rains, fair weather and crops. The other, Wodan—that is, the Furious—carries on war and imparts to man strength against his enemies. The third is Fricco, who bestows peace and pleasure on mortals. His likeness, too, they fashion with an immense phallus. But Wodan they chisel armed, as our people are wont to represent Mars. Thor with his sceptre apparently resembles Jove. The people also worship heroes made gods, whom they endow with immortality because of their remarkable exploits, as one reads in the *Vita* of Saint Ansgar they did in the case of King Eric.)[4]

Scholion 138 provides further information concerning the area near of the temple:

Prope illud templum est arbor maxima late ramos extendens, semper viridis in hieme et aestate, cuius illa generis sit, nemo scit. Ibi etiam est fons, ubi sacrificia paganorum solent exerceri et homo vivus inmergi. Qui dum non invenitur, ratum erit votum populi. (*Gesta Hammaburgensis* scholion 138)

(Near this temple stands a very large tree with wide-spreading branches, always green winter and summer. What kind it is nobody knows. There is also a spring at which the pagans are accustomed to make their sacrifices, and into it to plunge a live man. And if he is not found, the people's wish will be granted.)[5]

Scholion 139 describes the temple building and its surroundings in more detail:

Catena aurea templum circumdat pendens supra domus fastigia lateque rutilans advenientibus, eo quod ipsum delubrum in planitie situm

---

[4] The text is from Bernhard Schmeidler's 1917 edition. Translation by Francis J. Tschan 2002, but slightly modified.

[5] This scholion as well as scholia 139–41 are preserved in the oldest manuscript A2 (ca.1100). See Hultgård 1997a: 15. The last sentence in scholion 141 (*hoc sacrificium fit circa aequinoctium vernale*) is only attested late in the tradition of manuscripts, more precisely in manuscript A3 from 1434 (Hultgård 1997a: 30).

montes in circuitu habet positos ad instar theatri. (*Gesta Hammaburgensis* scholion 139)

(A golden chain goes round the temple. It hangs over the gable of the building and sends its glitter far off to those who approach, because the shrine stands on level ground with mountains all about it like a theatre.)

In 4, 27, the cultic activities are described in more detail as well as the ritual places where the sacrifices took place:

Sacrificium itaque tale est ex omni animante, quod masculinum est, novem capita offeruntur, quorum sanguine deos [tales] placari mos est. Corpora autem suspenduntur in lucum, qui proximus est templo. Is enim lucus tam sacer est gentilibus, ut singulae arbores eius ex morte vel tabo immolatorum divinae credantur. Ibi etiam canes et equi pendent cum hominibus, quorum corpora mixtim suspensa narravit mihi aliquis christianorum LXXII vidisse. (*Gesta Hammaburgensis* 4, 27)

(The sacrifice is of this nature: of every living thing that is male, they offer nine heads, with the blood of which it is customary to placate gods of this sort. The bodies they hang in the sacred grove that adjoins the temple. Now this grove is so sacred in the eyes of the heathen that each and every tree in it is believed divine because of the death or putrefaction of the victims. Even dogs and horses hang there with men. A certain Christian informed me he had seen seventy-two miscellaneous bodies suspended there.)

In examining Adam's account of the Uppsala sanctuary, including the scholia, one readily forms the impression that the cultic site was comprised of several ritual places and cultic elements. In addition to the temple building itself and the holy grove, where the sacrificial objects were hung, a specific holy tree and a spring are mentioned. During the springtime, Adam informs us, the pagans made their human sacrifices. An additional note (scholion 139) states that the shrine (*delubrum*) stands on level ground, surrounded by mountains (*montes*). In my opinion it is not impossible that Adam had, in fact, heard about the royal funeral mounds situated in Old Uppsala when he describes these "mountains" as located close to the sanctuary (see Sundqvist 2016: 436).

Adam's description of the Uppsala sanctuary is without doubt a highly controversial resource in today's research environment. In the past, some historians of religion and other scholars made the argument that his testimony was reliable since it was contemporary with the events it described.[6] In fact, Adam based his text on secondary information, although his informants were eyewitnesses. The Danish king, Svein Estridsson (in Old Norse, Sveinn Ástriðarson, also called Sveinn Úlfsson), was one of them. As it happened, in his youth, during the reign of the Swedish king Anund Jacob (perhaps around the 1030s and 1040s), the king had lived in exile among the Svear for about 12 years; thus, King Svein was likely quite familiar indeed with the customs of the Svear, at least during the period he was among them. Most likely, Bishop Adalvard the Younger of Sigtuna was also an important informant for Adam regarding the sanctuary at Uppsala (Sundqvist 2016: 121). Recent research, however, has turned more skeptical, arguing that Adam's text is permeated with rhetorical embellishments and missionary strategies.[7] Some scholars have also found mythical elements in it (Bruun and Finnur Jónsson 1909; Alkarp 1997, 2007). The temple, the tree and the well, for instance, are actually descriptions of a mythical landscape, i.e., a literary *topos* found in Old Norse traditions. These authorities argue that Adam misunderstood the mythical traditions surrounding Valhǫll, Yggdrasill, and the well of Urðr and confused them with reality. Therefore, they believe that Adam's text cannot be accepted as a trustworthy source on Viking Age sanctuaries.

In my opinion, these connections may lead to another conclusion. In what follows, I will argue that the mythical references in Adam's description render a cultic reality. The temple, the tree, and the well may deliberately have been arranged as a reminder of the mythical landscape. This is not unique to Uppsala, as this same practice can be seen at cultic places in other parts of Scandinavia and on the Continent as well. In my opinion, these cosmic references in Uppsala had significance for local rulers. Uppsala was not only a place for the famous temple, it was also a political and economic center. The rulers of Uppsala used mythical traditions about the cosmos and the divine world in order to gain

---

[6] See e.g. de Vries 1956–1957: §290. See also Nils Lid, who stated: "Ein må gå ut frå at dei einskilde ting Adam fortel om, har eit faktisk grunnlag" (Lid 1942: 86) (One must assume that the specific things Adam speaks of have a factual basis). Folke Ström wrote: "I en berömd och ofta citerad skildring har Adam av Bremen återgett ett ögonvittnes berättelse om de offer och ceremonier som utspelades i Uppsala vart nionde år" (Ström 1985: 79) (In a famous and oft-cited account Adam of Bremen cites an eyewitness account of the sacrifices and ceremonies that took place every nine years in Uppsala), while Anne Holtsmark argued: "Detta är en autentisk skildring av gudadyrkan i Norden i slutet av den hedniska tiden" (Holtsmark 1992: 17). For a more thorough survey of the debate, see Sundqvist 2016: 113–27.

[7] E.g. Hallencreutz 1997; Hultgård 1997a; Göthberg and Lovén 2010. For a very radical opinion about Adam's text, see Henrik Janson's work. Janson argues that that the account of the sanctuary in Uppsala should not be read literally but as a satirical attack on the Gregorians who opposed Adam's friend, Archbishop Liemar of Hamburg-Bremen (Janson 1997, 1998). Critically considered by e.g. Sundqvist 2002, 2013, 2016 and Reuter 2002.

legitimacy and power. For instance, the members of the famous family of the Ynglings viewed themselves as the god Freyr's offspring (Sundqvist 2002, 2004, 2007, 2013, 2016).

Theory and Methods

That the sanctuary at Uppsala might mirror cosmic elements of Svea religion is an idea largely derived from Mircea Eliade, who argues that temples, cult places, and towns in several societies reflect mythical symbolism (Eliade 1974, 1987, 1991 (1949)). In his famous book, *The Myth of the Eternal Return*, Eliade writes:

> The temple in particular—pre-eminently the sacred place—had a celestial prototype. On Mount Sinai, Jehovah shows Moses the "form" of the sanctuary that he is to build for him [...] And when David gives his son Solomon the plan for the temple buildings, for the tabernacle, and for all their utensils, he assures him that "All this [...] the Lord made me understand in writing by his hand upon me, even all the works of this pattern" (I Chronicles 28: 19). Hence he had seen the celestial model. (Eliade 1991: 7)

Such symbolism is evident in several cultures around the world, according to Eliade (for instance, in early Christian basilicas and medieval cathedrals). Modern scholarship sometimes views Eliade's ideas as problematic, criticizing him for his universal perspectives and for his general inattentiveness to specific cultural contexts (e.g., Flood 1999; Smith 2000; Hellman 2011; Sundqvist 2016). A number of scholars also point out, and disagree with, Eliade's apolitical and decontextualized interpretation of cosmic myths (e.g., Smith 1987; McCutcheon 1997). Despite these criticisms, Eliade's basic idea about cosmic symbolism at sanctuaries need not be rejected in a general sense in comparative studies, since different specialists have observed similar phenomena in many cultures and religions (see, e.g., Widengren 1961: 87f. and 1969: 340ff.), including ancient Scandinavia (e.g., Hedeager 2001 and 2011).

Still, there are other problems with Eliade's approach for a Scandinavianist, mainly concerning the sources, insofar as detailed descriptions of cosmology and mythical landscapes are not preserved in Eastern Scandinavian traditions. Accounts of this type are known only in West Norse texts, those written down in thirteenth- and fourteenth-century Iceland. We cannot know how accurately these materials describe phenomena outside of medieval Iceland, or whether such things ever existed in Viking Age Uppsala. Nothing like a centralized pre-Christian religious institution existed, nor was there an organized priesthood similar to the *sacerdotes* of the Roman Catholic Church that could have formulated normative worldviews, a "canon" of mythical accounts, or "official" ritual practices throughout Scandinavia (Sundqvist 2016: 204, 163–98).

On the other hand, one can easily imagine that certain religious themes spread over wide geographic areas and were stable over time. Ideas and concepts of this sort might have been transmitted by aristocrats who made contact with each other via marriages, (cultic) feastings in halls, law meetings, gift-giving systems, and trade. Is it possible to discover whether such mythic-cosmic aspects are indeed embedded in the landscape? Perhaps we can find out by using a method that employs not only the mythic traditions preserved in medieval Icelandic texts, with their various problems, but also the evidence of the ritual structure at Uppsala, in comparison with other cultic sites as preserved in different kinds of sources.

In other words, a comparison of several well-established Iron Age sanctuaries, as evidenced in different types of source materials related to Scandinavia and Germanic Europe, should reveal recurrent elements and features from which we could justifiably draw conclusions about the sites' central or common character. In my opinion, such configurations reflect aspects of a "common cultural model", used by those constructing the sanctuary. These actual cultic configurations—empirical, material, and visible—should thus be understood to relate in some sense to a common cosmology, that is, general ideas of how mythical and human cultic sites were to be structured and conceived. Very likely, the material nature of such sites was intended to express the mythical world in the first place.[8] These early manifestations of what a mythical sanctuary should be like increasingly served as prototypes or models of what a cultic site should be like and were subsequently projected on all later constructions of ritual structures in the real world (Sundqvist 2016: 204).

Turning to Adam's description of the site and the scholarly discussion of whether there are connections between myth and the real cultic topography of Uppsala, I want to set Adam's text against available archaeological evidence in Old Uppsala. And, finally, I will turn to descriptions and archaeological evidence of other cultic sites in order to see if Uppsala reflects a common model. The comparisons that will be made in the present study are restricted to what Jens Peter Schjødt calls the first two levels of comparison, i.e., comparisons

---

[8] Whether the ritual landscape was based on a mythical model created in a pre-material way, or the mythic traditions were composed with the mundane sanctuaries in mind, is actually impossible to say. Surely a centuries-old reflexive action of mutual influence between the mythic and the physical is the explanation. The major point here is that both myths and sanctuaries were structured according to a common model or broad tradition. On the theories of materiality and the ontological turn in the study of religion, see, e.g., Miller 2005; Henare et al. 2007; Engelke 2012. In this new scholarly tradition, the significance of material culture is emphasized while the meaning behind the things is toned down.

with information from the Scandinavians and their neighbors, in this case, the Germanic people living in the south and the people living in the West Slavic areas, just across the Baltic Sea in the Southeast.[9]

The Temple

In Book 4, 26, as quoted above, Adam describes the temple at Uppsala as being totally adorned with gold. Inside it, the people worship statues of three gods. The mightiest of them, Thor (Þórr), has his throne in the middle, and Wodan (Óðinn) and Fricco (Freyr) sit on either side. In a marginal note, we are told that a golden chain surrounds the temple, hanging over the gables of the building, glowing brilliantly towards those who approach. This description (see above for more detail) resembles mythical conditions. In *Gylfaginning*, Snorri Sturluson describes a *hof*-building at a place called Glaðsheimr, which was decorated with nothing but gold:[10]

> Var þat hit fyrsta þeira verk at gera hof þat er sæti þeira standa í, tólf ǫnnur en hásætit þat er Alfǫðr á. Þat hús er bezt gert á jǫrðu ok mest. Allt er þat útan ok innan svá sem gull eitt. (*Gylfaginning* ch. 14)

> (It was their [the gods] first act to build the temple that their thrones stand in, twelve in addition to the throne that belongs to All-father [Óðinn]. This building is the best that is built on earth and the biggest. Outside and inside it seems like nothing but gold.)

This building seems to be identical with "the gold-bright Valhǫll" mentioned in the eddic poem *Grímnismál* in stanzas 8 and 23:[11]

> Glaðsheimr heitir inn fimti, þars en gullbiarta,
> Valhǫll víð of þrumir (*Grímnismál* st. 8)
> (Glaðsheimr a fifth is called,
> there gold-bright Valhǫll
> rises peacefully, seen from afar)

---

[9]   Schjødt differs between comparisons on four levels: (1) comparisons with information from the Scandinavian (Old Norse) speaking areas; (2) comparisons with neighbouring cultures of Scandinavia (e.g. Sámi peoples in the North, the Germanic people in the South); (3) comparisons with Indo-European speaking areas; and (4) comparative study of religious phenomena, i.e. world-wide comparisons (Schjødt 2012). In one sense the West Slavic areas also refer to comparisons with Indo-European speaking areas (level 3), since the Slavic language can be connected to this broad language family. In this case, however, I primarily regard the West Slavic people as neighbors to the Scandinavians when conducting comparisons.

[10]   Text from *Snorra Edda*, edited by Anthony Faulkes (1988). Translation by Faulkes 1987.

[11]   Text from The Poetic Edda by Neckel and Kuhn (1983). Translation by Caroline Larrington (2008).

Fimm hundruð dura oc um fiórom togom,
svá hygg ec at Valhǫllo vera (*Grímnismál* st. 23)
(Five hundred doors and forty
I think there are in Valhǫll)

The number of doors indicates that it is large and therefore can be seen from afar. As does the Uppsala temple, this house has seats for the deities. Óðinn has the high-seat there, and the *einherjar* (slain human heroes) can drink their fill there every day. According to chapter 36 of *Gylfaginning* and stanza 36 of *Grímnismál*, which is in fact quoted in Snorri's text, the valkyries (*valkyrjur*) serve ale to the *einherjar* there.

The parallels between the Uppsala temple and Valhǫll are striking. Most obviously, in both places the gods are enthroned in a mighty gold-adorned building. There are also other, subtler, similarities. When Adam described the temple in Uppsala, he probably did not aim at describing a building exclusively intended for idols and ritual objects. Behind the term *templum*, a great multi-functional hall building could be concealed, i.e., a room for banquets, which reminds one of Valhǫll. It has been noticed that Adam applied the term *triclinium* when describing the room where the idols stood (see Dillmann 1997). In both classical and medieval Latin, this term denotes "dining-room" and "room for ceremonial banquets". According to Adam, libation rituals were made to the three images there:

> Si pestis et fames imminet, Thor ydolo lybatur, si bellum, Wodani si nuptiae celebrandae sunt, Fricconi. (*Gesta Hammaburgensis* 4, 27)

> (If plague or famine is nigh, a libation is made to the idol of Thor, if war, to Wodan, if marriage is to be solemnized, to Fricco.)

In this quotation the Latin verb *libo* (< *libare*) must be interpreted in its more precise meaning, i.e. "to perform a libation sacrifice to the deity" (Dillmann 1997: 66). It thus seems as if the worship of the gods in the banqueting room (*triclinium*) was intimately associated with drinking rituals, perhaps with the ruler sitting in his high-seat. The sacrificial terminology (e.g. *libo*) used by Adam and the concept *triclinium* emphasize the connection between the Uppsala temple and Valhǫll further, i.e., as places where ritual drinking and ceremonial banquets were performed.[12]

---

[12] Scholars have also argued that the last element in the name *Uppsala* refers to "banqueting halls" (pl.). E.g. B. Gräslund 1993; Brink 1999: 38–39, 48–49n15; Herschend 2001: 39–60. For a more recent treatment on the name *Uppsala*, see Vikstrand 2013.

Archaeologists have found remains of structures in Old Uppsala that may be related to a ceremonial building. In 1926, Sune Lindquist discovered post-holes beneath the current stone church, which he interpreted as the remains of a rectangular temple. New investigations have shown, however, that this interpretation must be rejected (see Nordahl 1996). Remains of a Merovingian period hall north of the church were, however, discovered in the late 1980s (Nordahl 1996). It was located on a plateau and thus elevated in the landscape and visible from public roads; new excavations at Old Uppsala in the summer of 2011 indicate that the hall was 50 meters in length. This hall, however, burned down around 800 and therefore cannot be identical with the temple mentioned by Adam.

The hall in Uppsala had probably been embellished with spiral decorations, made in iron. It seems further that these spirals were deposited in the post-holes of the house and along the walls after the building burned down in the early Viking Age (Ljungkvist 2013; Ljungkvist and Frölund 2015; Sundqvist 2013, 2016). These decorations and ritual deposits indicate that the house had a special function. Even the discovery that the interior of the house was white-limed shows that it was special. Most likely this hall building was used for public meetings, including ceremonial banquets. Knowledge of this Merovingian period hall (or a subsequent hall in Uppsala not yet discovered) may have reached Adam through his informants and inspired his description of the temple.

In recent research, it has been emphasized that Iron Age halls had cultic functions in Scandinavia (Herschend 1993, 1998, 1999). Sometimes they appear at places with sacred place names, such as *Helgö* "the holy island", in Uppland, Sweden, and *Gudme* "the home/district of the gods", in Fyn, Denmark (on these names, see Vikstrand 2001; Brink 2011). Archaeological finds suggest that these buildings were occasionally adorned with gold, like Valhǫll. Melted gold was discovered in connection with one of the post-holes of the hall at Gudme. Frands Herschend has hypothesized that the posts at Gudme were decorated with gold, which melted in a fire and trickled into the post-hole (see Herschend in Anne-Sofie Gräslund 1997: 108–9). The Gudme hall was very large, about 50 meters in length, and probably visible from afar (Hedeager 2001, 2011; Jørgenssen 2009, 2011). The cultic hall of Helgö was smaller (ca. 21 meters long), but situated on a plateau, and thus located in an exposed position within the surrounding landscape. We may here recall that the large decorated Merovingian hall in Uppsala was similarly located on a plateau.

It thus appears that such hall buildings in Scandinavia typically occupied a prominent position in the landscape. It also stands to reason that the sovereignty of these halls was underscored and reinforced by their spectacular size, ornamentation, and architecture. Key, elevated—and thus highly visible—locations and great size were likely to have been associated with ideological elements and derived from a deliberate strategy of association with the divine and mythical world. Most of the features just enumerated in relation to ceremonial buildings and halls are to be seen in descriptions of such foundational "mythical houses" as Valhǫll. In *Grímnismál*, we hear, for instance, thus:

- er blíð regin silfri þǫcþo sali; Valasciálf heitir (where the cheerful Powers roofed the hall with silver; Valasciálf it is called) (st. 6)
- þars en gullbiarta Valhǫll víð of þrumir (there gold-bright Valhǫll rises peacefully) (st. 8)
- Breiðablic (the far-shining one) (st. 12)
- Glitnir (the shining one) (st. 15)

Perhaps these recurrent features and correspondences indicate an "ideal state", the existence of a "common model", and/or a cosmic symbolism of the ceremonial buildings in Uppsala and other late Iron Age cultic sites of Scandinavia (see also Sundqvist 2016: 205–19).

The Tree and the Well

As discussed above, in scholion 138 of *Gesta Hammaburgensis*, the author comments on the surroundings of the Uppsala temple, saying that near the temple there stands a very large tree with wide spreading branches, always green, whether winter or summer, and a spring at which the pagans make their sacrifices. This description also resembles information from mythical traditions about the Norse "world tree" Yggdrasill and its wells. According to Snorri's *Gylfaginning*, Yggdrasill was, of all trees, the biggest and the best:

> Askrinn [Yggdrasill] er allra tréa mestr ok beztr. Limar hans dreifask yfir heim allan ok standa yfir himni. Þrjár rœtr trésins halda því upp ok standa afar breitt [...] ok undir þeiri rót er Hvergelmir [...] En undir þeiri rót er til hrímþursa horfir, þar er Mímis brunnr [...] Þriðja rót asksins stendr á himni, ok undir þeiri rót er brunnr sá er mjǫk er heilagr er heitir Urðar brunnr. (*Gylfaginning* ch. 15)

> (The ash is of all trees the biggest and best. Its branches spread out over all the world and extend across the sky. Three of the tree's roots support it and extend very, very far [...] and under that root is Hvergelmir [...] But under the root that reaches towards the frost-giants, there is where Mímis brunnr is [...] The third root of the ash extends to heaven, and beneath that root is a well which is very holy called Urðar brunnr.)

From this description, it seems as if one of the tree's roots reached down towards *Mímis brunnr* (Mímir's well), where Óðinn deposited his eye in order to drink of the knowledge that the well contained, while a second root was located among the gods at *Urðar brunnr* (Urðr's well), and a third root ran down to the well called *Hvergelmir*. Even if Snorri meant to describe three different wells, these three springs are usually interpreted today as different names for one and the same mental image, that is, the cosmic well (see, e.g., Simek 2006: 167). It is worth noting that the tree and well are mentioned in eddic lays as being related to each other: in *Vǫluspá*, for example, it is said that the tree Yggdrasill is always green and stands beside the well of Urðr.

> Asc veit ec standa, heitir Yggdrasill,
> hár baðmr, ausinn hvítaauri;
> þaðan koma dǫggvar, þærs í dala falla,
> stendr æ yfir, grœnn, Urðar brunni. (*Vǫluspá* st. 19)
> (I know that an ash-tree,
> stands called Yggdrasill,
> a high tree, soaked
> with shining loam;
> from there come the dews
> which falls in the valleys,
> ever green, it stands over
> Urðr's well.)

According to *Hávamál*, Urðr's well was situated besides the "High-One's hall", i.e. Valhǫll:

> Mál er at þylia þular stóli á,
> Urðar brunni at;
> . . . .
> Háva hǫllo at, Háva hǫllo í;
> heyrða ec segia svá: (*Hávamál* st. 111)
>
> (It is time to declaim from the sage's high-seat,
> at Urðr's well;
> . . . .
> at the High One's hall, in the
> High One's hall;
> thus I heard them speak:)

These similarities between Uppsala and the mythical traditions have, as mentioned above, been taken by some scholars in the past as indications that

Adam based his account on myth and confused it with reality (e.g., Bruun and Finnur Jónsson 1909; Alkarp 1997).[13] Thus, they argue that Adam's account cannot be taken seriously. In opposition to this view, I think that Adam's description is reliable. The existence of trees and wells is very common to Germanic sacred sites. In the ecclesiastical polemics against pagan customs the expression *arbor et fons* "tree and spring" seems to announce a pagan cultic place. It appears in normative documents and letters from the sixth century to the *capitularia* in the age of Charlemagne (see, e.g., Boudriot 1928: 34–35, 38–40; Homann 1976; Nilsson 1992; Sundqvist 2016). A document from the council of Tours in 567 CE reports how recently converted people, who still perform pagan ritual actions, should be treated and punished. Some of them worshipped mountains, trees and wells ("...ut, quoscumque in hac fatuitate persistere viderint vel ad nescio quas petras aut arbores aut ad fontes" (*Concilium Turonense* p. 133)). In a letter from Gregory I to Queen Brunhilde in 597, the pope states that the pagan cult of trees does not exist any longer ("ut [...] cultores arborum non existant" (*Registrum Epistolarum* 2: 3, 7));[14] however a Langobardic law, compiled during King Liutprand's reign in 727, perscribes fines for those who worshipped trees and wells ("Simili modo et qui ad arbore, quam rustici sanctiuum uocant, atque ad fontanas adorauerit" (*Liutprandi Leges*, Anni 15, ch. 84, in *Leges Langobardorum* p. 139)).[15] At Concilium Germanicarum, led by Saint Boniface in the year 743, basic Carolingian mission strategies were worked out, including regulations against pagan customs. Some of these regulations were presented in the text *Indiculus superstitionum et paganiarum* (*Index of Superstitions and Pagan Practices*). In this text, we read about prohibited customs related to trees and wells, in, for instance, chapter 6, "De sacris silvarum, quae nimidas vocant" and chapter 11, "De fontibus sacrificiorum" (*Indiculus Superstitionum et Paganiarum* pp. 222–23; see also *Fontes Historiae Religionis Germanicae* pp. 42–43). These regulations indicate that a pagan cult of trees and wells was still widespread in Carolingian areas in the first half of the eighth century. In *Capitulatio de partibus Saxoniae* (769 CE) as well, the cult of wells and trees was forbidden. Sacrifices at groves in a heathen fashion and the custom of making meals in honor of the demons were also rejected ("Si quis ad fonts aut arbores vel lucos votum fecerit aut aliquit more gentilium obtulerit et ad honorem daemonum commederet" (*Capitulatio de partibus Saxoniae* p. 69)).

---

[13] Anders Hultgård argues that the description in scholion 138 is basically poetic-mythical and that the motif may be based on a common mythical heritage. He does not, however, comment on the possibility that the cultic place in Uppsala may be based on a mythical model (Hultgård 1997a: 26). For a more thorough investigation of possible ritual representations of mythical trees at cultic sites, see Sundqvist 2016: 250–59.

[14] See also *Fontes Historiae Religionis Germanicae* p. 30.

[15] See also *Fontes Historiae Religionis Germanicae* p. 38.

Sometimes the cosmic pillar or *axis mundi*, a fundamental structure present in many mythological systems, is represented by a tree trunk in these texts. A pre-Christian sanctuary situated in a stronghold called Eresburg (present-day Obermarsberg) is reported in several sources concerning Charlemagne's campaign in Saxony. In 772 CE, he conquered and destroyed this pagan cultic site and replaced it with a church. Rudolf of Fulda (ca. 865), for instance, describes this pagan sanctuary and mentions that the Saxons worshipped wells and green groves. In this sanctuary there was a huge tree trunk erected in the open air:

> Frondosis arboribus fontibusque venerationem exhibebant. Truncum quoque ligni non parvae magnitudinis in altum erectum sub divo colebant, patria eum lingua Irminsul appellantes, quod Latine dicitur universalis columna, quasi sustinens omnia. (*Translatio S. Alexandri* p. 676)

> (They [the Saxons] worship green trees and wells. They also worship a large tree trunk, erected under the naked sky; in native language they call it Irminsul, which in Latin means world-pillar, since it supports everything [in the world].)[16]

Rudolf's text is built on older narratives, and is thus not a direct or primary source; moreover, there seem to be secondary elements in it, such as the explanation of the name Irminsul (Palm 1948: 86–88; see however Springer 2000). The information Rudolf relates about Irminsul being a big tree trunk or pillar appears, however, to be reliable, since the name *Irmin-sul* (ON *jǫrmun-* + *súla*) means "large pillar".[17] Widukind, who was a monk in Corvey during the tenth century, has a slightly different version. He records in his chronicle *Rerum gestarum Saxonicarum* (ca. 967) that a cultic image made as a pillar was devoted to the god Irmin ("effigie columpnarum [...] Hirmin [...] dicitur" *Rerum Gestarum Saxonicarum* pp. 20–21, 21n3).[18] The information that Irmin was a god or forefather is considered uncertain (cf. Simek 2006: 175). In my opinion, it is more likely that Irminsul refers to "a great pillar or tree trunk" than to "the pillar of the god Irmin", since the name suggests this. In either case, Irminsul was an important cultic object at the chief sanctuary of the Saxons, and most likely it

---

[16] See also *Fontes Historiae Religionis Germanicae* pp. 60–61. My translation.

[17] Cf. ON *jǫrmun-*, OE *eormen-* "large", "enormous", "elevated", "wide"; in *jǫrmungandr*, "the big [enormous] stave", i.e. the Miðgarðsormr; in OE *eormengrund* "wide world"; and in a *heiti* of Óðinn, *Jǫrmunr.* See e.g. Fritzner 1954 2: 244; Clark Hall 1916: 93; Palm 1948: 92–93; Maier 2000; Drobin and Keinänen 2001: 141.

[18] See also e.g. Palm 1948: 89–91; Simek 2006: 175–76; Maier 2000; Drobin and Keinänen 2001: 140–41.

included some kind of cosmic symbolism (see e.g. Simek 2006: 175–76; Maier 2000; Sundqvist 2016: 252–57).

Cultic trees and cosmic pillars are also attested in Nordic contexts. The U-version of *Hervarar saga* reports that a sacrificial tree, called *blóttré*, stood at the assembly place of the Svear, perhaps located in Uppsala. When the people there oppose King Ingi Steinkelsson (ca. 1080–1110), who refuses to sacrifice to the gods on their behalf, his brother-in-law Sveinn steps forward. Sveinn tells them that he will perform sacrifices on their behalf if they will give him the kingdom. All assent to that proposal: "Þá var fram leitt hross eitt á þingit ok höggvit í sundr ok skipt til áts, en roðit blóðinu blóttré" (*Hervarar saga* ch. 16) (A horse was led to the meeting place, dismembered and distributed for eating, and the sacrificial tree was reddened with the blood). This late text, which dates to ca. 1300, is usually regarded as an uncertain source on pre-Christian religion, but the information about a cultic tree harmonizes with Adam's text (see Sundqvist 2016: 254).

Sacred trees and groves have been searched for in Old Uppsala, but so far without positive results. Whether the recently discovered holes for large pillars with deposited animal bones reflect traces of *axis mundi* symbols must be regarded as very unlikely (see further below on their function) (Beronius Jörpeland et al. 2013; Sundqvist 2013; Jonas Wikborg, pers. comm.).[19] The dating of these posts is unclear, but most likely some of them were erected during the monumentalization process in Old Uppsala during the early Merovingian Period (ca. 600), when the royal mounds and the great hall were built (cf. Ljungkvist 2013).

There is, however, archaeological support for cultic trees in other places of Sweden. Excavations beneath the altar of the church of *Frösön* "the island of the deity Freyr", in Jämtland, revealed large quantities of animal bones in association with a decayed birch stump. Approximately 60 percent of the bone remains had come from wild animals, such as bears, while 40 percent consisted of domestic animal bones. Both the bone materials and the stump have been dated to the tenth century (Iregren 1989; Magnell and Iregren 2010). That the birch root was found under the altar of the church suggests a cosmological continuity of the site (Andrén 2014: 37). In a document from 1408, the church on Frösön was called *Hoffs kirkio*, and still today, a place southeast of the church is called *Hov*. Per Vikstrand, an onomastics specialist, has argued that such *hov*-names in Jämtland refer to structures where cult practices were carried out (Vikstrand 1993). Thus, we may well have a configuration at Frösön similar to that in Uppsala, that is, a cultic house situated close to a cultic tree (Sundqvist 2016: 254).

---

[19] Jonas Wikborg, pers. comm. See also www.arkeologigamlauppsala.se (last accessed on May 1, 2014).

Cultic trees need not always have been real trees, as in the case of Frösön. The archaeologist Anders Andrén has suggested that the triangular stone-settings (Swedish "treuddar", sg. treudd), which have been found at several locations in Scandinavia, are to be interpreted as symbolic expressions of the world-tree Yggdrasill with its three roots (Andrén 2004, 2014).[20] One such Viking Age treudd, this one with concave sides, is situated just outside the cultic hall at Helgö, in Uppland, Sweden (Zachrisson 2004a, 2004b). It contained ritual depositions that included surgical instruments, crucibles, bread, arrowheads, whetstones, birch-bark containers, ice nails, flint and pottery. An Arabic silver coin of *terminus post quem* 819 CE and some potsherds indicate that this stone-setting was constructed during the early Viking Age (Zachrisson 2004b: 148–49). Under this configuration, in the middle, one single post-hole was found, dating to the early Merovingian Period. It too had remains of depositions, again including surgical instruments, suggesting rituals of healing at this site (Zachrisson 2004b: 157–58; Andrén 2014: 43). Perhaps a cosmic pillar of the Irminsul-type or a cultic representation of the mythic Yggdrasill stood there, before the stone setting was made (cf. Sundqvist 2016: 255).

Scholars have also searched for Adam's sacred spring (*fons*) in Old Uppsala (cf. Sundqvist 2016: 258). The archaeologist David Damell suggested that this *fons* is identical with what is today the drained little lake at Myrby träsk near the Old Uppsala cathedral—a high content of phosphorus has been detected at this location (Damell 1980; cf. Duczko 1993: 21). New investigations made by means of dendrochronological analysis indicate that the so-called "Odens brunn" (Óðinn's well), situated beside the middle mound in Old Uppsala, is to be dated to the twelfth century. Although this spring has been interpreted as a sacrificial well connected with the cult of Saint Erik (Per Frölund, pers. comm. 2013),[21] it cannot be ruled out that it had a pre-Christian background. Bountiful evidence exists of the existence of sacrificial lakes and bogs, as well as of cultic springs and wells, in Scandinavia from different times and places (cf. Sundqvist 2016: 258–62). In the most recent archaeological investigations from Old Uppsala, at least one Late Iron Age sacrificial well has been found just outside the royal estate in the eastern part of the site (Seiler and Magnell, forthcoming).

In the context of the present argument, the most intriguing of these bodies of water is the lake called Tissø "lake dedicated to the god Týr", on Zealand (Jørgensen 2002, 2009; see Brink 2001: 97 and Holmberg 1986 on the place name). Several Late Iron Age finds, interpreted as sacrificial objects, have been made

---

[20] Tricorns have mainly been found in southern and central Sweden and in southern Norway (see Myhre 2005).

[21] See also: http://arkeologiupplandsmuseet.worpress.com/2013/10/11/gamla-uppsala-nytt-ljus-over-gammal-offerbrunn-2/. Accessed on 1 May, 2014.

there. Local elite had raised a huge ceremonial hall just beside the lake, where it is likely cultic feasts took place. A small building—interpreted as a cultic house— appears in connection with the south-western part of the hall. This building was enclosed by a palisade. A similar pattern is also in evidence at the Late Iron Age settlement of Järrestad, Scania, with a hall, an enclosed area with a small cultic building, and beside this hall, sacrificial wells and springs (Söderberg 2003, 2005: 211–13, 238, 252–54).

Similar conditions are to be found at Late Iron Age central places in the Mälaren region of Sweden. At Tuna in Vendel, for example, a ceremonial hall was positioned on a platform, near the spot of the present church and the famous boat graves. A farm with the name *Torsmyra* is situated just north of Tuna. Per Vikstrand has interpreted the name as meaning "the bog dedicated to the god Þórr" (Vikstrand 2000). If so, we can surmise that wetland sacrifices took place there; however, we have no archaeological support for such interpretation. A well called *Odensbrunn* "Óðinn's well" exists southwest of Tuna in Vendel. Both Johannes Bureus and Johan Rhezelius report its existence in the seventeenth century; in the seventeenth-century Rannsakningar (an accounting of ancient artifacts deemed worthy of preservation), it is described as a sacrificial well.[22] One of the seventeenth-century sources gives the name in a reduced form, as *Onsbrönn*, which suggests that the name is old and authentic (Vikstrand 2001: 127). As far as I know, however, there are no finds from there, which makes a cultic interpretation uncertain at best. It is not impossible to imagine, however, that the topography of these sites, like Uppsala, was structured according to a certain mental figuration or mythical model (Sundqvist 2016: 260).

As at Tissø and Järrestad, the sanctuary at Uppsala may have been ritually demarcated by a long row of posts, appearing both south and north of the site. The demarcated ritual area of Uppsala, or the *temenos*,[23] could be identical with the shrine (*delubrum*) mentioned in Adam's text, scholion 139 (see above). The post alignments could, on the other hand, also be markers of a processional road (Beronius Jörpeland et al. 2013; Sundqvist 2013: 89–90; Jonas Wikborg, pers. comm.).[24] As in the cases of the tree and the well, the long row of posts could also be part of a common cultural model for sanctuaries in Northern Europe. A similar Iron Age linear monument of posts, as at Uppsala, has also been found in, for instance, Degeberga, Scania (Björk and Wickberg 2013).

---

[22] For quotations from Bureus, Rhezelius, and the Rannsakningar, see Vikstrand 2001: 127.

[23] The concept *temenos* refers actually to ancient Greek temple areas. The word τέμενος is in Liddell and Scott translated to "a piece of land marked off from common uses and dedicated to a god, precinct" (1958: 1774).

[24] See also www.arkeologiaamlauppsala.se (last accessed on May 1, 2014).

West Slavic Sanctuaries

The mythical-ritual configuration of temple, tree, and well is also visible at cult sites in Continental Europe, especially among northwestern pre-Christian Slavic people. In comparison to the materials available to the historian of Scandinavian religion, the picture of Slavic temples is impressive (Slupecki 1993, 1994, 2002, 2006; cf. Palm 1937). There is good evidence in written sources for temples at, for instance, Radogosc, Szczecin, Wolin, Wolgast, Garz, and Gutzkow. In addition to these sites, possible sanctuaries have been found by archaeologists at Feldber, Wolin, Groß Raden, Ralsiek, Parchim, and Wroklaw.

From the perspective of the present essay, a description of the Triglav temple at Szczecin (Stettin), Pommern, is particularly interesting. It was written in the twelfth century by Herbord in his biography of Bishop Otto of Bamberg and is based on eyewitness information (Slupecki 1993: 250, 265–67, 2002: 31–32; Hultgård 1997a: 27). According to Herbord, there were four temples (*continae*) in Stettin when Otto arrived.[25] The principal one was called the temple of Triglav and was, according to Herbord, built with amazing reverence and skill. Herbord's Latin *continue* (sg. *contina*) is equivalent to Old Slavic *kañcina* "temple" (Moszynski 1992: 117–20). After describing the principal temple and a three-headed idol of Triglav, Herbord states:

> Erat praeterea ibi quercus ingens et frondosa et fons subter eam amoe-nissimus, quam plebs simplex numinis alicuius inhabitatione sacram aestimans magna veneratione colebat. (*Herbodi Vita Ottonis* 2, 32–33, pp. 89–90)

> (There was also a huge oak tree with lots of leaves there, and a most pleasant spring near it. The simple people regarded it as seat of a deity and held it in great esteem.)

Similar information about this temple is reported in other sources (*Herbordi Vita Ottonis* 3, 22–23; *Ebonis Vita Ottonis* 3, 18; *Vita Prieflingensis* 3, 11). As at Uppsala, Stettin was also a site for rulers. The palace was situated on the mountain of Triglav (Slupecki 1993: 267). Perhaps cosmic symbolism, including the ceremonial building, the tree, and the well, also played an ideological role in Stettin.

Sacred trees and springs in the twelfth century West Slavic area are also attested elsewhere. For example, Helmold of Bosau reports on the pagan revival among the Wends in 1134. On a trip to Wagria, he saw oak trees enclosed within a courtyard surrounded by a fence of stakes: "Among very old trees we saw

---

[25] "Erant autem in civitate Stetinensi continae quator" (*Herbordi Vita Ottonis* 2, 32–33, pp. 89–90).

there the sacred oaks devoted to the god of that country, called Prove. They were encircled by a yard and a dense wooden fence with two gates" (Slupecki 2002: 28–29 (orig. *Chronica Slavorum* 1, 84). In a different passage, Helmold mentions some deities who inhabit forest and groves, for example Prove, the god of Oldenburg ("Prove deus Aldenburgensis terrae" (*Chronica Slavorum* 1, 52)). In the eleventh century, Thietmar mentions a holy spring situated no more than two miles from Elbe, called Glomac: "Its waters create a large morass on which, as the people from the area claim, strange events happen" (Slupecki 2002: 27 (orig. *Chronik* 1, 3)). Leszek Slupecki suggests that offerings may have been made in Glomac (Slupecki 2002: 27–28). Baltic people also worshipped trees and springs. In a papal letter from Innocentius III, the pre-Christian Latvian cult was described on the basis of missionary reports: "qui honorem Deo debitum animalibus brutis, arboribus frondosis, aquis limpidis, virentibus herbis et spiritibus immundis impendunt" (qtd. Mannhardt 1905 1: 28) (The honor they owe to God, they give (instead) to irrational animals, verdant trees, clear springs, medical herbs and unclean spirits).

Since we do not know much about the ancient Slavic worldview it is hard to know if the ritual elements of Stettin and at other cult places corresponds with the sort of mythic symbolism proposed here. It is possible that the cultic sites among northwestern Slavs had been established under the influence of Scandinavian or Germanic tribes (Palm 1937; critically considered by Slupecki 1994: 21, 2002: 30ff.). Supporting this conclusion are several facts: Stettin is located close to the Baltic Sea, not far from Bornholm. The ninth-century hagiography *Vita Anskarii* mentions that both Swedish and Danish people plundered in the south coast of the Baltic Sea, both in Slavic and Baltic areas, during the same century (*Vita Anskarii* ch. 19 and 30). There is also archaeological evidence of Scandinavians in this area during the Late Iron Age. Merovingian period artifacts with Gotlandic and Swedish origin were discovered at three cemeteries outside a town called Grobin close to Liepaja (Libau), on the Latvian coast (Nerman 1958; Stenberger 1971: 646–48). It is also possible that Baltic people, Slavs and Scandinavians influenced each other in a reciprocal way as regards the ritual structures of cultic sites.

Concluding Remarks

The question the present study addresses is whether the descriptions of pre-Christian sanctuaries in Scandinavia were based on a literary *topos* found in Old Norse sources or if they reflect real cultic conditions. In my opinion, Adam's description of Uppsala, at least fundamentally if not in every detail, cannot be ruled out despite the lack of clear archaeological evidence from the Late Iron Age (cf. Sundqvist 2016: 263). Evidence from other sources and comparative materials supports such an argument. Since cultic buildings are repeatedly found at other sites in combination with specific trees/axis mundi-symbols and/or wells, lakes or bogs, I suggest that this composition reflects a kind of cultural model, i.e., a widespread mythic-cosmological tradition. Aspects of such symbolism and ideology are also observable at other rulers' sites in Scandinavia, and perhaps also on the Continent.

Most likely this cosmic configuration (or model) could be extended with other ritual structures, such as sacred mounds, workshops, and enclosures, which also play symbolic roles in the mythical tradition. The mythic-cosmic symbols seen at Uppsala in Adam's text had several functions. On a religious level, they indicated that this site was a threshold to the divine world. At this place, man could meet the divine powers by means of performing rituals, such as sacrifices. Beyond this religious purpose, the configuration also had important ideological and power implications for the rulers of Uppsala. When the ruler appeared, the scene needed to be set with specific properties. Religious symbols, such as representations of the cosmic hall, tree, and well, created the appearance that the ruler's authority came from a realm beyond politics, society, and the natural world (cf. Lincoln 1994).

Works Cited

Primary Sources

Capitulatio de partibus Saxoniae
Capitulatio de partibus Saxoniae. Ed. Alfredus Boretius. Monumenta Germaniae Historica. Legum Sectio II. Capitularia Regum Francorum I. Hanover: 1883.

Chronica Slavorum
Helmoldi presbyteri Bozoviensis Chronica Slavorum. Ed. Heinz Stoob. Berlin: 1963.

Chronik
Thietmar of Merseburg. *Chronik.* Ed. and transl. Werner Trillmich. Ausgewählte Quellen zur deutschen Geschichte des Mittelalters: Freiherr vom Stein-Gedächtnisausgabe, 9. Darmstadt: 1957.

Concilium Turonense
Concilium Turonense. Ed. Fridericus Maasen. Monumenta Germaniae Historica. Legum Sectio III Concilia I. Concilia Aevi Merovingici. Hanover: 1893.

Ebonis Vita Ottonis
Ebonis Vita S. Ottonis episcopi Bambenbergensis. Ed. Jan Wikarjak and Kazimierz Liman. Pomniki Dziejowe Polski Series 2. Vol. 7, pt. 2. Warsaw: 1969.

Fontes Historiae Religionis Germanicae
Fontes historiae religionis germanicae. Ed. Carolus Clemen. Fontes Historiae Religionum, III. Berlin: 1928.

Gesta Hammaburgensis Ecclesiae Pontificum
Adam of Bremen. *Hamburgische Kirchengeschichte.* Ed. Bernhard Schmeidler. Scriptores Rerum Germanicarum in usum scholarum ex Monumentis Germaniae Historicis Separatim Editi. Magistri Adam Bremensis Gesta Hammaburgensis Ecclesiae Pontificum. Hannover & Leipzig: 1917.

TRANSLATION
Adam of Bremen: History of the Archbishops of Hamburg-Bremen. Transl. Francis J. Tschan. Records of Civilization: Source and Studies. New York: 2002. Orig. pub. 1959.

Grímnismál: see *Poetic Edda*

Gylfaginning: see *Snorra Edda*

Hávamál: see *Poetic Edda*

Herbordi Vita Ottonis
Herbordi Dialogus de vita Ottonis episcopi bambenbergensis / Ex recensione Rudolfi Köpke. In usum scholarum ex Monumentis Germaniae historicis recudi fecit Georgius Heinricus Pertz. Hanoverae: 1868.

Hervarar saga
Hervarar saga ok Heiðriks. Ed. Gabriel Turville-Petre. Viking Society's Text Series, 2. London: 2006. Orig. pub. 1976.

Indiculus Superstitionum et Paganiarum
Indiculus Superstitionum et Paganiarum. Ed. Alfredus Boretius. Monumenta Germaniae Historica. Legum Sectio II. Capitularia Regum Francorum. Vol. 1. Hanover: 1883.

Leges Langobardorum
Leges Langobardorum 643–866. Ed. Franz Beyerle. Göttingen: 1962. Orig. pub. 1947.

Poetic Edda

Edda: Die Liederdes Codex regius nebst verwandten Denkmälern. Ed. Gustav Neckel and Hans Kuhn. Germanische Bibliothek, Vierte Reihe. Heidelberg: 1983.

TRANSLATION
The Poetic Edda. Transl. Carolyne Larrington. Oxford World's Classics. Oxford: 2008.

Registrum Epistolarum

Gregorii I. Papae [Pope Gregory I]. *Registrum Epistolarum.* Vol. 2, pt. 1. Ed. Ludovicus M. Hartmann. Monumenta Germaniae Historica. Hanover: 1899.

Rerum Gestarum Saxonicarum

Widukind of Corvey. *Rerum Gestarum Saxonicarum.* Ed. Paulus Hirsch with Hans-Eberhard Lohmann. Vol. 3. Scriptores Rerum Germanicarum in Usum Scholarum ex Monumentis Germaniae Historicis. Hanover: 1935.

Snorra Edda

Snorri Sturluson. *Edda: Prologue and Gylfaginning.* Ed. Anthony Faulkes. London: 1988.

TRANSLATION
Edda. Transl. by Anthony Faulkes. London: 1987.

Translatio S. Alexandri

Rudolf of Fulda. *Translatio S. Alexandri.* Ed. Georgius Heinricus Pertz. Monumenta Germaniae Historica. Scriptorum II. Hanover: 1829.

Vita Anskarii

Rimbert, Saint Archbishop of Hamburg and Bremen. *Vita Anskarii auctore Rimberto. Accedit Vita Rimberti.* Ed. Georg Waitz. Monumenta Germaniae Historica. Scriptores rerum Germanicarum in usum scholarum separatim editi, 55. Hanover: 1884.

TRANSLATION
Anskar, the Apostle of the North: 801–865. Transl. Charles H. Robinson. London: 1921.

Vita Prieflingensis

Sancti Ottonis episcopi Babenbergensis Vita Prieflingensis. Ed. Kazimierz Liman and Jan Wikarjak. Pomniki dziejowe polski, Ser. 2, Vol. 7, pt. 1. Warsaw: 1966.

Vǫluspá: see *Poetic Edda*

Secondary Sources

Alkarp, Magnus. 1997. "Källan, lunden och templet—Adam av Bremens Uppsalaskildring i ny belysning." *Fornvännen* 92: 155–61.

———. 2007. "…men där är också mycken galenskap—Adam av Bremen, arkeologin och Gamla Uppsala." In *Kult, guld och makt: Ett tvärvetenskapligt symposium i Götene.* Ed. Ingemar Nordgren. Historieforum Västra Götaland, Serie B, Vetenskapliga rapporter och Småskrifter, 4. Skara. Pp. 198–220.

Andrén, Anders. 2004. "I skuggan av Yggdrasil: Trädet mellan idé realitet i nordisk tradition." In Andrén, Jennbert, and Raudvere 2004: 389–430.

———. 2014. *Tracing Old Norse Cosmology: The World Tree, Middle Earth, and the Sun in Archaeological Perspectives.* Vägar till Midgård, 16. Lund.

Andrén, Anders, Kristina Jennbert, and Catharina Raudvere, eds. 2004. *Ordning mot kaos—studier av nordisk förkristen kosmologi.* Vägar till Midgård, 4. Lund.

Beck, Heinrich et al., eds. 1968–2008. *Reallexikon der Germanischen Altertumskunde.* 2nd ed. 37 vols. Berlin.

Beronius Jörpeland, Lena et al. 2013. "Monumentala stolprader i Gamla Uppsala." *Fornvännen* 108: 278–81.

Björk, Tony, and Ylva Wickberg. 2013. "Linear Iron Age Monuments at Degeberga in Scania and Elsewhere in Sweden: Evidence for a Radical Transformation of the Ritual Landscape." *Fornvännen* 108: 93–108.

Boudriot, Wilhelm. 1928. *Die altgermanische Religion in der amtliches kirchlichen Literatur des Abendlandes vom 5. bis 11. Jahrhundert.* Untersuchungen zur allgemeinen Religionsgeschichte, 2. Bonn.

Brink, Stefan. 1999. "Fornskandinavisk religion—förhistoriskt samhälle: En bosättningshistorisk studie av centralorter i Norden." In *Religion och samhälle i det förkristna Norden: Et symposium.* Ed. Ulf Drobin et al. Odense. Pp. 11–55.

———. 2001. "Mythologizing Landscape: Place and Space of Cult and Myth." In Stausberg, Sundqvist, and van Nahl 2001: 76–112.

———. 2011. "Gudme—The Toponymic Evidence (or Rather Challenge)." In Grimm and Pesch 2011: 15–24.

Bruun, Daniel, and Finnur Jónsson. 1909. "Om hove og hovudgravninger på Island." *Aarbøger for nordisk Oldkyndighed og Historie* 2 (24): 245–316.

Clark Hall, John R. 1916. *A Concise Anglo-Saxon Dictionary for the Use of Students.* Cambridge.

Damell, David. 1980. "Om en fosfatkarta över fornminnesområdet vid Gamla Uppsala." In *Inventori in honorem: En vänbok till Folke Hallberg.* Ed. Åke Hyenstrand. Stockholm. Pp. 64–67.

Dillmann, Francois-Xavier. 1997. "Kring de rituella gästabuden i fornskandi-navisk religion." In Hultgård 1997b: 51–73.

Drobin, Ulf, and Marja-Liisa Keinänen. 2001. "Frey, Veralden olmai och Sampo." In Stausberg, Sundqvist, and van Nahl 2001: 136–69.

Duczko, Wladyslaw. 1993. "Introduktion till Gamla Uppsala." In *Arkeologi och miljöekologi i Gamla Uppsala: Studier och rapporter.* Ed. Wladyslaw Duczko. OPIA 7. Uppsala. Pp. 9–37.

Eliade, Mircea. 1974. *Patterns in Comparative Religion.* Transl. R. Sheed. New York. Orig. pub as *Traité d'historie des réligions.* 1949.

———. 1987. *The Sacred and the Profane: The Nature of Religion.* Transl. W. R. Trask. San Diego. Orig. pub. as *Das Heilige und das Profane.* 1957.

———. 1991. *The Myth of Eternal Return: Or, Cosmos and History.* Transl. W. R. Trask. Princeton. Orig. pub. as *Le Mythe de l'éternel retour: Archétypes et répétition.* 1949.

Engelke, Matthew. 2012. "Material Religion." In *The Cambridge Companion to Religious Studies.* Ed. Robert A. Orsi. Cambridge. Pp. 209–29.

Flood, Gavin. 1999. *Beyond Phenomenology: Rethinking the Study of Religion.* London.

Fritzner, Johan. 1954 (1883–1896). *Ordbog over det gamle norske sprog.* 3 vols. Oslo.

Göthberg, Hans, Christian Lovén, and Göran Dahlbäck. 2010. "Domkyrkan i Gamla Uppsala." In *Domkyrkan i Gamla Uppsala: Nuvarande domkyrkans omgivningar.* Vol. 2 of *Uppsala Domkyrka.* Ed. Ronnie Carlsson et al. Sveriges kyrkor, 228. Uppsala. Pp. 11–64.

Grimm, Oliver, and Alexandra Pesch, eds. 2011. *The Gudme/Gudhem Phenomenon.* Neumünster.

Gräslund, Anne-Sofie. 1997. "Adams Uppsala—och arkeologins." In Hultgård 1997b: 101–15.

Gräslund, Bo. 1993. "Folkvandringstidens Uppsala: Namn, myter, arkeologi och historia." In *Kärnhuset i riksäpplet: Upplands fornminnesförening och hembygdsförbunds årsbok.* Ed. Kent Blent et al. Uppsala. Pp. 173–208.

Hallencreutz, Carl Fredrik. 1997. "Missionsstrategi och religionstolkning: Till frågan om Adam av Bremen och Uppsalatemplet." In Hultgård 1997b: 117–30.

Hedeager, Lotte. 2001. "Asgard Reconstructed? Gudme—A 'Central Place' in the North." In *Topographies of Power in the Early Middle Ages.* Ed. Mayke de Jong and Frans Theuws, with Carine van Rhijn. Leiden. Pp. 467–507.

———. 2011. *Iron Age Myth and Materiality: An Archaeology of Scandinavia AD 400-1000.* London.

Hellman, Eva. 2011. *Vad är religion? En disciplinteoretisk metastudie.* Religionshistoriska forskningsrapporter från Uppsala, 21. Nora.

Henare, Amira, Martin Holbraad, and Sari Wastell. 2007. "Introduction: Thinking Through Things." In *Thinking Through Things: Theorising Artefacts Ethnographically*. Ed. Amiria Henare, Martin Holbraad, and Sari Wastell. London. Pp. 1–31.

Herschend, Frands. 1993. "The Origin of the Hall in Southern Scandinavia." *Tor* 25: 175–99.

———. 1998. *The Idea of the Good in Late Iron Age Society*. OPIA, 15. Uppsala.

———. 1999. "Halle." In Beck et al. 13: 414–25.

———. 2001. *Journey of Civilisation: The Late Iron Age View of the Human World*. OPIA, 24. Uppsala.

Holmberg, Bente. 1986. "Den hedenske gud Tyr i danske stednavne." In *Mange bække små: Til John Kousgård Sørensen på tresårsdagen 6.12.1985*. Ed. Vibeke Dalberg and Gillian Fellows-Jensen. Copenhagen. Pp. 109–26.

Holtsmark, Anne. 1992. *Fornnordisk mytologi: Tro och myter under vikingatiden*. Transl. Henrik Williams. Lund. Orig. pub. as *Norrøn mytologi: Tro og myter i vikingtiden*. 1970.

Homann, H. 1976. "Baumkult." In Beck et al. 2: 107–10.

Hultgård, Anders. 1997a. "Från ögonvittnesskildring till retorik: Adam av Bremens notiser om Uppsalakulten i religionshistorisk belysning." In Hultgård 1997b: 9–50.

———, ed. 1997b. *Uppsalakulten och Adam av Bremen*. Nora.

Iregren, Elisabeth. 1989. "Under Frösö kyrka—ben från en vikingatida offerlund?" In *Arkeologi och religion: Rapport från arkeologidagarna 16–18 januari 1989*. Ed. Lars Larsson and Bożena Wyszomirska. Lund. Pp. 119–33.

Janson, Henrik. 1997. "Adam av Bremen, Gregorius VII och Uppsalatemplet." In Hultgård 1997b: 131–95.

———. 1998. *Templum Nobilissimum: Adam av Bremen, Uppsalatemplet och konfliktlinjerna i Europa kring år 1075*. Avhandlingar från Historiska institutionen i Göteborg, 21. Gothenburg.

Jørgensen, Lars. 2002. "Kongsgård—kusted—marked: Overvejelser omkring Tissøkompleksets struktur og funktion." In *Plats och praxis—studier av nordisk förkristen ritual*. Ed. Kristina Jennbert, Anders Andrén, and Catharina Raudvere. Vägar till Midgård, 2. Lund. Pp. 215–47.

———. 2009. "Pre-Christian Cult at Aristocratic Residences and Settlement Complexes in Southern Scandinavia in the 3rd–10th centuries AD." In *Glaube, Kult und Herrschaft: Phänomene des Religiosen im 1. Jahrtausend n. Chr. in Mittel- und Nordeuropa; Akten des 59. Internationalen Sachsensymposions und der Grundprobleme der frühgeschichtlichen Entwicklung im Mitteldonauraum*. Ed. Uta von Freeden, Herwig Friesinger, and Egon Wamers. Kolloquien zur Vor- und Frühgeschichte, 12. Bonn. Pp. 329–54.

————. 2011. "Gudme-Lundeborg on Funen: As a model for northern Europe?" In Grimm and Pesch 2011: 77–90.

Lid, Nils. 1942. "Gudar og gudedyrkning." In *Religionshistorie*. Nordisk kultur, 26. Oslo. Pp. 80–153.

Liddell, Henry Georg, and Robert Scott. 1958 (1843). *A Greek-English Lexicon: A New Edition*. Oxford.

Lincoln, Bruce. 1994. *Authority: Construction and Corrosion*. Chicago.

Ljungkvist, John. 2013. "Monumentaliseringen av Gamla Uppsala." In Sundqvist and Vikstrand 2013: 33–67.

Ljungkvist, John, and Per Frölund. 2015. "Gamla Uppsala—The Emergence of a Centre and a Magnate Complex." *Journal of Archaeology and Ancient History* 16: 2–29.

Magnell, Ola, and Elisabeth Iregren. 2010. "Veitstu hvé blóta skal? The Old Norse Blót in Light of Osteological Remains from Frösö Church, Jämtland, Sweden." *Current Swedish Archaeology* 18: 223–50.

Maier, Bernhard. 2000. "Irminsul. § 2. Sprachliche Deutung. § 3 Religions-geschichtliche." In Beck et al. 15: 505–06.

Mannhardt, Wilhelm. 1904–1905. *Wald- und Feldkulte*. 2 vols. Berlin. Orig. pub. 1874–1875.

McCutcheon, R. T. 1997. *Manufacturing Religion: The Discourse on Sui Generis Religion and the Politics of Nostalgia*. New York.

Miller, Daniel. 2005. "Materiality: Introduction." In *Materiality*. Ed. Daniel Miller. Durham. Pp. 1–50.

Moszynski, Leszek. 1992. *Die vorchristliche Religion der Slaven im Lichte der slavischen Sprachwissenschaft*. Bausteine zur slavischen Philologie und Kulturgeschichte, Reihe A: Slavistische Forschungen, Neue Folge, 1. Cologne.

Myhre, Bjørn. 2005. "Krossane på Ullandhaug, Døds-sjødno på Sele og Fem dårlige jomfruer på Norheim: Symboler for Yggdrasil—livets tre?" *Frá haug ok heiðni* 2005 (3): 3–10.

Nerman, Birger. 1958. *Grobin-Seeburg: Ausgrabungen und Funde*. Kungl. Vitterhets Historie Antikvitets Akademien. Stockholm.

Nilsson, Bertil. 1992. "Till frågan om kyrkans hållning till icke-kristna kult-fenomen: Attityder under tidig medeltid i Europa och Norden." In *Kontinuitet i kult och tro från vikingatid till medeltid*. Ed. Bertil Nilsson. Projektet Sveriges Kristnande Publikationer, 1. Uppsala. Pp. 9–47.

Nordahl, Else. 1996. *... templum quod Ubsola dicitur ... i arkeologisk belysning*. Aun, 22. Uppsala.

Nyberg, Tore. 1984. "Stad, skrift och stift: Några historiska inledningsfrågor." In *Adam av Bremen: Historien om Hamburgstiftet och dess biskopar*. Transl. Emanuel Svenberg. Stockholm. Pp. 295–339.

Palm, Thede. 1937. *Wendische Kultstätten: Quellenkritische Untersuchungen zu den letzten Jahrhunderten slavischen Heidentums.* Lund.

———. 1948. *Trädkult: Studier i germansk religionshistoria.* Skrifter utgivna av Vetenskaps-Societeten i Lund, 33. Lund.

Reuter, Timothy. 2002. "Introduction to the 2002 Edition." In *Gesta Hammaburgensis Ecclesiae Pontificum.* Pp. xi–xxi.

Sawyer, Peter H. 1991. *När Sverige blev Sverige.* Transl. Birgit Sawyer. Occasional Papers on Medieval Topics, 5. Alingsås. Orig. pub. as *The Making of Sweden.* 1989.

Schjødt, Jens Peter. 2012. "Reflections on Aims and Methods in the Study of Old Norse Religion." In *More than Mythology: Narratives, Ritual practices and Regional Distribution in Pre-Christian Scandinavian Religions.* Ed. Catharina Raudvere and Jens Peter Schjødt. Lund. Pp. 263–87.

Seiler, Anton, and Ola Magnell. Forthcoming. *Til árs ok friðar - gårdsnära rituella depositioner i östra Gamla Uppsala.*

Slupecki, Leszek P. 1993. "Die Slawischen Tempel und die Frage des sakralen Raumes bei den Westslawen in vorchristlichen Zeiten." *Tor* 25: 247–98.

———. 1994. *Slavonic Pagan Sanctuaries.* Warsaw.

———. 2002. "Pagan Religion and Cultural Landscape of Northwestern Slavs in the Early Middle-Ages." *Siedlungsforschung: Archäologie, Geschichte, Geographie* 20: 25–40.

———. 2006. "The Temple in Rhetra-Riedegost: West Slavic Pagan Ritual as Described at the Beginning of Eleventh Century [sic]." In *Old Norse Religion in Long-Term Perspectives: Origins, Changes, and Interactions.* Ed. Anders Andrén, Kristina Jennbert, and Catharina Raudvere. Vägar till Midgård, 8. Lund. Pp. 224–28.

Simek, Rudolf. 2006. *Dictionary of Northern Mythology.* Transl. Angela Hall. Cambridge. Orig. pub. as *Lexikon der germanischen Mythologie.* 1993.

Smith, Jonathan Z. 1987. *To Take Place: Towards Theory in Ritual.* Chicago.

———. 2000. "In Comparison a Magic Dwells." In *A Magic Still Dwells: Comparative Religion in the Postmodern Age.* Ed. Kimberley C. Patton and Benjamin C. Ray. Berkeley. Pp. 23–44.

Söderberg, Bengt. 2003. "Järnålderns Järrestad." In *Järrestad: Huvudgård i centralbygd.* Ed. Bengt Söderberg. Riksantikvarieämbetet: Arkeologiska undersökningar Skrifter, 51. Stockholm. Pp. 109–74.

———. 2005. *Aristokratiskt rum och gränsöverskridande: Järrestad och sydöstra Skåne mellan region och rike 600–1100.* Riksantikvarieämbetet: Arkeologiska undersökningar Skrifter, 62. Lund.

Springer, M. 2000. "Irminsul. § 1. Historisches." In Beck et al. 15: 504–05.

Stausberg, Michael, Olof Sundqvist, and Astrid van Nahl, eds. 2001. *Kontinuitäten und Brüche in der Religionsgeschichte: Festschrift für Anders Hultgård zu seinem 65. Geburtstag am 23.12.2001*. Berlin.

Stenberger, Mårten. 1971. *Det forntida Sverige*. Stockholm. Orig. pub. 1964.

Ström, Folke. 1985. *Nordisk hedendom: Tro och sed i förkristen tid*. Gothenburg. Orig. pub. 1961.

Sundqvist, Olof. 2002. *Freyr's Offspring: Rulers and Religion in Ancient Svea Society*. Acta Universitatis Upsaliensis Historia Religionum, 21. Uppsala.

——. 2004. "Uppsala och Asgård: Makt, offer och kosmos i forntida Skandinavien." In Andrén, Jennbert, and Raudvere 2004: 145–79.

——. 2007. *Kultledare i fornskandinavisk religion*. OPIA, 41. Uppsala.

——. 2013. "Gamla Uppsala som förkristen kultplats: en översikt och en hypotes." In Sundqvist and Vikstrand 2013: 69–111.

——. 2016. *An Arena for Higher Powers: Ceremonial Buildings and Religious Strategies for Rulership in Late Iron Age Scandinavia*. NuS, 150. Leiden.

Sundqvist, Olof, and Per Vikstrand, eds. 2013. *Gamla Uppsala i ny belysning*. Religionsvetenskapliga studier från Gävle, 9. Gävle.

Tschan, Francis J. 2002. "Introduction." In *Gesta Hammaburgensis Ecclesiae Pontificum*. xxv–xlvi.

Vikstrand, Per. 1993. "Förkristna sakrala ortnamn i Jämtland." *Namn och bygd* 81: 49–84.

——. 2000. "Konungen och helgedomen." In vol. 2 of *Oluf Rygh: Rapport fra symposium på Stiklestad 13.-15. Mai 1999*. Ed. Berit Sandnes et al. Uppsala. Pp. 43–54.

——. 2001. *Gudarnas platser: Förkristna sakrala ortnamn i Mälarlandskapen*. Acta Academiae Regiae Gustavi Adolphi 77. Uppsala.

——. 2013. "Namnet Uppsala." In Sundqvist and Vikstrand 2013: 135–60.

de Vries, Jan. 1956–1957. *Altgermanische Religionsgeschichte*. 2 vols. Grundriss der germanischen Philologie, 12 (1–2). Berlin.

Widengren, Geo. 1961. *Kungar, profeter och harlekiner: Religionshistoriska uppsatser*. Stockholm.

——. 1969. *Religionsphänomenlogie*. Berlin.

Zachrisson, Torun. 2004a. "Det heliga på Helgö och dess kosmiska referenser." In Andrén, Jennbert, and Raudvere 2004: 343–88.

——. 2004b. "The Holiness of Helgö." In vol. 16 of *Excavations at Helgö: Exotic and Sacral Finds from Helgö*. Ed. Bo Gyllensvärd et al. Kungl. Vitterhets Historie och Antikvitets Akademien. Stockholm. Gustavi Adolphi, 77. Studier till en svensk ortnamnsatlas, 17. Uppsala. Pp. 143–75.

The Mythic Sun
An Areal Perspective

Thomas A. DuBois
University of Wisconsin-Madison

Abstract: Old Norse materials regarding the sun present conflicting stories about its identity and nature. These contradictions are examined in light of folk song materials and other evidence from Balto-Finnic, Sámi, and Baltic cultures to investigate to what extent a shared mythic narrative of a female sun (or sun's daughter) may have existed as a common element in Nordic/Baltic mythologies and whether that figure enters into marriage with other astral figures (e.g., the moon, the stars). Methodologically, the paper investigates the extent to which folk song materials—central in the reconstruction of Finnish and Baltic mythologies but largely rejected in the field of Old Norse studies—can serve as useful tools in reconstructing ancient myths in the region.

Anyone familiar with Old Norse mythology will have noticed certain discrepancies with respect to conceptualizations of the sun. In a region beset with extreme shifts in the daylight regimen and long, frigid winters, one would think that the sun would be one astral being about which much would be said, and that, as a result, the sun's mythological representation would show a great deal of consistency and continuity. Instead, however, as I hope to demonstrate in the following discussion, the sun in Old Norse mythology seems to be depicted in differing, contradictory fashions. The sun is sometimes described as an unpersonified flame or disk, while in other cases, the sun figures as a female deity, or a deified earthling consigned to the sky. Perennially chased by wolves, the sun will eventually be swallowed or extinguished in the tumultuous events at the end of the world. Before her demise, however, she will have given birth to a daughter, who will follow in her footsteps in the reconstituted new cosmos (*Vafðrúðnismál* st. 47; *Gylfaginning* p. 54).

My question in surveying this range of accounts of the sun and her fate is to ask to what extent an areal—Nordic-Baltic—perspective can in some ways shed light on the seeming contradictions in the sun's image and treatment described above. In the following, I sketch the main lines of sun mythology in Old Norse, Balto-Finnic, Sámi, and Baltic (Latvian) traditions, with an eye to understanding whether there could have been, if not downright borrowing of mythic ideas from one culture to the next in the Nordic-Baltic region, then at least an *awareness* of neighboring peoples' understandings of the sun, awareness that could have translated into the incorporation of mythic elements that do not necessarily cohere logically, but that account for the various conceptualizations of the sun operative in the region.

In order to make an areal comparison, I need to examine, and to some extent accept, the validity of research methods in Finnish, Karelian, Estonian, Sámi, and Latvian scholarship that make use of song materials committed to writing long after the end of the Middle Ages. I do so with the cognizance that medievalists tend to avoid using such evidence, and that much may have changed in *detail* from the thirteenth century of Snorri Sturluson to the eighteenth or nineteenth centuries of folklorist collectors like Elias Lönnrot, F. Reinhold Kreutzwald, Anders Fjellner, or Krišjānis Barons. But I would like to suggest that we can posit certain *continuities* nonetheless, particularly if we keep our analysis on the level of broad formations rather than minute details, and provided we follow the well-founded judgments of scholars in these fields regarding measures of likely antiquity—broad distribution, continuity between earliest and later recordings of a given motif, and careful appraisal of possible borrowings from written or adjacent oral traditions over time. What I would like to suggest is that the folk songs sung by non-literate Latvian, Estonian, Karelian, Finnish and Sámi singers over a broad geographic expanse are probably qualitatively quite distinct from the Scandinavian ballad tradition to which they are often compared and should be regarded as a valuable potential source of comparative evidence for illuminating aspects of pre-Christian Nordic mythology.[1]

---

[1] For an overview of the contents and style of songs in the Finnish "Kalevala meter", see the excellent anthology *Finnish Folk Poetry: Epic*, edited by Matti Kuusi, Keith Bosley, and Michael Branch (1977). The origins and distinctiveness of Kalevalaic (trochaic tetrameter) meter in particular have been ably discussed by Mikko Korhonen (1994) and Pentti Leino (1994) in articles published in English. These scholars build on Matti Sadeniemi's (1953) important study of the meter, available in German. Anna-Leena Siikala has explored thematic connections between the Kalevalaic songs and Old Norse poetry in her *Mythic Images and Shamanism* (2002). The classic exploration of the relationship between Finland's archaic Kalevalaic song tradition and the stanzaic, rhymed song tradition that displaced it during the later Middle Ages and after can be found in Matti Kuusi's chapter "Keskiajan kalevalainen runous" and Matti Hako's follow-up chapter "Riimilliset kansanlaulut" in Kuusi's edited volume *Suomen kirjallisuus I: Kirjoittamaton kirjallisuus* (1963). Musicological aspects of the traditions are aptly surveyed in Anneli Asplund's chapters

The Sun in Old Norse Sources

Images apparently of the sun figure prominently on the Gotlandic picture stones, where they are accorded a prominent place at the top center of the stones, a placement later occupied by images of the god Óðinn, or later still, by the Christian Cross (Andrén 2014). The images of these earliest Gotlandic stones, which date to the early Viking Age or even before, suggest a sun understood as a swirling flame, a pinwheel of fire. In two places in *Skáldskaparmál*, Snorri enumerates a wide range of sun epithets that closely match this unpersonified flame. In one passage, he calls the sun "Eldr himins" and "[eldr] lopts " (*Skáldskaparmál* p. 39) (fire of sky, fire of air) (Faulkes 1987: 93). He also furnishes a wider catalogue, including the following terms:

Sunna	Sun
Rǫðull	Disc
Eyglóa	Ever-glow
Alskír	All-bright
Sýni	Seen
Fagrahvél	Fair-wheel
Líknskin	Grace-shine
Dvalins leika	Dvalin's toy
Álfrǫðull	Elf disc
Ífrǫðull	Doubt disc
Mýlin	Ruddy

(*Skáldskaparmál* p. 85; translation: Faulkes 1987: 133–34)
At least some of these epithets recall, however cryptically, mythic events, e.g., Dvalins leika, (Dvalin's toy), a name that occurs also in the eddic poem *Alvíssmál* and suggests a narrative of fatal dwarf dealings with the sun (*Alvíssmál* st. 16). But even with such apparently narrative-referential epithets, the sun acts apparently not as a personified being, but rather simply as the luminous astral body that presides over the day and proves lethal when seen by dwarfs. As the pedantic Alvíss explains in response to Þórr's question:

> Sól heitir með mǫnnum   enn sunna með goðom,
>   kalla dvergar Dvalins leica
> eygló iǫtnar   álfar fagrahvél
>   alscír ása synir. (*Alvíssmál* st. 16; *Prose Edda* p. 126)

"Kalevalaiset laulut" and "Riimilliset kansanlaulut" in the volume she edited with Matti Hako entitled *Kansanmusiikki* (1981).

> (Sun it's called by men
> And sunshine by the gods,
> for the dwarfs it's Dvalin's deluder
> The giants call it overglow
> The elves the lovely wheel
> The sons of the Æsir all-shining. (Larrington1996: 111))

The sun, called either *sól* or *sunna*, is a bright and glowing disc, a fire in the sky, perhaps wheel-like in its roundness and movement, but not, apparently, a personified being. It should be noted that in many instances, the Old Norse material, like the Hebrew accounts in Genesis 1: 3 and 1: 14–18, seems to separate the sun-as-flame from the light of day, which is seen to have a separate, independent existence. So the sun in these epithets is a shining, welcome, but potentially dangerous, astral body, not a deity *per se* and not directly the source of the world's periodically plentiful light. It is interesting that the final speakers enumerated in Alvíss's catalogue above are the *ása synir*, "sons of the Æsir", a group not mentioned elsewhere in *Alvíssmál*, but an epithet which figures prominently, as we shall see, in Latvian song traditions connected with the sun.

Snorri presents the genesis of the sun in terms that similarly underscore this unpersonified, naturalistic imagery. In describing the formation of the cosmos out of the primordial void, Snorri recounts in his *Gylfaginning*:

> Þau tóku þeir síur ok gneista þá, er lausir fóru ok kastat hafði ór Múspellsheimi, ok settu í miðjan Ginnungahimin bæði ofan ok neðan til at lýsa himin ok jǫrð. Þeir gáfu staðar ǫllum eldingum, sumum á himni, sumar fóru lausar undir himni, ok settu þó þeim stað ok skǫpuðu gǫnga þeim ... (*Gylfaginning* p. 12)

> (Then they took molten particles and sparks that were flying uncontrolled and had shot out of the world of Muspell and set them in the middle of the firmament of the sky both above and below to shine on heaven and earth. They fixed all the lights, some in the sky, some moved in a wandering course beneath the sky, but they appointed them positions and ordained their courses ... (Faulkes 1987: 12))

The sun is a spark, fixed in the sky by the gods, and consigned to its predictable course by the divine will of others.

In one of the same passages of *Skáldskaparmál* quoted above, however, Snorri mentions other epithets, ones which he privileges by listing them ahead of unpersonified names like "Fair-wheel" and "Elf-disc". Not only is the sun a disc or flame, in other words, but also "Dóttur Mundilfœra", "Systur Mána", and

"Kona Glens" (*Skáldskaparmál* p. 39) (Daughter of Mundilfæri, Sister of Moon, Wife of Glenr) (Faulkes 1987: 93).

Snorri quotes the eleventh-century Icelandic skald Skúli Þorsteinsson regarding the sun's mysterious spouse Glenr mentioned in this listing:

> Glens beðja veðr gyðju
> goðblíð í vé, síðan
> ljós kemr gótt með geislum,
> gránserks ofan mána. (*Skáldskaparmál* p. 39)

(God-blithe bedfellow of Glen steps to her divine sanctuary with brightness; then descends the good light of grey-clad moon. (Faulkes 1987: 93))

Here, the setting sun is described as sinking into her bed, her nightly sanctuary, leaving the sky to the light of the moon. The identity or nature of Glenr beyond his marriage to the sun however, remains unexplicated.

In *Skáldskarparmál*, then, the sun is accorded a female gender (matching the grammatical gender of the Old Norse term *sól*) and a kinship network: she is the daughter of one Mundilfæri, the sister of the moon, and the wife of someone named Glenr. In the eddic poem *Vǫluspá*, it is noted that at the beginning of creation, "Sól þat né vissi hvar hon sali átti ... " (lit., the sun did not know where she had her hall (*Vǫluspá* st. 3))—a similar ascription of human or divine attributes and behaviors to an astral body that other textual references describe as simply a spark, flame, or wheel. Snorri draws his *Skáldskaparmál* terms in part from another eddic poem, *Vafðrúðnismál*, in which the giant Vafðrúðnir declares:

> Mundilfœri heitir   hann er Mána faðir
>   ok svá Sólar iþ sama;
> himin hverfa   þau scolo hvergian dag,
>   ǫldum at ártali. (*Vafðrúðnismál* st. 23)

(Mundilfæri he is called   the father of Moon
and likewise of Sun;
they must pass through the sky, every day
to count the years for men. (Larrington 1996: 43))

Sun and moon are female and male, linked by the same father and destined to parallel daily treks across the sky. A little later in the same poem, the genders of day and night are reversed, as we read of another father, Dellingr, and his son Dagr (day) and daughter Nor (night):

> Dellingr heitir, hann er Dags faðir
>   enn Nótt var Nörvi borin;
> ný och nið   skópo nýt regin
>   öldum at ártali. (*Vafðrúðnismál* st. 25)

> (Delling he is called, he is Day's father,
> and Night was born of Norr;
> new moon and dark of the moon the beneficent Powers made
> to count the years for men. (Larrington 1996: 44))

In order to accommodate the sun's female gender and kinship relations with the competing image of the sun as an unpersonified flame, Snorri supplies what seems like a somewhat convoluted tale:

> Sá maðr er nefndr Mundilfœri, er átti tvau bǫrn. Þau váru svá fǫgr ok fríð at hann kallaði annat Mána, en dóttur sína Sól, ok gifti hana þeim manni, er Glenr hét. En guðin reiddusk þessu ofdrambi ok tóku þau systkin ok settu upp á himin, létu Sól keyra þá hesta, er drógu kerru solarinnar þeirar er guðin hǫfðu skapat til at lýsa heimana af þeiri síu er flaug ór Múspellsheimi. (*Gylfaginning* p. 13)

> (There was a person whose name was Mundilfæri, who had two children. They were so fair and beautiful that he called the one Moon and his daughter Sun, and gave her in marriage to a man named Glen. But the gods grew angry at this arrogance and took the brother and sister and set them up in the sky. They made Sol drive the horses that drew the chariot of the sun which the gods had created, to illuminate the worlds, out of the molten particle that had flown out of the land of Muspell. (Faulkes 1987: 14))

Here the personified sun, Sól, a human being unwisely named by her overweening father, is made the driver of a sun chariot that draws the unpersonified flame or disc, síu, that is the sun in its most primal essence. So there are two "Suns", one the actual flame, the other a human attendant. Such a situation may be reflected also in the far earlier Trundholm sun chariot (ca. 1400 BCE), which depicts a large upright disk (the sun?) drawn by a horse on wheels, albeit with no driver (see discussion below).

It should be noted that this account is markedly masculine in its characters and ideology: the gods (*guðin*)—presumably the three Æsir credited with creating the land and sky in Snorri's account, i.e., Óðinn, Vili, and Vé—perform all consequential actions, from the establishment of the earth and sky from the body of the murdered frost giant Ymir, to the appointment of the sun and establishment of the solar path. It is they who punish the human father Mundilfæri when he transgresses by naming his children after the sun and moon. It is Mundilfæri, the father, who is punished by the consignment of his children to perpetual astral servitude. Sól has no independent latitude of action of her own, be she the actual sun or the sun's human chauffeur. She eventually marries, but Snorri tells us nothing of her courtship, wedding, or marriage, until he supplies the detail that she has given birth to a replacement sun at Ragnarǫk. This decidedly masculine narrative contrasts markedly with the myths known from the Sámi, Balto-Finnic, and Baltic traditions, as discussed below.

The progress of the sun, chariot or otherwise, is not serene: both sun and moon are pursued by wolves. *Grímnismál* states:

> Scǫll heitir úlfr, er fylgir ino scírleita goði
> til varna viðar;
> Enn annarr Hati hann er Hróðvitnis sonr,
> sá scal fyr heiða brúði himins. (*Grímnismál* st. 39)

> (Skoll a wolf is called who pursues the shining god
> to the protecting woods;
> and another is Hati, he is Hrodvitnir's son,
> who chases the bright bride of heaven. (Larrington 1996: 57))

I note in passing that the beset sun here is described as *brúði himins* (bride of heaven/the sky), a name that underscores the sun's personified identity as well as her entry into marriage with a being of the sky, or at least *in* the sky. She is not described as an attendant of the *real* sun, as in Snorri's account, but as a goddess, an image paralleled, as we shall see, in Latvian tradition. Snorri includes the image of the panicked, pursued sun and moon in *Gylfaginning*, noting that the wolf will eventually catch the sun *hana*, "her", but not clarifying if this capture is of the flame, the chariot, or its human driver (*Gylfaginning* p. 14; Faulkes 1987: 14–15). *Grímnismál*, too, describes such a pursuit, mentioning a defender as well:

> Svǫl heitir hann stendr sólo fyrir
> sciǫldr, scínanda goði
> biǫrg oc brim ec veit at brenna scolo
> ef hann fellr ífrá (*Grímnismál* st. 38)

> (Svalin is the name of a shield which stands before the sun
> before the shining god;

> mountain and sea I know would burn up
> if it fell away from in front. (Larrington 1996: 57))

This mysterious defender Svǫl ("Cooler"; Larrington's Svalin)—be it an anthropomorphized being or a physical shield—is not mentioned in Snorri's accounts. It is certainly possible to interpret Svǫl as a personified deity standing in defense of a presumably personified sun. Whatever the case, Svǫl is ultimately unsuccessful, for, as Snorri recounts, the sun is eventually swallowed by one of the pursuing wolves: "Þá verðr þat er mikil tíðindi þykkja, at úlfrinn gleypir sólna, ok þykkir mǫnnum þat mikit mein" (*Gylfaginning* p. 49) (Then something will happen that will be thought a most significant event: the wolf will swallow the sun, and people will think this a great disaster (Faulkes 1987: 53)). Here, again, Snorri does not differentiate between the sun as flame, the chariot, or its human driver. Drawing on *Vafðrúðnismál*, however, he recounts the sun's eventual rebirth. As the eddic poem puts it:

> ... eina dóttur   berr Álfrǫðull
>   áðr hana Fenrir fari;
> sú scal ríða   þá er regin deyja
>   móður brautir mær. (*Vafðrúðnismál* st. 47; *Gylfaginning* p. 54)

(A daughter shall Álfrǫðull [Elf-disc] bear before Fenrir catches her. She shall ride, when the powers die, the maiden, her mother's road. (Faulkes 1987: 57))

Vafðrúðnismál thus describes a sun named with a disc epithet, consciously riding along an established route and capable of giving birth to a sun being like herself. Such an act implies the shining essence of the sun as flame, the presence of some sort of wagon or wheels, and a reproductive anatomy. At some point in her daily (or nightly) travels, in other words, the sun has engaged in sexual reproduction, perhaps as a result of her conjugal relations with her husband (Glenr) or possibly through her dealings with her (amorous?) defender Svǫl.

In summary, then, we can see in the Old Norse material at least two competing images of the sun: one as an unpersonified flame or wheel, set in its place by deities, and the other as a conscious, anthropomorphized woman or female deity, capable of marriage, fear, and reproduction. Between these two images we find a human driver, possibly Snorri's interpolation so as to reconcile the conflicting accounts: this Sól is the victim of her father's hubris and may be the being who gives birth to the reborn sun at the end of the world.

Balto-Finnic Tradition

As John Lindow argues in his contribution to this volume, songs collected from illiterate Finnish and Karelian peasants in the nineteenth century provide useful comparative evidence for the student of Old Norse mythology. These songs are best known to an international audience through their literary adaptation into the Finnish national epic *Kalevala*, a project undertaken in the 1830s and 40s by the folklorist and doctor Elias Lönnrot (1802–1884).[2] Although Lönnrot's literary rendering changed many details of the traditional songs that Lönnrot and other scholars collected, the collectors' original notations and field recordings survive in the archives of the Finnish Literature Society (Suomalaisen Kirjallisuuden Seura) and have been partially published in a massive anthology *Suomen Kansan Vanhat Runot* (Ancient Songs of the Finnish People)[3] (SKVR). In the wake of the 1835 publication of the *Kalevala*, a long succession of folklorists undertook further fieldwork expeditions to rural tracts of northern and eastern Finland, Ingria, and Karelia to collect additional songs, so that Finnish archives today possess a great wealth of carefully collected songs from the nineteenth century. Similarly, in Estonia, the romantic ideas of Johann Gottfried von Herder (1744–1803) and the intellectual excitement occasioned by the appearance of the *Kalevala* led to parallel collection efforts in Estonia and the eventual literary epic *Kalevipoeg*, created by Friedrich R. Kreutzwald (1803–1882).[4]

Although these songs were first recorded in writing only in the nineteenth century, several factors point to their likely antiquity. Firstly, the collected songs are widespread in the Balto-Finnic culture area, occurring with certain significant variations in Finnish, Karelian, Ingrian, Votic, and Estonian languages. Secondly, they possess a conservative meter and alliterative system that helped maintain the texts over time. The marked language barrier that separated Finnic speakers from the lore and languages of other European populations, and the low literacy rate of peasants in the era when the songs were collected, further limited cross-cultural diffusion of European ballad and other musical traditions from Scandinavia and

---

[2]   For a detailed discussion of the relation of Lönnrot's epic to its oral antecedents, see (in Finnish) Anttila 1985, Kaukonen 1939–1945, and Kuusi and Anttonen 1995. For further detail of the antecedent song traditions see especially Harvilahti 1992 and (in English) Tarkka 2013. For useful examinations in English, see Pentikäinen 1989, DuBois 1995, and Virtanen and DuBois 2000. For a useful and accurate translation of the *Kalevala* into English, see Bosley's translation, listed in the primary sources section of this chapter.

[3]   Translations are my own unless otherwise indicated.

[4]   For valuable examinations of Estonian folk song traditions and the *Kalevipoeg*, see especially Tedre 1969, Annist 1966, and (in English) *Kalevipoeg* (Kurman 1982) and Oinas 1985.

Low German. And, finally, the intriguing thematic linkages of the songs with mythic themes found in other North Eurasian and even North American culture areas, argue for contacts and diffusion processes occurring over many centuries. Balto-Finnic song traditions are qualitatively different, in other words, from the Scandinavian ballad traditions with which they are sometimes compared, traditions that, as modern research has shown, were frequently shaped by clerical, literate, and literary forces that do not seem to have operated to the same degree within the peasant communities on the northern and southern shores of the Gulf of Finland. This is not to say that new ideas or motifs did not occasionally diffuse into these song traditions, as we shall see below. But it is relatively safe to suggest that a song common to Finnish, Karelian, and Estonian song traditions, widely distributed and displaying the characteristics of the alliterative song tradition, is likely to be of significant antiquity, reaching back at least into the medieval era.

The epic songs and incantations collected among Finns, Karelians, Ingrians, Votes, and Estonians during the nineteenth century contain a number of myths concerning the sun and the heavens. In the southern range, i.e., the areas in closest long-term contact with Baltic cultures, images of solar courtship and marriage occur, as we shall see below. More fundamental within the Balto-Finnic tradition, however, appear to be variants of a bird-egg myth, in which the origin of the cosmos results from the recovery of one or more fractured eggs, laid on a small outcropping of land (or hero's limb) above the wide expanse of a primordial sea, and eventually sundered to create the land, sky, clouds, sun, moon, and all other heavenly bodies. In Estonian, Votic, and Ingrian versions, the bird responsible for this feat is often referred to as a migratory swallow, bat, waterfowl, or *päivälintu*, "sunbird" (Valk 2000). A song collected in the village of Halliste, Estonia, in 1889 recounts:

> Pääsukeine, päevalindu—
> tei ta pesa söödu pääle.
> Munne kolmi muna sisse:
> üits sai aoss alla ilma,
> teine päevas pääle ilma,
> kolmas sai kuusse taevasse. (Tedre 1969 I: 15)

> (Little swallow, sunbird—
> built a nest upon a field.
> She laid three eggs inside:
> One became the dawn light for the lower world
> The second the sun for the upper world
> The third the moon in the sky.)

Here, as in the Old Norse material, the sun—*päeva*—is distinguished from the light of dawn, which exists separately from it. In 1883, V. Porkka collected a similar song from Paroi, Saku's wife, in Hevaa, Kaprio, Ingria:

> Pääsköilintu päivöilintu
> haravoi meroin kokkoon
> kaikki ruokot meroista
> ja kaikki kaislat kaislikosta.
> Löysi puolet ruskeaista
> toisen puolen valkeaista
> kolmaas kelloin karvallista:
> mikä puolet oli ruskeaista
> se kuuksi kumoittamaan,
> mikä puoli valkeaista
> se päivöiksi paistamaan,
> mikä kelloin karvallista
> se pilviksi pakeneviksi. (SKVR 4(2) no. 1821; Kuusi et al. 1977: 84)

> (The swallow bird, the sun bird
> raked the seabed together
> all the seaweed from the seas
> all the reeds from the marshes.
> She found a part that was ruddy
> Also a part that was white
> A third part that was yellow:
> That which was ruddy
> Became the moon to glow;
> That which was white
> Became the sun to shine;
> That which was yellow
> Became the clouds to drift.)

In other versions of such songs, the sun is formed from the yolk of the egg or eggs which the bird recovers (Tedre 1969 I: 13–15; Valk 2000). The sun is thus created at the same time as all other elements of the sky, which come to supplement the primordial sea and mythic beings like the bird and whatever gods or other figures assist her in the recovery of the shattered fragments. The sun is not preeminent and is not personified, although the myth as a whole has a decidedly female cast in that it depicts key events in the creation of the heavenly bodies as the result of a mother seeking restoration of her lost offspring.

In some areas, e.g., in the Karelian song traditions, figures like the hero/god Väinämöinen are included as ancillary or even central actors in this creation narrative. Väinämöinen's knee or some other appendage serves as the nesting place for the bird (often an eagle, hawk, or duck), and he uses words to transform the shattered eggs into celestial bodies (Kuusi 1963a: 64–71; Pentikäinen 1989: 131–32; Honko et al. 1993: 96–97; Tarkka 2013: 209–13). The instigator of the egg's destruction in such more northerly versions—as often in the versions collected in Estonia and Ingria as well, if specified—is a male deity, Ukko (a god of thunder and/or the sky), or Jumala, the term used in modern Finnish for the supreme deity of Christianity. Occasionally, the toppling of the eggs is attributed to Väinämöinen. The rake that the bird employs, like the heavens themselves in other epic songs, may be described as the work of the god Ilmarinen. Parallels to the Balto-Finnic egg myth are found in other parts of the world, including the eastern Mediterranean, South Asia, the Malay Archipelago, Oceania, and Australia (motif A641 in Stith Thompson's index), although Ülo Valk suggests that the particular myth as reflected in Balto-Finnic songs may be of independent origin and predate Indo-European arrival in the Nordic region (Valk 2000: 154). Matti Kuusi posits that Finno-Ugric mythology may have contained a key dichotomy in a god of the heavens (Ilmarinen) and a god of the waters (Väinämöinen), and that the production of the sun may represent a transfer of items from the watery realm to the sky (Kussi 1963: 71).

Another widespread myth related to the sun in Balto-Finnic song traditions relates its theft and eventual restoration (Kuusi 1963a: 70–71; Kuusi et al. 1977: 195–204). Like the cosmogonic egg myth, this narrative has parallels in many other parts of the world (motif A721.1 "Theft of the Sun" and A1411 "Theft of Light" in Thompson 1932–1936). In Balto-Finnic songs, the sun (sometimes also the moon) disappears from the sky or is stolen, to be restored by the heroic acts of the song's main character. In a song collected from an unidentified singer in Paltamo, Finland sometime before 1825, for instance, the sun is imprisoned in a rock:

> Minne, sano, meiltä päivä peäty
> kunnas meiltä kuu katosi?
> Päivä peäty kalliohon. (SKVR 12(2) no. 99; Kuusi et al. 1977: 195)

> (Say where our sun has been taken
> where has our moon disappeared to?
> The sun has been taken into a rock.)

The hero, who must release the sun by hammering the rock, may be Väinämöinen, as in the above song, or sometimes Jesus (SKVR 4(2) no. 1838; Kuusi et al. 1977: 200–4) but is not always divine or male. In a version of the song collected from a female singer named Natelia in Soikkola in 1883, for instance, the rescuing hero is a smith's wife:

> Sepoin nain selvä nain
> nii joutui omille maille.
> Oli isoin ikkunalla
> oli kasvant kultain koivu
> oli kasvant hoppiia honka:
> sinne tuo laati päivyeen
> ja laati kuun kumattammaa. (SKVR 3(1) no. 1150; Kuusi et al. 1977: 199)

> (The smith's wife, a clear-headed woman
> thus made it to her own lands.
> There was at the window of her fathers
> There a golden birch had grown
> There a silver pine had grown
> That is where she placed her sun
> and set the moon to shine.)

The woman sets the sun in a tree for the benefit of her community (Thompson motif A714.2). In such songs, the widespread international myth of the theft and release of the sun can be discerned (A721.1); in these myths the sun, unpersonified in itself, is a boon to be rescued and restored to the sky (or first placed in the sky) by the benevolent actions of a likely or unlikely culture hero, often a trickster. Often in Balto-Finnic songs, the rescue is also accompanied by the imagery of a bridal quest (Thompson motif R225), in which the culture hero must elude the pursuit of some guardian(s) of the sun who would sequester the sun again. Pursuit recurs in these songs, as in the Old Norse wolf myths, but the outcome is better: in the end, the sun survives to shine in the sky and illuminate the earth.

A third key sun-related myth found in the Balto-Finnic song complex is the story of a giant oak that for a time so completely screens the light of the sun that the world is plunged into darkness (Honko et al. 1993: 98–100). Pentikäinen (1989: 164–65) regards it as related to the myth of the world tree, something which has plentiful parallels in the Norse tradition and is implicated in Bronze Age solar myths, as discussed below. It is noteworthy that the Finnish word for

January, *tammikuu*, literally "oak moon", reflects this myth, and that Latvian *dainas* collected by Krišjānis Barons (as discussed below) occasionally reference mythic oaks in relation to the sun.[5] In this song complex, the sun is not a personified being but rather a source of light, obscured by a massive tree. As Anders Andrén notes, the Bronze Age biotope of the Nordic-Baltic region was dominated by deciduous trees: the coniferous dominance and relative rarity of oaks within the region today was not always the case (Andrén 2014: 46).

A fourth, less prominent mythic tendency in some of the Balto-Finnic songs is to refer to the sun as a female deity *Päivätär*, parallel to a similarly female moon deity *Kuutar* (Turunen 1981: 270). In wedding songs, both beings are described weaving wedding clothes of gold and silver. Anna-Leena Siikala notes that Karelian bathing charms, such as those used to ensure fertility of the bride in wedding preparations and for other healing or protective functions, often subsume Päivätär into the figure of the Virgin Mary (Siikala 2002: 118, 197). Perhaps related to these details is the reference to the mythical land *Päivölä*, visited by the epic hero Lemminkäinen as part of a bridal quest. As Siikala has shown, these Päivölä songs contain striking shamanic elements and can be regarded as an epic account of shamanic cosmic travel (Siikala 2002: 270–71). At the same time, it is travel that is tied to a marriage quest, one in which the culture hero aims at obtaining for himself a bride from the land of the sun or the daughter of the sun. Such is exemplified in the opening of a song collected in Kiimasjärvi in 1872 in which the impetuous Lemmingäine calls for raiment to outfit him for his quest:

> Oi on emo kandajaizen
> tuo tänne sodisobani
> kannas vainovoattieni
> piiruloissa piettäväni
> häissä häilyteldäväni:
> lähem Päivöläm pidoho
> suarijoukon juomingihi! (SKVR 1(2) no. 716; Kuusi et al. 1977: 207)

> (Oh mother who bore me
> bring here my war gear
> fetch my killer clothes
> that I can wear at the party
> that I can show off at the wedding

---

[5] For *dainas* incorporating this motif, see the Barons database: http://www.dainuskapis.lv/meklet/Ozols-auga%20Daugav%C4%81 (accessed April 4, 2015).

I'm leaving for the feast in the Land of the Sun
for the drinking bout of the island crowd.)

Lemminkäinen's reception at Päivölä makes it evident that he has come as a suitor or wedding guest, albeit one who is very unwelcome. In this song complex, in other words, the sun seems to be equipped with human societal characteristics like a realm, a court, and a family. Siikala points out that otherworldly courting sites like Päivölä in Balto-Finnic songs are generally presided over by women rather than men: although a hero like Lemminkäinen may eventually battle a male host, he is initially greeted and rejected by the presiding woman of the house, the *emäntä* (Siikala 2002: 322). Siikala also points out that in some Ingrian songs, a son of the sun (Päivän poika) heads to the land of the dead (Tuoni) in quest of a bride (Siikala 2002: 315). Here the solar associations remain, although the sun has become attached to the suitor instead of the bride, a detail shared with the Estonian song discussed below.

A divergent depiction of the sun appears in the Estonian song known as "Tähemõrsja" (The Star Bride) (Tedre 1969 II: 18–19). Here, a human maiden Salme is courted by male astral figures: the sun, the moon, and a star. She rejects the sun and moon but eventually consents to marry the star suitor. Felix Oinas has examined this song's variants and motifs in detail and suggests that it represents not an ancient part of the Balto-Finnic song tradition but rather a medieval or post-medieval loan from Russian Orthodox song traditions, a finding which helps explain its different portrayal of the sun and the limited distribution of the song to only the Estonian tradition (Oinas n.d.).

To summarize, then, in most Balto-Finnic mythic songs the sun appears usually as an object, produced, stolen, or regained by other beings: female birds, male deities, or human women. The myths feature male deities more prominently in the more northerly reaches of the tradition (e.g., in Finnish and Karelian songs), while female beings—female birds, a farmwife, female wedding attendants, and so on—play more central or uncontested roles in more southerly reaches (e.g., in Ingrian, Votic, and Estonian songs). Songs related to the recovery of the sun sometimes employ bridal quest imagery, and wedding songs and fertility incantations occasionally refer to the sun as a personified goddess, weaving clothing and ensuring the fertility of the bridal couple. The figure of Päivätär and the land of Päivölä indicate a more personified notion of the sun, one with parallels to the personified sun descriptions in Old Norse and, more particularly, to those found in Sámi and Baltic materials. In both the Balto-Finnic and Old Norse traditions, however, these personified sun images exist alongside a more prominent unpersonified image of the sun as a source of light or flame.

Sámi Tradition and Anders Fjellner's Poetry

Sámi pre-Christian beliefs are known primarily through seventeenth- and eighteenth-century missionary accounts of pagan "backsliding", as well as certain items of material culture, such as the seventy-some shamanic drums that survived decay and willful destruction from this same era. The status of the sun in these materials has been meticulously examined by Bo Lundmark (1982, 1985), building on the authoritative two-volume survey of Sámi shamanic drums provided by Ernst Manker (1938, 1950). All of these materials have been recently reviewed and reanalyzed by, among others, Juha Pentikäinen (1995) and Hans Mebius (2003).

The sun (North Sámi *beaivi*, South Sámi *biejjie*) figures prominently on Sámi shamanic drumheads surviving from the eighteenth century (Manker 1938, 1950; Mebius 2003). Here, the sun often occupies a central area (Manker 1950: 58–59). In many drums produced in the South Sámi area, the sun is depicted as rhomboid, with rays emanating outward in four directions, rays which in turn are populated by various personified deities (Manker 1950: 62–68). In other drums produced farther to the North, however, the sun is depicted as round or as a wheel, as for instance on the drum now preserved at the Vatican (Pentikäinen 1995: 128). Images of the sun could also figure on the back side of drums. Such round or wheel-like suns are reminiscent of the Old Norse unpersonified sun terms, and the sun on such objects may have played a role in cosmic navigation, i.e., in helping the *noaidi* (shaman) account for or depict the different astral and underworld realms with reference to the visible world. Yet it may also have been the object of entreaties, as missionary accounts of ritual practices indicate (see below). And many deities on the drumheads are depicted with images that do not imply personification even though they were viewed in anthropomorphic terms: as Manker has shown, for instance, the important male deity known variously as Ipmel, Raedie (ruler), Raedieaehtjie (ruler's father), Máilmmeraedie (world ruler), or Vearelden ålmaj (man of the world) is usually represented as some sort of building topped with crosses (Manker 1950: 76–89). Whatever the broader meaning of such depictions, for the purposes of the present discussion, the main lesson conveyed by the drumheads is that the sun played a central role in the cosmology and ritual life of the *noaidi*.

In his 1671 overview of Sámi culture and religious practices, Samuel Rheen (d. 1680) asserts:

> Den tredie Afgudh lapparna offra är Sohlen, den dhe för een Moder hålla för alle lefwande diur, Conservera deras Rehnfoster och medhela them then naturlige warman att the wäll må trijwas, hvarföre the och

offra henne Unge Reenar, och särdeles the som ähro af waijo kiönet. (Quoted in Mebius 2003: 75)

(The third false god to whom the Sámi make offerings is the Sun, which they regard as the mother of all living creatures, one who takes care of their young reindeer and provides them with natural warmth so that they may thrive. For this [service] they offer her young reindeer, and especially ones of the female sex.)

Rheen had entered university at Uppsala in 1633 and served as a minister/preacher in both Jokkmokk and Kvikkjokk from 1666 to 1671. His study's sixteen chapters include three on Sámi religious practices, shamanic drums, and bear rituals. His account has been regarded as a careful and apparently accurate account of practices then current among Lule Sámi people (Mebius 2003: 32). It is also clear, however, that his status as a minister made it difficult for him to obtain a full account of Sámi pre-Christian traditions. Nevertheless, his emphasis on the feminine nature of the sun and her status as a mother to all creatures is a characterization that squares well with other evidence regarding Sámi beliefs regarding the sun.

An important ritual associated with the sun and described in various sources consisted of preparing and consuming a porridge made of the inner bark of pine trees. The missionary Hans Skanke (1679–1739), drawing on the notes of Thomas von Westen (1682–1727), describes the production of such porridge on midsummer night's eve (Lundmark 1985: 183). Although Skanke's account focuses primarily on the South Sámi area, other parallel accounts, along with the scar evidence on surviving Scots pine trees, indicates the widespread nature of the custom (Bergman et al. 2004). The sun is a deity of fertility and nourishment, one lovingly entreated for help in the lean moments of the North Nordic early spring.

In the mid-nineteenth century, the Sámi minister Anders Fjellner (1795–1876) produced several extended poems, constructed, apparently, of narratives he knew from his childhood South Sámi tracts or his adult life in North and Lule Sámi parishes (Lundmark 1979). Fjellner's works are authored poems, reflective of Fjellner's literary aspirations. Yet they probably also reflect at least some of the concepts of the sun common to the communities he lived in. His explicit aim in creating these poems was to celebrate Sámi cultural identity and oral literature, aims that, one might posit, would have led him to attempt in some way to stay close to his source tradition.

In the poem "Biejjie-baernien såangoe Jeahnaj eatnamisnie" (North Sámi "Beaivvi bártni soagŋu Jiehtanasaid máilmmis") (The Sons of the Sun in the

Thomas A. DuBois

Land of the Giants), one of the sons of Gállá (a Sámi name for the stars of Orion's belt) or perhaps Gállá himself (the Sámi name for the star Sirius) embarks on a bridal quest to the land of the giants (Fjellner 2003: 3). He charms the giant's daughter and with her help accomplishes marriage trials to win her hand. After the couple have had their wedding and have embarked on their homeward journey with plentiful wedding gifts, the girl's brothers pursue them, leading to an exciting chase and the release of magic winds. The bride and groom become the progenitors of the Sámi. Even more interesting is the lyric poem Fjellner composed (or, possibly, recorded) regarding the death of the "daughter of the Sun", "Biejjie-neijten sealadimmie" (North Sámi "Beaivvi Niedda jápmin") (The Death of the Daughter of the Sun) (Gaski 2006). The poem depicts the dying moments of the daughter of the sun, who has lived on earth a lifetime and now yearns to return to the sky:

> Beaivi luoitá, gumppet bohtet
> ihkku njáhket bivdimin
> Čiehkádallet seavdnjadasas
> Iđit boahtá, iigo dáidde?
>
> ....
> Johtá goitge
> Beaivvi nieida Beaivvi lusa
> Váldá Beaivvi mánáid mielde
> Iđit boahtá, iigo dáidde? (Quoted in Gaski 2006: 15)
>
> (The Sun/day gives way, wolves approach
> hunting in the night
> lurking in the dark
> Morning comes, will it not?
>
> ....
> But she proceeds
> the Sun's daughter, home to the Sun
> takes along the Sun's children
> Morning comes, will it not?)

Here, the wolf imagery so prevalent in the Old Norse material recurs. We are reminded of why such a metaphor would arise: wolves come out as darkness sets in, posing threats to the Sámi reindeer herd and to the domestic livestock of medieval Scandinavians alike. As the poem relates, the sun's daughter returns to the heavens, ending her mythic sojourn on earth—presumably the result of a mythic marriage.

Fjellner's poems, along with other corroborating evidence, suggest a strong tendency in the Sámi material to view the sun, or at least the sun's daughter, as a female deity, one who entered into marital relations with a hero from the sky and who became a progenitor of the Sámi people. It is important to point out, as Bo Lundmark notes, that in the Kola region, Sámi traditions often represented the sun in particular as male, making the sun the father of the "Biejjien niejde" known in North and South Sámi traditions (Lundmark 1985: 187). In a sense, this view of the sun as masculine is a logical outgrowth of the notion of a sun daughter or sun bride, one expectable in a culture in which fathers played a central role in negotiating and securing their daughter's marriages. It may also reflect Russian Orthodox influence, as might the Estonian "Tähemõrsja" discussed above. The fact that Sámi has no grammatical gender probably helped facilitate this logical progression or gender ambiguity in a manner that may have been hampered in Germanic and Baltic languages, where the words for the sun are of feminine gender. Crucially, as in the Old Norse and Balto-Finnic cases, we find in these Sámi materials both an apparently unpersonified sun image and a personified one. But here, the balance seems to shift decidedly toward the personified, as the sun becomes both overtly female and an ancestor of the Sámi themselves.

Latvian Myths

Like their Finno-Ugric neighbors to the north, the Latvians developed elaborate song traditions. A particularly strong tradition was ritual songs, sung at various times of the year and in key life cycle moments like weddings.[6] In fact, in Latvian wedding songs in particular, the sun figures as a frequent and richly described character. The comprehensive and acclaimed six volumes of published *dainas*, collected and edited by Krišjānis Barons and appearing in print between 1894 and 1915 (and now available digitally) are even more recent additions to the textual record (Barons nd). Yet, like the Balto-Finnic songs, they evince strong evidence of antiquity, and Baltic scholars—both Latvian and Lithuanian—have been unanimous in regarding them as prime sources for the reconstruction of pre-Christian Baltic mythology. Foremost among these scholars has been Haralds Biezais, whose richly nuanced studies examine the vast store of recorded *dainas* for recurring details and a unifying logic (Biezais 1954, 1961, 1972, 1976).

---

[6] For an excellent overview of the Latvian *daina* tradition, see the various articles in the edited volume *Linguistics and Poetics of Latvian Folk Songs* (Vīķe-Freiberga 1989).

In the various *dainas* collected during the nineteenth century, the sky god Dievs is often involved in one way or another in an astral wedding featuring the sun. The sun's suitors include Dieva dēli, "the sons of Dievs", Mēness, "the moon", Mēnesnieks, "moonlight", and "Auseklis", a term that may refer to either the light of dawn or the morning star (Venus). Typical of these short but evocative songs is the following, in which the sun's suitors are referred to as the sons of Dievs:

> Dieva dēli, Saules meitas
> Vidū gaisa kāzas dzēra;
> Mēnesnīca tekādama
> Tā pārmija gredzeniņus. (Biezais 1976: 514)

> (The Dieva dēli [sons of Dievs], and Saules meita [daughter
>   of the sun]
> Celebrated their wedding up in the air.
> The landscape was moonlit as they proceeded
> Exchanged dear/little rings.)

Another song describes an evening sky in which the morning star (Auseklis) is absent since he has gone to attend the sun's wedding:

> Mēnesītis zvaigznes skaita,
> Vai ir visas vakarā.
> Visas bija vakarā,
> Auseklīša vien nebij.
> Auseklītis aztecēja,
> Saules meitas kāzas dzert.
> Dieviņš ņēma Saules meitu,
> Pērkons jāja vedībās. (Biezais 1961: 125)

> (Mēnesītis [moon] counts the stars
> [to see] if they are all there in the evening.
> All are there in the evening
> Only Auseklis [morning star] is not.
> Auseklis has gone
> To celebrate the wedding of the daughter of the sun.
> Dievs takes the daughter of the sun as his bride,
> Pērkons [thunder] makes up part of the groom's party.)

In many songs, and paralleled by the human rituals at earthly weddings at which such songs were traditionally performed, the sun prepares her daughter for marriage, dressing and adorning her appropriately for the event and providing wedding gifts to all attendees. In the following *daina*, the sun provides dowry gifts to the forest trees:

> Kam tie tādi kumeliņi
> Sudrabiņa podziņām?
> Dieva dēla kumeliņi,
> Saules meita vedamā.
> Pate Saule pūru veda,
> Visus mežus veltīdama:
> Ozolam raibi cimdi,
> Liepai mēļu vilnainīte,
> Smalkajam kārkliņam
> Apzeltīti prievietiņi (Biezais 1961: 126)

> (Who has such horses
> With silver buttons?
> the horses of Diev's son
> come for the daughter of the sun.
> The sun herself provided the dowry
> Gave gifts to all the forest:
> Colorful gloves for the oak,
> A dark blue little woolen kerchief for the linden
> For the fine little willow bush
> Gilded stocking garters.)

With all attendees properly gifted, the community prepares for a wedding celebration that, like its human counterpart in Latvian folk custom, will last for days: "Trīs dieniņas, trīs naksiņas/Dieviņam kāzas dzēra" (Biezais 1961: 126) (Three days, three nights, was Diev's wedding celebrated). Here it is easy to imagine parallels with the eddic poem *Skírnismál*, where the bride, as in the Sámi poem described above, is described as a giant's daughter, and the marriage (or sexual encounter) is one of male god and female earth, the core of the mythic *hieros gamos* tradition. In Latvian songs, however, the bride is unambiguously described as the sun or the sun's daughter, and her home is in the sky, not on the earth. She marries another denizen of the sky, and her wedding holds significance for all the cosmos, heavens and earth combined.

Haralds Biezais points out that the term *Saules meita* places the word for sun, *saule*, in the genitive, where it can mean either of two things. As an appellative genitive, the term would mean "the maiden, the sun": i.e., the sun herself would be the maiden bride (Biezais 1962: 127; 1972: 184–90). This appellative use of the genitive is common in Latvian folksongs, where, for instance, the Virgin Mary can be called "Maṛas jumpraviṇa" (literally, "the virgin of Mary") (Biezais 1962: 128). As a possessive genitive, however, *Saules meita* would mean "the daughter *of* the sun", in which the maiden is the sun's child, whose wedding is being arranged and celebrated by a loving astral parent. Perhaps we can see in *Saule* and *Saules meita* a mother-daughter relationship much as in the Old Norse texts discussed above, in which the sun (Álfrǫðull or Sól) will give birth to a daughter, who will follow in her mother's path in the world after Ragnarǫk. In any case, the distinction between the sun and the sun's offspring is perhaps not as significant as it might at first seem, since in Latvian weddings—and in the mythology that these songs seem to suggest—a daughter is a metonym for her family, a product and fulfillment of her natal household, the entirety of which is implicated in marriage. In a sense she *is* her family, at least in the act of marriage.

The female sun and her daughter are described in rich detail in the various *dainas*. Their clothing and jewelry is enumerated and beauty praised. Their activities include greeting the suitors, who, as in the above-quoted text, tend to arrive on horseback (Biezais 1972: 204). The sun or her daughter also owns and uses horses and wagons (Biezais 1972: 207), particularly when traversing the mountain of the sky (Biezais 1972: 211, 236–48). The sun owns a boat as well (Biezais 1972: 212), a detail paralleled, as Anders Andrén notes, by Bronze Age petroglyphs as well as Gotlandic picture stones, as I will discuss below (Andrén 2014: 123). In the night the sun travels back to the East by crossing a sea (Biezais 1972: 278–302), riding in a ship or wading:

> Mēnestiņis tā vaicāja:
> Kur, Saulīte, nakti guli?
> Sak' Saulīte raudādama:
> Vai es arī nakti gulu?
> Dienu teku zaļu birzi,
> Nakti zelta laiviņā (Biezais 1972: 289).

> (Mēnestiņis [moon] asked thus:
> Where, Saulīte [sun], do you sleep at night?
> Says Saulīte [sun] weeping:
> Do I sleep at night?
> In the daytime I run in a green grove
> In the night in a golden boat.)

Although this image has connections with solar myths reaching back to the Bronze Age, as we shall note below, the sun is also frequently depicted wading her way through the sea:

> Saules meita jūru brida,
> Ne matiņus neredzēja;
> Dieva dēli gan redzēja,
> Kur met jūŗa burbulīšus. (Biezais 1972: 279)

> (Saules meita [daughter of the sun] wades in the sea
> Her hair was not seen
> Dieva dēli [Diev's sons] saw indeed
> Where the sea casts foam.)

Sometimes, as the above *daina* indicates, this wading is such that the maiden is almost completely submerged, with only her crown showing above the surface of the water:

> Saules meita jūrā slīka
> Vainadziņu vien redzēja;
> Dieva dēls kalniņa
> Zelta krustu vēcināja. (Biezais 1972: 279)

> (Saules meita [daughter of the sun] sank in the sea
> Only her crown was visible;
> Dieva dēls [Diev's son] on the little mountain
> Dangled a golden cross.)

This image makes particular sense in the West of Latvia and Lithuania, where the setting sun is seen to sink into the Baltic Sea, reemerging in the East at dawn, having traversed an unseen sea or underworld in her return to her starting place.

In Latvian folk custom, similes likening the astral and human bridal couple were flattering to the families involved in the wedding, but they also, according to Biezais, preserved mythic concepts that had survived from the ancient past regarding the sun. As in Germanic languages, Baltic sun terms are grammatically feminine, a fact which must have helped preserve or even intensify the goddess imagery within the song tradition. In any case, we find in the Latvian material virtually no tendency to regard the sun as an unpersonified flame, wheel, or spark. Instead, the sun is consistently depicted as a female deity, fully anthropomorphized and explicitly likened to a human bride, or mother of a bride, through the ritual use of sun *dainas* in wedding celebrations.

Areal Comparison

What this survey of the varying sun images of the Nordic-Baltic region demonstrates, I believe, is that two different understandings of the sun have prevailed in the region and that these show geographic concentrations as well as areas of overlap. We can tabulate these differences with respect to particular cultures as follows:

	flame	disk	released	pursued	chariot	bridal quest	bride	suitor	goddess
Old Norse	+	+	-	+	+	-	(+)	(+)	(+)
Balto-Finnic	+	+	+	(+)	-	(+)	(+)	(+)	(+)
Sámi	-	(+)	-	(+)	-	+	+	+	(+)
Latvian	-	-	-	(+)	+	+	+	+	+

In the above listing, a plus sign means that the listed mythic motif is clearly present within the culture's recorded materials. A plus sign within parentheses denotes cases in which the motif is only weakly evidenced but is nonetheless logically expectable, given other present motifs. And a minus sign means that the motif is seldom or never found in the tradition, at least as far as we can tell from extant evidence. As can be seen, the Old Norse and Balto-Finnic traditions show a strong cluster of features on the unpersonified side of the listing, with some evidence of bridal and goddess imagery as well. The Sámi and Latvian traditions show an opposite skewing, with a strong clustering of features on the personified, female side of the listing and only sporadic inclusion of unpersonified images related to the sun. Both the Balto-Finnic and Sámi examples show a mediating array of features, although it is noteworthy that the details of the Sámi and Latvian traditions seem a good deal closer to each other than to the Balto-Finnic or Old Norse. In particular, the Sámi myth of an astral hero embarking on a quest to marry an astral bride seems startlingly close to the Latvian tradition. And the fact that Sámi, like the Balto-Finnic languages, possesses no grammatical gender makes the striking feminine attributes of the Sámi sun myths all the more significant. It is also noteworthy that if we separate the Balto-Finnic traditions to songs collected north of the Gulf of Finland from those common to the South, we find a stronger tendency toward feminine imagery in the southern area than in the North.

The possibility of cultural diffusion here seems plausible, in which an eastern Baltic goddess myth has diffused productively northward at an early period, to be strongly adopted in Sámi traditions (and transformed into a distinctively Sámi myth) and combined in the Balto-Finnic song tradition with a similarly feminine bird egg myth. Some of the stray epithets described in the Old Norse materials—e.g., *Alvíssmál's ása synir*, "sons of the gods" and *Grímnismál's brúði himins*, "bride of the sky"—suggest that the Norse mythology may have come in contact with or shared such a marriage myth to some extent, whether it be as a result of contact with Latvians, Balto-Finns, or Sámi, or through an independent Germanic development arising from the grammatical gender of sun terms in Old Norse. In any case, by the era during which the eddic poems were composed or written down, the sun was also known to have a father, brother, and husband, and to ride in a chariot pursued by wolves.

One way to account for contradictions in the Old Norse mythological conceptions of the sun is to posit an evolution of ideas. Changes in understandings of the sun can occur over time, and to some extent these can be discerned through archaeological data, as Anders Andrén has shown in his important study *Tracing Old Norse Cosmology* (2014). For Andrén, Norse, Sámi, and Baltic cultures share an underlying set of cosmological understandings concerning the sun that date at least to the Bronze Age. Drawing on Flemming Kaul (2004), Andrén sees the Bronze Age itself (ca. 1500 BCE) as witnessing the development of a concept of the sun drawn in a chariot pulled by one or two horses, an image that finds its most stirring embodiment in the Bronze Age Trundholm sun chariot (Andrén 2014: 126). The sun chariot construct finds partial replication in several other finds, including horse sculptures recovered at Tågaberg (Skåne) and Järfälla (near Stockholm), as well as some petroglyphs and bronze razor decorations. As Kaul argues, the existence of such chariots and horses does not necessarily imply the existence of an anthropomorphized god or goddess as a driver, and it is notable that the Bronze Age depictions do not seem to include such figures (Kaul 2004: 341). Where personified beings are included, Kaul argues, they seem to be dawn and dusk helpers, perhaps equivalent to the mythic twins of Greek and Roman tradition, the Dioscuri (Kaul 2004: 80). Bronze Age petroglyph images of ships as well as Gotlandic picture stones also seem to indicate that the sun returns to the East overnight by sailing a ship across the dark sea of night (Andrén 2014: 123).

A further stirring image of the sun from ca. 500 BCE is the Eskelheim sun disc, excavated in western Gotland, where it was deposited with a large number of bronze horse bits and fittings. The bronze object, consisting of five concentric rings connected by small spikes, was probably imported into the Nordic region from the South. It appears to depict a sun and may have been attached to a harness or carriage shaft, its attached bronze pieces creating a tinkling sound to accompany movement. Writes Andrén: "This gives us an unusual illustration of a sun symbol in its functional, and probably ritual, context" (Andrén 2014: 133). The disc also shows the addition of waterfowl images and serpent shapes that supplement earlier solar symbols from about 1100 BCE onward. As noted, images of a ship—understood as the means of the sun's nocturnal return journey—also begin to appear in Nordic petroglyphs from around the same period as the Eskelheim sun disc, and appear to be a counterpart to the diurnal chariot image.

According to Andrén, the archaeological record is silent on sun representations for some centuries thereafter (i.e., ca. 500 BCE–200 CE), but sun imagery rises again to prominence in the period ca. 200–550 CE, along with notions of the sun's daily travels, interaction with the world tree, and a return journey through an underworld by ship (Andrén 2014: 165). In Iron Age metalwork as well as early Gotlandic picture stones, swirling sun images figure prominently, as on the Sanda stone, dated to ca. 400 CE (Andrén 201: 138). *Sol-* place-names, widespread in various parts of mainland and insular Scandinavia, appear to indicate a widespread ritual and mythic tradition (Andrén 2014: 159–60). Andrén suggests that this evolving image of a personified sun in Old Norse mythology may have undergone further influence from the rise of the cult of Sol Invictus in late Roman paganism: "It is also possible that the old solar myths were renewed with inspiration from the contemporary Roman world [...] The Roman Dioscuri, as well as the imperial cult of Sol Invictus, which was introduced in the early third century, may have stood as models for local reinterpretations of earlier mythologies" (Andrén 2014: 166). Norse bracteates made in imitation of Roman medallions witness this process of adaptation (Andrén 2014: 179).

In concert with Bo Gräslund (2007) and Daniel Löwenborg (2012), Andrén sees the solar dust veil catastrophe of 535–537 CE as causing a decisive break with earlier solar ideologies.[7] Association with a now-fickle sun seems to have become a political liability that leaders wished to avoid in a context of massive depopulation, settlement abandonment, and social restructuring. In its place, and possibly in imitation of Roman practices associated with temples, villas, and camp forts, there arose a new court-based aristocracy reliant on control of large tracts of land, equipped with larger, more class-differentiated military troops,

---

[7]   Large volcanic eruptions can produce enough atmospheric particulates to alter weather patterns and cool the global climate. These occurrences are now called "dust veil events".

and asserting royal genealogies tied to masculine sky gods distinct from the sun. In a concrete sense, the Old Norse mythological images of gods inhabiting grand halls and engaging in periodic feasts can be tied to this new social system, which seems to have arisen from roughly 550 CE onward (Carlie 2004; Skre 1998; Brink 2001; Myhre 2002; Zachrisson 2011; Fabech and Näsman 2013; Andrén 2014: 187). It may be in this context that unpersonified images of the sun took on a new currency, reinforced by the notion of an inanimate sun within the expanding and influential Christian worldview.

Yet, at the same time, as the above discussion shows, images of a personified sun—particularly envisioned as a celestial bride who will eventually give birth to a new sun—lived on alongside such unpersonified images, reflecting a different, competing cosmological understanding. An areal examination of the mythic traditions of the Nordic-Baltic region suggest that this alternative conceptualization was paralleled or perhaps buttressed in Norse tradition by the myths of neighboring peoples with whom the Norse were engaged in frequent close trade and cultural exchange for millennia. It is difficult to know for certain whether the evidence presented above from late pagan Old Norse tradition and agrarian early modern or modern Sámi, Balto-Finnic, and Baltic cultures are precisely contemporaneous. In accordance with scholars in Sámi studies, Balto-Finnic folklore studies, and Baltic folklore studies, I believe that many of the images described above were extant among Sámi, Balto-Finnic, and Baltic peoples in the era before Christianization, even if their modern recording in folkloric texts and artifacts undoubtedly also reflects later Christian influences. If we accept the folkloric and philological assertions of the antiquity of such widespread and apparently stable images in the North and East of the Nordic-Baltic region, we can conclude that they permit us to look at a multilingual cultural region in which images of an unpersonified flame or disc sun co-occurred with images of a personified sun goddess or anthropomorphic sun.

Conclusion

Focusing on sun imagery within the Nordic-Baltic region allows us to sense the intercultural relations that tied Nordic-Baltic peoples together, despite their differing languages and economies. In other words, although the Norse, Sámi, Balto-Finns, and Balts all spoke different languages, they seem to have known, and perhaps been influenced by, each others' traditions. In the Mediterranean world, it should be noted, an areal perspective on mythology is fully accepted: intercultural borrowing and adaptation of neighboring cults was common and fully normative prior to (or even after) the rise of Christianity. Roman emperors made use of the deities and rituals of neighboring peoples in order to enhance their own authority and demonstrate control over subjugated peoples. In late Roman paganism, the Egyptian Isis, Middle-Eastern variants of Sol Invictus, Judaism, and the Persian god Mithra were all the focus of popular cults, sometimes strongly endorsed by Roman authorities, sometimes merely tolerated, sometimes suppressed. In any case, an openness to religious sharing was regarded as understandable and useful in the sometimes challenging work of uniting peoples into a multiethnic state or empire.

In the small, decentralized communities of the Nordic-Baltic region, such conscious, organized borrowing on the level of statecraft may seem improbable at least prior to the advent of Christianization, when the new faith certainly became a tool for the consolidation of states and royal dynasties. Archaeological evidence from after 550 CE seems to indicate, as Andrén shows, an embrace of gods like those celebrated in Old Norse materials as parallels to a new kind of aristocracy developing in the mid-sixth century (Andrén 2014). But there were also plentiful settlements far less unified or controlled within the Nordic-Baltic area, particularly among the non-Norse populations of the North and East. In such areas, archaeological evidence also makes clear the extent of human exchange across cultural lines. The intensive practice and maintenance of trade relations across the region meant that communities easily became aware of the religious traditions of their neighbors and could easily choose, consciously or unconsciously, to incorporate foreign elements into their ritual practices and mythic conceptions. In the more decentralized Sámi, Balto-Finnic and Baltic communities (as well as in *landnám*-era Iceland), family units played a central role as an organizing principle, and marriages between families were of tremendous importance. In this social context, it makes sense that marriage and weddings were reflected within the mythic system as well. Thus, the female-centered, marriage quest myths of the eastern regions reflect a different, perhaps prior, social system, one just as normative to Sámi or Latvians as the male-dominated court-based myths of Snorri's *Prose Edda* were to late pagan Norse.

An areal perspective here thus provides valuable insights into the potential development, diffusion, or maintenance of competing, contrasting myths within a single region. It acknowledges the fact that Norse, Finno-Ugric (Sámi and Balto-Finnic), and Baltic cultures have lived in close and continuous contact for millennia and have had ample opportunities through the centuries to compare their understandings of the cosmos. Such comparisons are natural when one considers the importance of the sun to all these cultures and their associated livelihoods, be they hunters, fishermen, traders, herders, or farmers. In the process of comparison, mythic elements transfer from one culture to the next, and clearly demarcated categories could become blurred with subtle or striking contradictions. Such does not imply decay or disarray, however, but rather, a process of ongoing evolution, in which new ideas come to dwell along-side older ones in a widening of understandings and mythic models that seek to incorporate or assimilate foreign ideas that are in some way attractive or memorable. In this way, the abstract and seemingly fanciful details of mythic narrative become reflective of the concrete world of intercultural contacts, interactions, and exchange.

•••

Many thanks to both Anders Andrén and Guntis Šmidchens for their comments and advice on earlier drafts of this paper.

Works Cited

Primary Sources

Alvíssmál: see *Poetic Edda*

Grímnismál: see *Poetic Edda*

Gylfaginning: see *Prose Edda*

Kalevala
The Kalevala: An Epic Poem after Oral Tradition. Compiled by Elias Lönnrot. Transl. Keith Bosley. Oxford: 1989.

Kalevipoeg
Kalevipoeg: An Ancient Estonian Tale. Ed. and transl. Jüri Kurman. Compiled by Fr. R. Kreutzwald. Moorestown, NJ: 1982.

Krišjāņa Barona Dainu skapis
Barons, Krišjānis. *Krišjāņa Barona Dainu skapis.* http://dainuskapis.lv/ (accessed April 4, 2015).

Poetic Edda
Edda: Die Lieder des Codex regius nebst verwandten Denkmälern. Ed. Gustav Neckel and Hans Kuhn. Germanische Bibliothek, Vierte Reihe. Heidelberg: 1962.
Translation
The Poetic Edda. Transl. Carolyne Larrington. Oxford: 1996.

Prose Edda
Snorri Sturluson. *Edda: Prologue and Gylfaginning.* Ed. Anthony Faulkes. London: 2005.

Snorri Sturluson. *Edda: Skáldskaparmál.* Vol. 1: Introduction, Text and Notes. Ed. Anthony Faulkes. London: 1998.

TRANSLATION
Snorri Sturluson. *Edda.* Ed. and transl. Anthony Faulkes. London: 1987.

Skáldskaparmál: see *Prose Edda*

Skírnismál: see *Poetic Edda*

SKVR
Suomen Kansan Vanhat Runot. 34 vols. Ed. A. R. Niemi et al. Helsinki: 1908.

Vafðrúðnismál: see *Poetic Edda*

Vǫluspá: see *Poetic Edda*

Secondary Sources

Andrén, Anders. 2014. *Tracing Old Norse Cosmology: The World Tree, Middle Earth, and the Sun in Archaeological Perspectives.* Vägar till Midgård 16. Lund.

Annist, August. 1966. *Friedrich Reinhold Kreutzwaldi muinasjuttude algupära ja kunstiline laad.* Tallinn.

Anttila, Aarne. 1985. *Elias Lönnrot: Elämä ja toiminta.* Helsinki.

Asplund, Anneli, and Matti Hako, eds. 1981. *Kansanmusiikki.* Helsinki.

Asplund, Anneli. 1981a. "Kalevalaiset laulut." In Asplund and Hako 1981: 18–43.

———. 1981b. "Riimilliset kansanlaulut." In Asplund and Hako 1981: 64–124.

Bergman, Ingela, Lars Östlund, and Olle Zackrisson. 2004. "The Use of Plants as Regular Food in Ancient Subarctic Economies: A Case Study Based on Sami Use of Scots Pine Innerbark." *Arctic Anthropology* 41(1): 1–13.

Biezais, Haralds. 1954. *Die Religionsquellen der baltischen Völker und die Ergebnisse der bisherigen Forschungen.* Uppsala.

———. 1961. *Die Gottesgestalt der lettischen Volksreligion.* Stockholm.

———. 1972. *Die Himmliche Götterfamilie der alten Letten.* Uppsala.

———. 1976. *Lichtgott der alten Letten.* Stockholm.

Brink, Stefan. 2001. "Mythologizing the Landscape: Place and Space of Cult and Myth." In *Kontinuität und Brüche in der Religionsgeschichte.* Ed. M. Stausberg. Berlin. Pp. 76–112.

Carlie, Anne. 2004. *Forntida byggnadskult in tradition och regionalitet in södra Skandinavien.* Stockholm.

DuBois, Thomas A. 1995. *Finnish Folk Poetry and the Kalevala.* New York.

Fabech, Charlotte, and Ulf Näsman. 2013. "Ritual Landscapes and Sacral Places in the First Millennium AD in South Scandinavia." In *Sacred Sites and Holy*

Places: Exploring the Sacralization of Landscape through Time and Space. Ed. Sæbjørg Walaker Nordeide and Stefan Brink. Turnhout. Pp. 53–109.

Fjellner, Anders. 2003. *Biejjien baernie. Beaivvi bárdni. Sámi Son of the Sun by Anders Fjellner*. Ed. Harald Gaski. Karasjok.

Gaski, Harald, ed. 2006. *25 sámi čáppa- ja fágagirjjálaš sátneduojára*. Kárášjohka.

Gräslund, Bo. 2007 "Fimbulvintern, Ragnarök och klimatkrisen år 536–537 e. Kr." *Saga och Sed*: 93–123.

Hako, Matti. 1963. "Riimilliset kansanlaulut." In Kuusi 1963a: 410–46.

Harvilahti, Lauri. 1992. *Kertovan runon keinot: Inkeriläisen runoepiikan tuottamisesta*. Helsinki.

Honko, Lauri, Senni Timonen, and Michael Branch, eds. 1993. *The Great Bear: A Thematic Anthology of Oral Poetry in the Finno-Ugrian Languages*. Helsinki.

Kaukonen, Väinö. 1939–1945. *Vanhan Kalevalan kokoonpano*. 2 vols. Helsinki.

Kaul, Flemming. 2004. *Bronzealderens religion: Studier af den nordiske bronzealders ikonografi*. Copenhagen.

Korhonen, Mikko. 1994. "The Early History of the Kalevala Meter." In Siikala and Vakimo 1994: 75–90.

Kuusi, Matti, ed. 1963a. *Suomen kirjallisuus I: Kirjoittamaton kirjallisuus*. Helsinki.

———. 1963b. "Keskiajan kalevalainen runous." In Kuusi 1963a: 273–410.

Kuusi, Matti, Keith Bosley, and Michael Branch. 1977. *Finnish Folk Poetry: Epic*. Helsinki.

Kuusi, Matti, and Pertti Anttonen. 1995. *Kalevala-lipas*. Helsinki.

Leino, Pentti. 1994. "The Kalevala Metre and Its Development." In Siikala and Vakimo 1994: 56–74.

Lundmark, Bo. 1979. *Anders Fjellner—Samernas Homeros och diktningen om Solsönerna*. Acta Bothniensia Occidentalis 4. Umeå.

———. 1982. *Bæi'vi mánno nástit: Sol och månkult samt astrala och celesta föreställningar bland samerna*. Acta Bothniensia Occidentalis. Skrifter i västerbottnisk kulturhistoria 5. Umeå.

———. 1985. "'They Consider the Sun to Be a Mother to All Living Creatures': The Sun-Cult of the Saamis." *Arv* 41: 179–88.

Löwenborg, Daniel. 2012. "An Iron Age Shock Doctrine—Did the AD 536-7 Event Trigger Large-Scale Social Changes in the Mälaren Valley Area?" *Journal of Archaeology and Ancient History* 4: 3–29.

Manker, Ernst. 1938. *Die lappische Zaubertrommel. Eine Ethnologische Monographie. Vol I. Die Trommel als Denkmal materieller Kultur*. Acta Lapponica 1. Stockholm.

———. 1950. *Die lappische Zaubertrommel. Eine Ethnologische Monographie. Vol II. Die Trommel als Urkunde geistligen Lebens*. Acta Lapponica 6. Stockholm.

Mebius, Hans. 2003. *Bissie: Studier i samisk religionshistoria*. Östersund.

Myhre, Bjørn. 2002. "Landbruk, landskap og samfunn 4000 f. Kr-800 e. Kr." In *4000 f.Kr.-1350 e.Kr.: jorda blir levevei*. Vol. 1 of *Norges landbrukshistorie*. Ed. Bjørn Myhre and Ingvild Øye. Oslo. Pp. 1–214.

Oinas, Felix. 1985. *Studies in Finnic Folklore*. Helsinki.

———. n.d. "Tähemõrsja." http://www.folklore.ee/rl/folkte/myte/kalev2/tahemorsja.html (accessed April 4, 2015).

Pentikäinen, Juha. 1989. *Kalevala Mythology*. Transl. Ritva Poom. Bloomington & Indianapolis.

———. 1995. *Saamelaiset—Pohjoisen Kansan Mytologia*. Helsinki.

Sadeniemi, Matti. 1951. *Die Metrik des Kalevala-verses*. FF Communications 139. Helsinki.

Siikala, Anna-Leena. 2002. *Mythic Images and Shamanism: A Perspective on Kalevala Poetry*. FF Communications 130. Helsinki.

Siikala, Anna-Leena, and Sinikka Vakimo, eds. 1994. *Songs Beyond the Kalevala: Transformations of Oral Poetry*. Helsinki.

Skre, Dagfinn. 1998. *Herredømmet: Bosetning og besittelse på Romerike 200–1350 e Kr*. Oslo.

Tarkka, Lotte. 2013. *Songs of the Border People: Genre, Reflexivity, and Performance in Karelian Oral Poetry*. FF Communications 305. Helsinki.

Tedre, Ülo, ed. 1969. *Eesti Rahvalaulud. Antologia*. 2 vols. Tallinn.

Thompson, Stith. 1932–1936. *Motif-Index of Folk Literature; A Classification of Narrative Elements in Folk-Tales, Ballads, Myths, Fables, Mediaeval Romances, Exempla, Fabliaux, Jest-Books, and Local Legends*. FF Communications 106–9, 116–17. Helsinki.

Turunen, Aimo. 1981. *Kalevalan sanat ja niiden taustat*. Helsinki.

Valk, Ülo. 2000. "*Ex Ovo Omnia*: Where Does the Balto-Finnic Cosmogony Originate?" *Oral Tradition* 15: 145–58.

Vīķe-Freiberga, Vaira, ed. 1989. *Linguistics and Poetics of Latvian Folk Songs: Essays in Honour of the Sesquicentennial of the Birth of Kr. Barons*. Kingston & Montreal.

Virtanen, Leea, and Thomas DuBois. 2000. *Finnish Folklore*. Studia Fennica Folkloristica 9. Helsinki.

Zachrisson, Torun. 2011. "Property and Honour—Social Change in Central Sweden, 200–700 AD, Mirrored in the Area around Old Uppsala." In *Det 61. Internationale Sachsensymposion 2010 Haderslev, Danmark: Arkæologi i Slesvig*. Ed. L. Boye. Neumünster. Pp. 141–56.

Comparing Balto-Finnic and Nordic Mythologies

John Lindow
University of California, Berkeley

Abstract: This paper briefly considers several points of comparison between Balto-Finnic ("Kalevaic") and Nordic mythology: time depth; form; content, including larger structures and specific comparisons; shamanism. Although these points are easy to locate, in the end they bear little weight. However, the breadth and depth of the Balto-Finnic materials, collected as they were with better recording and archiving techniques, suggest an original comparable breadth and depth for the Nordic materials.

Introduction

As is well known, Finnish literature to some degree brought along with it, from the very beginning, Finnish mythology. Mikael Agricola, the "father of Finnish literature", included as a preface to his 1551 translation of the "Psalter of David" lists of the "gods" of Häme and Karelia, and such lists imply the existence of a mythology.[1] Just to be clear, and because definitions of myth and mythology vary so greatly, here is my own definition of mythology:

> Mythology comprises not just a corpus of narratives, but a system of related narratives with implicit cross-referencing. This system is therefore intertextual: all or most of it is latent in each part of it. Furthermore, the narratives within the system must be set away from the here and now: in the distant past—that is, a past that is recognizably not today, and in a place that is not recognizably here. The characters in them cannot be from today's world, and they may not play by the

---

[1] Recent contextualization of Agricola's lists can be found in Anttonen 2012.

same rules as we do. For this reason gods often feature in them. Thus
although they sometimes pass for "sacred narratives", as my Berkeley
colleague Alan Dundes felicitously termed them (Dundes 1984), they
need not necessarily be. The narratives in a mythology frequently are
foundational, in that some aspects of today's world may be traced back
to them, including the origins of objects, behaviors, and structures;
and, finally, they should be good to think with.

Anyone who has read either the *Kalevala* or the underlying poems from oral
tradition will recognize that this definition fits them,[2] and will recognize many
of the characters in Agricola's lists. Indeed, centuries after Agricola compiled his
lists, when (or perhaps before?) Johann Gottfried Herder's ideas of the nation
were beginning to be felt in Finland (Pulkkinen 1999), the term mythology
was explicitly used, namely in Christfrid Ganander's 1789 *Mythololgia Fennica*
(Ganander 1984), which despite its Latin title is a work in Swedish, the language
of the kingdom of which Finland had long been a part. As the subtitles of the
original make clear, Ganander drew his material from oral traditions, most of
which were narrative. According to the title page, his sources comprised: "de
äldre finska troll-runor, synnyt, sanat, sadut, arwotuxet &c" (the older Finnish
magic songs, origins, words, tales, riddles, etc), and he quotes a certain amount
of narrative poetry. In his preface, Ganander draws frequent comparisons with
classical mythology, but he does profess an interest in two other mythologies
from within the kingdom, the Sámi and the Swedish. Indeed, insofar as he promises comparison among these three mythologies, Ganander is the first scholar
to attempt a comparison of Balto-Finnic and Scandinavian materials, although
his actual comparisons in the alphabetical listings within the *Mythologia* deal
either with earlier scholars' attempts to create Swedish prehistory out of Old
Norse and classical writings, or the so-called "lower mythology", or "folk belief"
of the time.

Most of the world is familiar with Balto-Finnic mythology from the epic
Elias Lönnrot created in the 1849 *Kalevala*, all or parts of which have been translated well over 100 times in over 50 languages. In its oral form, this mythology
was embedded in relatively short songs, ranging from a few lines in their
recorded forms up to several hundred. A vast amount of it has been collected,
and the corpus published by the Finnish Literary Society, *Suomen kansan vanhat
runot* (old runic songs of the Finnish people) fills dozens of thick volumes. Areas

---

[2]   Thus, for example, Lotte Tarkka can read the nineteenth-century corpus of song from
Vuokkiniemi in Archangel Karelia in a way that fits the spirit of this definition (Tarkka 2013).
Note too the titles of Holmberg 1927 and Pentikäinen 1997.

of distribution include Finland, Karelia, Ingria, and Estonia, whence the designation Balto-Finnic mythology.

Time Depth

An initial point of comparison comprises the long time depth of the sources. Although the sources of Old Norse mythology were written down primarily in the thirteenth century, most scholars (if not quite all) would agree that the mythological structures are older and probably extend back to the Viking Age and perhaps even the Migration Period or beyond. They would also agree that although the texts are mostly recorded in Iceland, they can tell us about myth (and religion) elsewhere in the northern world. The same thing is surely true for Balto-Finnic mythology. Although the texts were recorded mostly in the nineteenth century and are the products of individual singers, their mythological structures are older and probably were not limited to the narrow region where the singer lived and was recorded. We can point to the list of native gods by Agricola, many of which are quite recognizable in the epic songs collected centuries later. This point of comparison should hardly surprise us, since we are dealing with two oral cultures.

Formal Comparison

The meter of the Balto-Finnic epic songs is trochaic tetrameter. Without examining the issue in detail, it is notable that there are ordinarily two stresses per half line, as in *fornyrðislag* ("old meter", used primarily in eddic poetry) and West Germanic poetry, often with a caesura.

Itse laulan, | millon kuulen

kuta kuulen, | niin kujerran (sung by Arhippa Perttunen; collected
     by Elias Lönnrot in 1834 in Latvajärvi in the parish of
     Vuokkiniemi, Archangel Karelia)
(Myself I sing, when I hear;
what I hear, I coo (text and translation in *Finnish Folk Poetry* p. 81))

Hljóðs bið ec allar | helgar kindir

meiri oc minni, | mǫgo Heimdalar (*Vǫluspá* st. 1)

(I ask for a hearing from all the holy peoples,
greater and lesser, the sons of Heimdallr.)[3]

There are similarities beyond the two stresses per half line: in Balto-Finnic, extra syllables can accrue at the beginning of the a-lines, as in *fornyrðislag* and West Germanic alliterative poetry; there is a tendency toward variation, as in West Germanic alliterative poetry; and alliteration is very common, although it does not play a structural role, as it does in Germanic poetry. Add all these, and the similarities are certainly thought-provoking. I am not making any argument here about mutual influence or even areal stylistics; but I do think persons from one tradition area could probably hear familiar features in the poetry of the other area, even if they could not understand a word. Probably the initial word stress in both language families caused some of these similarities, but this is not the place to engage in comparative metrics.

There were, of course, extensive contacts across the Baltic, and these from an early date. Central Sweden (the Mälar region), especially, has connections with Finland, and the Vendel Period and Viking Age contacts are widely accepted by historians and archaeologists alike. There had to be a fair amount of bilingualism, so there probably were people who could appreciate Swedish and Balto-Finnic poetry. In addition, runic inscriptions certify alliterative poetry from Sweden throughout the Viking Age—for example, the Rök stone from Östergötland in the early ninth century and the snatches of poetry on some eleventh-century stones from farther north in the Mälar region. The fact that the Finnish mythological songs go by the name *runo*, perhaps a Germanic loan, certainly suggests cultural contact.

Unlike eddic poetry, but like West Germanic poetry, the form of this Balto-Finnic poetry was stichic. And Balto-Finnic poetry was sung, whereas the Old Norse verb *kveða* and its cognates, the operative verb for the oral performance of poetry, operates equally well for ordinary speech (e.g., "Þá qvað þat Þrymr, þursa dróttinn" (*Þrymskviða* st. 22, 25, 30) (Then Þrymr said that, the lord of monsters)) and has no etymological association with singing or even chanting.

Content

Both these metrical traditions could be used for various kinds of content. The variety is more obvious in the Balto-Finnic area, which attests a robust array of narratives, charms, and laments in trochaic tetrameter. Although what remains of Germanic poetry is primarily narrative, there are certainly also charms, in both Old English and eddic poetry. The laments left fewer traces, but they too

---

[3] Translations are my own unless otherwise indicated.

can be located. Egill's *Sonatorrek* is perhaps the primary example (*Egils saga* ch. 80), but scholars have long recognized the category of elegy in Old English, (e.g., Schücking 1908; Sieper 1915) and Old Norse (Sprenger 1992; Sävborg 1997). Indeed, Joseph Harris has assembled a coherent argument for the presence of elegy and lament across Germanic tradition (Harris 1982, 1988, 1994). While both charms and laments clearly form part of religion,[4] they attach to myth (according to my definition) only in their narrative aspects.

The short mythological poems of both traditions tend to focus on a single narrative scene. Many such scenes are to be found in both traditions. These include such obvious parallels as cosmogonies or etiological stories, verbal duels, the acquisition of precious objects, seeking women from an out-group, and the issue of the permanence of death, to name a few. These are staples of mythologies. One sees them not only in such familiar Indo-European traditions as Greek and Roman, but also outside the Indo-European area, as for example in Knud Rasmussen's collections of Greenlandic oral tradition (1921–1925).

Larger Structures

The short, usually mono-episodic poems of both the Balto-Finnic and eddic traditions could be strung together to make a mythic curve, a coherent master narrative moving from creation to mythic actions to an *Endzeit*.[5] We do not know who had the idea, in the middle of the thirteenth century in Iceland, to piece together existing and new written forms of the oral poetry about gods and heroes, but the result was what is probably still the most famous book in Iceland, namely the Poetic Edda. I stress that it starts with a poem that gives us a cosmogony (*Vǫluspá*), that it gradually replaces the gods, called the Æsir, with humans, and that it ends with what might easily be called a heroic Ragnarǫk (Clark 2007), namely the demise of the offspring of Guðrún, ultimately of the (human) family of the hero Sigurðr.

When Elias Lönnrot first strung together cycles about Lemminkäinen, Väinämöinen, and one of wedding songs (the unpublished "Proto-Kalevala" of 1833), he was no doubt motivated by the spirit of the 1817 statement by Kaarle Akseli (Carl Axel) Gottlund that captured the Zeitgeist in Russian Finland:

---

4 I define religion here as a way of thinking that allows for a world or worlds outside of the world of living human beings, other worlds with which some sort of communication is possible. Thus charms attempt to influence events in the human world through communication with the world of the spirits, and laments, at least when attached to ritual, may ease the transition from life to death.

5 This point is treated at length in Tolley 2013, which draws many apt parallels between *Kalevala* and the Poetic Edda. I take the term *Endzeit* from Klingenberg 1974.

> If one should desire to collect the old traditional songs (*nationalsånger*) and from these make a systematic whole, there might come from them an epic, a drama, or whatever, so that from this a new Homer, Ossian, or Nibelungelied might come into being. (Gottlund 1817; transl. in Magoun 1963: 350)

The so-called *Old Kalevala* of 1835 realized this dream in print, but what we now know is the 1849 "classical" or "canonical" *Kalevala*. It differs from the *Old Kalevala* in that the cosmogonic songs are placed in the beginning, and it plays up the agonism between the people of Kalevala and those of Pohjola. Finally, it ends with the departure of Väinämöinen, who belonged to that old era, just as Hamðir, Sǫrli, and Erpr (Guðrún's sons) did. Just as there are numerous formal and thematic comparanda in both traditions, so too, the raw material in both could be worked into a single grand mythological narrative.

Specific Comparisons

Specific comparison of content between Balto-Finnic and Nordic mythology has a long history, going back at least to Matthias Alexander Castrén, who argued in the last chapter of his 1853 lectures on Finnish mythology that the major players in that mythology had in fact once been gods.[6] He ends his treatment by pointing out the correspondence of the divine trilogy Väinämöinen, Ilmarinen, and Lemminkäinen with a divine trilogy Óðinn, Þórr, and Týr:

> Wir haben hier die merkwürdige Göttertrilogie, die aus Wäinämöinen, der dem Odin entspricht, aus Ilmarinen, der eine Uebereinstimmung mit Thor zeigt, und aus Lemminkäinen, der durch seinen kühnen und kriegerischen Sinn mit Tyr [sic] verglichen werden könnte, besteht. (Castrén 1853b: 313)[7]

> (Here we have the noteworthy divine trilogy that consists of Väinämöinen, who corresponds to Óðinn, Ilmarinen, who shows a correspondence with Þórr, and Lemminkäinen, who can be compared to Týr through his brave and warlike character.)

Castrén then documents the correspondences between Lemminkäinen and Baldr, both killed by a blind man with a strange weapon:

---

[6] For an analysis of Castrén"s methodology and fidelity to his sources, see Lukina (2014).

[7] I quote from the far more widely available German edition rather than the original Swedish (Castrén 1853a). An English translation is apparently to be undertaken in the near future (Joonas Ahola, personal communication).

Lemminkäinen erinnert übrigens durch seinen Tod auch an Balder, denn wie dieser durch den blinden Höder mit einem Mistelspross erschossen wird, so wurde auch der Lempi-Sohn durch den blinden Hirten von Pohjola mit einer dem Aussehen nach sehr unschuldigen Waffe—einem zugeschlossenen Rohr getötet. (Castrén 1853b: 313).

(Through his death, Lemminkäinen is reminiscent of Baldr, since just as he was shot through by the blind Hǫðr with a mistletoe, the son of Lempi was also killed by the blind shepherd of Pohjola with a weapon quite harmless in its appearance—a reed that was flung.)

And there was more. Not content to expose the similarities of individuals, Castrén expanded his gaze to the general populations of the two mythological systems.

All diese drei Götter können im Allgemeinen mit den Asen vergli-chen werden, wie von der andern Seite die Bewohner von Pohjola viel Aehnlichkeit von den Riesen haben. Uebrigens erinnert Louhi, die Pohjola-Wirthen, sowohl durch ihren Namen als auch durch ihre feindliche Stellung zu den übrigen Asen, an Loki. (Castrén 1853b: 313)

(All three of these gods can in general be compared with the Æsir, just as from the other side the inhabitants of Pohjola bear great similarity to the giants. Furthermore, Louhi, the hostess of Pohjola, is reminis-cent of Loki, both in her name and in her enmity to the Æsir.)

Castrén thought that the occupants of Pohjola look like the *jǫtnar* "giants" of Old Norse, and that Louhi seems reminiscent of Loki, both with respect to her enmity toward the Æsir (that is indeed how he puts it, not the people of Kalevala) and the similarity of name forms. That horse has had long legs, and one still sometimes sees Louhi turning up in the debate on Loki.

But Castrén's ending is the best part of this discussion.

Doch wir wollen diese Vergleiche nicht weiter verfolgen, denn dieser Pfad ist schlüpfrig und leitet leicht in die Irre. Ausserdem ist die altnor-dische Mythologie noch nicht gehörig erörtert und für die finnische nicht einmal das Material vollständig gesammelt. (Castrén 1853b: 313)

(However, we do not wish to pursue these comparisons further, since this path is slippery and easily leads to confusion. Furthermore, Old Norse mythology is not fully commented on and on the Finnish side the material is not even fully collected.)

229

Comparison is still a slippery path that can easily lead us astray. But the path is clearer now that Old Norse mythology is closer to having been considered properly and the Finnish material has been more thoroughly collected.

Following Castrén, I will start with the apparent similarities between Väinämöinen "eternal sage" (Haavio 1952) and at least some of the characteristics of Óðinn. Both are masters of verse, wanderers who seek and acquire wisdom. The oldest sources seem to suggest that crafting verse was a primary feature for Väinämöinen. In his list of the gods of Häme, Agricola wrote "Äinemöinen wirdhet tacoi" (Äinemöinen forged songs), and Ganander has an entire entry on "Wäinemöinen or Äinemöinen" as poet (Ganander 1984: 203–4). Included in this entry is the information that (like Óðinn in *Ynglinga saga* ch. 6) Väinämöinen can have a protective function in battle; Väinämöinen offers protection with his cloak, however, not through anything like "battle-fetters"—making his enemies deaf and consumed with fear. Ganander goes on to report that Väinämöinen sang of the deeds of great heroes, of the foundation of the world, of the origin of fire, of the nature of things—that is, that he possessed precisely the kind of cosmic knowledge possessed by Óðinn, knowledge that was realized in verse, that is, *frœði* "wisdom". Alluded to in this entry, and spelled out in the entry on Joukavainen, is the duel with this figure (styled as Joukahainen in the *Kalevala*). In songs recorded later from oral tradition, as taken up in the *Kalevala*, this duel is a singing contest, which is easily likened to the contest of wisdom Óðinn undertakes with the giant Vafþrúðnir in the Poetic Edda (*Vafþrúðnismál*). Although Ganander reports that Joukavainen is indeed a giant, the duel as he describes it is at first resolved with a spear with which Väinämöinen stabs Joukavainen. Thereafter, however, Nuori-Joukawainen (Young Joukavainen) calls upon Väinämöinen to sing, and this has cosmic results: the doors of darkness open, the air resounds, cliffs crumble. But in the song recorded in 1825 by A. J. Sjögren in Archangel Karelia from the renowned singer Ontrei Malinen (the basis of part of runo 3–4 in the *Kalevala*), young Joukavainen and old Väinämöinen really do contest in wisdom, along a road ("Ken on tiiolta pahempi / sen on tieltä siirtyminen" (*Finnish Folk Poetry* p. 102) (He whose knowledge is the worse / must move aside from the road)). Väinämöinen bests Joukavainen's knowledge because Väinämöinen has first-hand knowledge of cosmogonic events, which were his doing. Väinämöinen sings Joukavainen into the ground but frees him from this death when Joukavainen promises Väinämöinen his sister. Thus, like Óðinn, Väinämöinen participates in cosmogony.

In some other songs, Väinämöinen's participation in cosmogony is spelled out, and here the parallel with Óðinn becomes less strong. The Balto-Finnic material operates primarily with the conception of the earth-egg creation story (common to several mythologies, but not found in Norse), and sometimes

Väinämöinen is connected to it by providing a site, often the crook of his knee, where the egg rests before it hatches. Väinämöinen's role is passive, not active, as is Óðinn's. In *Vǫluspá* Óðinn kills the proto-giant to create the cosmos, and is also involved in animating human beings (*Vǫluspá* st. 3–4, 18; cf. *Gylfaginning* ch. 7–9). At least in the extant materials, that is not part of Väinämöinen's job description. Sometimes he does shape the seabed floor, but no more. As for the contest of wisdom, the circumstances are quite different there as well. *Vafþrúðnismál* is the prototypical contest of wisdom in Old Norse mythology, and there Óðinn's journey is deliberate; he goes to test his wisdom against the wisest of giants. Väinämöinen, on the other hand, simply encounters Joukavainen on the roadway. The closest narrative analogue is actually the folktale of "The Shepherd Substituting for the Clergyman Answers the King's Questions",[8] in which the clergyman and king meet on the road and the shepherd (or sexton) has to save the parson's life in a verbal exchange with the king. Another contrast between the Old Norse and Balto-Finnic materials is that we do not actually get to hear the wisdom when Väinämöinen meets Joukavainen; we simply learn that Väinämöinen sang Joukavainen down into the ground—and that in some versions, as noted, Joukavainen promises his sister to Väinämöinen in exchange for being sung up out of the ground.

Castrén's next point of comparison was between Ilmarinen and Þórr. Agricola had this to say of Ilmarinen, listed like Väinämöinen under the rubric of the gods of Häme: "Ilmarinen Rauhan ja ilman tei / ja Matkmiehet edheswei" (Ilmarinen made the calm and the air / and advanced travelers). There is certainly little here that suggests Þórr, unless we interpret "calm and air" as having reference to thunder and thus to the etymology of Þórr's name, if not to his actions in the mythology that has come down to us. Ganander makes Ilmarinen the brother of Väinämöinen, which could perhaps recall the family relationship of Óðinn and Þórr, although there it is father and son. More to the point, Ganander too lists Ilmarinen as god of the air ("luft-guden"), also ruling fire and water, and indeed he cites the verse from Agricola (Ganander 1984: 19). Air, fire, and water may suggest smithing, and Ganander confirms this notion, citing several lines of rune poetry in which Ilmarinen is smithing. Certainly this smithing could suggest alignment with Þórr, for it is not difficult to discern aspects of the blacksmith in the Norse deity, not least in his handling of molten metal in the myth of his encounter with Geirrøðr (*Skáldskaparmál*, ch. 18).

---

[8] The tale is classified as ATU (Aarne-Thompson-Uther) type 922 (Uther 2004, v. 1: 552–53). Because of the popularity of the version by P. C. Asbjørnsen and Jørgen Moe, with two iconic illustrations by Erik Werenskiold, it is often also called "Presten og klokkeren" (The parson and the sexton) (Asbjørnsen and Moe 1936, v. 1: 152–53).

Making the connection between Ilmarinen and Þórr was easy for nature mythologists, since *ilma* means air, the place where Þórr would heave around his thunderbolts. Both were thus easily seen as sky gods. Both have a hammer, and although Þórr uses his as a weapon, it is the smith's tool; correspondingly, a common epithet for Ilmarinen is "eternal hammerer". Ilmarinen has extensive connections with cosmogony, and Þórr has a few: the valleys that dot the path to Útgarðar, caused by his hammer strokes against his giant traveling companion, calling himself Skrýmir (*Gylfaginning* ch. 44–47); the stars from the eyes of the giant Þjazi, cast into heaven, apparently by Þórr, according to the early Viking Age skald Bragi Boddason.[9]

However, as the eternal hammerer, Ilmarinen is forever making *things*: the cosmos, the sampo (a most mysterious item at the center of Lönnrot's *Kalevala*), a metal woman (she proves unsatisfactory as a sexual partner), and so forth. Þórr, on the other hand, never makes much of anything. Frankly, Ilmarinen does better in a comparison with Wayland the smith of Germanic tradition (Vǫlundr in Norse), although the idea of Ilmarinen as unlucky in love, which would parallel Vǫlundr's loss of his swan-maiden wife in the eddic poem *Vǫlundarkviða*, was largely the product of Lönnrot's editing of the *Kalevala*. And indeed, twentieth-century scholarship, when considering the figure of the smith, tended to look first at Óðinn among the gods (e.g., Davidson 1969; Motz 1973; cf. Hauck 1977, who postulates a visual trope of smith and valkyries). Moreover, when Maths Bertell put Þórr in a more general Nordic context, his point of comparison in Finnish mythology was with Ukko, not Ilmarinen (Bertell 2003).

Finally, Castrén's desire to equate Lemminkäinen with Týr is a far greater stretch than his other two proposed points of comparison. Although Lemminkäinen is not found in the lists of Agricola and, with his epithet "lieto" (reckless), is mentioned by Ganander only for rowing Väinämöinen's new boat, Lemminkäinen in the poems hardly seems centered on a model of a "brave and warlike" nature. Furthermore, that description of Týr may also be misleading. It is of course true that in *Gylfaginning* Hár introduces Týr as "djarfastr ok bezt hugaðr ok hann ræðr mjǫk sigri í orrostum" (*Gylfaginning* ch. 25) (bravest and most valiant, and he has great power over victory in battles (Faulkes 1995: 24)). It is also, of course, true that Týr equates with Mars in the *interpretatio Germanica* of the weekdays' names. But his mythological function is very spare, and although it may be brave indeed to put one's hand into the mouth of a slavering wolf (*Gylfaginning* ch. 25), we do not see Týr in battle.

---

[9]   The stanza in question is found in *Skáldskaparmál* (34) and attributed to Bragi. Scholars usually edit it as part of Bragi's sequence of stanzas on Þórr''s fishing up the Midgard serpent.

Both mythologies do show a desire of the in-group males to marry or otherwise obtain out-group females (see Tarkka 2013: 259–326, on courtship poems and courtship cycles in the Kalevaic material, which usually involve a journey to an Other world). However, the lust of the giants for the women of the Æsir has no real analogy in the Balto-Finnic material, and, even more important, the system of social interaction that privileges the movement of females from giants to Æsir and blocks it in the other direction—what Margaret Clunies Ross called "negative reciprocity" (1994: 103–43)—is missing in the Balto-Finnic materials. Lönnrot and the painter Akseli Gallen-Kalella combined to make Väinämöinen's lust famous, but Lönnrot invented Aino, the object of Väinämöinen's lust, and even more to the point, Óðinn's purpose-oriented sex—to get the mead from Gunnlǫð (*Skáldskaparmál* ch. 58; *Hávamál* st. 104–10), to sire an avenger on Rindr (best documented in *Gesta Danorum* 3, 4)—has nothing to do with lust. It is true that Lemminkäinen and Kaukomainen are involved with sexuality, but not in a way that fits any Old Norse figures.

A relationship between Lemminkäinen and Baldr, the son of Óðinn whose death starts the end of the world in Norse eschatology, was mentioned by Castrén and has remained a scholarly staple (Krohn 1905; Fromm 1963; but cf. Lindow 1977). Recently it was the topic of a long and far-ranging dissertation by Frog, who again argued direct influence of the Baldr cycle on inchoate notions of Lemminkïanen within a general circum-Baltic context (Frog 2010: 352–64). While Frog certainly succeeds in locating numerous heretofore unnoticed parallels and in very thoroughly collating the Finno-Karelian material, his model, like all such models, requires a good deal of postulating hypothetical early stages of narrative clusters. In this Frog to some degree follows the tradition within Finnish scholarship to assign dates confidently to the origin of various themes within the mythological poetry, mostly as the result of outside influences, considerably removed from the dates of the collection of the material. Nevertheless, his argument on behalf of direct influence in particular cultural and narrative contexts is powerful and subtle.

I do think that there is a similarity between the binaries of the Æsir and *jǫtnar* in Old Norse mythology and the Kalevala and Pohjola people in *Kalevala*, but that is, I think, exactly what Castrén noticed: the similarities in *Kalevala* (he was probably one of the few who could read it in the original). Unfortunately, that was another of Lönnrot's manipulations. While the underlying oral tradition naturally relies on a distinction between in-group and Others, a clearly defined ethnic binary is lacking.

Shamanism

One way to think about possible comparison between Old Norse mythology and Balto-Finnic mythology is that both to some degree represent narrative traditions informed to a greater or lesser extent by notions of shamanisms (see, e.g., Siikala 2002). Journeys to other worlds, as a response to various sorts of crises, would especially be expected in such narrative traditions, as might verbal duels. However, Clive Tolley (2009) has cast doubt on the existence of shamanism in the Old Norse materials, and even if one takes a less strict view than that of Tolley, there are significant differences of the degree of what appears to be shamanic in the two traditions.

Conclusion

Despite the apparent similarities taken up (all too briefly) in these pages, there remains a major distinction between the two mythologies, namely at the ideological level. Old Norse mythology, as we have it, betrays a very large amount of royal ideology, as opposed to Balto-Finnic, which betrays none. Freyr is king in Uppsala; Óðinn heads up royal genealogies, and aspects of the myths surrounding him seem to reflect the warrior bands adhering to chieftains who were the predecessors of kings. Valhǫll is not just any world of the dead; it is the military camp and palatial hall of a powerful chieftain.

My exposition may seem rather negative. The formal similarities between the two poetic systems are interesting, but do they tell us anything? The parallel between the Poetic Edda and *Kalevala* is interesting, but how much can it tell us about the material of either? And what about the similarities of content? Are they not for the most part vitiated by similar content in many mythologies, and, more importantly, by the royal ideology of Old Norse mythology?

And yet I think this comparison is important for those of us who work in Old Norse mythology. We can recognize that there are similarities of form, content, and what we might call the nineteenth- and twentieth-century reception of Nordic and Finnish-Karelian mythologies, and that these mythologies existed in more or less contiguous spaces around the Baltic. We can recognize also that the research field about contacts and influences in this region is still relatively underworked. However, my efforts emphasize distinctions that deal primarily with timing and scale. Old Norse mythology was for the most part recorded in a very specific time and place, namely medieval Iceland. Take away the eight manuscripts that contain versions of *Skáldskaparmál*, with its mythic narratives and skaldic stanzas; take away the four manuscripts that contain *Gylfaginning*, take away the one manuscript that is the Poetic Edda and its parallel, AM 748 4to, and we would know nearly as little about Scandinavian mythology as we know about, say, Anglo-Saxon mythology. Balto-Finnic mythology was also recorded in a specific time and place: in a nineteenth-century Europe that had discovered the value of traditions in the countryside and where national romanticism flourished. More than two thousand kilometers separate these places, and five centuries or so separate these times. One major difference is the technology of recording: it was easier to write with an ink pen than a quill, and it was easier to write in a little notebook than on vellum; and of course it only got easier. An even greater difference was what I will call information technology, with the Balto-Finnic material being not only assiduously collected but also systematically archived. The Balto-Finnic mythological material shows clearly how much material was out there, not just—as the archives show—in places where Balto-Finnic languages are spoken, but also—as I am arguing we should accept—in areas where Germanic languages were spoken. If modern collecting conceptions and technologies had been available eight centuries ago, we might have as many lines of verse about Óðinn, Þórr, and Freyr, and as varied and subtle pictures of these mythological figures as we do about Väinämöinen, Ilmarinen, and Lemminkäinen. We might see extensive variation of names, as we do with these figures (e.g. Ilmarine, Ilmoninen, Ilmorini, and the like), and scholars would not need to expend quite so much philological energy when confronted with three versions of the name Mimir, Mímr, and Mími, or seemingly incompatible versions of what characters are or do (Kvasir provides a good example). Most scholars accept at least in principle the idea of variation within the overall system in the Germanic material. If we had a corpus even 10 percent the size of the Finnish-Karelian, we would see variation so clearly that it would presumably cease to be an issue. At the same time, we would see the consistencies. They would show even more clearly than now the "semantic core" of various deities. The system would be more nuanced, more complex, but still presumably clear and systematic, in keeping with the definition of myth presented above. In the end, that is something valuable that Balto-Finnic mythology can teach us about Old Norse and indeed Germanic mythology.

Works Cited

Primary Sources

Agricola, *Psalter of David*
Agricola, Mikael. *Mikael Agricolan psalttari 1551*. Ed. Kaisa Häkkinen. Wanhan suomen arkisto, 3. Turku: 2010.

Egils saga
Íslenzk fornrit, 2. Ed. Sigurður Nordal. Reykjavík: 1933.

TRANSLATION

"Egil's saga." In *The Sagas of Icelanders: A Selection*. Transl. Bernard Scudder. London, etc.: 2000. Pp. 3–184.

Finnish Folk Poetry
Finnish Folk Poetry: Epic: An Anthology in Finnish and English. Ed. and transl. Matti Kuusi, Keith Bosley, and Michael Branch. Helsinki: 1997.

Gesta Danorum
Saxo Grammaticus. *Saxo Grammaticus: Gesta Danorum: The History of the Danes*. Ed. Karsten Friis-Jensen and transl. Peter Fisher. Oxford Medieval Texts. Oxford: 2015.

TRANSLATION

Saxo Grammaticus: The History of the Danes: Books 1-9. Ed. Hilda Ellis Davidson and transl. Peter Fisher. Cambridge: 2008.

Gylfaginning
Snorri Sturluson. *Edda: Gylfaginning*. Ed. Anthony Faulkes. London: 2005.

TRANSLATION

Edda. Transl. Anthony Faulkes. London: 1995.

Hávamál: see *Poetic Edda*

Kalevala
Kalevala taikka wanhoja karjalan runoja suomen muinosista ajoista. Helsinki: 1835. *Kalevala*. Helsinki: 1849.

TRANSLATIONS

The Old Kalevala: And Certain Antecedents. Compiled by Elias Lönnrot and transl. Francis Peabody Magoun. Cambridge, MA: 1969.

Kalevala, Or Poems of the Kaleva District. Compiled by Elias Lönnrot and transl. Francis Peabody Magoun, Jr. Cambridge, MA: 1963.

Poetic Edda
Edda: Die Lieder des Codex regius nebst verwandten Denkmälern. Ed. Gustav Neckel and Hans Kuhn. Germanische Bibliothek, Vierte Reihe. Heidelberg: 1962.

TRANSLATION

The Poetic Edda. Transl. Carolyne Larrington. Oxford: 1996.

Skáldskaparmál
Snorri Sturluson. *Snorri Sturluson: Edda: Skáldskaparmál*. 2 vols. Ed. Anthony
Faulkes. London: 1998.

TRANSLATION
Snorri Sturluson: Edda. Transl. Anthony Faulkes. London: 1987.

Skírnismál: see *Poetic Edda*

Suomen kansan vanhat runot
Suomen kansan vanhat runot. 34 vols. Helsinki: 1908–1948.

Vafþrúðnismál: see *Poetic Edda*

Vǫlundarkviða: see *Poetic Edda*

Vǫluspá: see *Poetic Edda*

Ynglinga saga
Íslenzk fornrit, 26. Ed. Bjarni Aðalbjarnarson. Reykjavík: 1941. Pp. 9–83

Þrymskviða: see *Poetic Edda*

Secondary Sources

Anttonen, Veikko. 2012. "Literary Representation of Oral Religion: Organizing
Principles in Mikael Agricola's Lists of Mythological Agents in Late
Medieval Finland." In *More than Mythology: Narratives, Ritual Practices and
Regional Distribution in Pre-Christian Scandinavian Religions*. Ed. Catharine
Raudvere and Jens Peter Schjødt. Lund. Pp. 185–223.

Asbjørnsen, Peter Christian, and Jørgen Moe. 1936. *Samlede eventyr: Norske
kunstneres billedutgave*. 3 vols. Oslo.

Bertell, Matthias. 2003. *Tor och den nordiska åskguden*. Stockholm.

Castrén, Matias A. 1853a. *Nordiska resor och forskningar af M. A. Castrén. Vol. 3:
Föreläsningar i finsk mytologi*. Helsinki.

———. 1853b. *Vorlesungen über die finnische Mythologie*. St. Petersburg.

Clark, David. 2007. "Kin-Slaying in the Poetic Edda: The End of the World." *Viking
and Medieval Scandinavia* 3: 21–41. Repr. in *Gender, Violence, and the Past in
Edda and Saga*. Ed. David Clark. Oxford: 2012.

Clunies Ross, Margaret. 1994. *Prolonged Echoes: Old Norse Myths in Medieval Society.
Vol. 1: The Myths*. Viking Collection, 7. Odense.

Davidson, H. R. Ellis. 1969. "The Smith and the Goddess: Two Figures on the
Franks Casket from Auzon." *Frühmittelalterliche Studien* 3: 216–26.

Dundes, Alan, ed. 1984. *Sacred Narrative: Readings in the Theory of Myth.* Berkeley & Los Angeles.

Frog, [Etunimetön]. 2010. *Baldr and Lemminkäinen: Approaching the Evolution of Mythological Narrative through the Activating Power of Expression: A Case Study in Germanic and Finno-Karelian Cultural Contact and Exchange.* PhD diss., University College London.

Fromm, Hans. 1963. "Lemminkäinen und Balder." In *Märchen, Mythos, Dichtung: Festschrift zum 90. Geburtstag Friedrich von der Leyens am 19. August 1963.* Ed. Hugo Kuhn and Kurt Schier. Munich. Pp. 287–302.

Ganander, Christfrid. 1984. *Mythologia Fennica.* Helsinki. Orig. pub. 1789.

Gottlund, Carl Axel. 1817. Review of Friedrich Rühs, *Finland och dess invånare,* 1811–1813. *Svensk literaturtidning* 25 (June 21): 385–400.

Haavio, Martti. 1952. *Väinämöinen, Eternal Sage.* FF Communications, 144. Helsinki.

Harris, Joseph. 1982. "Elegy in Old English and Old Norse: A Problem in Literary History." In *The Vikings.* Ed. R. T. Farrell. Chichester. Pp. 157–64. Repr. in *The Old English Elegies: New Essays in Criticism and Research.* Ed. Martin Green. Rutherford, NJ: 1983.

———. 1988. "Hadubrand's Lament: On the Origin and Age of Elegy in Germanic." In *Heldensage und Heldendichtung im Germanischen.* Ed. Heinrich Beck. Ergänzungsbände zum Reallexikon der Germanischen Altertumskunde, 2. Berlin. Pp. 81–114.

———. 1994. "A Nativist Approach to Beowulf: The Case of Germanic Elegy." In *Companion to Old English Poetry.* Ed. Henk Aertsen and Rolf H. Bremmer. Amsterdam. Pp. 45–62.

Hauck, Karl. 1977. *Wielands Hort: Der sozialgeschichtliche Stellung des Schmiedes in frühen Bildprogrammen nach und vor dem Religionswechsel.* Antikvariskt arkiv, 64. Stockholm.

Holmberg, Uno. 1927. *Finno-Ugric, Siberian.* The Mythology of All Races, 4. Boston.

Klingenberg, Heinz. 1974. *Edda—Sammlung und Dichtung.* Beiträge zur nordischen Philologie, 3. Basel.

Krohn, Kaarle. 1905. "Lemminkäinens Tod < Christi > Balders Tod." *Finnische-Ugrische Forschungen* 5: 83–138.

Lindow, John. 1997. "Baldr and Lemminkäinen." *Journal of Finnish Studies* 1 (2): 37–47.

Magoun, Francis P. 1963. Appendix D. In *Kalevala, Or Songs of the Kalevala District.* Compiled by Elias Lönnrot and transl. Francis Peabody Magoun, Jr. Cambridge, MA. Pp. 363–79.

Motz, Lotte. 1973. "New Thoughts on Dwarf-Names in Old Icelandic." *Frühmittelalterliche Studien* 7: 100–17.

Pentikäinen, Juha. 1997. *Kalevala Mythology*. Expanded and transl. Ritva Poom. Bloomington.

Pulkkinen, Tuija. 1999. "One Language, One Mind: The Nationalist Tradition in Finnish Political Culture." In *Europes's Northern Frontier: Perspectives on Finland's Western Identity*. Ed. Tuomas M. S. Lehtonen and transl. Philip Landon. Jyväskylä. Pp. 118–37.

Rasmussen, Knud. 1921–1925. *Myter og sagn fra Grønland*. 3 vols. Copenhagen.

Schücking, Levin Ludwig. 1908. "Das angelsächische Todenklagelied." *Englische Studien* 39: 1–13.

Sieper, Ernst. 1915. *Die altenglische Elegie*. Strasbourg.

Siikala, Anna-Leena. 2002. *Mythic Images and Shamanism: A Perspective on Kalevala Poetry*. FF Communications, 280. Helsinki.

Sprenger, Ulrike. 1992. *Die altnordische heroische Elegie*. Ergänzungsbände zum Reallexikon der Germanischen Altertumskunde, 6. Berlin.

Sävborg, Daniel. 1997. *Sorg och elegi i Eddans hjältediktning*. Stockhom Studies in History and Literature, 36. Stockholm.

Tarkka, Lotte. 2013. *Songs of the Border People: Genre, Reflexivity and Performance in Karelian Oral Poetry*. FF Communications, 305. Helsinki.

Tolley, Clive. 2009. *Shamanism in Norse Myth and Magic*. 2 vols. FF Communications, 296–97. Helsinki.

———. 2013. "The Kalevala as a Model for Our Understanding of the Composition of the Codex Regius of the Poetic Edda." In *Viisas matkassa, vara laukussa: Näkökulmia kansanperinteen tutkimukseen*. Ed. T. Hovi et al. Turun Yliopiston Folkloristikan Julaisuja, 3. Turku. Pp. 114–43.

Uther, Hans-Jörg. 2004. *The Types of International Folktales: A Classification and Bibliography*. 4 vols. FF Communications, 284–87. Helsinki.

PART THREE

GLOBAL TRADITIONS

Snorri and the Jews

Richard Cole
University of Notre Dame

Abstract: This essay considers the mythological writing of Snorri Sturluson (d. 1241) in its most temporally proximal comparative context: the intellectual culture of thirteenth century Christian Europe, specifically one particular area of the High Medieval imagination: Christian narratives about Jews. Particular attention is paid to Snorri's use of anti-Jewish typology in his depiction of Loki and the *Muspellssynir* "The Sons of Muspell" (the agents of the apocalypse who break loose at the end of the world). The essay argues that Snorri's configuration of Loki's status amongst the Æsir might well have been drawn from contemporary thinking about the status of the Jew amongst Christians: both were considered outsiders, whose presence was tolerated because they were thought to have special abilities, even while they were widely held to be untrustworthy and deleterious to society. Loki's apocalyptic comrades, the *Muspellssynir*, obviously originate in the eddic poem *Vǫluspá*, but I argue that Snorri's account of them is strongly colored by the medieval motif of the "Red Jews", menacing Jewish warriors who would break out of their subterranean tomb during the Last Days and ride forth into Christendom with warlike intent.

For medieval Scandinavians, it was a religion that belonged to the past. Perhaps it had once offered spiritual truths, but that was before the coming of Christianity, a belief system which had swept it aside and utterly superseded the old ways. People had believed in it only because Christ had not yet come to them. That, in itself, was blameless, but once the Good News had been spread, only the most stubborn and malevolent mind would refuse to convert to the one true faith. Nonetheless, it had left behind a precious trove of worthy narratives, tales of heroic deeds, and beautiful poetry. A good medieval Christian could certainly appreciate that, but he ought to feel nothing but disdain for any remaining adherents of this backwards creed. In the literature of the thirteenth century, its followers were frequently depicted as witches, troublemakers, and ne'er-do-wells; relics of a bygone age, waiting either for conversion or the righteous violence of the pious. These are perceptions reasonably attached to paganism, as it would have been understood by thirteenth-century intellectuals such as Snorri Sturluson. In this study, however, we will consider the valence of such attitudes to Judaism, the "superseded" religion upon whose abjection the foundations of medieval Christian identity were built.[1]

Hostility towards Jews was an unpleasant and recurrent feature of thirteenth-century European life.[2] The continent's Jewish population, numbering perhaps some 450,000 (Baron 2007: 389), were subjected to rhetorical attacks by Christian preachers, repressive laws, and occasional outbreaks of violence. To frame this chronology of persecution within the life and times of Snorri Sturluson, we might begin by noting that *Snorra Edda* was written just a few years after the ruling of the Fourth Lateran Council in 1215. This edict included the infamous proclamation that Jews and Muslims "utriusque sexus in omni christianorum provincia et omni tempore qualitate habitus publice ab aliis populis distinguantur" (*Decreta* p. 266) (of both sexes in all Christian provinces and at all times shall be differentiated from other peoples in the public's eyes by the manner of their dress). The ruling ultimately led to the enforced wearing of yellow badges or hats in many countries. As I have pointed out previously (Cole 2014: 239), Snorri's lifetime saw blood libel accusations and massacres against the Jews in Bristol, Bury St. Edmonds, Fulda, London, Oxford, Winchester and York. By the time Snorri died in 1241, England had been driven into disorder by anti-Jewish pogroms following the coronation of Richard the Lionheart in 1189; crusading mobs had slain over 2,500 Jews in northern France; and Pope Gregory IX had put the Talmud on trial in Paris (Mentgen 2005: 155; Yuval 1998: 113–16).

My aim in this paper, then, is to situate Snorri in what is arguably his most proximal comparative context: that of intellectual culture in the thirteenth

---

[1] Indeed, in a sense there is more Old Norse writing concerning these "worthy narratives" from the Bible than there are reproductions of pagan narratives. *Stjórn, Gyðinga saga*, and the Old Testament *exempla* from *Konungs Skuggsjá*, for example, dwarf *Snorra Edda* and the Eddic poems. For an argument connecting all three of the former to one author, Brandr Jónsson, see Ian Kirby (1986: 169–81), although cf. Wolf (1990). Studies of Snorri's attitudes towards paganism are numerous, but the reader may profitably be directed to Wanner (2008: esp. 140–61) and Faulkes (1983).

[2] The initial description of medieval Europe as a "persecuting society" was provided by R. I. Moore. He pays particular attention to the twelfth and thirteenth centuries in the second edition of his book, *The Formation of a Persecuting Society* (2006: 144–71).

century.[3] Specifically, I will focus on the meditations on Judaism, and often anti-Judaism and anti-Semitism, which pervaded that culture. During this period serious thinkers could hardly avoid engagement with the questions prompted by the ongoing interaction between Christianity and Judaism. Even if they only treated the topic tangentially, the place of the Jews as characters in the Gospels, popular accusations of Jewish perfidy, the pervasive typological associations of "the Jew" in Christian exegesis, and awareness of Christianity's historical beginnings as a Jewish sect meant that most of the important writers of the thirteenth century made use of the Jewish *topos*. We might cite any number of examples here: Albertus Magnus (fl. 1245), William of Auvergne, (fl. 1228) and Robert Grosseteste (fl. 1220s) are all demonstrative of this trend (Liebeschutz 2007a: 591, 2007b: 64; on Grosseteste, his anti-Judaism and his problematic Hebraism, see McEvoy 2000: 120–32; Friedman 1934; cf. Roth 1951: 121, 126–27).

Snorra Edda obviously does not feature any Jewish characters proper, but, to employ a distinction coined by Jeffrey Jerome Cohen in his study of Margery Kempe (Cohen 2006, 2003: 185), there are several figures who are "Jew-ish". That is to say, they are not intended to be direct comments upon the Jews or their religion, but they do freely make use of the potent typological armory of anti-Judaism.[4] I use the word "typology" here in a sense that encompasses both its literary and exegetical meanings. The most obvious typological project in Christian narrative is the foreshadowing of Christ projected back into the Old Testament, an endeavour that began with the authors of the New Testament and which was enthusiastically continued by the church. Romans 5: 14 is an early example, and the one that gives us the word "type": "Nevertheless death reigned from Adam to Moses, even over them that had not sinned after the similitude of Adam's transgression, who is the figure of him that was to come" (Koiné: τύπος τοῦ μέλλοντος; Vulgate: *forma futuri*). Importantly, the business of figurative interpretation was also applied to non-Biblical texts and concepts. As Eric Auerbach put it concerning the case of Dante Alighieri's (d. 1321) *Divina Commedia*:

> Not only the world of the Christian religion, but also the ancient world
> is included in Dante's figural system; the Roman empire of Augustus is
> for Dante a figure of God's eternal empire, and the prominent part Virgil
> plays in Dante's work is based on this assumption. Dante is not the first

[3] Of course, this is not a novel proposal. See, for example, Fidjestøl (1997: 343–50) or Faulkes (1993: 59–76).

[4] I have deployed Cohen's category of "Jew-ishness" before, although I would now reconsider the previous suggestions of Hebraist influence in the case of Mǫkkurkálfi offered there: Cole 2014: 257–58.

to subject all the material of human history to the figural conception [i.e. typological reading]; biblical history, Jewish and Christian, came to be seen as universal human history, and all pagan historical material had to be inserted and adapted to this framework. (Auerbach 1952: 6)

Typology in this sense becomes the pursuit of what St. Augustine called "obscura quaedam figura rerum" (the obscured figure of the thing) (*Enarrationes* col. 1788). For the typologically-minded reader, all narrative elements can be aligned with a predictive type, drawn from the rich *dramatis personae* of Christian tradition. The identity of this type will then serve as a predictor for the qualities and behaviors of the character to whom it has been appended. For instance, the Roman Empire is aligned with the Kingdom of Heaven, and therefore becomes a state charged with safeguarding spiritual perfection. Rahab becomes aligned with Ecclesia (Auerbach 1952: 3–4), and thus the scarlet rope she hangs from her window becomes a symbol of Christ's blood: the sacrifice that saves Ecclesia just as the rope saves the harlot of Jericho. For the purposes of this study, we will focus on the manipulation of one type, namely the Jew(s) as perceived by thirteenth-century Christendom, and its potential influence upon Snorri Sturluson's *Edda*, a literary product of that age. Snorri borrows from a given tradition where its imagery inspires or the typological allusion is particularly striking, but it should be stressed that I do not believe he was dealing in allegory *per se*. This is especially true in the case of Snorri's use of the anti-Jewish tradition. Snorri did not intend to enter into anti-Jewish polemic, much as the more astute in his audience might have drawn that inference. Rather, amongst a myriad of other, more innocent influences, he was inspired by contemporary ideas about Jews and Judaism, and he then deployed those ideas, liberated from their original frame of reference, in the fantasy world of his *Edda*.

Praise for the Jews in the Codex Wormianus

While there are no Jewish personalities in the *Edda*, the Jews as a collective do make an explicit appearance in one particular recension, namely the Codex Wormianus from the middle of the fourteenth century. There, in the prologue, we find the following elaboration on the device of euhemerism:

> Enn sem nofnín fiǫlguðuz. þa tyndiz með þui sanleikrinn. Ok af fyrstu uillu þa blotaði huerr maðr epterkomandí sinn formeistara dyr eða fugla loptin ok himintunglín ok ymisliga dauðlega lutí þar til er þessi uilla gekk um allan heím ok sua uandlegha tyndu þeir sannleiknum at æingi uissi skapara sinn. utan þeir æínir menn sem toluðu ebreska tungu þa sem gekk firi stǫpul smíðina (Wormianus p. 3)

(And as the names [for God] multiplied, the true one was lost. And from the initial heresy every man and his descendants worshipped as their master animals or birds, the sky and the heavenly bodies and various inanimate objects until this heresy went all around the world, and so they habitually lost the truth, so that no-one knew his Creator, except for those men who had spoken the Hebrew language preceding the construction of the tower [of Babel])

Coming from an interpolation found solely in the Codex Wormianus, this episode is surely "Eddic" even if it probably is not "Snorric". Nonetheless, it is enlightening for our understanding of (one particular) *Edda*'s connections to the Christian conception of the Jews. There is a reminder here of the antiquity of Judaism, and implicit therein is a nod to St. Augustine's paradigm of "Jew as Witness" (Cohen 1999: 23–65). That is to say, this apparently casual remark stresses to the reader that the Jews had been the guardians of God's law even while Scandinavians and the other gentile nations had been distracted into worshipping "inanimate objects" (*dauðligar hlutir*). There is almost a tone of esteem for Jews in the narrative voice, versus a mocking admonishment towards pagans. It is significant that the Jews are not referred to by any of their usual names in Old Norse, e.g. *gyðingr* or *júði*. The somewhat oblique appellation of "men who had spoken the Hebrew language" seems to anticipate any negative connotations which might have accompanied the word "Jew". The separation of the Jews from their language was a common psychological mechanism in medieval Christianity which accommodated anti-Judaism with reverence for one of the languages of scripture. Christian Hebraists who revered the Hebrew language were still capable of anti-Jewish moments, e.g., St. Jerome, who attacked Jewish ritual clothing (Signer 2004: esp. 26; Itzkowitz 2007: 563–72). We can observe this "doublethink" elsewhere in Old Norse literature. For example, in the *Messuskýringar* (commentaries on the symbolism of liturgy) we find the statement: "Því er á inu vinstra horni alltaris miðhlutr messu sunginn, at nú standa aðrar þjóðir undir trú. Enn þeir eru nú mjǫk útan brautar gyðingarnir" (pp. 47–48, my standardization) (This is why the Mass is sung on the left side of the altar, so that other nations might submit to faith. But those Jews are now strayed far from the path). This is in no way at odds with the commentator's previous joyous assertion that: "ina æðztu tungu er ebreska" (pp. 45–46) (the highest language is Hebrew). That being said, there is no reason to suppose that the author was attempting such anti-Jewish intellectual gymnastics in the prologue of the Codex Wormianus. It might be an aside, but his intent is clear. To summarize it colloquially: "you may not like the Jews, but they were a great deal closer to God than we were, back when we were worshipping Óðinn, rocks, puddles or who-knows-what-other-*dauðligar-hlutir*". The Codex Wormianus thus attests an *Edda* tempered with a degree of warmth towards Jews.

Loki the Jew?

Snorri himself, as opposed to the Wormianus scribe, tends to borrow from the more dramatic, hostile perception of Jews. The example of Snorri's putative anti-Judaism that has probably received the most attention concerns the role of Christian typology in Snorri's account of Baldr's death and abortive resurrection. It is worth noting as an aside that elsewhere scholars have also investigated parallels and perhaps even borrowings from medieval Jewish literature in *Snorra Edda* (see Bugge 1881–1898: 45; Turville–Petre 1964: 119; O'Donoghue 2005: 90–91; Cole 2014), although space does not allow for further discussion of this trend here. Baldr's Christ-like credentials are well known, which begs the question: which character in Snorri's narrative then represents the people whom medieval Christians widely saw as Christ's killers, the Jews? Noting the long-standing characterization of "Synagoga" as blind, Arthur Mosher proposed that Hǫðr must have been intended to refer to the Jews, with Loki, as the orchestrating power, acting as a cipher for Satan (Mosher 1983: 313–14). Mosher's overtly Christological interpretation of this episode has not been universally accepted (e.g., Liberman 2004: 24–25). His hypothesis can perhaps be modified and enhanced with some concomitant examples of the tropes he discusses. To my knowledge, Jews are described as blind five times in the surviving Old Norse corpus, including one reference in the *Old Icelandic Homily Book* (*Maríu saga* pp. 890–93, 963–65; *HMS* 1 pp. 302–08, 308–11; *Homiliubók* pp. 57–58). In addition to these textual attestations, one pictorial depiction of the blind Synagoga survives from the Old Norse-speaking period on an altar panel from Kinsarvik, Norway (see Figure 1). Moreover, the Gospel motif of the Jews as unwitting instruments for Satan's plan to kill Christ also features in *Niðrstigningar saga*, the Old Norse translation of the apocryphal *Gospel of Nichodemus*, which Christopher Abram (2006: 13, 2011: 220) has argued may have inspired Snorri elsewhere in the *Edda*, specifically his account of Hermóðr's *Helreið* (ride to Hel). In *Niðrstigningar saga* it is written that the Devil "ęggiat gyþing[a] lyþ fiandscapar viþ hann" (*HMS* 2 p. 16; cf. pp. 3–4, 19) (incited the Jewish nation to enmity against Him).

I therefore agree that it is not unreasonable to adduce that Snorri would have been familiar with the trope. But Mosher's argument is open to criticism on two fronts. Firstly, it implies that *Snorra Edda* is a sort of *roman à clef*, where each character is a façade for one discrete referent. As I have elsewhere argued concerning the similarity between Surtr, the *Døkkálfar*, and *blámenn* (Cole 2015b), such narrow literalism is not how Snorri's mind worked. Behind

a single character may lie a genealogy including any number of influences—
"authentically" pagan or otherwise—and a single influence may manifest itself
in many different characters simultaneously. Secondly, Mosher does not draw on
the most tangible and credible source of typology for Snorri's writing, namely
the kind of preaching material now best exemplified by the *Old Icelandic Homily
Book*. Abram, who also argues for the presence of incognito Jews in Snorri's
work, says this on the matter:

Figure 1. Blind Synagoga with St. Paul, Antependium from Kinsarvik Church,
Norway, c. 1200. Image courtesy of Norsk Folkemuseum.
Interestingly, many of the published images of this altar frontal are cropped in
such a way as to remove her.

In [Gregory the Great's (590–604)] eighth homily on the Gospels, [...] [he] specifies that not quite *everything* acknowledged Christ's divinity by their sorrow at his death. Gregory enumerates the ways in which the different elements of creation—including the rocks, sea and sun—perceived Christ as Lord [...] But, continues Gregory, the Jews who turned away from Christ were harder hearted even than rocks, refusing "to acknowledge him whom [...] the elements proclaimed to be God either by their signs or by being broken" [...] When combined with the relatively well-known idea that all creation wept at Christ's death, Gregory's homily may lead us to suspect that at some point in the transmission of the Baldr myth it has been susceptible to Christian influence. Gregory's homilies were known in Iceland and translated into Old Norse, and they provided an important source for the types of sermon that Snorri might have heard preached each Sunday in church. (Abram 2011: 219–20)

Abram's argument is fortified when we confirm that the relevant excerpt from the Gregorian homily he describes is indeed attested in an Old Icelandic sermon on the Apparition of Christ:

En oss er þeckianda i ꜵllom tócnom þeim er sýnd ero bǽþe at bornom drótne oc deyianda. hve mikil illzca hever veret i hiortom neqverra gyþinga er hvártke keNdosc þeir viþ gvþ fyr spár ne fyr iarteiner. þuiat *allar hofoþskepnor vóttoþo komet hafa scapera siN. J þui keNdo himnarner guþ. er þeir sendio stiornona. Hafet* keNde hann. *þuiat þat spratt eige vndan fótom hans þa er hann geck yver þat. Jorþen kende hann. þuiat hon skalf at honom deyianda. Sólen kende hann. þuiat hon gerþe eigi skína. Steínar* keNdo hann. *þuiat þeir sprungo a tíþ daúþa hans. Helvíte kende hann. þuiat þat varþ aftr at selia þa dauþa meN es þat helt áþr.* En þóat allar hofoþskepnor váttaþe hann guþ vera. þa villdo ꝍllvngis eige hiorto ótrúra gyþinga trúa hann guþ vera. oc harþare steinom villdo þau eige kliúfasc til iþronar. oc vilia eige iáta þeim er allar skepnor skilia guþ vera. (*Homilíubók* p. 58, my emphasis)

(It is known to us in all wonders, those which were seen both at the Lord's birth and death, how much evil has been in the hearts of some Jews, who neither acknowledge God for prophecies nor for miracles. Because *all the elements affirmed that their creator had come. The heavens acknowledged God, for they sent the stars. The sea acknowledged Him, because it did not part under his feet when he walked over it. The earth acknowledged Him, because it shook upon his death. The sun acknowledged Him, because it did not shine. The stones acknowledged Him, because they cracked at the time of His death.* Hell acknowledged Him, because it came again to deliver back those dead men, whom previously it held. But even though all of the elements attested that He was God, then the hearts of the faithless Jews would by no means believe Him to be God, and harder than stones they would not be cracked for [their] repentance, and would not yield to Him, whom all of creation understands to be God.)

Considered alongside Snorri's own words, the influence from this scene on the *Edda* becomes quite transparent:

Því næst sendu Æsir um allan heim ørindreka at biðja at Baldr væri grátinn ór Helju. *En allir gerðu þat, menninir ok kykvendin ok jǫrðin ok stein-arnir ok tré ok allr málmr, svá sem þú munt sét hafa at þessir hlutir gráta þá er þeir koma ór frosti ok í hita.* Þá er sendimenn fóru heim ok hǫfðu vel rekit sín eyrindi, finna þeir í helli nokkvorum hvar gýgr sat. Hon nefndisk Þǫkk. Þeir biðja hana gráta Baldr ór Helju. Hon segir:

"Þǫkk mun gráta / þurrum tárum / Baldrs bálfarar. / Kyks né dauðs / nautka ek karls sonar: / haldi Hel því er hefir".

En þess geta menn at þar hafi verit Loki Laufeyjarson er flest hefir illt gert með Ásum. (*Gylfaginning* pp. 47–48, my emphasis)

(The next thing that happened, the Æsir sent word around the whole world, asking for Baldr to be wept out of Hel. *And everyone did so, humans and animals and the earth and the stones and trees and every kind of metal-work, as you will have seen that these things weep when they are brought out of the cold and into the warm.* Then when the messengers came home and had almost completed their task, they find a giantess sitting in a certain cave. She was called Þǫkk. They ask her to weep for Baldr, to get him out of Hel. She says:

"Þǫkk will cry / dry tears / at Baldr's funeral. / Living nor dead, / I did not delight in the old man's son [Baldr] / May Hel keep what she has."

But most people think this was really Loki, son of Laufey, who committed the most evil against the Æsir.)

Besides the allusion to Gregory's homily, there are other factors in Snorri's account contributing to Loki's Jew-ishness. There appears to be a subtle irony in the choice of Loki's alter ego. Þǫkk means "thanks" or "gratefulness". Richard

Richard Cole

Cleasby and Guðbrandur Vigfusson assert that this is a coincidence, and that Þǫkk's name must originally have a different root (Cleasby and Vigfusson 1874: 756). But for typological purposes, this double meaning is quite appropriate. After all, from a medieval Christian perspective, it was gratefulness that was sorely lacking when Christ revealed himself to the Jews. As Christians told the history of the early Church, the Jews had been given a great gift, yet they had rejected it. In the end, it was the gentiles who would show appreciation, and so form the Church. As the *Old Icelandic Homily Book* says: "iorsala lýþr oc gyþingar georþesc vinstre handar men. þat ero recningar fyr ótrú sína. en hann valþc epter písl sóma heógre handar men sér af heiþnom monnom ór norþre" (*Homilíubók* p. 37) (the people of Jerusalem and the Jews were made left-hand-men [i.e. enemies], that is a sign of their faithlessness, and after his crucifixion he chose for the honor of his right-hand-men heathen peoples from the North).

Furthermore, there is something very Jew-ish in Loki's function amongst the Æsir. Loki in Ásgarðr and the Jew in Western Christendom are both positions predicated on the notion of "being in service". From Augustine describing the Jews as book-carrying servants for Christian students, to Emperor Frederick II's designation of Jews as *servi camere nostre* "servants of our chamber", to the possessive servitude exhibited in the Anglo-Norman *Judei Nostri*, the doctrine of the "Jew in Christian Service" permeated medieval thinking about Jews (Rowe 2004: 16; Krummel 2011: 28–36; Abulafia 2011). But in both cases, the servant is held in contempt, perceived as antisocial and disloyal. Like the Jew amongst Christians, Loki is an ethnic Other, because his father Fárbauti belongs to the race of the *jǫtnar* (giants).[5] And in both cases, the cunning, magic-wielding outsider is tolerated only because of his unique qualities. If Loki only insulted and tricked the gods, and did not at all assist them when they fell into unfortunate predicaments, his presence in Ásgarðr would surely not be sustained. The parallel also extends perfectly to the way "the Jew" and Loki are treated. Both are righteously abused for the profit of their masters. Robert Grosseteste, a contemporary of Snorri, succinctly articulated the consensus regarding the status of the Jew within Christendom:

[5] The relationship could even be conceived of in postcolonial terms. Miriamne Krummel reads the "Red Jews" motif in *The Travels of Sir John Mandeville* as an anxiety that the Christian oppression of the Jews will be inverted during the apocalypse (Krummel 2011: 80–87). Ragnarøkr will also see the Æsir fall prey to the giants they have oppressed for so long, led by Loki, a half-giant in their midst.

[...] et justæ pœnæ inflictio est ut terram laboriose operetur, quæ etsi ex operatione illius populi fructificet, non tamen fert illi fructus suos, sed principibus sub quibus captivatur. (*Epistolae* p. 35)[6]

([...] it is the infliction of a just punishment that this people labour hard at tilling ground that, although it produces abundantly from their efforts, nevertheless bears its fruits not for them, but for the princes under whom they are held captive (*Letters* pp. 67–68))

This is a metaphor which could just as well be applied to Loki under the Æsir.

The Sons of Muspell and the Red Jews: Two Harbingers of the Apocalypse

Loki's Jew-ish credentials are further enhanced when we consider his fate at the end of the world. When the Æsir suspect his role in Baldr's death, their vengeance is grisly in the extreme. There is a brief allusion to the fact that Loki has been bound in stanza 14 of *Baldrs draumr*: "er lauss Loki líðr ór bǫndom" (Poetic Edda p. 279) (when Loki gets free from his bonds). Some details are also given in the prose epilogue to *Lokasenna* in the Codex Regius, which corresponds quite closely to the description provided by Snorri. *Snorra Edda*, however, is our chief source for the details of the scene. As Hár explains to Gangleri:

"Nú var Loki tekinn griðalauss ok farit með hann í helli nokkvorn. Þá tóku þeir þrjár hellur ok settu á egg ok lustu rauf á hellunni hverri. Þá váru teknir synir Loka Váli ok Nari eða Narfi. Brugðu Æsir Vála í vargs líki ok reif hann í sundr Narfa bróður sinn. Þá tóku Æsir þarma hans ok bundu Loka með yfir þá þrjá steina - einn undir herðum annarr undir lendum, þriði undir knésfótum - ok urðu þau bǫnd at járni. Þá tók Skaði eitrorm ok festi upp yfir hann svá at eitrit skyldi drjúpa ór orminum í andlit honum. En Sigyn kona hans stendr hjá honum ok heldr mund-laugu undir eitrdropa. En þá er full er mundlaugin þá gengr hon ok slær

---

[6] The anti-Semitic image of the Jew as a duplicitous servant, making cloying pledges and boasting indispensable special skills even while he undermines his master's society, is also brilliantly exemplified by the words Thomas of Monmouth (fl. c. 1149) puts into the mouth of an imaginary Jewish lawyer: "Nos iudei tui sumus, tui quotennes tributarii, tuisque crebro necessarii necessitatibus, tibi siquidem semper fideles regnoque tuo non inutiles" (*The Life and Miracles of St. William of Norwich* p. 100) (We are your Jews, your yearly payers of tribute, and to you we are necessary whenever you are in need, for we are always true to you and not at all useless to your realm (my translation)). That the William of Norwich legend was apparently known in Iceland and Norway, and that Archbishop Eysteinn (d. 1188) would have been in Bury during the alleged martyrdom of Robert of Bury, are the matter for a separate study.

út eitrinu, en meðan drýpr eitrit í andlit honum. Þá kippisk hann svá hart við at jǫrð ǫll skelfr. Þat kallið þér landskjálpta. Þar liggr hann í bǫndum til ragnarøkrs". (*Gylfaginning* p. 49)

("Now, without mercy, Loki was taken and brought to a certain cave. Then they took three slabs and turned them on their edges and drilled a hole in each. Then the sons of Loki were taken, Váli and Nari or Narfi. The Æsir transformed Váli into the shape of a wolf and he tore his brother Narfi to shreds. Then the Æsir took his entrails and bound Loki with them over the three stones—one under his shoulders, the second under his hips, the third under his knees, and they turned those bonds into iron. Then Skaði took a poisonous serpent and secured it above him so that the poison would drip out of its mouth onto his face. And Sigyn, his wife, stands by him and holds a cup under the dripping poison. But when the cup is full then she goes and throws the poison away, and in the meantime the poison drips onto his face. Then he thrashes so hard that the whole earth shakes. That's what you call an earthquake. He lies there in his bonds until Ragnarøkr".)

And when Ragnarøkr[7] comes, this is what happens:

Í þessum gný klofnar himinninn ok ríða þaðan Muspells synir. Surtr ríðr fyrst ok fyrir honum ok eptir bæði eldr brennanndi. Sverð hans er gott mjǫk. Af því skínn bjartara en af sólu. En er þeir ríða Bifrǫst þá brotnar hon sem fyrr er sagt. Muspells megir sœkja fram á þann vǫll er Vígríðr heitir. Þar kemr ok þá Fenrisúlfr ok Miðgarðsormr. Þar er ok þá Loki kominn ok Hrymr ok með honum allir hrímþursar, en Loka fylgja allir Heljar sinnar. En Muspells synir hafa einir sér fylking; er sú bjǫrt mjǫk. (*Gylfaginning* p. 50)

(In this clamor, the sky splits in two and the sons of Muspell ride forth. Surtr rides out first, before and after him there is burning fire. His sword is very great. The shine from it is brighter than the sun. And as they ride on Bifrǫst, then it breaks as previously said. The troops of Muspell head forth to the field which is called Vígríðr. Fenrisúlfr and Miðgarðsormr also arrive. Loki has also arrived, and Hrymr, and with

---

[7] I use the spelling Ragnarøkr throughout as it is specifically Snorri's version of events, as depicted in chapters 50–51 of *Gylfaginning*, to which I am referring. On this problem, see Haraldur Bernharðsson (2007). I am particularly grateful to one of my anonymous peer reviewers for recommending this source.

him all the Ice Giants, and all the champions of Hel follow Loki. And the sons of Muspell have a *fylking* all to themselves. It shines a great deal.)[8]

Snorri quotes stanza 51 of *Vǫluspá* as his source here:

> Kjóll ferr austan
> koma munu Muspells
> og lǫg lýðir,
> en Loki stýrir.
> Þar ró fíflmegir
> með freka allir
> Þeim er bróðir
> Býleists í fǫr (*Gylfaginning* p. 51; cf. Poetic Edda p. 12)

> (A ship journeys from the East
> [the sons] of Muspell are coming
> across the waves
> There are the monstrous brood
> with all the wolves
> Those are the brothers
> of Býleist, on their way)

But Snorri's description of the imprisonment and counter-attack of the Muspellssynir also has much in common with another popular medieval narrative. "The Red Jews" is a motif, seeming to emanate most forcefully from German-speaking Europe in the twelfth century (e.g. Gow 1995: esp. 91-95), in which a nation of Jews are imprisoned in a remote area, often in a mountain tomb somewhere around the Caucasus. Upon their release in the build-up to the apocalypse, the Red Jews will attack Christendom, resulting in an apocalyptic bloodshed that will bring on the End of Days. There are many variants to the legend—sometimes the Red Jews are identified with Gog and Magog, sometimes the Lost Ten Tribes of Israel. Sometimes, as in *The Travels of John Mandeville* (c. 1350s), they will seek out the Jewish Diaspora, and act as a globally coordinated threat. Sometimes they are directly answerable to the Anti-Christ or they ride

---

[8] It may be noted that Snorri's conclusion of his account of the Muspellssynir on the march with the words *er sú bjǫrt mjǫk* (It shines a great deal) or more closely (It is very bright) is remarkably similar to the description of the Red Jews on the march in *Der Göttweiger Trojanerkrieg* (1280): *Ir helm waren hartte glantz* (Their helmets had a frightful gleam) (*Der Göttweiger Trojanerkrieg* p. 273). However, as the Middle High German account is much later than *Snorra Edda* there can be no possibility of direct influence. The most we can say about this resemblance is that it is indicative of the similar mental images both the Muspellssynir and the Red Jews were conjuring during the thirteenth century.

with the Four Horsemen of the Apocalypse. Elsewhere, they are in league with the forces of Islam (Gow 1995). The first textual witness to a group of people actually referred to as "Red Jews" is *Der Jüngere Titurel* (c. 1272) but the motif is undoubtedly dependent on much earlier material from Alexander romances, going back as far as the tenth century *Historia de Preliis Alexandri Magni* (Gow 1995: 70–76). Precursor groups to the Red Jews appear in St. Jerome's *Commentariorum in Hiezechielem* (c. 380), Lamprecht's *Alexander* (c. 1130), and the *Historia Scholastica* (1160s) amongst other Latin and German sources (see Gow 1995: 300–1, 305–6, 308). The Red Jews proper are not attested in the West Norse corpus, although an antecedent tradition does appear in the Old Norse *Elucidarius* (c. 1200)[9]:

> Anti christus man berast i babílon hínní miclu or kẏni dan fra port kono [...] Oll tacn hans ero lẏgín. Hann man endr nya hína fornu iorsala borg. þat er íherusalem. oc lata sic þar gofga sem guð. Við honum monu gẏðingar taka fegensamlega. oc koma til hans or ollum heímí. En þeír monu snuast til tru af kenníngum enocs oc elias. Oc taka mioc sua aller harðar píníngar fyrir guðs nafne. (*Elucidarius* p. 84)

> (The Anti-Christ will be born in Greater Babylon to a woman of easy virtue from the tribe of Dan [...] All his miracles are false. He will rebuild the ancient *Jórsalaborg*, that is to say, Jerusalem, and have himself worshipped there as God. The Jews will receive him eagerly, and they will come to him from all over the world. But they will be converted to the faith by the teachings of Enoch and Elijah. And they will receive very harsh punishments in the name of God.)

There is no suggestion here that the Jews have been contained, or that they will embark on a premeditated annihilation of Christendom. Crucially, though, there is the notion that the Jews will unite all over the world, and that they will act in a coordinated fashion in the service of the Anti-Christ until Enoch and Elijah show them the errors of their ways. These "proto-Red Jews" are a noteworthy example of the kind of thinking about Jews that was circulating in the Old Norse world. As shall be seen, it appears that Snorri had access to a more mature version of the Red Jews legend, which he then allowed to color his perception (or depiction) of the Muspellssynir: e.g., both Snorri's "sons of Muspell" and the Red Jews are held underground until the end of times, both ride on horseback, etc. If we are in search of a strain of the Red Jews tradition

---

[9]   I am grateful to Arngrímur Vidalín for pointing out to me that this tradition was still current in the early fourteenth century, as it is repeated in *Hauksbók* (pp. 170–71).

which is more analogous to the apocalyptic agents of *Snorra Edda*, we must look beyond Icelandic sources.

As the continental material concerning the Red Jews is so diverse, any decision over which particular source to quote as exemplary will be more or less arbitrary. Therefore, I have opted to compare Snorri's Muspellssynir with the tradition as it appears in Old Swedish.[10] Doubtless, there can be no suggestion of direct transmission between the two, as the Swedish *Konung Alexander* (c. 1380) is over a century younger than *Snorra Edda*. However, the particular Latin text of which it is substantially a translation, the *Historia de Preliis Alexandri Magni*, dates from the tenth century. The Old Swedish account thus has the advantage of having a strong connection to one of the oldest known ancestors of the Red Jews. Furthermore, owing to the linguistic affinity between Old Swedish and Old Norse it can also give us a hint at what a rendering of the Red Jews tale might have looked like in Snorri's own language—not that there necessarily was a written vernacular version. The tale could well have been told by foreign guests or cosmopolitan scholars at the Norwegian court of King Hákon Hákonarson, for example. We know that people in that very circle were discussing—and evaluating the plausibility of—another Orientalist fantasy, namely the *Letter of Prester John*. Written at the court of King Hákon for the king-in-waiting, Magnús Hákonarson, *Konungs skuggsjá* (c. 1250s) refers to "þá bok er gior var a indija landi [...] þar sie margt vndarliga j sagt" (*Konungs skuggsiá* p. 13; see also Larrington 2004: 96–97) (that book which was made in India [...] in which many wondrous things are said). Indeed, it ought to be noted that some versions of the *Letter* actually contained references to the Red Jews (Gow 1995: 307, 309–10). Obviously we are in the realm of the deeply speculative here, but it does not seem unthinkable that a discussion similar to the one hinted at in *Konungs skuggsjá* might also have taken place concerning the Red Jews.

[Old Swedish]
han foor thådhan ower sitiam
óster borter ij wårlina fram
enkte land laa thiit wt mere
ther man wiste aff sighia flere
han fan ther folk wårre ån trull
th3 hafdhe tho råt månniskio hull
rådhelikith ok mykith oreent
them gat ångin opa seet

---

[10] An overview of this tradition in East Norse more broadly is provided by Jonathan Adams (2013: 75–77). On *Konung Alexander* and the sources of the *Historia* see Mitchell (1996: 37–38), Zingerlie (1977) and Gow (1995: 77).

the hafdho syyn å swa grym
at ånghin thordhe se a them
thȝ lifdhe alt widh trulla sidh
ångin månniskia fik ther fridh
thȝ aat folk mȝ huld ok krop
inbyrdhis hwart annath op
ok alla handa creatwr
håst ok wargh foghil ok diwr
hwath som fôdhis a iordh åller wådher
thȝ åta the alt saman mådher
....

the plågha enkte thera iordha
the åtar them op a thera bordhe
hwath man kan hålȝt lifwande nåmpna
....

orena gerninga margha handa
sa alexander aff them ganga
ther lofflika åra skriffwa
thȝ år alt ont thȝ the drifwa
Rôdhe iudha mon thȝ heta
swa finder han ån hwa them wil leta
tha alexander hafdhe thetta seet
badhe hôrt ok widha leet
at thetta folk dreff tholik last
han thånkte ij sinom hoghe rast
vtan thetta folk forgaar
al wårlin åpter dôme faar
ok smittas ij tholik gerning snôdh
all wårlin hafwer thås stora nôdh
om thȝ skal ganga sin fram gang
åpter thera sidh tha smittas mang
ok lifwa ij thera åpter dôme
thȝ ware båtra at man them gôme
Alexander fan et ful got raadh
thȝ folkith han saman drifwa badh
ij en flok badhe mån ok qwinna
swa then mera som then minnda
swa at enkte ater bleff

nor ij wårlina alla them dreff
swa langan wågh råt ij nor
at thiit ångin fara thỏr
Thᴣ war alexanders idhelik bỏn
til gudh som allom gifwer lỏn
at wårlin skulle ekke smittas
aff tholikt lifwerne ekke hittas

....

han badh swa långe gudh hỏrdhe han
gudh giordhe vnder the åra san
ey stort fore alexanders saka
vtan månniskio helso til maka
han bỏdh tvem berghom the standa ån
ganga til saman badhin ij sån
the waro hỏgh ok mykith lang
gingo saman vtan alt bang

....

ther år stort rwm innan til
som et ganᴣt land iak thᴣ sighia wil

....

bårghin åra alt kringom brant
som annar mwr thᴣ år sånt
the åra som andre mwrwåggia hỏghia
ther kan ångin op fore ỏghia
the rỏdha iudha åra ther inne
badhe flere ok swa minne (*Konung Alexander* 130–33)

[English]
(He goes from there over Scythia.
Away, far to the East of the world.
There was no land out there any more
that anyone knew of. Many say
there he found a people worse than
trolls
Although they had human skin
angry and most unclean
No one could bear to look upon them
They had such an ugly appearance

that no one dared to look upon them
they all lived in the manner of trolls.
No human there could find any peace.
They ate people with skin and body
including each other
and all kinds of creatures,
horses and wolves, birds and beasts,
whatever lives on earth or sea,
they ate it all in the same way

....

they do not tend to their land.
On their tables, they eat up
whatever living thing you can name.
The committing of many impure deeds [spells?]
Alexander saw them do.
There, it is written in law
that everything they do is evil.
They are called "Red Jews"
so he seeks them, and wants to see them.
When Alexander had seen that,
both heard it and clearly observed,
that this people behaved in such a way
he thinks in his booming voice
all the world will be judged
unless this people are destroyed
and will be smote by such sordid actions.
The whole world is in great need.
If things were to go their own way
according to their custom many would be smitten
and live ever after in their power.
It would be better if one could hide them away
Alexander had a great idea.
He had that people rounded up
in one group, both men and women,
the short and the tall,
so that not one was left behind at all.
He had them driven north in the world,
such a long way north,

that no one would dare to go there.
It was Alexander's pious prayer
to God who rewards all
that the world would not be smitten
and never encounter such a way of life

....

he prayed so long that God heard him.
God did it, it's true,
not for Alexander's sake alone
but for the good of all humankind.
He commanded two mountains—they still stand—
to come together as one.
They were tall and very long.
They went together without any noise

....

Inside there is a lot of space
like a huge country, I should say

....

the mountains are steep all around
like another wall, it's true.
They are like other tall walls.
No one can climb it.
The Red Jews are in there,
both short and tall.)

There are several striking affinities between the coming of the Muspellssynir according to Snorri and the Red Jews according to the Alexander romances. Both are imprisoned underground: Loki in a cave, the Red Jews in the mountains. Both engage in cannibalism. The Red Jews "aat folk mʒ huld ok krop / inbyrdhis hwart annath op" (eat people and their flesh and blood / they'll even munch each other up). Similarly, according to Snorri, Loki's son Váli eats his brother, Narfi. The release of either the Red Jews or the Muspellssynir is a precursor to the apocalypse. Alexander, as a Christianized king in the medieval tradition, can pray to the one true God and prevent it from happening. Snorri's tragically flawed pagan deities, on the other hand, must vainly await their doom. Indeed, concerning one important detail, *Snorra Edda* is closer to the Red Jews motif than it is to *Vǫluspá*. In the eddic poem, the Muspellssynir approach over water with a ship, a *kjóll*. But in *Snorra Edda*, despite the citation of the original

Figure 2. Der Antichrist, fol. 14v (1480).
Image courtesy of Die Bayerische Staatsbibliothek.

poem, the accompanying prose clearly states that they ride on horseback towards Ásgarðr. This suggests that the image of the Muspellssynir conjured by Snorri's mind's eye probably resembled something like the example provided in Figure 2, rather than the nautical setting that would have been drawn from *Vǫluspá* alone.

If one did not know the actual context for this image (and did not know how relatively few artistic depictions there are of Old Norse myth from the Middle Ages versus, say, Christian devotional art), one might very well describe these horse-mounted warriors and their malevolent leader as the Sons of Muspell and Loki, as depicted by Snorri: "ríða þaðan Muspells synir" (the Sons of Muspell ride forth) (*Gylfaginning*, p. 50). Of course, it is actually a depiction of the Red Jews from *Der Antichrist*, fol. 14v (1480). The queen of the Amazons is also amongst the horde. A similar image can also be found in Ms. Germ 2mo 129, fol. 15v (c. 1320). Otherwise, the earliest surviving pictorial representation pertaining to the Red Jews shows the entombed Gog and Magog eating human flesh, from the *Ebstorf World Map* (1235). See Gow 1995: 383–390.

	Muspellssynir in Vǫluspá	*Muspellsynir in Snorra Edda*	*The Red Jews*
Appear at the apocalypse?	Yes	Yes	Yes
How will they arrive at the apocalypse?	Sea, by boat (*kjóll*)	By land, on horseback (*at ríða*), and on foot	By land, on horseback, and on foot
Where are they prior to the apocalypse?	Muspell, more specific whereabouts unknown	Underground, inside a cave	Underground, inside a mountain
Depicted as a military force?	Uncertain, described as fíflmegir, 'monstrous men', perhaps intended here as 'monstrous brood' rather than 'monstrous troops'. However, the point seems obscure.	Yes. They march in a *fylking*, a medieval defensive formation. They are also referred to as the *Muspells megir*, 'men of Muspell', perhaps intended here in the sense of 'troops of Muspell' (but cf. *fíflmegir*).	Frequently, as in e.g. the Gottweiger *Trojanerkrieg* late 1200s): "Dar ringe gantz / Ir ringe gantz / Ir helm waren hartte glantz" (Gow 1995: 193) [There under [their armor] they wore huge steel rings / their helmets had a fearful gleam]

As is so often the case with Snorri's work, the sons of Muspell are not drawn exclusively from any one tradition. *Vǫluspá* clearly provided the basic structure upon which Snorri could build his own narrative of Ragnarøkr. But Snorri does seem to be permitting his ancient, pagan materials to draw color from the potent images of the high medieval cultural canon in which he was immersed. Snorri was not insulated from the intellectual climate to which he was contributing, and thus could no more avoid being influenced by the powerful typologies of anti-Judaism than he could avoid any other aspect of the medieval Christian *Weltanschauung*. Indeed, the emphasis on the "sons of Muspell" as a descent group based on lineage makes them feel more like a contemporary ethnic group than a venerable cosmological fixture.[11] As if to highlight the originality of the

---

[11] On the notion of descent and race in the Middle Ages, see Robert Bartlett (2001). On the importance of lineage for understanding Jewishness in Old Norse literature, see Richard Cole (2015a: 239–68).

thirteenth-century eddic hybrid he has created, it is only Snorri (and the singular example of stanza 48 in *Lokasenna*) who employs the name "Muspellssynir" to refer to these agents of the apocalypse. In *Vǫluspá*, they are elliptically named *Muspells,* lit. "Of Muspell". One might rather optimistically attribute the uniqueness of Snorri's appellation by proposing that he is the only surviving witness of a naming tradition which was already at least two centuries old by the time he wrote it down, having apparently survived in oral record from some time around Iceland's official conversion in the year 1000 until the 1220s. More soberly, we might consider Snorri's own era and consider if there were any group in the thought of that period whose presence was associated with the apocalypse and who were known as *synir,* (sons of). Readers will note the similarity between the phrases *Muspells synir* and *Isræls synir,* the term frequently used in thirteenth century works—such as *Stjórn*—to refer to the Jews. Both are based on the formula of geographical location + *synir.* They are also phonologically similar. In Snorri's days the /els syni:r/ of *Muspells synir* would have made a half rhyme with the /ɛ:ls syni:r/ of *Isræls synir.* Admittedly, the proposition that there are resonances of anti-Jewish imagery in *Snorra Edda* may be unpalatable, but it is a crucial to considering Snorri in his comparative context. Much as scholars may employ *Snorra Edda* to recover details of the pagan past, it is also necessary to acknowledge Snorri's Christian present. Thinking about the Jews was an inalienable aspect of that experience.

Works Cited

Primary Sources

Decreta
Conciliorum Oecumenicorum Decreta. Ed. J. Alberigo et al. Bologna: 1973.

Der Antichrist
Der Antichrist und Die fünfzehn Zeichen vor dem jüngsten Gericht. Faksimile der ersten typographischen Ausgabe eines unbekannten Straßburger Druckers, um 1480. Hamburg: 1979.

Der Göttweiger Trojanerkrieg
Pseudo-Wolfram von Eschenbach. *Der Göttweiger Trojanerkrieg.* Ed. Alfred Koppitz. Deutsche Texte des Mittelalters, 29. Berlin: 1926.

Elucidarius
The Old Norse Elucidarius. Ed. Evelyn Scherabon Firchow. Columbia: 1992.

Enarrationes
St. Augustine of Hippo. *Enarrationes in Psalmos*. Ed. J. P. Migne. Patrologia Latina, 37. Paris: 1845.

Epistolae
Robert Grossteste. *Roberti Grosseteste Episcopi Quondam Lincolniensis Epistolæ*. Ed. Henry Richards Luard. Rerum Britannicarum medii aevi scriptores, 25. London: 1861.

TRANSLATION
The Letters of Robert Grosseteste, Bishop of Lincoln. Transl. F. A. C. Mantello and Joseph Goering. Toronto: 2010.

Gylfaginning: see *Snorra Edda*

Hauksbók
Hauksbók. Udgiven efter de Arnamagnæanske håndskrifter no. 371, 544 og 675, 4o. 1. Ed. Finnur Jónsson. Copenhagen: 1892.

Heilagra Manna Søgur [= HMS]
Heilagra Manna Søgur, fortællinger og legender om hellige mænd og kvinder. 2 vols. Ed. C.R. Unger. Christiania: 1877.

Homiliu-Bók
Homiliu-Bók. Isländska Homilier efter en Handskrift från Tolfte Århundradet. Ed. Theodor Wisén. Lund: 1872.

Konung Alexander
Konung Alexander. En Medeltids Dikt från Latinet Vänd i Svenska Rim. Ed. G.E. Klemming. Stockholm: 1862.

Konungs Skuggsjá
Konungs Skuggsiá. Ed. Ludvig Holm-Olsen. Norrøne tekster, 1. Oslo: 1983.

Letters: see *Epistolae*

The Life and Miracles of St. William of Norwich
Thomas of Monmouth. *The Life and Miracles of St. William of Norwich*. Ed. and Transl. Augustus Jessopp and Montague Rhodes James. Cambridge: 1896.

Maríu saga
Mariu Saga. Legender om Jomfru Maria og hendes jertegn, efter gamle haandskrifter. Ed. C.R. Unger. Christiania: 1871.

Messuskýringar
Messuskýringar. Liturgisk Symbolik frå Den Norsk-Islandske Kyrkja i Millomalderen.
  Vol. 1. Ed. Oluf Kolsrud. Oslo: 1952.

Poetic Edda
Edda: Die Lieder des Codex Regius nebst verwandten Denkmälern. Vol. 1. Ed. Gustav
  Neckel & Hans Kuhn. Heidelberg: 1983.

Snorra Edda
Snorri Sturluson. *Edda. Prologue and Gylfaginning.* Ed. Anthony Faulkes. London:
  1988.

Stjórn
Stjórn. Tekst etter håndskriftene. 2 vols. Ed. Reidar Astås. Norrøne tekster, 8. Oslo:
  2009.

Wormianus
Edda Snorra Sturlusonar. Codex Wormianus AM 242, fol. Ed. Finnur Jónsson.
  Copenhagen: 1924.

Secondary Sources

Abram, Christopher. 2006. "Snorri's Invention of Hermóðr's *helreið*." In *The
  Fantastic in Old Norse / Icelandic, Sagas and the British Isles: Preprints of the
  Thirteenth International Saga Conference.* Ed. John McKinnell, David Ashurst,
  and Donata Kick. Durham. Pp. 22–31.
———. 2011. *Myths of the Pagan North: The Gods of the Norsemen.* London.
Abulafia, Anna Sapir. 2011. *Christian-Jewish Relations, 1000-1300. Jews in the Service
  of Medieval Christendom.* London.
Adams, Jonathan. 2013. *Lessons in Contempt: Poul Ræff's Publication in 1516 of
  Johannes Pfefferkorn's The Confession of the Jews.* Odense.
Auerbach, Eric. 1952. "Typological Symbolism in Medieval Literature." *Yale
  French Studies* 9: 3–10.
Berenbaum, Michael, and Fred Skolnik, eds. 2007. *Encyclopedia Judaica.* 22 vols.
  Detroit.
Baron, Salo W. 2007. "Population." In Berenbaum and Skolnik 2007 16: 381–400.
Bartlett, Robert. 2001. "Medieval and Modern Concepts of Race and Ethnicity."
  Journal of Medieval and Early Modern Studies 31(1): 39–56.
Bugge, Sophus. 1881–1898. *Studier over de nordiske Gude- og heltesagns Oprindelse.*
  Christiania.
Cleasby, Richard, and Gudbrand Vigfusson. 1874. *An Icelandic-English Dictionary.*
  Oxford.

Cohen, Jeffrey Jerome. 2003. *Medieval Identity Machines.* Minneapolis.

———. 2006. "Was Margery Kempe Jewish?" *In the Middle.* Blog. April 21. http://www.inthemedievalmiddle.com/2006/04/was-margery-kempe-jewish.html (accessed on March 1, 2015).

Cohen, Jeremy. 1999. *Living Letters of the Law: Ideas of the Jew in Medieval Christianity.* Los Angeles.

Cole, Richard. 2014. "The French Connection, or Þórr versus the Golem." *Medieval Encounters* 20(3): 238–60.

———. 2015a. "*Kyn / Fólk / Þjóð / Ætt*: Proto-Racial Thinking and its Application to Jews in Old Norse Literature." In *Fear and Loathing in the North: Jews and Muslims in Medieval Scandinavia and the Baltic Region.* Ed. Cordelia Heß and Jonathan Adams. Berlin. Pp. 239–68.

———. 2015b. "Racial Thinking in Old Norse Literature: The Case of the *Blámaðr.*" *Saga-Book* 39: 21–40.

Faulkes, Anthony. 1983. "Pagan Sympathy: Attitudes to Heathendom in the Prologue to *Snorra Edda.*" In *Edda: A Collection of Essays.* Ed. R. J. Glendinning and Haraldur Bessason. Winnipeg.

———. 1993. "The Sources of Skáldskaparmál: Snorri's Intellectual Background." In *Snorri Sturluson: Kolloquium anlasslich der 750: Wiederkehr seines Todestages.* Ed. Alois Wolf. Tübingen. Pp. 59–76.

Fidjestøl, Bjarne. 1997. "Snorri Sturluson—European Humanist and Rhetorician." In *Selected Papers.* Ed. Odd Einar Haugen and Else Mundal. Transl. Peter Foote. Odense. Pp. 343–50.

Friedman, Lee M. 1934. *Robert Grosseteste and the Jews.* Cambridge, MA.

Gow, Andrew Colin. 1995. *The Red Jews: Antisemitism in an Apocalyptic Age 1200–1600.* Leiden.

Haraldur Bernharðsson. 2007. "Old Icelandic *ragnarök* and *ragnarøkkr.*" In *Verba docenti: Studies in historical and Indo-European linguistics presented to Jay H. Jasanoff.* Ed. Alan J. Nussbaum. Ann Arbor. Pp. 25–38.

Holm-Olsen, Ludvig, and Kjell Heggelund. 1974. *Fra Runene til Norske Selskab.* Vol. 1 of *Norges Litteratur Historie.* Oslo.

Itzkowitz, Joel B. 2007. "Jews, Indians, Phylacteries: Jerome on Matthew 23.5." *Journal of Early Christian Studies* 15(4): 563–72.

Kirby, Ian. 1986. *Bible Translation in Old Norse.* Geneva.

Krummel, Miriamne Ara. 2011. *Crafting Jewishness in Medieval England. Legally Absent, Virtually Present.* New York.

Larrington, Carolyne. 2004. "'Undruðusk þá, sem fyrir var': Wonder, Vínland and Medieval Travel Narratives." *Mediaeval Scandinavia* 14: 91–114.

Liberman, Anatoly. 2004. "Some Controversial Aspects of the Myth of Baldr." *Alvíssmál* 11: 17–54.

Liebeschutz, Hans. 2007a. "Albertus Magnus." In Berenbaum and Skolnik 2007 1: 591.

———. 2007b. "William of Auvergne." In Berenbaum and Skolnik 2007 21: 64.

McEvoy, James. 2000. *Robert Grosseteste.* Oxford.

Mentgen, Gerd. 2005. "Crusades." In vol. 1 of *Antisemitism: A Historical Encyclopedia of Prejudice and Persecution.* Ed. Richard S. Levy. Oxford. Pp. 152–55.

Mitchell, Stephen A. 1996. "The Middle Ages." In *A History of Swedish Literature.* Ed. Lars G. Warme. Lincoln, NE. Pp. 1–57.

Moore, R.I. 2006. *The Formation of a Persecuting Society: Authority and Deviance in Western Europe 950-1250.* New York.

Mosher, Arthur D. 1983. "The Story of Baldr's Death: the Inadequacy of Myth in the Light of Christian Faith." *Scandinavian Studies* 55 (4): 305–15.

O'Donoghue, Heather. 2005. "What has Baldr to do with Lamech? The Lethal Shot of a Blind Man in Old Norse Myth and Jewish Exegetical Traditions." *Medium Ævum* 72: 82–107.

Roth, Cecil. 1951. *The Jews of Medieval Oxford.* Oxford.

Rowe, Nina. 2004. *The Jew, the Cathedral and the Medieval City: Synagoga and Ecclesia in the Thirteenth Century.* Cambridge.

Signer, Michael A. 2004. "Polemics and Exegesis: The Varieties of Twelfth Century Christian Hebraism." In *Hebraica Veritas? Christian Hebraists and the Study of Judaism in Early Modern Europe.* Ed. Allison Coudert. Philadelphia. Pp. 21–32.

Turville-Petre, E. O. G. 1964. *Myth and Religion of the North: the Religion of Ancient Scandinavia.* London.

Wanner, Kevin J. 2008. *Snorri Sturluson and the Edda: The Conversion of Cultural Capital in Medieval Scandinavia.* Toronto.

Wolf, Kirsten. 1990. "Brandr Jónsson and *Stjórn.*" *Scandinavian Studies* 62 (2): 163–88.

Yuval, Israel Yacob. 1998. "Jewish Messianic Expectations towards 1240 and Christian Reactions." In *Toward the Millennium: Messianic Expectations from the Bible to Waco.* Ed. Peter Schäfer and Mark R. Cohen. 105–21. Leiden.

Zingerlie, Oswald. 1977. *Die Quellen zum Alexander des Rudolf von Ems.* New York.

Creation from Fire in Snorri's *Edda*

The Tenets of a Vernacular Theory of Geothermal Activity in Old Norse Myth

Mathias Nordvig
University of Colorado, Boulder

Abstract: This article argues that Snorri's version of the creation myth in Snorri's *Edda* contains imagery from volcanic activity described in terms of a "vernacular theory of geothermal activity". The vernacular theory of geothermal activity mythologizes natural events, volcanic and otherwise, and describes them in terms of relatable analogical and metaphorical imagery sampled primarily from the cultural vault of Nordic mythology. There are several natural aspects of Snorri's creation myth, which seem to not fully make sense if compared with the usual analogies of the natural behavior of ice and fire. These inconsistencies are fully explained if one turns to another analogy, namely the low discharge effusive eruptions, which are so common in Iceland. These processes cannot, however, be described in the vernacular vocabulary without analogies to ice and water, and this is why there is confusion about the details of the process. Lacking such words as "lava" or even "eruption", the Icelandic creation myth in Snorri's *Edda* turns to analogies such as "ice" and "river" to describe these phenomena. The end result is a creation myth based on indigenous theories on volcanic activity, and aspects of Neoplatonism inherited from continental philosophy.

Introduction

The purpose of this article is to give insight into the ways in which early Icelanders communicated their experience of volcanic eruptions in myths and legends. It is my theory that if the early Icelanders had a vocabulary able to express the experience of volcanic eruptions, it was not particularly detailed. Therefore, early Icelanders may have used mythic language and linguistic tropes to express what they saw in eruptions. This theory relies on observations by scholars and scientists working with different cultures in many parts of the world, and it is a theory that has also been carefully suggested by Oren Falk in connection with the Icelandic material in his article, "The Vanishing Volcanoes" (Falk 2007). Falk has dubbed it the vernacular theory on geothermal activity (see below), and I find this designation clear and broadly applicable. To demonstrate how the vernacular theory of geothermal activity in early Iceland may have functioned, I will analyze the convergence of fire and ice in the creation myth in Snorri's *Edda* as a sequence that borrows from the nature of a common Icelandic low discharge volcanic eruption. I will comment on some inconsistencies in the natural image of the creation myth, pointed out by Anne Holtsmark in her 1964 study *Studier i Snorris mytologi*. I will argue that the inconsistencies that Holtsmark had some difficulties reconciling are in fact explainable if the natural image of the convergence of fire and ice is compared with a lava flow. To strengthen this argument, I make use of the only medieval Icelandic source that describes the details of a volcanic eruption, the poem *Hallmundarkviða*. I approach the texts as medieval literature, which contains, on the one hand, ancient myth from oral culture, and, on the other hand, contemporary reflections on the part of the authors, based in medieval Icelandic culture and Continental teaching. First, I will contextualize this analysis with a brief overview of volcanism in Iceland and a survey of research into the connection between volcanism and Old Norse myths. I will then expound on the details of Snorri's creation myth, focusing mainly on the language and descriptions associated with the components of *Élivágar* and *eitr*.

Volcanism in Iceland

Icelandic volcano types are highly varied. They range from shield volcanoes such as the infamous Eyjafjallajökull, which erupted in 2010; stratovolcanoes like Hekla; calderas; spatter cones; scoria cones; tuff cones; lava shields; chasms such as Eldgjá; mixed cone rows such as Laki; and, finally, rows of tuff cones and maars (Þorvaldur Þórðarson and Ármann Höskuldsson 2008: 201). Icelandic eruptions are as complex as the various volcano types. They can be explosive or effusive, or a mixture of both (Þorvaldur Þórðarson and Ármann Höskuldsson 2008: 202), and their eruption styles range from Surtseyan to Phreatoplinian in the case of wet eruptions, and in the case of dry eruptions, from Strombolian to Plinian (Þorvaldur Þórðarson and Ármann Höskuldsson 2008: 200). Naturally, the many eruption types have varied effects on the landscape, but the most frequent lava-producing eruptions create the type of rubbly pāhoehoe that is characteristic of the landscape in Iceland (Þorvaldur Þórðarson and Ármann Höskuldsson 2008: 207). Large-scale tephra-producing events are less frequent.

The impact of Icelandic volcanism ranges from local to hemispheric. Minor eruptions in Iceland can affect humans who live in the immediate vicinity of the volcano, but do not necessarily have an effect on the life of residents elsewhere in the region. Major eruptions, on the other hand, have been known to disturb Europe and even Asia. The hazards of Icelandic volcanism include lava flows, ash clouds and ash depositions, debris flows, gas emissions, lightning, and glacier bursts, also known as *jökulhlaups*. Magma that is exposed to water or ice erupts especially violently as the rapid cooling of the magma generates phreatic activity and large quantities of ash, which is deposited in a wide area. The generated meltwater from subglacial eruptions creates *jökulhlaups*, which can be highly debris-charged and lahar-like (Tweed 2012: 218).

While the stratovolcano Hekla remains the historically widest known volcano in Iceland—it is one of only a handful mentioned in the medieval Icelandic *Annales Regii* (pp. 76–155)—the two most severe eruptions of Iceland, in the little over 1100 years that the island has been inhabited, are the fissure eruptions of Eldgjá in 934 CE and Laki in 1783–1784 CE (Zielinski et al. 1995: 129). Eldgjá emitted some 19.6 cubic kilometers of lava and dispersed tephra across roughly 20,000 square kilometers. The eruption may have lasted as long as six years, until 940 CE. Laki emitted 15.1 cubic kilometers of lava and caused around 8,000 square kilometers of tephra fall. It lasted for eight months (Þorvaldur Þórðarson and Ármann Höskuldsson 2008: 212). The Laki fissures occurred in the 28 kilometer-long vent complex stretching from the southwestern tip of Vatnajökull to the icecap covering Katla. The eruption column in Laki was 12–15 kilometers high, and the height of the fire fountains was between 800 and 1400 meters high (Þór Þórðarson and Self 1993: 233). This also seems to have been the case in the Eldgjá eruption, which was even more violent (Zielinski 1995: 132).[1]

Except for a single reference to "an eruption" that displaced the settler Molda-Gnúpr in *Landnámabók* ch. 329, the Eldgjá event is not mentioned in written sources from Iceland. This means that there are no indications of the impact of the eruption locally, but based on historical sources from Europe, the Middle East (Stothers 1998), and from as far away as China (Fei and Zhou 2006), it can be concluded that the global climatic impact was severe. The 1783–1784 CE Laki eruption was likewise a great menace to the European climate, causing crop failure and famine (Grattan and Pyatt 1993; Grattan 1995), as well as elevated mortality rates as a result of air pollution (Grattan, Durand, and Taylor

---

[1]   Strangely, *Annales Regii* does not recount the Eldgjá eruption (see *Annales Regii* p. 103).

2003; Courtillot 2005; Grattan et al. 2005). The famine following Laki caused a mortality rate as high as 25 percent in the Icelandic parishes that were most affected by the eruption (Vasey 1991: 342). Based on that, we may only guess what calamities Eldgjá brought with it in Iceland. Inferring from these events, the settlers coming from Scandinavia must have been terrified by the experience of fire fountains rising higher than the skyline of any modern city, roaring noises, which must have been audible in a large area, and an all-engulfing darkness caused by ashes in the atmosphere, blocking out the sun.

Situated on the mid-Atlantic ridge with approximately thirty singular volcanoes (Þorvaldur Þórðarson and Ármann Höskuldsson 2008: 199–200), Iceland is the most geologically active region in the world. It is estimated that over the last 1100 years, as long as there has been human settlement in Iceland, there have been approximately 250 large and small eruptions (Tweed 2012: 217). From the decade just before the *landnám* (the settlement period in the ninth century) until the mid-fourteenth century, there were roughly fifty-six verified eruptions. Thirty-nine of these occurred before 1220, the approximate time Snorri Sturluson wrote down his *Edda*, a prose collection of mythological narratives. Of these, four were effusive events, an additional four were of mixed effusive and explosive nature, and twenty-four were explosive events (Þór Þórðarson and Larsen 2007: 137). In the period from 1179 to ca. 1200, both an explosive and an effusive event occurred in the Katla system (Þór Þórðarson and Larsen 2007: 134), and in the period 1201–1220, two mixed eruptions and one explosive one were recorded to have occurred "somewhere in Iceland" (Þór Þórðarson and Larsen 2007: 137).

Thus nearly every generation of Icelanders, from the time of the *landnám* to the time when the mythology was recorded in writing, would have had the chance to experience volcanic eruptions. In these eruption types, there is sufficient material to inspire the imagination of Icelanders attempting to give accounts of the subterranean processes particular to the region. With so much geological activity, it is perhaps no wonder that the question of a volcanic imprint on the premodern literature of Iceland has occasionally boggled the minds of some scholars since at least the beginning of the twentieth century.

Research Survey

In 1905, Bertha S. Phillpotts published the article "Surt" in *Arkiv för nordisk filologi*, arguing that the fire-giant Surtr was indeed a volcano-giant, and that his mythical role as the antagonist of the Æsir, who sets the world on fire, is reminiscent of observations of volcanism in Iceland. This argument served the greater purpose of arguing that the eddic poem *Vǫluspá* is originally an Icelandic poem. Sigurður Nordal welcomed this argument in his analysis of the poem in *Vǫluspá* from 1927. The interpretation has been widely accepted, though not universally (Falk 2007: 7). Nevertheless, Rudolf Simek reiterates the notion in the *Dictionary of Northern Mythology* (Simek 2007: 303–04).

Dorothy B. Vitaliano also investigates the question of volcanism in premodern Icelandic narratives in her book on geomythology, entitled *Legends of the Earth* (1973). Her focus is on a mix of medieval narratives, primarily the *Kristni saga* account of the eruption that created Kristnitökuhraun, and folk legends, such as one about the cause of eruptions in Katla volcano. Vitaliano's investigations are unfortunately marred by a general lack of theoretical knowledge about literary genres, myth as a genre, and a critical grasp of premodern Icelandic literature.

More recently, Oren Falk has revisited the question in the article "The Vanishing Volcanoes: Fragments of Fourteenth-Century Icelandic Folklore" (2007). Falk provides an encompassing survey of the different narratives of Old Norse-Icelandic literature that can be associated with volcanism. He concludes his article by proposing an interpretation of certain passages in the saga literature, arguing that, for instance, images of dragons lying on gold hoards are expressions of a "vernacular geothermal theory" in a genre that, according to Falk, dares not speak of volcanoes (Falk 2007: 10–12).

In his article "Perception of Volcanic Eruptions in Iceland", geologist Þorvaldur Þórðarson has made a case for a special pragmatic conception of volcanoes in premodern Iceland. He argues that pre-Christian Icelanders were less prone to react with awe and supernatural interpretations of the volcanic phenomena than their later Christian descendants were. This argument is based on his readings of Vitaliano's interpretation of the story about the Kristnitökuhraun eruption compared with Herbert the monk's fantastic descriptions of volcanic eruptions in Iceland in *Liber Miraculorum* from ca. 1170 CE (Þorvaldur Þórðarson 2010).

Archaeologists Bo Gräslund and Neil Price, in the article "Twilight of the Gods? The 'Dust Veil Event' of AD 536 in Critical Perspective", discuss the theme of a natural disaster, possibly of volcanic origin, affecting the mythology of the Scandinavians in the Migration Age (Gräslund and Price 2012). Already in 2009, Gräslund suggested that the Fimbulvetr and related eschatological images in *Snorra Edda* have affinity to a volcanic catastrophe (Gräslund 2009: 318–26).

The most recent publication combining Old Norse mythology with volcanic eruptions is geologist Árni Hjartarson's thorough comparison of the images of *Hallmundarkviða* with volcanic eruptions in his article "Hallmundarkviða, eldforn lýsing á eldgósi" (2014). Aside from pointing out that myths have been used to convey experiences of volcanic activity in a European context as far back as Greek mythology (Árni Hjartarson 2014: 28), he meticulously explains the connection between the poem, eruptions, and certain mythical figures in the narrative.

In this context, it should be mentioned that the idea that literary and oral traditions can shed light on natural phenomena and geological events has been gaining increasing acceptance across a wide spectrum of scholarly disciplines. The archaeologist-folklorist pair Elizabeth W. Barber and Paul T. Barber have provided an extensive interpretive method for understanding how oral societies relate superior geological events in their book *When They Severed Earth from Sky* (2004). Likewise, the anthology *Myth and Geology*, edited by L. Piccardi and W.B. Masse, reveals the potential of myths to yield data of value to the geological sciences. Scholars continue to find examples of how myths and legends narrate experiences of geological events. The most well-known example may be the myth (as much as 7,675 years old) of the Klamath tribe in northwestern North America about the eruption of Mount Mazama (Zdanowich, Zielinski, and Germani 1999). Most recently, a team of Australian researchers in geology and linguistics has discovered that indigenous Australians have retained up to 10,000-year-old stories about sea-level change in southern Australia (Reid, Nunn, and Sharpe 2014). My approach to the idea of a vernacular theory on geothermal activity in early Iceland can be expressed with the following quotation by M. Juneja and G.J. Schenk:

> Nature is commonly perceived as an entity distinct from humans, possibly inhabited by the divine forces, endowed with degrees of power, a potentially dangerous—or alternatively sublime—force, to be domesticated, appeased, controlled by technology, in general a field of flux marked by a shifting relationship between humans, the environment and god(s). Local cosmologies provide an entry point into this relationship which they articulate through specific cultural media—texts, images and objects. (Juneja and Schenk 2014: 10)

This suggests that we can expect that the early settlers of Iceland, within the parameters of their worldview, would have attempted to exert some form of cultural control over the geo-activity that they faced. Old Norse mythology is a local cosmology in Iceland of the kind mentioned by Juneja and Schenk. It can therefore function as an entry point to the relationship between early Icelanders and the volcanic activity of the region. In light of this, and that millennia-old stories about geological events seem to occur worldwide (Vitaliano 1973; Barber and Barber 2004; Piccardi and Masse 2007; Cashman and Cronin 2008; Hamacher and Norris 2011), it should not be controversial to assume that the premodern Icelandic literary material may contain more data on volcanism than is commonly recognized.

Method of Approach

The early Scandinavian settlers of Iceland presumably did not have much vocabulary with which they could express their experiences of volcanic events; they migrated to the highly volcanically active island of Iceland from the geologically stable Scandinavian region. They must immediately have been forced to find words for the phenomena. It is possible that in order to convey such experiences, and share them with posterity, myths and mythic language, functioning as master narratives, were employed to construct a meaningful and coherent account of eruptions. In *When They Severed Earth from Sky*, Barber and Barber describe a common human communicative strategy associated with geological and volcanic events. Oral narrative processing often takes the form of analogical tales, which describe the event in anthropomorphic terms: the mountain is a living entity or the dwelling of a being, and the eruption is caused by a supernatural being, a god, a demiurge, or a demon. The various details of eruptions are described in terms of comprehensible known objects. Lava, for instance, can be a "river of fire" (Barber and Barber 2004: 43). In more recent colloquialisms, the sound of a volcanic explosion has been described as "artillery", the shockwave of an explosion as a "blizzard" (Barber and Barber 2004: 72–75). Tephra (rock fragments) can be described as "dry snow" (Beaudoin and Oetelaar 2006a, 2006b). Indeed, the word lava originates in the Latin *lavare* (to wash), and magma is originally Greek for "ointment". That early Icelanders had trouble finding exact words to describe the various aspects of volcanism is attested in the use of interchangeable words and phrases for volcanic events in the annals and in *Landnámabók*, for instance *jarðeldr*, lit. "earth-fire" and *eldzuppkváma*, lit. "fire-up-throw". The widely used Icelandic word for lava, *hraun*, is imprecise: it originally meant "little island", "rubble", or "stone ground" (de Vries 1961: 252)—a meaning that is still intact in other Scandinavian languages.

This is the essence of the so-called vernacular geothermal theory proposed by Falk. He writes: "[but] neither does it seem far-fetched [...] to see the glowing dragons and their hoard as a stylised depiction of a volcanic crevice, and the devastating poisonous fire and blood as euphemisms for lava" (Falk 2007: 11). Upon presenting even more examples, Falk suggests that reformulating volcanic events in terms of a gold treasure that may burn, swallow, or in other ways kill you, relates to a certain hostility in both Icelandic law and the sagas to buried treasure (Falk 2007: 12). A taboo seems to have shrouded geothermal activity as much as the activity of burying treasure, but, Falk writes:

This folk tradition never quite got off the ground as a saga narrative motif. Whether as superstition or as proverb, such folklore would certainly have served useful social functions. Besides helping to explain to Icelanders the natural environment they saw all around them, a literal belief of this sort would have helped dissuade both treasure-hunters and would-be hoarders [...] As metaphor, meanwhile, the equation of molten rock with burning gold would have had an even wider potential amplitude, whose full range, now lost to us, we can only imagine. (Falk 2007: 12)

Barber and Barber's theory of linguistic modulation of geological phenomena in *When They Severed Earth from Sky* is very similar to that of Falk. They call it the Analogy Principle: "If any entities or phenomena bear some resemblance, in any aspect, they must be related" (Barber and Barber 2004: 34–40). In the case above, a glowing dragon, its gold hoard, blood, and poisonous fires all bear some resemblance to the products of an eruption. This principle of analogy is, in fact, expressed quite explicitly in context of Old Norse mythology. According to Snorri's *Edda*, when the god Loki is bound in the underground after having caused the death of Baldr, it is said that he causes earthquakes. As Loki jerks his bonds whenever his wife Sigyn does not protect his face from the poison dripping from the venomous snake above him, he makes the ground shake. Hár, who is telling this story to King Gylfi, says "Þat kallið þér landskjálpta" (*Gylfaginning* p. 49) (That is what you call an earthquake).[2] This may be an example of a vernacular theory of earthquakes particular to Iceland, seeing as the medieval Norwegian *Konungs Skuggsjá* explains earthquakes as the result of winds entering caves in the ground and making the earth shake. This is a notion that has its origins in traditional classical literature, and can be found in, among other texts, Ovid's *Metamorphoses* (Nordvig 2013: 166). The two explanations are quite different from one another, and it seems that the one including Loki may be of Scandinavian origin, whereas the other one is not. In the following, I will employ this interpretative strategy in connection with the creation myth in Snorri's *Edda*, and address some inconsistencies in the myth, which Holtsmark found puzzling in her 1964 analysis.

The Nature Image in Snorri's Creation Myth

Snorri's creation myth describes how the cosmos was created from fire and ice. There was a cold world called Niflheimr with a well in the middle, which was named Hvergelmir. From this well, eleven ice-cold rivers flowed. In the southern

---

[2] Unless otherwise stated, all translations are my own.

part of the cosmos, there was another world, which was hot and fiery. It was called Muspell or Muspellzheimr, and it was guarded by a *jǫtunn* "giant" who brandished a flaming sword. The convergence of the cold from the icy rivers from Niflheimr and the heat and sparks from Muspellzheimr created a milder climate in the center, a region called Ginnungagap. When the water and the sparks met there, the world was eventually created (*Gylfaginning* pp. 9–10).

Several scholars have argued that the creation myth in Snorri's *Edda* relies fully or in part on classical Latin learning, and that it is inspired either by the notion of the four elements (Holtsmark 1964: 29–30) or by Neoplatonic dualism (Dronke and Dronke 1977: 172; Faulkes 1983: 288; von See 1988: 53; Guðrún Nordal 2001: 273–77). While this may be the case, there are parts of the descriptions of the natural image of the convergence of heat and cold that are not entirely harmonic or, rather, seem to contest the normal rules of nature. It was Holtsmark who initially took notice of them. They occur in relation to the description of the rivers flowing from Hvergelmir, which reads as follows:

> Þá mælir Hár: "Ár þær er kallaðar eru Élivágar, þá er þær váru svá langt komnar frá uppsprettunni at eitrkvikja sú er þar fylgði harðnaði svá sem sindr þat er renn ór eldinum, þá varð þat íss, ok þá er sá íss gaf staðar ok rann eigi, þá héldi yfir þannig úr þat er af stóð eitrinu ok fraus at hrími, ok jók hrímit hvert yfir annat allt í Ginnungagap." (*Gylfaginning* ch. 5)

> (These rivers that are called Élivágar, when they had come far enough away from the source, so that the poisonous flow that followed hardened like the cinders that run out of the fire, then it turned to ice, and when this ice stopped and did not run, then the vapor that stood off the poison froze to rime on top of it in the same direction, and this rime increased in layers all over Ginnungagap.)

In the following, I will concentrate on interpreting two important elements in this description of water and ice in the creation myth: *eitr* and the Élivágar. Initially, I will treat the term *eitr*, because this term has most potential to illuminate the vernacular theory of geothermal activity.

Eitr

Holtsmark has some difficulties reconciling what happens with the *eitrdropar* "drops of poison" and the described process of smelting, quickening, and freezing. She writes:

> Naturbilledet er ikke slående: elver som fryser til is, frostrøk over isen
> som rimer, det går an; men rim over hele Ginnungagap som senere blir
> beskrevet som *hlætt sem lopt vindlaust* er merkelig; det spørs om isen
> og *eitrdropar* fra *Élivágar* ikke tar omveien om rimet bare for å forklare
> navnet *hrímþursar*. (Holtsmark 1964: 30–31)

> (The image of nature is not obvious: rivers freezing over, rime over the
> ice, that is reasonable; but rime over the whole of Ginnungagap, which
> is later described as *hlætt sem lopt vindlaust* [mild as a windless sky] is
> strange; one wonders if not the ice and *eitrdropar* from *Élivágar* take a
> detour over the rime only to explain the name *hrímþursar* [frost-giant].)

Holtsmark proceeds to attempt an explanation based on examples of the use of
eitr in other instances. *Eitr* does not only mean "poison" but may also denote pus
from a wound. It is also used in a word for a special type of glaciers in Norway
and Iceland, which are called *eitrár*. The use of *eitr* can then be explained as a
function that refers to a frozen waterfall coming over a cliff (Holtsmark 1964:
31). Holtsmark goes on to discuss the term *sindr* "slag". Similarly, while she
accepts the image of *sindr* as reasonable to anyone who has seen the process of
iron ore smelting, she goes on to wonder:

> Men der kommer jo motsetningen inn igjen, *Élivágar* er kalde, og en
> blåstermile er varm, og *sindr* størkner når det kommer i kaldere luft,
> mens eiter-elvene skulle fryse til is når de kom fra selve kulden ut i det
> varmere strøk, i Ginnungagap. (Holtsmark 1964: 31)

> (But here comes the contradiction again, *Élivágar* are cold and the wind
> gust is warm, and the *sindr* quicken when it comes into colder air, while
> the *eitr*-rivers are supposed to freeze when they come from the cold
> itself into the warmer region of Ginnungagap.)

The image projected is that of the rivers flowing from a cold source and freezing
when they have flowed far enough from their well. From this flow of *eitr*, vapor
rises and turns to rime that builds layer upon layer over Ginnungagap. This rime
persists in Ginnungagap even though the region is mild as a windless sky. The
flow of *eitr* is compared, not to water freezing over, but to the cinders flowing
from a smelter. As Holtsmark points out, this does not add up—at least not if
the terminology relates to water and ice. However, if we consider lava and ash
ejected from an eruption, the nature image may become more palatable.

A lava flow from an effusive eruption behaves like water turning to ice.
To understand this image, it is useful to consult a scientific description of the

behavior of certain eruption types. Geologists Þór Þórðarson and Larsen explain the formation of lava shields in Iceland:

> Lava shields are the principal representatives of low-discharge (≤ 300 m³/s) flood lava eruptions. These eruptions produce vast pahoehoe flow fields (up to 20 km³) that are fed by a lava lake residing in the summit crater. The lava cone of each shield is essentially constructed by fountain-fed flows and overspills from the lake, whereas the surrounding lava apron is produced by tube-fed pahoehoe where insulated transport and flow inflation enables great flow length [...] The high-discharge (> 1000 m³/s) flood lava events, such as the 1783–1784 A.D. Laki and 934–938 A.D. Eldgjá fissure eruptions, represent some of the greatest spectacles of Icelandic volcanism. (Þór Þórðarson and Larsen 2007: 131)

A volcano's lava flows from a lake in its newly formed crater and advances upon an area where it quickens. This results in the creation of a *hraun*, a lava field. The rubbly pāhoehoe caused by pulsating discharges characterizes the most common basalt flow types of Iceland (Þór Þórðarson and Larsen 2007: 131).

Strip the geologists' description of its scientific discourse and it may be reduced to the following: a liquid substance flows from a reservoir; it quickens and creates a *hraun*. Moreover, the liquid itself is poisonous (*eitr*), it flows (*at renna*) from its source (*uppspretta*), and it becomes hard like the slags (*sindr*) from the smelter (*eldr*). Vapor (*úr*) rises from the flow, it lands—it freezes (*at frjósa*)— on top, becoming rime (*hrím*) that builds in layers.

The term *eitr* is ambiguous. It refers both to poison and to ice-cold rivers. However, based on what Holtsmark remarks above, it does not seem to refer to the quality of being cold in relation to the *eitrár*, but rather to the color yellow and a thick flowing substance. Holtsmark herself mentions that the common reference between frozen ice and pus is the color (Holtsmark 1964: 31). *Eitr* is poisonous and yellow—just like lava. That volcanoes and related phenomena can be poisonous (from gasses) was known to medieval Icelanders. This is attested in *Konungs Skuggsjá* (ch. 17–21). As noted above, the emission of hydrogen fluoride was the main culprit in the Laki eruption in 1783–1784, and it has also been observed in relation to eruptions in Hekla (Haraldur Sigurðsson et al., 1985: 1003). Saxo, giving a detailed description of the wonders of Iceland, mentions deadly wells there: "Illic etiam fama est pestilentis undę laticem scaturire, quo quis gustato perinde ac ueneno prosternitur" (*Gesta Danorum* Praefatio, 2,7) (It is also told that there are springs up there with water that is so dangerous that if you taste it you die instantly, as if it were poison). If the *eitr* is in fact lava, there should be nothing contradictory in the notion of it flowing from a well and freezing up when it flows too far, even though, as Holtsmark notes, it flows into a warmer climate. Neither is there any conflict between the image of the *eitr*–rivers and the image of the slags flowing from a smelter; they are analogous.

The vapor that freezes and turns to rime did not as such cause Holtsmark any distress, but there is one problem with this image: the rime builds layer upon layer as if it were ice. Rime is an accumulation of already frozen moisture particles in the air, and does not generally build in layers. Ice may do so, and when one interprets this image as a process of an ice formation, this inconsistency is easily overlooked. I will presumptuously suggest that if the author were looking for a frozen watery substance to build in layers across Ginnungagap, the image of snow would have been more suitable. Where rime would start depositing on the surface and keep accreting in a leeward direction, snow builds layers upon layers across any exposed surface. However, snow melts in the warmth, and Holtsmark noted the inconsistency between Ginnungagap being mild as a windless sky and the rime building layers there.

Relying on Árni Hjartarson's verdict on the contents of *Hallmundarkviða*, aspects of the poem can be useful in terms of certain words, phrasings, and analogies pertaining to volcanism. As *Hallmundarkviða* describes an eruption, it provides an early vocabulary that can clarify the meaning of some of the imagery expounded in the creation myth. Árni Magnússon copied *Hallmundarkviða* in 1686 from the *Vatnshyrna* manuscript, which perished in the Copenhagen fire in 1728. It is preserved in *Bergbúa Þáttr*, and consists of twelve stanzas in *dróttkvætt* meter. The language has been dated to either the twelfth or the thirteenth century (*Bergbúa Þáttr* pp. cciii–ccv). If nothing else, this puts the poem in the same period as *Snorra Edda*.

By consulting the language of *Hallmundarkviða*, the image of the rime is no longer an unresolvable inconsistency. *Hrím* has a secondary meaning, namely "soot", and the *jǫtunn*-name Hrímnir can mean "sooty" or "the one that causes soot" (i.e., fire) (Finnur Jónsson 1966: 284–85). Hrímnir appears in *Hallmundarkviða* in connection with the eruption. The ashes are called *mjǫll* "newly fallen snow" (*Hallmundarkviða* st. 11). This confirms the prevalence of an analogy between the ejecta from a volcanic eruption and frozen precipitation. Unlike rime, soot and ash build up, layer upon layer, when ejected in an eruption and unlike snow (and rime), soot and ash persist even though it enters a milder climate: it cools down rather than heating up. In "The Day the Dry Snow Fell: The Record of a 7627-year-old Disaster", archaeologists Alwynne Beaudoin and Gerald Oetelaar provide some interesting points of comparison with the image of rime, vapor, and *eitr* (Beaudoin and Oetelaar 2006a). The First Nation peoples of the Alberta and Saskatchewan provinces in Canada relate a tale of the 7,627-year-old cataclysmic Mazama eruption in modern-day Oregon. The Mazama event is remembered as "the day the dry snow fell"; the legend recounts that it fell for days from a darkened sky. It built up in layers, and when you walked in it, dust (ON *úr*) would rise up and choke you (*eitr*), and rain would turn the dust into a thick and slimy substance that eventually dried to a crust (*sindr, aurr, íss*) (Beaudoin and Oetelaar 2006a: 41–43).

   This comparison may explain the apparent inconsistencies that Holtsmark noted in the ice and rime, which did not behave as these elements are supposed to. The creation myth in *Gylfaginning* draws upon images of ice and water because there is nothing in the vocabulary to provide an independent description of a volcanic eruption. In the same way that tephra became "dry snow" to the First Nation peoples in Alberta and Saskatchewan, the ashes of an Icelandic eruption became *hrím* and *úr* in Snorri's *Edda* and *mjǫll* in *Hallmundarkviða*. Such a description is provided as a consequence of the principle of analogy in the vernacular theory of geothermal activity.

Élivágar

Élivágar is a term for a body of ice-cold waters that occurs in a couple of medieval narratives, namely the eddic poem *Hymiskviða* and the prose story *Þorsteins þáttr bœjarmagns*. In *Hymiskviða*, it seems to be synonymous with the sea encircling the world (Finnur Jónsson 1966: 117) and in *Þorsteins þáttr bœjarmagns* it is an ice-cold river that separates Miðgarðr (the human world) from Jǫtunheimar (the land of giants). Élivágar is also mentioned in *Vafþrúðnismál*, another eddic poem, and *Hallmundarkviða*, but whether it is a term for a body of ice-cold water is not clear. We have already seen how the *eitr* in Snorri's creation myth may connote lava, rather than water so cold that it is poisonous. In Snorri's creation myth, it seems natural to assume that both the *eitr* and its source, the Élivágar, are extremely cold bodies of liquid. However, the association with extreme cold is caused by a series of juxtapositions that can be attributed to the author. According to *Snorra Edda*, Hvergelmir is situated in Niflheimr, and this is the source of the rivers. In the eddic poem *Grímnismál*, water flows from the hart Eikþyrnir's horns into the well of Hvergelmir, and this is the source of all the water in the world (*Grímnismál* st. 26). The river names that are recounted in Snorri's creation myth are borrowed from *Grímnismál* (st. 27–28), but it seems that the connection to Élivágar is only established through the narrative of *Gylfaginning*. There is no precedence for this connection elsewhere (Simek 2007: 73). One of the rivers flows past the Hel-gates, the deepest part of the underworld. At this point in Snorri's narrative, it is not mentioned that Niflheimr is cold; in fact the text immediately proceeds to describe the fiery realm of Muspell and its guardian Surtr. After this description, and a citation from *Vǫluspá inn skamma*, the Élivágar are described as flowing from some place (*Gylfaginnning* ch. 5). It is not stated directly that the Élivágar come from Hvergelmir, but the phrasing "Ár þær er kallaðar eru Élivágar" (*Gylfaginning* ch. 5) (These rivers, which are called Élivágar) naturally leads to this assumption on part of the reader. This is most likely the intention of the text, but it is important to note that Snorri has not yet defined Niflheimr as cold, the description of the Élivágar is not precisely pinned to Niflheimr, and most importantly, the Élivágar do not seem to be an original name for the rivers that flow from Hvergelmir. They have individual names in *Grímnismál*, whereas *Vafþrúðnismál* tells a different story about Élivágar. It may therefore be possible that the direct association of Élivágar with a cold body of water does not underlie Snorri's creation myth.

Vafþrúðnismál may facilitate an alternative understanding of Élivágar. It is one of the most prominent sources for *Gylfaginning* (*Gylfaginning* p. xxv) and also most probably contains the oldest attestation of the term "Élivágar." It does not give any clear reason to assume that the Élivágar are cold. In *Vafþrúðnismál*, the god Óðinn asks the wise giant Vafþrúðnir where the primordial *jǫtunn* Aurgelmir came from. Vafþrúðnir answers: "Ór Élivágom stucco eitrdropar, svá óx unz varð ór iǫtunn" (*Vafþrúðnismál* st. 30) (From Élivágar sprang poison drops, so they grew until there came a *jǫtunn* from them). This stanza is also included in *Gylfaginning*, but it is interpolated after Snorri announces that Niflheimr is cold. In this manner, the idea that the Élivágar are cold is established. Undoubtedly, the reference to Aurgelmir's offspring as *hrímþursar* in stanza 33 plays a role here, but as I noted above, *hrím* may well refer to soot, not rime or ice. If we stay with the volcanic image of the flowing *eitr* from *Gylfaginning*, the image in stanza 30 of *Vafþrúðnismál* fits well. The *eitr* in this instance springs from its source, the Élivágar, and build up until they become a figure, Aurgelmir.

Snorri claims that Aurgelmir and Ymir are the same, i.e. the primordial giant. According to *Grímnismál* (st. 40–41) and *Vafþrúðnismál* (st. 21), the human world is made from the body of Ymir. *Gylfaginning* also relates this creation myth but insists (in discord with *Vafþrúðnismál*) that Aurgelmir and Ymir are the same being. It is possible that this connection between the two figures is established through the relationship of extreme cold. *Vafþrúðnismál* relates that Ymir was ice-cold: "ins *hrímkalda* iǫtun[s]" (*Vafþrúðnismál* st. 21) (the *rime-cold* giant) (emphasis added). There are strong indications that this association of the two figures is a conscious construction, designed to polarize the *jǫtunn* race into hot and cold in the creation myth (Clunies Ross 1983: 51). This could, in accordance with Klaus von See's theory (1988: 52–55), be an attempt to reconcile elements of a seemingly pagan complex of mythos with medieval Neoplatonic theories.

Underneath this attempt, a widespread terminology that can be associated with volcanism can be detected: the first part of the name Aurgelmir is probably *aurr*- "wet sand, gravel" (Simek 2007: 24). *Vafþrúðnismál* says that Aurgelmir fathered Þrúðgelmir, who fathered Bergelmir (st. 29). *Þrúð*- seems to mean "power" (Simek 2007: 329), and the first part of Bergelmir, *ber(g)*-, may mean "bear" (Finnur Jónsson 1966: 44) or "mountain" (Simek 2007: 34). The last part of these names, *-gelmir*, means "roarer" (Simek 2007: 24). This word is also associated with wells and rivers such as Hvergelmir (*hverr*- meaning "kettle-roarer" [Finnur Jónsson 1966: 300]) and Vaðgelmir (Finnur Jónsson 1966: 587). If *-gelmir* refers to the roaring, churning commotion of the rivers and wells of the underworld, the image of roaring, churning, violent gravel and sand is highly interesting, as it is so readily applicable to a jökulhlaup, a lahar, or other volcanic ejecta. The powerful roars of Þrúðgelmir and Bergelmir, whether the latter means "bear-roarer" or "mountain-roarer", is similarly easy to apply to volcanism, but the association of these names to volcanism does not rest on this assumption alone.

The *jǫtunn* Aurnir is a figure in *Hallmundarkviða*. He appears in stanza 9, where he receives an iron-braced stone boat from the *bergbúi* "mountain-dweller" who is relating the course of the eruption. In the last stanza, the *bergbúi* says that Aurnir's well is not yet dry. In other words, the *jǫtunn* presides over a well, which seems to be the source of eruptions. Aurnir's name is probably derived from the same *aurr*- as Aurgelmir (Simek 2007: 252).[3] This notion coincides with stanza 7, where the *bergbúi* describes the eruption of lava with the term *aurr* "clay": "aurr tekr upp at fœrask undarligr ór grundu" (*Hallmundarkviða* st. 7) (a strange clay begins to flow from the ground). This word was already known to the tradition from its association with Aurgelmir as the man who was built from the *eitr* of the Élivágar. The term Élivágar also occurs in *Hallmundarkviða*. In stanza 7, the underground commotion is described as a fight in Élivágar (*bág, í Élivága*). In this way, there is a direct association between the Élivágar and volcanism. In *Vafþrúðnismál* the Élivágar produce a figure whose name is closely associated with a term for lava, and in *Hallmundarkviða* they are the site of a battle in the course of an eruption. Presumably, they are to be understood as a euphemism for underground lava—just like Aurnir's well. Both Aurgelmir and Aurnir may then be personifications of lava, and the material in jökulhlaups, on the same terms as Hrímnir, can be a personification of soot and ash, and Surtr can be a personification of volcanic fire.

---

[3]   In fact, there are several *jǫtunn* names derived from *aurr*- and *berg*- (Finnur Jónsson 1966: 24, 44-45).

Conclusion

In Snorri's version of the creation myth, we find a possible vernacular theory of geothermal activity embedded in the image he paints of nature. The nature-image makes use of references to ice and water, but, as Holtsmark has pointed out, the image is not convincing when treated on the parameters offered by the natural behavior of ice and water. Instead, it makes sense when it is treated with consideration of the observable aspects of the commonly occurring Icelandic low discharge effusive eruptions, where lava gushes out from its source and flows like a raging river until it hardens and adds new layers to the landmass. The term *eitr* refers to the qualities of the lava as a glowing hot, yellow-red substance that is poisonous (or harmful) in every way. This substance flows from the caldera as a river and becomes "ice". From the flow there are fumes—vapors—which rise and crystallize like snow and ice, and fall down again to build layers of this strange "ice" in the primordial void. These processes cannot be described in the vernacular vocabulary without analogies to ice and water, and this is why there is confusion about the details of the process. The creature that is produced from this flow of lava is, in the original story in *Vafþrúðnismál*, Aurgelmir "clay-roarer". In *Vafþrúðnismál*, the primeval *jǫtunn* was originally created from lava, referred to as *eitr*, but a conscious effort on behalf of the author of *Gylfaginning* reconfigures the information from the poetry, and rearranges the semantics of the nature-image in the creation myth. Aurgelmir is professed to be the same as Ymir, and inspired by Neoplatonic philosophy, Snorri infers a dichotomy between fire and ice. The creation myth in *Gylfaginning* looks to be an attempt to align a vernacular theory of geothermal activity—and the creation of the world—with the teachings of continental philosophy of the twelfth and thirteenth centuries.

The tendency to formulate mythic stories and legends with a basis in the theme of geology has been observed among many peoples who live in close proximity to volcanoes. These stories are more or less transparent to individuals who are outsiders to the culture in question. One of the factors that can obscure a narrative layer centered on geological aspects in a myth or legend is vernacular vocabulary. Such vocabulary may be very culture-specific. In the case of Old Norse myths, if one operates under the assumption that these narratives reflect, at least in part, aspects of the worldview of pre-Christian Scandinavians, there is a strong possibility that these myths can be considered entry points into the relationship between early Icelanders and their environment.

Works Cited

Primary Sources

Annales Regii
Islandske Annaler indtil 1578. Ed. Gustav Storm. Christiania: 1888.

Bergbúa Þáttr
Íslenzk fornrit, 13. Ed. Þórhallur Vilmundarson and Bjarni Vilhjálmsson. Reykjavík: 1991. Pp. 441–50.

Gesta Danorum
Saxo Grammaticus. *Gesta Danorum.* Ed. Karsten Friis-Jensen. Transl. Peter Zeeberg. 2 vols. Copenhagen: 2005.

Grímnismál: see *Poetic Edda*

Gylfaginning
Snorri Sturluson. *Edda: Prologue and Gylfaginning.* 2nd ed. Ed. Anthony Faulkes. London: 2011.

Hallmundarkviða: see *Bergbúa Þáttr*

Hymiskviða: see *Poetic Edda*

Kristni Saga
Kristnisaga, Þáttr Þorvalds ens víðförla, Þáttr Ísleifs biskups Gizurarsonar, Hungrvaka. Ed. Bernhard Kahle. Altnordische Saga-Bibliothek, 11. Halle an der Saale: 1905.

Konungs Skuggsjá
Konungs Skuggsiá. Ed. Ludvig Holm-Olsen. Oslo: 1945.

Landnámabók
Íslenzk fornrit, 1. Ed. Jakob Benediktsson. Reykjavík: 1986. Pp. 29-397.

Liber Miraculorum
Herbert von Clairvaux und sein Liber Miraculorum. Die Kurzversion eines anonymen bayrischen redaktors. Ed. Gabriela Kompatscher Gufler. Lateinische Sprache und Literatur des Mittelalters, 39. Berlin: 2005.

Metamorphoses
Metamorphoses, P. Ovidi Nasonis. Ed. Richard J. Tarrant. New York: 2004.

Poetic Edda

Edda. Die Lieder des Codex Regius nebst verwandten Denkmälern. 3rd ed. Ed. Gustav Neckel and Hans Kuhn. Heidelberg: 1962.

Vafþrúðnismál: see Poetic Edda

Vǫluspá: see Poetic Edda

Secondary Sources

Árni Hjartarson. 2014. "Hallmundarkviða, eldforn lysing á eldgósi." Náttúrufræðingurinn 84 (1–2): 27–37.

Barber, Elizabeth W., and Paul T. Barber. 2004. When They Severed Earth from Sky: How the Human Mind Shapes Myth. Princeton.

Beaudoin, Alwynne B., and Gerald A. Oetelaar. 2006a. "The Day the Dry Snow Fell: The Record of a 7627-year-old Disaster." In Alberta Formed Alberta Transformed. Ed. Michael Payne, Donald Grant Wetherell, and Catherine Anne Kavanaugh. Edmonton. Pp. 36–53.

———. 2006b. "Darkened Skies and Sparkling Grasses: The Potential Impact of the Mazama Ash Fall on the Northwestern Plains." Plains Anthropologist 50 (195): 285–305.

Cashman, Kathy, and Sean Cronin. 2008. "Welcoming a Monster to the World: Myths, Oral Tradition, and Modern Societal Response to Volcanic Disasters." Journal of Volcanology and Geothermal Activity 176: 407–18.

Clunies Ross, Margaret. 1983. "Snorri Sturluson's Use of the Norse Origin-legend of the Sons of Fornjótr in his Edda." Arkiv för nordisk filologi 98: 47–66.

Courtillot, Vincent. 2005. "New Evidence for Massive Pollution and Mortality in Europe in 1783–1784 may have Bearing on Global Change and Mass Extinctions." C. R. Geoscience 337: 635–37.

Dronke, Ursula, and Peter Dronke. 1977. "The Prologue of the Prose Edda: Explorations of a Latin Background." In Sjötiu Ritgerðir: Festskrift til Jakob Benediktsson. Ed. E. G. Pétursson and J. Kristjánsson. Reykjavík. Pp. 153–76.

Falk, Oren. 2007. "The Vanishing Volcanoes: Fragments of Fourteenth-century Icelandic Folklore." Folklore 118 (1): 1–22.

Faulkes, Anthony. 1983. "Pagan Sympathy: Attitudes to Heathendom in the Prologue to Snorra Edda." In Edda: A Collection of Essays. Ed. R. J. Glendinning and H. Bessason. Manitoba. Pp. 283–314.

Fei, Jie, and Jie Zhou. 2006. "The Possible Climatic Impact in China of Iceland's Eldgjá Eruption Inferred from Historical Sources." Climatic Change 76: 443–57.

Finnur Jónsson, ed. 1966. *Lexicon Poeticum Antiquae Linguae Septentrionalis: Ordbog over det Norsk-Islandske Skjaldesprog*. 2nd ed. Copenhagen.

Grattan, John. 1995. "An Amazing and Portentous Summer: Environmental and Social Responses in Britain to the 1783 Eruption of an Iceland Volcano." *The Geographical Journal* 161: 125–36.

Grattan, John, and F. Brian Pyatt. 1993. "Acid Damage to Vegetation Following the Laki Fissure Eruption in 1783—an Historical Review." *The Science of the Total Environment* 151: 241–47.

Grattan, John, M. Durand, and S. Taylor. 2003. "Illness and Elevated Human Mortality in Europe Coincident with the Laki Fissure Eruption." In *Volcanic Degassing*. Ed. Clive Oppenheimer, David M. Pyle, and Jenni Barclay. Geological Society of London Special Publication, 213. London. Pp. 401–14.

Grattan, John, Roland Rabartin, Stephen Self, and Þorvaldur Þórðarson. 2005. "Volcanic Air Pollution and Mortality in France 1783-1784." *Comptes Rendus—Geoscience* 337: 641–51.

Gräslund, Bo. 2009. "*Ekki nýtr solar*. När himlen färgades röd av gudarnas blod." In vol. 1 of *Á austrvega: Saga and East Scandinavia. Preprint papers of the 14th International Saga Conference Uppsala, 9th-15th August 2009*. Ed. Agneta Ney, Henrik Williams, and Fredrik Charpentier Ljungqvist, et al. Gävle. Pp. 318–26.

Gräslund, Bo, and Neil Price. 2012. "Twilight of the Gods? The 'Dust Veil Event' of AD 536 in Critical Perspective." *Antiquity* 86: 428–43.

Guðrún Nordal. 2001. *Tools of Literacy*. Toronto.

Hamacher, Duane W., and Ray P. Norris. 2009. "Australian Aboriginal Geomythology: Eyewithess Accounts of Cosmic Impacts?" *Archaeoastronomy* 22 (2009): 62–95.

Haraldur Sigurðsson et al., eds. 1985. *Encyclopedia of Volcanoes*. New York.

Holtsmark, Anne. 1964. *Studier i Snorres Mytologi*. Oslo.

Juneja, Monica, and Gerrit J. Schenk. 2014. "Viewing Disasters: Myth, History, Iconography, and Media Across Europe and Asia." In *Disaster as Image: Iconographies and Media Strategies across Europe and Asia*. Ed. Monica Juneja and Gerrit J. Schenk. Regensburg. Pp. 7–40.

Nordvig, A. Mathias V. 2013. *Of Fire and Water: The Old Norse Mythical Worldview in an Eco-Mythological Perspective*. PhD diss., Aarhus University.

Phillpotts, Bertha S. 1905. "Surt." *Arkiv för nordisk filologi* 21: 14–30.

Piccardi, Luigi and W. Bruce Masse, eds. 2007. *Myth and Geology*. Geology Society Special Publications, 273. London.

Reid, Nick, Patrick Nunn, and Margaret Sharpe. 2014. "Indigenous Australian Stories and Sea-level Change." In *Indigenous Languages and their Value to the Community: Proceedings of the 18th Foundation for Endangered Languages Conference.* Ed. Patrick Heinrich and Nicholas Ostler. Bath. Pp. 82–87.

von See, Klaus. 1988. *Mythos und Theologie im skandinavischen Hochmittelalter.* Heidelberg.

Sigurður Nordal. 1927. *Völuspá.* Copenhagen.

Simek, Rudolf. 2007. *Dictionary of Northern Mythology.* Suffolk.

Stothers, Richard B. 1998. "Far Reach of the Tenth Century Eldgjá Eruption, Iceland." *Climatic Change* 39: 715–26.

Tweed, Fiona S. 2012. "'Now that the Dust has Settled ...' the Impacts of Icelandic Volcanic Eruptions." *Geology Today* 28 (6): 217–23.

Vasey, Daniel E. 1991. "Population, Agriculture, and Famine: Iceland, 1784–1785." *Human Ecology* 19 (3): 323–50.

Vitaliano, Dorothy B. 1973. *Legends of the Earth.* Bloomington.

de Vries, Jan. 1961. *Altnordische etymologisches Wörterbuch.* Leiden.

Zdanowicz, C. M., G. A. Zielinski, and M. S. Germani. 1999. "Mount Mazama Eruption: Calendrical Age Verified and Atmospheric Impact Assessed." *Geology* 27: 621–24.

Zielinski, Gregory et al. 1995. "Evidence of the Eldgjá (Iceland) Eruption in the GISP2 Greenland Ice Core: Relationship to Eruption Processes and Climatic Conditions in the Tenth Century." *The Holocene* 5 (2): 129–40.

Þór Þórðarson. 2010. "Perception of Volcanic Eruptions in Iceland." In *Landscapes and Societies: Selected Case.* Ed. I. P. Martini and Ward Chesworth. New York. Pp. 285–96.

Þór Þórðarson and G. Larsen. 2007. "Volcanism in Iceland in Historical Time: Volcano Types, Eruption Styles and Eruptive History." *Journal of Geodynamics* 43: 118–52.

Þór Þórðarson and S. Self. 1993. "The Laki (Skaftár Fires) and Grimsvötn Eruptions in 1783–1785." *Bulletin of Volcanology* 55: 233–63.

Þorvaldur Þórðarson and Ármann Höskuldsson. 2008. "Postglacial Volcanism in Iceland." *Jökull* 58: 197–228.

Óðinn, Charms, and Necromancy

Hávamál 157 in Its Nordic and European Contexts

Stephen A. Mitchell
Harvard University

Abstract: Óðinn claims in stanza 157 of *Hávamál* that he is able to carve and color runes such that a hanged man will walk and talk with him. In this essay the central image of this the twelfth charm in the *Ljóðatal* section of *Hávamál* is examined in the context of parallels drawn from Iron Age archaeology, Old Norse literature, the wide-spread practice of "Charon's Obol", and Christian tradition.

Introduction

To modern sensibilities, few images are more disturbing in Old Norse mythology than the macabre claim made by Óðinn in stanza 157 of *Hávamál*:

> Þat kann ec iþ tólpta,   ef ec sé á tré uppi
> > váfa virgilná:
> svá ec ríst   oc í rúnom fác,
> > at sá gengr gumi
> > oc mælir við mic.

> I know a twelfth one   if I see, up in a tree,
> > a dangling corpse in a noose,
> I can so carve   and colour the runes
> > that the man walks
> > and talks with me.[1]

---

[1]   *Note*: A version of this essay was originally delivered in Zürich at the October 27–28, 2011 meeting of the Aarhus mythology conference.
Cf. Martin Clarke's translation (1923: 85):

To what belief system does this grisly presentation of necromancy—if, indeed, that is what it is—refer?[2] Does this "charm" (*ljóð*) project pure fantasy or might it reflect what was once an actual practice?

The following comments review possible backgrounds of, and influences on, the text's key claim that Óðinn can make a *virgilnár* speak. They build on the work of many earlier scholars who have considered the issue of the dead and dying in Old Norse mythology, from the pioneering studies by Helge Rosén (1918), Rolf Pipping (1928), H. R. Ellis Davidson (1943), Nora Chadwick (1946), and Folke Ström (1947) to the more recent work of Kirsi Kanerva (2011, 2013), Olof Sundqvist (2009, 2010), John McKinnell (2007) and Vésteinn Ólason (2003).[3] Specifically, the essay looks to place Óðinn's boast in the comparative contexts of native and non-native traditions, exploring on the one hand the Nordic basis for Óðinn's claim, as well as, on the other hand, the more distant but possibly related European reflexes for the charm, especially those linked to classical traditions of the so-called Ferryman's Fee (Thompson 1966: P613), and various Christian saint legends. By identifying more precisely the background against which this thirteenth-century text presents the Nordic world's master of magic making an assertion of this sort, i.e., that he can make a hanged man's corpse talk and walk through the use of runes, it may be possible to understand what

---

A twelfth I know: if I see on a tree aloft
    a corpse swinging from a halter,
I cut   and paint runes
    in such wise that the man walks
    and talks with me.

English dictionaries (i.e., Cleasby-Vigfusson 1982, Zoega 1975) do indeed gloss *virgill* as "halter" but in contemporary English, this term, when used in isolation (i.e., not in combination with "top" or "neck"), exclusively conveys the sense of a lead, something similar to a bridle, for securing and guiding livestock (at least in the North American dialects I know). By contrast, "noose", although technically referring narrowly to the knot (cf. its etymology), carries with it in common parlance the sense of a hangman's knot and of execution, hence, the expression, "to dangle from the end of a noose" or as Larrington has for *váfa virgilná*, "a dangling corpse in a noose". In line with this interpretation, Fritzner (1973) offers, "Strikke hvori Person hænges forat skille ham af med Livet".

2   Necromancy (< *necromantia*) properly refers to divination through the use of the dead (cf. Greek *nekros* "corpse" + *manteia* "divination"), practices associated with Óðinn in Nordic sources and with such figures as the witch of Endor (1 Sam. 28) in Judeo-Christian tradition; however, confusion, intentional or accidental, with *nigromantia* "black arts" has led to the term's more general sense of "sorcery" and "witchcraft", on which see especially Kieckhefer 1990: 151–75 and Kieckhefer 1997: 4, 19.

3   Scholarship on specific topics is, of course, indicated as appropriate, but with regard to the broader, and vast, scholarship on *Hávamál*, I refer readers to the discussion in Harris 1985, the items listed in Lindow 1983, and the forthcoming volume on *Hávamál* in the series Kommentar zu den Liedern der Edda (von See 1997–). As regards the literature concerned with various aspects of death and the afterlife in the Old Norse context, I refer readers to the discussion and comprehensive bibliography in Nordberg 2004: 313–39.

aspect of pre-Christian Nordic religion and mythology it is that we witness in *Hávamál* 157, how these views relate to pagan and Christian ideology, and just what they can tell us, both about such beliefs and, not least, our medieval religious texts.

Hávamál 157 in Its Nordic Setting

The significance of the dead in Nordic mythological texts has been the focus of substantial debate over the years.[4] In fact, a number of passages in extant Nordic sources allude to Óðinn interacting with the dead, occasionally in ways nearly as direct as that portrayed in *Hávamál* 157. Notably, on the one hand, there is the matter of postmortem conversations with Mímir,[5] and, on the other, there are the numerous references to Óðinn and others awakening and speaking with the dead, as presented in such poems as *Vǫluspá*, *Baldrs draumar*, *Hyndluljóð*, and *Grógaldr*.[6]

Allusions in *Gylfaginning* (ch. 17) and *Vǫluspá* (st. 28) to the story of Mímir's well, drinking from which Óðinn gains at the cost of an eye, support a general association of Mímir with wisdom and prophetic connections, but it is especially the story laid out in full in *Ynglinga saga* (ch. 4, 7), and referred to, e.g., in *Vǫluspá* (st. 46) and *Sigrdrífumál* (st. 14), that excites attention in the current context.[7] According to this tale, Mímir and Hœnir are sent as hostages to the Vanir as part of the exchange that helps end the war between this group of gods and the Æsir. The Vanir, believing that they have been defrauded—as Hœnir, when

---

[4] In addition to the works cited in the preceding section, cf. the argument by Andreas Nordberg with regard to the age of the *valhǫll* concept and the extensive review of related literature he provides (Nordberg 2004). Of related interest is the "mentalities" perspective Arnved Nedkvitne applies to the matter of pre-Christian Nordic views of the dead (2003: 19–47). As I write, publication of Neil Price's *Odin's Whisper: Death and the Vikings* has just been announced.

[5] On Mímir, see, e.g., the comments and overviews in Sigurður Nordal 1927: 91; de Vries 1956–1957: I: 245–248, II: 82; Halvorsen 1982; Lindow 2001: 230–32; and Simek 1993; on possible Celtic influence at work in the case of Mímir, as regards both his head and his well, and for a survey of the literature on the topic, see Simpson 1963–1964, as well as the recent review in Egeler 2013: 85–88.

[6] H. R. Ellis Davidson, in a discussion of necromancy, brings these poems together with Saxo's account of Harthgrepa. After describing the necromantic process (e.g., awakening, transmitting of knowledge), she notes: "The wisdom which is imparted is of two kinds. Either it consists of a revelation from the future or the past of what is normally hidden—the doom of the world, the fate of the individual or the line of dead ancestors behind a man of noble rank—or else it consists of spells which give power to the possessor, which can guard him against the baleful magic of others, or give him the power to overcome certain perils in his journeyings" (Davidson 1943: 156).

[7] The names Mímir and Mímr are both used; however, they occur in complementary distribution: "The form of the name in the formula 'Mímir's head' is always Mímr, otherwise the form is Mímir" (Simek 1993: 216).

not benefiting from Mímir's advice, proves to be less outstanding than they had thought—decapitate Mímir and send the head to Óðinn:

> Þá tóku þeir Mími ok hálshjoggu ok sendu hofuðit Ásum. Óðinn tók hofuðit ok smurði urtum þeim, er eigi mátti fúna, ok kvað þar yfir galdra ok magnaði svá, at þat mælti við hann ok sagði honum marga leynda hluti. (*Ynglinga saga* ch. 4)

> (Then they seized Mímir and beheaded him and sent the head to the Æsir. Óthin took it and embalmed it with herbs so that it would not rot, and spoke charms over it, giving it magic power so that it would answer him and tell him many occult things. (*Ynglinga saga* p. 8))

And a few chapters later, in the enumeration of Óðinn's magical abilities, the same text notes:

> Óðinn hafði með sér hofuð Mímis, ok sagði þat honum morg tíðendi or oðrum heimum, en stundum vakði hann upp dauða menn or jorðu eða settisk undir hanga. Fyrir því var hann kallaðr draugadróttinn eða hangadróttinn. (*Ynglinga saga*, ch. 7)

> (Óthin had with him Mímir's head, which told him many tidings from other worlds; and at times he would call to life dead men out of the ground, or he would sit down under men that were hanged. On this account he was called Lord of Ghouls or of the Hanged. (*Ynglinga saga* p. 11))

The story of Óðinn and Mímir's head holds a unique place in the mythology,[8] insofar as in opposition to other prophetic "talking heads" in Old Norse literature (e.g., *Eyrbyggja saga* ch. 43), it is specifically Óðinn's charm magic that allows or induces Mímir's head to produce its utterances.[9]

---

[8]   Cp. Davidson who suggests that the story of the *volsi* in *Flateyjarbók* (*Volsa þáttr*) may be the closest direct analogue to Mímir's head in that both call for the preservation of a body part later connected to occult knowledge (Davidson 1943: 157–58).

[9]   In *Eyrbyggia saga*, a certain Freysteinn, crossing a scree called Geirvor late one evening, encounters a severed human head, which volunteers a quatrain (*staka*) without any manipulation from Freysteinn:

Roðin es Geirvor	Geirvor is bloodied
gumna blóði,	by the gore of men,
hon mun hylja	she will hide
hausa manna.	human skulls.
(*Eyrbyggia saga* ch. 43)	(*Eyrbyggia saga* p. 116)

Clearly related to the same mythological complex that assumes that the "Lord of Ghouls" could call the dead to life are such scenes as the following in *Baldrs draumar*, where Óðinn speaks *valgaldr* "corpse-magic" (lit., "magic of the fallen or slain") in order to awaken the *vǫlva* from her postmortem sleep; she, in turn, utters *nás orð* "corpse-words":

Þá reið Óðinn   fyr austan dyrr
þar er hann vissi   vǫlo leiði;
nam hann vittugri   valgaldr qveða,
unz nauðig reis,   nás orð um qvað:(*Baldrs draumar* st. 4)

(Then Othin rode   to the eastern door,
There, he knew well,   was the wise-woman's grave;
Magic he spoke   and mighty charms,
Till spell-bound she rose,   and in death she spoke:
    (Larrington 2014: 235))

References in the medieval mythological texts to the summoned, prophesying dead (Thompson 1966: M301.14) naturally raise the question of whether these scenes might reflect beliefs about the dead in earlier periods. In fact, the possibility of pre-Christian traditions of such practices as ritual hanging and the gibbeting of enemies—or parts of enemies—killed in battle in northern Europe has been long bruited about. The most famous example comes half a dozen years after the battle of the Teutoburg Forest (9 CE), when a Roman army encounters the carnage left from the defeat of three of its legions:

medio campi albentia ossa, ut fugerant, ut restiterant, disiecta vel aggerata. Adiacebant fragmina telorum equorumque artus, simul truncis arborum antefixa ora. Lucis propinquis barbarae arae, apud quas tribunos ac primorum ordinum centuriones mactaverant. (*Annals* 1.61)

(In the plain between were bleaching bones, scattered or in little heaps, as the men had fallen, fleeing or standing fast. Hard by lay splintered spears and limbs of horses, while human skulls were nailed prominently on the tree-trunks. In the neighbouring groves stood the savage altars at which they had slaughtered the tribunes and chief centurions (pp. 348–49))

Freysteinn relates this vision (*fyrirburðr*) to Þorbrandr, to whom the episode portends important events (*þótti honum vera tíðenda-vænligt*).

This scene, gruesome as the spectacle of human skulls nailed on tree-trunks must have been, lacks some of the eeriness of the scenario of revivified dead hinted at in *Hávamál* 157, but it does suggest a frightening range of post-proelial manipulations of the dead in Iron Age northern Europe.[10]

And with that fact in mind, it is noteworthy that this twelfth charm, the mortuary charm reference of *Hávamál* 157, is embedded in a martial context: both the verse preceding it and the verse following it are specifically concerned with safety in battle. *Hávamál* 156 claims knowledge of a charm with which a leader could protect his troops such that they go safely to and *from battle*, and *Hávamál* 158 is concerned with protecting a young thane (*þegn*) *in battle*. The placement of verse 157 in *Hávamál* thus fits the mold shaped by both the material and textual evidence of Germanic rituals; indeed, classical writers describe with such vehemence the terrible things the northern tribes do with defeated enemies and their corpses that they might be easily dismissed as propagandistic *topoi*.[11] Yet in the light of modern archaeological research (e.g., Alken Enge in Jutland), scenes of the sort reported by classical writers about

---

[10] On the possibly related matter of animal skulls being ritually displayed, see the case of the Viking Age site at Hofstaðir, Iceland (Lucas and McGovern 2007) and the other examples cited there. The comments by Adam of Bremen regarding the pagan sacrifices in Uppsala bear mentioning in this context as well, "Ex omni animante, quod masculinum est, novem capita offeruntur, quorum sanguine deos placari mos est. Corpora autem suspenduntur in lucum, qui proximus est temple" (*Gesta Hammaburgensis* 4.27) (The sacrifice is of this nature: of every living thing that is male, they offer nine heads, with the blood of which it is customary to placate gods of this sort. The bodies they hang in the sacred grove that adjoins the temple (p. 208)).

[11] Against Tacitus' emotional and elegiac tone, one may, as something of a warning against over-reading, contrast the more blood-thirsty descriptions of other writers, as in the inflamed prose of Florus describing the events in the *Teutoburger Wald*:

Nihil illa caede per paludes perque silvas cruentius, nihil insultatione barbarorum intolerabilius, praecipue tamen in causarum patronos. Aliis oculos, aliis manus amputabant, uni os obsutum, recisa prius lingua, quam in manu tenens barbarus "tandem" ait "vipera sibilare desisti". (*Epitome* p. 340)

(Never was there slaughter more cruel than took place there in the marshes and woods, never were more intolerable insults inflicted by barbarians, especially those directed against the legal pleaders. They put out the eyes of some of them and cut off the hands of others; they sewed up the mouth of one of them after first cutting out his tongue, which one of the barbarians held in his hand, exclaiming, "At last, you viper, you have ceased to hiss". (pp. 339, 341))

Writing in a similar vein, Jordanes, in his sixth-century *Getica*, maintains that the Goths worshipped "Mars" with terrible rites, including slaying captives as sacrifices:

quem Martem Gothi semper asperrima placevere cultura (nam victimae eius mortes fuere captorum), opinantes bellorum praesulem apte humani sanguinis effusione placandum. (*Getica* 5.41)

(Now Mars has always been worshipped by the Goths with cruel rites, and captives were slain as his victims. They thought that he who is the lord of war needed to be appeased by the shedding of human blood. (p. 64))

the north European Iron Age may not be as farfetched as once thought.[12] On the other hand, although these instances may provide some opportunity for understanding the historico-cultural context of Óðinn's claim, they should be understood as no more than broad, if highly suggestive, typological parallels to the *Hávamál* image.

Yet a remarkable passage from the twelfth- or thirteenth-century Icelandic law code *Grágás* suggests that even in the Middle Ages the corpses of the deceased (or perhaps near-dead) were not merely the discarded husks of extinguished human life but could also be meaningful sites of debate, differentiation, and classification:

> Þeir menn ero ᴇɴ iiii. er náir ero kallaþir þott lifi. Ef maðr er hengðr eða kyrcþr eða settr i grof. eþa i scer. eða heptr afialle. eða i fløðar mále. Þar heitir gálg nár. oc graf nár. oc sker nár oc fiall nár. Þa menn alla scal iafnt aptr giallda niðgiolldom sem þeir se vegnir þott þeir lifi. (*Grágás* p. 202)

> (There are another four men who are called corpses even though they are alive. If a man is hanged or throttled or put in a grave or on a skerry or tied up on a mountain or below high-water mark, he is called "gallows-corpse" or "grave-corpse" or "skerry-corpse" or "mountain corpse". Those men are all to be atoned for by kindred payments as if they had been killed even though they are alive. (*Grágás* p. 182))

Some commentators (e.g., Joonas Ahola) understand this passage in practical terms,[13] but an earlier observer, Viktor Rydberg, saw the text in a different light, noting that the sense of *nár* as used in this section of *Grágás* is not merely "cadaver" and so on, but rather to those who are still conscious and can, for example, suffer.[14] One certainly senses thematic filiations between this and the previously

---

[12] Early reports on the project "The army and post-war rituals in the Iron Age—warriors sacrificed in the bog at Alken Enge in Illerup Ådal" suggest that here too there may have been ritual manipulations of the corpses (see, e.g., Lobell 2012). Further research will undoubtedly provide a conclusive answer (cf. Holst, Heinemeier, et al. Forthcoming), but as of the writing of this essay, that some real-world typological parallels existed to the comments made by classical writers may be more likely than once believed. See also "Alken Enge—The mass grave at Lake Mossø" (Museum Skanderborg 2013); "An Entire Army Sacrificed in a Bog" at ScienceNordic.com; and "Barbarisk fund: Vores forfædre bar ligrester på kæppe" (Persson 2014).

[13] "For acts that were not considered to be killing and therefore did not grant the right to prosecution, such as leaving someone helplessly on a skerry, mountain, cave, or hung (*Grágás*, 265), was likewise to be paid compensation (*wergild*), and the one at fault was responsible for that compensation" (Ahola 2014: 82).

[14] "Här tillämpas ordet nár således på varelser med medvetande och förmåga att lida, men under den förutsättning, att de äro sådana, som hemfallit under straff afsedda att icke upphöra, så länge de äro i stånd att förnimma dem" (Rydberg 1886: I: 324).

cited passages, but whereas *Hávamál* 157 uses *virgilnár* "halter corpse" or "noose corpse" (cf. n. 1 above), *Grágás* here uses the term "gallows corpse" (*galgnár*).[15]

Gallows in non-mythological medieval Nordic contexts generally show them being used for execution, as when in *Magnúss saga berfœtts*, Egill and Þórir are hanged for raising forces against the king (ch. 6; pp. 216–18). But, of course, once the execution phase of the process was over, hanged corpses, so positioned, transformed into highly effective and tactile warnings for others and could be left gibbeted, hanging—and visible—until they rotted off the rope, thus becoming public spectacles and expressions of authority visible for long distances, which, of course, accounts for the fact that they were often placed on heights (e.g., Galgberget [lit. "Gallows Hill"] in Södermalm, overlooking late medieval Stockholm) and near highly trafficked areas (e.g., crossroads).

Beyond the gallow's function in daily life as the ultimate legal sanction and as a potent demonstration of centralized power, gallows and the hanged are frequently mentioned in mythological and semi-mythological contexts that suggest that they also provided the means of torture, pain, and, as in the previous case, spectacle, both as an end in itself and as part of Odinic rituals of varying interpretations (e.g., initiation).[16] An example of the first type is found in *Hálfs saga ok Hálfsrekka*, when Hjǫrleifr is hung by his shoelaces between two fires. When he eventually escapes, Hjǫrleifr in turn hangs his enemy on the same gallows (*gálg*) which had been intended for his death.[17]

In other instances, such as *Gautreks saga*, when the mock sacrifice of King Víkarr turns real (ch. 7), the scene strikes most readers as being informed by a series of surviving narratives about those "hanging" between life and death: Óðinn's self-sacrifice on the World Tree; the comments in Saxo about sacrificial

---

[15] In addition to the probable synonymy of the two "corpse" terms, I note that even the devices from which they were suspended were likely to be thought of as equivalent: *galgtré* "gallows tree" is a relatively common collocation, used interchangeably with *galg* "gallows" (e.g., *Magnúss saga berfœtts* ch. 6). Although *tré* principally indicates arboreal organisms, it can also mean the products of them, such as "beam"—exactly what is needed to construct an H-shaped *galgtré*. On the other hand, Old Swedish and Old Danish sources tend to say that a thief should be hanged on either of the alliterative pair, *galgha œller gren* "gallows or limb", suggesting perhaps a perceived need for more immediate satisfaction of the death penalty than a constructed gallows would allow. Cf. the term *vargtré* "wolf [i.e., outlaw]-tree" for "gallows" in *Hamðismál* st. 17.

[16] Cf. Jens Peter Schjødt, who argues for the social reality of such a practice as a *rite de passage* within pre-Christian cultic practices (Schjødt 2008: 173–206; see also Sundqvist 2009, 2010). As Sundqvist notes, citing Bugge 1881–1889: 291–93, the picture is far from clear, as the medieval Latin *pendente in patibulo* "hanging in the gallows" was a common expression for the Crucifixion.

[17] "Hjǫrleifr konúngr var uppfestr í konúngs hǫll með skóþvengjum sínum sjálfs, millum elda tveggja," and "en Reiðar konúngr lèt hann hengja dauðan á gálga þann, er hann hafði honum ætlat" (*Hálfs saga ok Hálfsrekka* ch. 8). I read these two locations as being the same, although I recognize that the wording does not absolutely demand it. Cf. the "hanging" in *Hrafnkels saga Freysgoða* (ch. 5).

Figure 1. Detail from Lärbro Stora Hammars I. Photo by the author.

practices at Uppsala; the thanatological ritual in which Óðinn spouts numinous knowledge between the fires in *Grímnismál* (albeit a non-hanging image).[18] It is, of course, scenes of these types that many believe we see on one of the panels of the Lärbro Stora Hammars I stone on Gotland (Figure 1).[19] Whatever else the picture stone is meant to depict, it clearly means to show a warrior figure hanging from a tree in the context of a ritual.

Also significant in *Hávamál* 157 is the gallows-corpse (*virgilnár*) which Óðinn claims to be able to control: such a person might be a criminal or a sacrificial victim (perhaps even both). In fact, we meet not-quite-actually-dead cadavers in a variety of forms in the Old Norse world.[20] One type of undead dead populating Old Norse literature is the *haugbúi*, the mound-dweller, essentially always male, who seems to live in an almost humanlike way, occasionally in the company of

---

[18] As Hans-Joachim Klare suggests, the dead could know things even an otherwise all-knowing god would be eager to discover: "Die Toten wissen alles, was geschieht, sie sehen in die Zukunft, drum haben sie ein Wissen, das den nach Allwissen dürstenden Gott immer aufs neue reizt, sie zu befragen" (Klare 1933–1934: 16) (The dead know everything that happens, they see into the future, and thus they possess knowledge that excites that god thirsting for omniscience to question them). The literature in this area is vast: Ström 1947; Kragerud 1981; and Davidson 1988 remain useful portals into it; important recent studies include Schjødt 2008: 173–224; Patton 2009: 213–36; and Sundqvist 2009 and 2010.

[19] See, e.g., the discussion in McKinnell 2007.

[20] This topic has attracted much attention over the years; see Klare 1933–1934; Ohlmarks 1936; Davidson 1943; and Chadwick 1946.

others, within his mound. Among mound-dwellers, there seem to be a variety of types: at one extreme, there are the malicious, terrifying ones like the *haugbúi* Kárr inn gamli in *Grettis saga Ásmundarsonar* (ch. 18; pp. 56–59) who frightens all the farmers off the island until Grettir dispatches him (Vésteinn Ólason has called this type "the ungrateful dead"). At the other extreme are the benevolent undead like the mound-dweller Brynjarr in *Þorsteins þáttr uxafóts*, who significantly helps Þorsteinn. In between lie morally neutral types like the mound-dweller in *Kumlbúa þáttr*.[21]

Apparently a different category comprises the awakened dead female seeress or *vǫlva*, perhaps the best-known type to modern audiences (in, e.g., *Grógaldr*, *Vǫluspá*, *Baldrs draumar*). The division of these two types, the male *haugbúi* and the well-informed female *vǫlva*, although not absolute, is fairly consistent, with some important exceptions, as in *Hyndluljóð*, which features an awakened giantess who does not spew forth numinous knowledge in the manner of the *vǫlur* but rather engages, formally at least, in a wisdom contest with Freyja on their ride to Valhǫll (*Sennom við ǫr sǫðlom*, etc. v. 8). Another exception, in this case of stunning proportions, comes in Book I of Saxo's *Gesta Danorum*. Here, in a gender-reversing scene, we witness a recently dead man being used by a female worker of magic, when the giantess, Harthgrepa (significantly, perhaps, dressed as a man), and Hadingus come upon a house where the funeral of the master of the place, who has just died, is occurring.[22] Then, Saxo, continues, Harthgrepa calls his spirit in this manner, with the following results:

> Ubi magicę speculationis officio superum mentem rimari cupiens, diris admodum carminibus ligno insculptis iisdemque linguę defuncti per Hadingum suppositis hac uoce eum horrendum auribus carmen edere coegit:

> Inferis me qui retraxit, execrandus oppetat
> Tartaroque deuocati spiritus poenas luat! *etc.* (*Gesta Danorum* 1.6.4–5, 1: 108)

---

[21] On these types, see my comments in Mitchell 2009. In his fine, wide-ranging discussion of death and the dead in Icelandic literature, Vésteinn Ólason notes of the ungrateful dead, the sort we see in Kárr, that "they are resentful of the living, or some of them, and a strong desire to cause damage and destruction binds them to earthly life" (Vésteinn Ólason 2003: 169; on related concepts in Old Icelandic, such as the *draugr*, see Ármann Jakobsson 2011).

[22] I note here the similarity of this scene to that in *Hervarar saga ok Heiðreks* (ch. 3), when Angantýr's daughter, looking to fulfill a male warrior's role, goes to his mound and awakens him.

(Desiring to probe the will of the gods by magic, she inscribed most gruesome spells on wood and made Hading insert them under the corpse's
tongue, which then, in a voice terrible to the ear, uttered these lines:

Let the one who summoned me, a spirit from the underworld, dragged
me from the infernal depths, be cursed and perish miserably, *etc.* (p. 23))

This "spirit" eventually foretells their fate, but most of all he curses in direst
terms "the one who summoned me ... dragged me from the infernal depths."[23]

This scene is perhaps the closest we come to a literary presentation of what
Óðinn suggests in *Hávamál* 157, when he says of the *virgilnár* that "I can so carve
and colour the runes that the man walks and talks with me." In Saxo, the dead
man responds to Harthgrepa's use of runic magic, not only speaking with her
but also journeying back to the world of the living. Other loquacious corpses
occur in Old Norse literature, of course, such as Guðriðr's deceased husband,
Þorsteinn Eiríksson, in *Eiríks saga rauða* (ch. 6) and in *Grænlendinga saga* (ch. 6).
He too prophesies, but unlike the dead man in Saxo, his supernatural feats are
generally understood to relate to the Christian-themed tone of the saga, and in
any event, he is not responding to the manipulation of a magician.[24] The rune-
awakened corpse in Saxo does not walk, as Óðinn's comments might lead us to
expect, at least not in a normal sense, but he does move from the underworld to
our world, the world of the living. And certainly he talks, if reluctantly and with
ire, once the rune stick has been placed under his tongue. Saxo's presentation is
then not that distant from what *Hávamál* 157 suggests.

That this charm, among others, focuses on the tongue of the dead is not
surprising: after all, Old Norse *tunga* refers to the physical entity, as well as to
the general concept of a language (e.g., *á danska tungu*), that is, both to one of the
busiest muscular organs in the human body, the one necessary for the production of speech, *and* to the resulting product of such activity. It has been conjec-
tured that Óðinn's cognomen, "god of the hanged", a name that comes to us in

---

[23] On this passage, see further the comments in Davidson and Fisher 1980: 30, as well as my remarks
in Mitchell 2008b.

[24] Perhaps a more proximate example comes through the manipulations of Þrándr in *Færeyinga
saga*, when he apparently causes three dead men, or their apparitions, to appear in order to
discover the causes and places of their deaths. The description of his preparations includes
setting a large fire in the fire pit, making four trellises or frames, drawing nine squares, and
requesting that no one speak to him: "Þrandr hafde þa latit gera ellda mykla j ellda skala ok
grindanna fiorar lætr hann gera med fiorum hornum ok ix Ræita Ristr Þrandr alla uega vt fra
grindunum en hann setzst astol mille eldz ok grindanna hann bidr þa nu ekki vid sig tala ok þeir
gera suo" (ch. 40). (Thrand had had big fires made in the hearth-room, and he had four hurdles
[*frames*] set up with four corners, and he scratches nine squares all around out from the hurdles,
and he sits on a stool between the fires and the hurdles. Now he gives orders that nobody is to
talk to him, and they do as he says" (p. 81)).

a variety of forms (e.g., *hangatýr, hangaguð, hangadróttinn, heimþinguðr hanga*),[25] should be understood in relation to sacrificial hanging of the sort pictured on Figure 1 (Lärbro Stora Hammars I), especially where asphyxia (rather than breaking the cervical vertebrae) is understood as the cause of death. Hanging in this way typically causes a protruding, purplish tongue, just the sort of image useful, necessary even, for forced thanatological revelations of great secrets, of being "between two worlds" in Jens Peter Schjødt's evocative phrase (2008). It is also one of the reasons scholars have been inclined to believe that the one-eyed figure from the stave church at Hegge, Norway, should be understood with reference to Odinic belief systems (Figure 2[26]).

I note, however, that Saxo's reluctant, revelatory corpse is not the only case where tongues play an important role in stories involving interactions between the living and the dead. In fact, we have something of an inversion of Saxo's story pattern in *Þorleifs þáttr jarlsskálds*; here it is the dead poet, i.e., Þorleifr's *haugbúi*, who comes out of his mound, on which the aspiring but inadequate poet, Hallbjǫrn, regularly sleeps. Hallbjǫrn's attempts at composing poetry never go further than the opening line, "Here lies a poet" (*Hér liggr skáld*). Þorleifr pulls the tongue of the would-be poet (*togar hann á honum tunguna*), recites a verse for the aspirant to memorize, and instructs Hallbjǫrn to compose a poem praising Þorleifr and to be certain that the poem is complex with regard to both meter and metaphor. Hallbjǫrn succeeds and goes on to become a great skald (*Þorleifs þáttr jarlsskálds* ch. 5–8; pp. 222–29). Here, the tongue as the generative organ of speech, and thus of poetic production, is essentialized and its manipulation by the dead poet, Þorleifr, is the turning point in Hallbjǫrn's endeavor to acquire poetic ability.[27]

---

[25] *Víga-Glúms saga* ch. 27; Hávarðr halti ísfirðingr 14; *Ynglinga saga* ch. 7; *Heiðarvíga saga* ch. 26. Cf. the additional *heiti* enumerated in Falk 1924: 59–61, and his discussion concerning *haptaguð* "god of fetters" (?) (62).

[26] "Hegge stavkirke, maske på stav - 1" by John Erling Blad - Own work. Licensed under CC BY-SA 3.0 via Wikimedia Commons http://commons.wikimedia.org/wiki/File:Hegge_stavkirke,_maske_p%C3%A5_stav_-_1.jpg#/media/File:Hegge_stavkirke,_maske_p%C3%A5_stav_-_1.jpg

[27] Without wishing to strain the soup too thin, I note that Hallbjǫrn's poem specifically praises Þorleifr's libeling of Earl Hákon and that the story, which is, after all, about Þorleifr, follows with the comment that his brothers go to Norway the summer after his death, but it was not in the cards for them to kill Hákon, that is, "to have his head [lit., scalp; 'head-skin'] at their feet" (En þeim varð eigi lagið þá enn at standa yfir hǫfuðsvǫrðum Hákonar jarls (ch. 8)). When in *Óláfs saga Tryggvasonar*, Hákon is dispatched, is it then mere coincidence that the following scene takes place:

Sá hólmr var þá hafðr til þess at drepa þar þjófa ok illmenni, ok stóð þar gálgi, *ok lét hann þar til bera hǫfuð Hákonar jarls ok Karks*. Gekk þá til allr herrinn ok œpði upp ok grýtti þar at ok mæltu, at þar skyldi níðingr fara með ǫðrum níðingum. Síðan láta þeir fara upp í Gaulardal ok taka þar búkinn ok drógu í brott ok brenndu. (*Óláfs saga Tryggvasonar* ch. 50; emphasis added)

Figure 2. The one-eyed figure from the stave church at Hegge, Norway.
Photo by John Erling Blad/Wikimedia Commons, CC BY-SA 3.0.

The tongue and its relation to the production of speech also plays a key role in *Þorsteins þáttr uxafóts*. This story tells of how the hero of the *þáttr* enters a grave mound, where he finds there two fraternal *haugbúar* and their retinues.

(This island was at that time used for putting to death thieves and evildoers, and a gallows stood there. *The king had the heads of Earl Hákon and of Kark fastened to it*. Thereupon the whole multitude came with great shouts and stoned them, saying that they should fare thus like every other villain. Then they sent men up to Gaular Dale who hauled away Hákon's trunk and burned it. (p. 192, emphasis added))

The helpful brother, Brynjarr, explains that his brother Oddr, the evil one, has a special piece of gold that, when placed under the tongue of a dumb person, gives them the power of speech.[28] Importantly, Þorsteinn's mother, Oddný, had been born without the ability to speak and must respond to others by writing on a rune stick or *kefli* (*Oddný reist rúnar á kefli, því at hon mátti eigi mæla*). Þorsteinn wrests the gold piece from Oddr and gives it to his mother; when it is shortly thereafter placed "under the root of her tongue" (*undir tungurætr henni*), Oddný acquires and retains the power of speech.[29]

These plays on "tongue-power"—the gold object that cures Oddný, said to have been placed *undir tungurætr henni*; the gift of mantic speech in Saxo's *Gesta Danorum* that comes with the insertion of a rune charm under the tongue of the corpse; and so on—suggest that the various authors had degrees of familiarity with the same tradition from which *Hávamál* 157 derives. Of related interest to these later literary sources are examples of actual "tongue objects", or "Charon's obol" as archaeologists often term them (on which see below).

Such mortuary practices, although not common, are in evidence in early Scandinavian graves from, for example, Gotland and Sjælland. In fact, instances of the "Charon's obol" have been documented in Scandinavia dating back to at least the late Roman Iron Age (e.g., Almgren 1903; Shetelig 1908; Stjerna 1912: 101–02; Davidson 1943: 37; Gräslund 1965–1966). Summarizing much of this research, Signe Horn Fuglesang writes, "the best evidence for the custom in the Viking period comes from eastern Sweden, while it seems to have been rare in Denmark and the evidence from Norway and Finland is inconclusive" (Fuglesang 1989: 21–22). She notes further that "graves of the 13th and 14th centuries have documented [the practice] from Sweden, Scania and Norway" (Fuglesang 1989: 22). The tradition arguably continued even into modern folk beliefs, as there are graves from the 1700s that reflect the continuity of the practice.[30]

---

[28] "Oddr hefir at varðveita gull þat, er sú náttúra fylgir, at hverr maðr, sem mállaus er ok leggr þat undir tungurætr sér, þá tekr þegar mál sitt, ok af því gulli má móðir þín mál fá" (*Þorsteins þáttr uxafóts* ch. 6). (Odd keeps a piece of gold whose nature is that whatever dumb person puts that gold under the root of his or her tongue will then gain the power of speech and by means of that gold your mother will be able to speak (p. 346)).

[29] Noteworthy here are the Philolmela-like aspects of the story line in the *þáttr*, i.e., inability to speak, pregnancy, and so on.

[30] See especially Gräslund 1965–1966. The recent excavation of an early eighteenth-century site in which 14 small silver coins were found in 13 graves suggests the possibility that this practice continued up to modern times:
Myntfynden för tanken till den grekiska mytologin, som omtalar att färjekarlen Charon. [...] Att denna hedniska sedvänja kan ses i gravar från tidigt 1700-tal är ovanligt, och har möjligen att göra med att begravningarna inte ägde rum på den vanliga kyrkogården, och att de som begravts avlidit i en fruktad farsot. Mynten kan således ha fått följa de döda i graven som en extra försäkran om att man trots detta skulle få komma till himmelriket. (Jacobsson 2002: 17).

Hávamál 157 and the Learned and Ecclesiastical Tradition

As we have seen, there exists a rich native tradition that touches, or appears to touch, on the images suggested by *Hávamál* 157. But is that sufficient to explain the background against which Óðinn formulates his claim to know how to reanimate the dead and make them talk? Perhaps, but certainly there is more to the medieval cultural tapestry concerned with the dead and dying than these native traditions alone. In the end, we may decide that the influence of foreign learned and ecclesiastical materials is slight and favor instead the domestic traditions, but let us first examine the external materials and assess the effects they might have had.

As literature and as homily, a striking Judeo-Christian parallel to *Hávamál* 157 in which a dead person is raised and speaks specifically, like Mímir, for the purpose of prophesying, is the so-called "witch of Endor" (I Sam: 28), a narrative known to have been used in sermons in northern Europe (by, e.g., Ælfric [*Marcarius and the Magicians, Saul and the Witch of Endor*]). In this necromantic narrative, the spirit of the dead prophet Samuel is raised by a female medium; the shade converses with Saul and, like the spirit of the dead man in Saxo, he complains of having been disturbed and of having been "brought up", apparently out of the world of the dead.[31]

On a related issue, namely the role of the severed head, the story of John the Baptist's decapitation (Matt. 14: 1–11; Mark 6: 14–29) naturally meant that trunkless heads often played a key role in medieval Christian iconography. The Baptist is the most obvious figure of this sort to modern eyes; however, medieval hagiology includes a large number of saints whose legendary martyrdoms include decapitation. And among these, there are dozens of particular interest in the current discussion, such as the cephalophoric saints, that is those saints who, after being beheaded, pick up their detached heads and carry them, sometimes speaking as they go.

(The discoveries of coins makes one think of Greek mythology, which speaks of the ferryman Charon [...] That this pagan custom is to be seen in graves from the early 1700s is uncommon, and may be connected to the fact that the burials did not take place in a normal cemetery, and that those buried died in a dreaded plague. The coins may thus have followed the dead in their graves as extra assurance that one would despite that enter Heaven.)

[31] On this scene and Nordic mortuary beliefs, see Davidson 1943: 168–69. Cf. the comparison Clive Tolley makes between the biblical scene and *Vǫluspá*, in which he concludes that the echoes of the Bible in the poem are "clear and intentional" (Tolley 2009: 485–86). He goes on to say, in an excellent statement about the full range of purportedly pre-Christian materials, that this view "does not mean that the pagan elements [...] are not genuine, but it suggests these elements are being structured and perhaps interpreted in a way which may not have taken place in earlier, more purely pagan times."

Very likely the most famous of such saints in the Middle Ages was St. Denis, the first bishop of Paris and one of the city's patron saints, who was martyred in the mid-third century CE. Over time, the legend of St. Denis developed considerably (cf. Spiegel 1983) and by the thirteenth-century *Legenda aurea* of Jacobus de Voragine, it acquired the form in which it is best-known today: having been beheaded, St. Denis picks up his head and walks several miles to the site of the present cathedral basilica of Saint Denis, accompanied by the singing of angels (*Legenda aurea* p. 685).[32] Some later versions of the legend add that the head of St. Denis preached throughout the journey.[33] The point is, in other words, that there existed a notable emphasis in the Middle Ages on cephalic imagery in religion and law: this theme, as Esther Cohen argues, intensified over time, and by the high Middle Ages there is, as she writes, "a gradually growing shared perception of the head as the most important organ for life and identity, which derived from different fields of action and influenced different fields of knowledge" (Cohen 2013: 73).[34]

A similar type of decapitation narrative as that which came to signify St. Denis can be seen in the story of St. Edmund. According to the tenth-century *Passio Sancti Eadmundi* of Abbo of Fleury, the East Anglian king, Edmund, is martyred by the Danish army; according to the legend, he is tortured and beheaded due to his unwillingness to reject his Christian faith. The severed head of the martyr is deposited in a forest by the invaders and when the locals finally venture forth, they discover his headless body and begin a search for the missing head. In response to their cries, the head identifies its location by yelling, "Here, here, here!"[35]

---

[32] This part of the legend is faithfully reproduced in the Old Swedish translation of *Legenda aurea*, *Ett fornsvenskt legendarium*, here from Codex Bildstenianus (early 1400s):

Sidhan ledhis han ther wt ater (at / for) hedhan domara (mz sinom kompanom) at thola manga nya pinor: Ok halshuggus mz yxe. The thre. vm sidhe. Dyonisius ok hans compana rusticus ok eleutherius widher mercurii mønster. Sancti dyonisii (liikir / licame) reste sik wp siælfuir. Ok grep howdhit mz armomin. Ok gik æpter ængla ledsagh(ara) Ok himna liuse. thwo mila wægh fra halshuggeno som nu kallas martyrium biærgh til thæn stadh han ligger nu. (*Sagan om Sankt Dionysius* I: 344)

(Then he was led before a heathen judge with his companions and suffered many new torments. And the three, Dionyisius and his companions, Rusticus and Eleutherius, were beheaded with an axe at the temple of Mercury. The body of Saint Dionyisius raised itself up and grasped its head with its arms and followed angels and heavenly light for two miles from the place of the beheadings which is now called the hill of martyrs (i.e., Montmartre) to that place where he now lies. (My translation))

[33] I note, however, that I have not been able to identify this particular embellishment in any of the medieval sources.

[34] Cf. the many examples and themes covered by the essays in Tracy and Massey 2012; Gardeła and Kajkowski 2013 (many of which concern Old Norse topics); and Baert et al. 2013.

[35] Vispillonum sane more pluribus pedententim invia perlustrantibus, cum jam posset audiri loquens, ad voces se invicem cohortantium, et utpote socii ad socium alternatim clamantium,

This well-known motif (Thompson 1966: V229.25, "Severed head of saint speaks so that searchers can find it") appears to have had recognizable resonance in medieval Scandinavia, if in a modified version: in a legend first recorded ca. 1200 in the officium *Celebremus karissimi*, the eleventh-century English missionary, Sigfrid, undertakes conversion activity in Swedish Småland, at Växjö, accompanied by his nephews, Unaman, Sunaman, and Vinaman, all of whom are also ecclesiastics. They are engaged in the construction of a church at Växjö, dedicated, appropriately as it turns out, to John the Baptist. While Sigfrid is away in Västergötland, purportedly in order to baptize King Olof Skötkonung at Husaby, a group of pagans kills and beheads the three nephews. Their heads are placed in a wooden tub which is then weighed down with an enormous stone and sunk in the middle of the nearby lake. When Sigfrid returns, he is miraculously led to the heads' location in Lake Växjö when he sees three lights over the lake. The heads are floating on the water and speak to him. This legend gained traction quickly, and already by the end of the thirteenth century, the severed, and seemingly still bleeding, heads of the three nephews formed the seal of Växjö cathedral chapter.[36]

Thus, the idea of the recently dead being reanimated and regaining their capacity for speech and locomotion might not have been as farfetched or macabre to a medieval audience as it seems to us today. But these scenes apparently play out within the lives of saints as demonstrations of God's will, miracles with which to show the extent of God's power and love. Moreover, as noted above, there exists a long-standing Mediterranean tradition of "tongue objects", generally referred to as the "Ferryman's Fee" or "Charon's obol", special articles placed in the mouths of the dead. "Charon's obol" is, of course, a name that invokes the most famous classical example of this practice, but it is a tradition by no means limited to the world of the Greeks and Romans.[37] Indeed, the same

---

Ubi es? illud respondebat designando locum, patria lingua dicens, *Her, her, her*. Quod interpretatum Latinus sermo exprimit, Hic, hic, hic. (*Passio Sancti Eadmundi* p. 40)

(A number of the party, like corpse-searchers, were gradually examining the out-of-the-way parts of the wood, and when the moment had arrived at which the sound of a voice could be heard, the head, in response to the calls of the search party mutually encouraging one other, and as comrade to comrade crying alternately "Where are you?" indicated the place where it lay by exclaiming in their native tongue, Here! Here! Here! In Latin the same meaning would be rendered by Hic! Hic! Hic! (p. 41))

Subsequent reworkings of the passion, such as Ælfric's *Life of St Edmund* (II: 324–25), sometimes repeat and build on this scene.

[36] See the image in, e.g., Larsson 1975: 13. On the legend, see Schmid 1931; Lundén 1967; Larsson 1975; and *Celebremus karissimi* pp. 9–17.

[37] "Charon's fee: putting coin in dead person's mouth to pay for ferry across Styx" (Thompson 1966: P613). In her wide-ranging review of the literary and archaeological evidence for the practice in the classical world, Susan T. Stevens summarizes the phenomenon thus: "According to ancient authors, the custom of 'Charon's obol' has four characteristics, though there are some

practice of placing objects (often but not always coins) in the mouths of the dead was already known among the Egyptians, Phoenicians, and others from periods anterior to its use by the Greeks (see, e.g., Grabka 1953: 3, 6; Wolff 2002: 136).

It should be noted too that this concept, or at least something that looks very much like it, is not limited to the Old World but is also found in the pre-Columbian New World, as in the case of the Cañete valley of South America, where, for example, small copper discs were found in the mouths of Peruvian mummies.[38] Noting the existence of these cases is not, of course, meant to be an argument about *function*, which, to the extent we understand it, would likely have been quite discursive in these various instances; rather what interests us are the similar techniques, methods, operational elements, and outcomes of such practices.

From the perspective of our medieval data-points, perhaps the single most important aspect of the "Charon's obol" tradition is how it influenced Christian tradition, specifically, the Church's adaptation of the "Ferryman's Fee" into the so-called Last Rites, where the Eucharist is administered to the dying, the so-called *Viaticum*. The history of the relationship of the pagan *viaticum*, the provisions for the journey (< *via* "road") into the afterlife, and the Christian *Viaticum*, is complex, and it is a history not without its disputes (cf. Grabka 1953). In the early Church, such provisions or preparations might include baptism, prayers, or any other means that could help the dying in their transition into the next world. It could also refer to the Eucharist generally, until, in the words of the *Catholic Encyclopedia* in their entry on *Viaticum*, "finally it acquired its present fixed, exclusive, and technical sense of Holy Communion given to those in danger of death" (*Catholic Encyclopedia* 2003). It was, as Grabka has argued, *both* a Christian bulwark against the need to employ "Charon's obol" and an adaptation of that same tradition to Christian ritual.[39] But either way, whether

---

variations in their discussions: (1) a single low-denomination coin (2) is placed in the mouth (3) at the time of death (4) to pay Charon's fare" (Stevens 1991: 216). Among other motifs connected with this tradition are: A672.1.1, "Charon exacts fee to ferry souls across Styx"; E431.11, "Coin placed in mouth of dead to prevent return"; and E489.3, "Forgetting Charon's fee" (Thompson 1966). On the many, widely dispersed manifestations of the tradition, see Grinsell 1957.

[38] Regarding Peruvian practices in the Cañete valley, Kroeber and O'Neale write:
Most mummies had copper or occasionally silver sheets or ornaments bestowed about the head, most frequently perhaps in the mouth, but also about the ears or elsewhere on the face. Where the metal is entirely corroded it shows in green stains on the bone or teeth, as previously mentioned. This burial habit prevails for the Late period of all parts of the Peruvian coast which I have visited, from north of Trujillo to south of Nazca, frequently even as regards the graves of the poor. The most frequent disposal is of a round or oval sheet of thin metal about the size of a coin, apparently laid on the tongue—a sort of Charon's obol. (Kroeber and O'Neale 1926: 4: 247)

[39] The wide-ranging learning displayed by Grabka in his review of the traditions which led to the *Viaticum* does not, however, prevent him from seeming to hold two contradictory views of this history. Cp. "The ancient funeral rite of placing the *viaticum* coin in the mouth of the corpse

the custom was preemptive or adaptive, it was also about inserting something highly symbolic into the mouths of the dead and dying.

A final, further "learned" parallel to *Hávamál* 157 comes from the medieval world of natural magic, specifically the lapidary tradition. In this tradition, certain stones, when placed in the mouth, possessed the occult power to make the speaker reveal truths, including prophecies. Compendious works detailing the power of stones and gems are known already from antiquity, but the best-known example in medieval Europe was the eleventh-century *De Lapidibus* by Bishop Marbod of Rennes.[40] The earliest Nordic example I have found of this tradition of stones with prophetic properties being placed under the tongue comes from an Old Danish translation of Marbod (ca. 1300),[41] which reads in part:

Haldær man hanum [*Celonites*] undær ren tungæ. tha ma han spa.[42]
(*Stenbog* p. 191)

(If one places it under a clean [alt., pure] tongue then he may soothsay.)

The same belief later appears in Peder Månsson's Old Swedish translation of the late medieval *Speculum lapidum* of Camillus Leonardi, which similarly says that by taking *Celonites* and placing it under the tongue one can speak many

---

was responsible for the superstition in Christian burials of administering the *Viaticum* to the dead" (Grabka 1953: 42) *versus* "the pagan custom of placing a coin into the mouth of the dead as a *viaticum* for the journey of the soul to its after-life never gained a firm foothold among the Christians. They had their own *Viaticum* with which they provided their departing brethren: the Holy Eucharist" (Grabka 1953: 27) and "Seen in its essentials, the ancient Christian custom of providing the dying faithful with the Eucharist as their *Viaticum* for the journey to eternity was neither derived from nor inspired by the pagan *viaticum*; it was based on the revealed truths of Christianity" (Grabka 1953: 42).

40 On the learned tradition of magic in the Nordic world—lapidaries, alchemy, and so on—see esp. Mitchell 2008a, as well as Mitchell 2011.

41 On these translations, see *Stenbog*, LXVIII-CII, and Brix 1943: 38–39.

42 The complete entry under the heading Chelonites runs: "Silenites hetær en steen. oc føthæs af en snæghæl .i. brittani land. Han ær blalyk røth. Haldær man hanum undær ren tungæ. tha ma han spa. Thænnæ steen ma æi eld skathæ." (There is a stone called 'Silenites' which comes from a snail in Brittany. It is blueish[?] red. If one places it under a clean [alt., pure] tongue, then he may soothsay. This stone cannot be harmed by fire.) I take this opportunity to thank Henrik Jørgensen of Aarhus University for his advice on the treatment of *blalyk røth*. Ny. kgl. Samling 66, 8ᵛᵒ is a composite manuscript, which makes its dating difficult, but it is usually set to ca. 1300. In this instance, the description, although based on Marbod's lapidary poem, has been altered: India has become Brittany, and tortoise (*testudo*) has become a snail. Cf. Jespersen 1938: 164. Other manuscripts, e.g., Sth. K4, are fragmentary and do not contain an entry for "Chelonites/ Silenites." For a facsimile (and text) of Ny. kgl. Samling 66, 8ᵛᵒ [136v], see Det Danske Sprog- og Litteraturselskab's online site, *Tekster fra Danmarks middelalder 1100-1515*, at: http://middelalder-tekster.dk/harpestreng-nks66/3/58.

prophecies about things that will come to pass.[43] Although we cannot know with certainty whether this tradition exercised influence on the way Óðinn's powers are presented in our texts, it is likely that the existence of this parallel belief system would have been known among the clerics who possessed Latin learning and the other requirements necessary for engagement with natural magic.

Raising these points about the cephalophoric saints, the Ferryman's Fee, and the *Viaticum* and its history is not the same as claiming that these aspects of learned lore necessarily shaped the traditions we see in Saxo, *Hávamál*, or the other Nordic materials, but given the tendency to adduce parallels between the pre-Christian and Christian worlds, and to see in such analogues, prefigurations, and revelations of the Almighty's power, that such a parallel existed may well have reinforced the pre-existing concept and even allowed for its easier acceptance within clerical culture.

Conclusion

If we consider this problem operationally, as a ritual performed at some point in time, how was such a belief as that suggested by *Hávamál* 157 practiced, or believed to have been practiced? After all, we possess, so far as I know, no *kefli* "piece of wood" or other materials on which appropriate runic inscriptions have been carved to suggest such charms were ever used.[44] Even though there may exist no surviving recognizable runic inscriptions, we do have Church edicts and synodal statutes condemning the use of runes, listed in collocations with such things as magic, witchcraft, and superstitions. Presumably, mundane runic use was of little interest to the Church but precisely such things as charms to awaken the dead would have been what the bishops looked to eradicate. But, of course, this point is nothing but an inference.

We perhaps get a bit closer when we examine the provincial laws. Here, for example, the Older Law of Frostaþing speaks of those who are killed for various deeds, including witchcraft, visiting soothsayers, or sitting out in order to awaken spirits [lit., trolls] and thereby promote heathendom ("fordæðu scapi oc spáfarar oc útisetu at vecia tröll upp oc fremia heiðni með því", *Norges gamle Love* I: 182). This is just one of nearly a dozen such laws in Iceland and Norway specifying prohibitions against "sitting out." Sometimes the laws go one step further,

---

43 "Celonites är en sten som taks vth aff storom skölpaddom. [...] Hwilken som honom bär wndy twngonne han talar mangan spaadom som komma skal oc ske" (*Stenbok* p. 466). (Celonites is a stone taken from large turtles [...] Whoever bears it under his tongue can speak many prophecies of things that will come to pass. (My translation.))

44 Cf. modern narratives concerning "uppvakningar eða sendingar" in *Íslenzkar þjóðsögur og ævintýri* (I: 304–39), on all aspects of which see especially Gunnell 2012.

as in "So also those who attempt to awaken spirits (*draugar*) or mound-dwellers (*haugbúar*)" ("Sua oc þeir er freista draugha upp at ueckia æða haughbua", *Norges gamle Love* II: 326–27). This asserted practice brings to mind such developments in the mound as those presented in *Þorsteins þáttr uxafóts*, for example, as well as the commands used by saga characters that the seeresses and others should "awaken" (*vaki þú*).

Still, it is highly unlikely that anything like the sort of practice referred to in *Hávamál* 157 was ever practiced in the Christian Middle Ages and thus, our best presentation of such a performance derives from the surviving mythological materials. With respect to the poetry, *Baldrs draumar* provides the fullest information about how Óðinn accomplishes his task of compelling the dead to awaken and speak, as well as expressions in this instance of the *vǫlva*'s reluctance to be awakened and cooperate with the magician.[45] He rides to Hel and then to the seeress's resting place, where he undertakes a relatively detailed performance (at least compared to the general rule): Óðinn speaks, or more narrowly, chants or intones (past tense, *qvað*), various corpse-related items of word-power: *valgaldr* and *nás orð*, that is, literally, "slain-magic" and "corpse-words".[46] The *vǫlva* responds by asking who it is that has forced her to travel such difficult paths. The extant text does not specify that Óðinn does more than to vocalize these powerful charms in order to bend her to his will but we cannot know for sure. It would not be difficult to envision the carving of a *kefli* during the performance of such a charm, just as Harthgrepa does in forcing the corpse to speak in *Gesta Danorum* or as other characters do in performing rune magic, such as Skírnir in *Fǫr Scírnis* (see Mitchell 2007).

---

[45] How the dead person is raised in *Grógaldr* is unclear. Klare (1933–1934: 16) assumes that in awakening his mother from death and getting her willing assistance, Svipdagr does nothing more than speak ("er hatte nicht einmal Zaubermittel gebraucht. [...] Nun genügt ein Wort, sie kommt und hilft bereitwillig") (he does not even use a magic spell. [...] With just a word she comes and helps willingly). Although the poem gives no explicit information other than his command to "awaken", the audience here, and elsewhere, may, of course, have assumed other operations were in play. In the famous scene in *Hervarar saga ok Heiðreks* between live daughter and dead father (NB: gender-reversed compared to *Grógaldr*), referred to earlier, Hervǫr too appears to do no more than command that the dead man awaken (*vaki þú*) to begin their dialogue but there may have been much more to it. *Vǫluspá* is, if anything, even less clear than these other cases: the poem begins with the *vǫlva*'s calls for attention, not any act of Óðinn's. It is from the *comparanda* and such clues as her addresses to *Valfǫðr* about what he wants to know and her repeated phrase, "vitoð ér enn, eða hvat?" (do you understand yet, or what more) that scholars draw the reasonable inference that it is indeed cut from the same cloth as the others. And, in fact, rhythmically repeated questions of the "do you understand yet, or what more"-sort characterize most of these poems.

[46] Cleasby-Vigusson 1982, for example, glosses *valgaldr* as "*charms*, a kind of *necromancy* ascribed to Odin" and *nás orð* as "necromancy".

What happened when Nordic prophetic practices involving the dead encountered similar beliefs from the classical world or Christian interpretations of them? Nordic tradition could easily accommodate these views to its own, where the tongue object was not for the purpose of accompanying the dead into the afterlife but for the use of the living to look into the *arcana coelestia* which could only be known within a certain narrow mantic framework. Given the extensive *comparanda* over time and space, the practice of placing something in the mouth (and under the tongue) of a corpse need not be envisioned as having been borrowed from elsewhere, either the practices of the classical world or the Church, or indeed from adepts of natural magic. It is possible that these necromantic practices and belief systems had evolved in northern Europe over a very long time with ongoing reticulations between vernacular and learned belief systems.

Accusations of *Hávamál* being overly consistent are few for good reason. Certainly, in one respect, the earlier part of the poem may have even been *very* wrong: in verse 71, *Hávamál* claims "nýtr manngi nás" (a dead man is good for nothing). As we see from verse 157 and its cognate materials, apparently there existed a tradition according to which nothing could be further from the truth.

Works Cited

Primary Sources

Annals
(Cornelius) Tacitus. *Histories, Books IV–V; Annals Books I–III*. Tacitus Vol. 3. Transl. Clifford H. Moore and John Jackson. Loeb Classical Library, 249. Cambridge, MA & London: 1931.

Baldrs draumar: see *Poetic Edda*

Celebremus karissimi
S:t Sigfrid besjungen: Celebremus karissimi, ett helgonofficium från 1200-talet. Ed. Ann-Marie Nilsson. Runica et mediævalia. Scripta maiora, 6. Stockholm: 2010.

Eiríks saga rauða
Íslenzk fornrit, 4. Ed. Einar Ól. Sveinsson and Matthías Þórðarson. Reykjavík: 1957. Pp. 193-237.

TRANSLATION
Erik the Red's Saga. Transl. Keneva Kuntz. In *The Sagas of Icelanders: A Selection*. New York: 2000. Pp. 653–76.

Epitome of Roman History
Lucius Annaeus Florus, *Epitome of Roman History*. Ed. and transl. E. S. Forster. The
Loeb Classical Library. Cambridge, MA and London: 1929.

Eyrbyggia saga
Íslenzk fornrit, 4. Ed. Einar Ól. Sveinsson and Matthías Þórðarson. Reykjavík: 1957.
Pp. 1-184.

TRANSLATION
"The Saga of the People of Eyri." Transl. Judy Quinn. In vol. 5 of *The Complete
Sagas of Icelanders*. Reykjavík: 1997. Pp. 131–218.

Færeyinga saga
Færeyinga saga. Ed. Ólafur Halldórsson. Rit / Stofnun Árna Magnússonar á Islandi,
30. Reykjavík: 1987.

TRANSLATION
The Faroe Islanders' Saga. Transl. George Johnston. Ottawa: 1975.

For Scírnis: see *Poetic Edda*

Gautreks saga
Gautreks saga. In vol. 3 of *Fornaldar Sögur Nordrlanda, eptir gömlum handritum*. Ed.
Carl C. Rafn. Copenhagen: 1829–1830. Pp. 3–53.

TRANSLATION
Gautrek's Saga and Other Medieval Tales. Transl. Hermann Pálsson and Paul
Edwards. New York: 1968. Pp. 25–55.

Gesta Danorum
Saxo Grammaticus. *Gesta Danorum. Danmarkshistorien*. Ed. Karsten Friis-Jensen.
Transl. Peter Zeeberg [into Danish]. Copenhagen: 2005.

TRANSLATION
Saxo Grammaticus. *Saxo Grammaticus: The History of the Danes*. Vol. 1: *Text*. Ed. H.
R. Ellis Davidson. Transl. Peter Fisher. Cambridge: 1979.

Gesta Hammaburgensis ecclesiae pontificum
Adam of Bremen. *Adami Gesta Hammaburgensis ecclesiae pontificum*. Monumenta
Germaniae historica. Scriptores rerum germanicarum, 2. Hannover: 1876.

TRANSLATION
Adam of Bremen. *History of the Archbishops of Hamburg-Bremen by Adam of Bremen*.
Transl. F. J. Tschan. New York: 1959.

Grágás

Grágás, Konungsbók. Ed. Vilhjálmur Finsen. Odense: 1974. Facsimile ed. of text originally published in 1852.

TRANSLATION

Laws of Early Iceland: Grágás, the Codex Regius of Grágás, with Material from other Manuscripts. 2 vols. Ed. and transl. Andrew Dennis, Peter Foote, and Richard Perkins. University of Manitoba Icelandic Studies 3, 5. Winnipeg: 1980–2000.

Grettis saga Ásmundarsonar

Íslenzk fornrit, 7. Ed. Guðni Jónsson. Reykjavík: 1964. Pp. 3–290.

TRANSLATION

Grettir's saga. Transl. Denton Fox and Hermann Pálsson. Toronto: 1974.

Grímnismál: see Poetic Edda

Grænlendinga saga

Íslenzk fornrit, 4. Ed. Einar Ól. Sveinsson and Matthías Þórðarson. Reykjavík: 1957. Pp. 239-69.

TRANSLATION

The Saga of the Greenlanders. Transl. Keneva Kuntz. In The Sagas of Icelanders: A Selection. New York: 2000. Pp. 636–52.

Grógaldr

"Grógaldr." In De gamle Eddadigte. Ed. Finnur Jónsson. Copenhagen: 1932. Pp. 171–74.

TRANSLATION SEE POETIC EDDA

Gylfaginning

Snorri Sturluson. Edda. Prologue and Gylfaginning. Ed. Anthony Faulkes. 2nd ed. London: 2005.

TRANSLATION

Snorri Sturluson. Snorri Sturluson. Edda. Transl. Anthony Faulkes. London & Rutland, VT: 1995. Pp. 7–58.

Hálfs saga ok Hálfsrekka

Hálfs saga ok Hálfsrekka. In vol. 2 of Fornaldar Sögur Nordrlanda, eptir gömlum handritum. Ed. Carl C. Rafn. Copenhagen: 1829–1830. Pp. 23–60.

TRANSLATION

The Sagas of King Half and King Hrolf. Transl. W. Bryant Bachman and Guðmundur Erlingsson. Lanham: 1991.

Hamðismál: see *Poetic Edda*

Hávamál: see *Poetic Edda*

Hávarðr halti ísfirðingr
In *Rettet Tekst, 800-1200*. B1 of *Den norsk-islandske skjaldedigtning*. Ed. Finnur Jónsson. Copenhagen: 1973. P. 182.

Heiðarvíga saga
Íslenzk fornrit, 3. Ed. Sigurður Nordal and Guðni Jónsson. Reykjavík: 1938. Pp. 213–328.

TRANSLATION
Heidarvíga saga. Transl. W. Bryant Bachman and Guðmundur Erlingsson. Lanham: 1995.

Hervarar saga ok Heiðreks konungs
Saga Heiðreks konungs ins vitra. The Saga of King Heidrek the Wise. Ed. and transl. Christopher Tolkien. London, etc.: 1960.

Hrafnkels saga Freysgoða
Íslenzk fornrit, 11. Ed. Jón Jóhannesson. Reykjavík: 1950. Pp. 98–133.

TRANSLATION
"The Saga of Hrafnkel Frey's Godi." Transl. Terry Gunnell. In vol. 5 of *The Complete Sagas of Icelanders*. Reykjavík: 1997. Pp. 261–81.

Hyndluljóð
"Hyndluljóð." In *De gamle Eddadigte*. Ed. Finnur Jónsson. Copenhagen: 1932. Pp. 143–50.

TRANSLATION SEE *POETIC EDDA*

Íslenzkar þjóðsögur og ævintýri
Íslenzkar þjóðsögur og ævintýri. Ed. Jón Árnason. 2nd rev. ed. Reykjavík: 1954–61.

Getica
Iordanis Romana et Getica. Ed. Theodor Mommsen. Monumenta Germaniae historica. Auctores antiquissimi, 5: 1. Berlin: 1961.

TRANSLATION
The Gothic History of Jordanes in English version. Transl. Charles C. Mierow. 2nd ed. Cambridge: 1966.

Kumlbúa þáttr
Íslenzk fornrit, 13. Ed. Þórhallur Vilmundarson and Bjarni Vilhjálmsson. Reykjavík: 1991. Pp. 451–55.

TRANSLATION

"The Tale of the Cairn-Dweller." Transl. Marvin Taylor. In vol. 2 of *The Complete Sagas of Icelanders*. Reykjavík: 1997. Pp. 443–44.

De Lapidibus
Marbod of Rennes, "De lapidibus," considered as a Medical Treatise with Text, Commentary, and C. W. King's Translation, together with Text and Translation of Marbode's Minor Works on Stones. Ed. John M. Riddle. Sudhoffs Archiv. Beihefte, 20. Wiesbaden: 1977.

Legenda aurea
Jacobi a Voragine. *Legenda aurea vulgo Historia lombardica dicta.* Ed. Johann Georg Theodor Grässe. 2nd ed. Lipsiae: 1850.

TRANSLATION

The Golden Legend: Readings on the Saints. Transl. William Granger Ryan. Princeton: 1993.

Life of Saint Edmund
Ælfric. "Passio Sancti Eadmvndi Regis et Martyris." In vol. 2 of *Ælfric's Lives of Saints, being A Set of Sermons on Saints' Days Formerly Observed by the English Church.* Ed. and transl. Walter W. Skeat. Early English Text Society. Original series, no. 76, 82, 94, 114. London: 1881. Pp. 314–35.

Magnúss saga berfœtts
Íslenzk fornrit, 28. Ed. Bjarni Aðalbjarnarson. Reykjavík: 1979. Pp. 210–37.

TRANSLATION

Snorri Sturluson. *Heimskringla: History of the Kings of Norway by Snorri Sturluson.* Transl. Lee M. Hollander. Austin: 2005. Pp. 668–87.

Marcarius and the Magicians, Saul and the Witch of Endor
Ælfric. "Marcarius and the Magicians, Saul and the Witch of Endor." In vol. 2 of *Homilies of Ælfric: A Supplementary Collection.* Ed. John Collins Pope. Early English Text Society, 259. London and New York: 1967. Pp. 786–98.

Norges gamle Love
Norges gamle Love indtil 1387. Ed. Rudolf Keyser and Peter Andreas Munch. Christiania: 1846–1895.

TRANSLATION

The Earliest Norwegian Laws: Being the Gulathing Law and the Frostathing Law. Transl. Laurence M. Larson. 1935.

Óláfs saga Tryggvasonar

Íslenzk fornrit, 28. Ed. Bjarni Aðalbjarnarson. Reykjavík: 1979. Pp. 225–372.

TRANSLATION

Snorri Sturluson. Heimskringla: History of the Kings of Norway by Snorri Sturluson. Transl. Lee M. Hollander. Austin: 2005. Pp. 144–244.

Passio Sancti Eadmundi

Abbo of Fleury. Corolla Sancti Eadmundi. The Garland of Saint Edmund, King and Martyr. Ed. and transl. Lord Francis Hervey. London: 1907. Pp. 10–59.

Poetic Edda

Edda: Die Lieder des Codex regius nebst verwandten Denkmälern. Ed. Gustav Neckel and Hans Kuhn. Germanische Bibliothek. 5th rev. ed. Heidelberg: C. Winter, 1983.

TRANSLATION

The Poetic Edda. Transl. Carolyne Larrington. Oxford World's Classics. 2nd ed. Oxford: 2014.

Sagan om Sankt Dionysius

In vol. 1 of Ett Forn-Svenskt Legendarium, innehållande Medeltids Kloster-Sagor om Helgon, Påfvar och Kejsare ifrån det 1:sta till det XIII: de Århundradet. Ed. George Stephens and F.A. Dahlgren. Svenska Fornskrift-Sällskapets Samlingar, 7. Stockholm: 1847–1874. Pp. 339–345.

Speculum lapidum

Camillus Leonardi. Les pierres talismaniques: Speculum lapidum, livre III. Ed. and transl. Claude Lecouteux and Anne Monfort. Traditions & Croyances. Paris: 2003.

Stenbog

Henrik Harpestræng. In Gamle danske Urtebøger, Stenbøger og Kogebøger. Ed. Marius Kristensen. Universitets-Jubilæets danske Samfund. Copenhagen: 1908. Pp. 174–93 (Ny kgl. Saml. 66, 8vo).

Stenbok

Peder Månssons skrifter på svenska. Ed. Robert Geete. Svenska Fornskrift-Sällskapets Samlingar, 43. Stockholm: 1913–1915. Pp. 457–530.

Sigrdrífumál: see *Poetic Edda*

Víga-Glúms saga
Íslenzk fornrit, 9. Ed. Jónas Kristjánsson. Reykjavík: 1956. Pp. 1–98.

TRANSLATION

"Killer-Glum's Saga." Transl. John McKinnell. In vol. 2 of *The Complete Sagas of Icelanders*. Reykjavík: 1997. Pp. 267–327.

Vǫlsa þáttr
"Vǫlsa þáttr." In *Stories from the Sagas of the Kings, with Introduction, Notes and Glossary*. Ed. Anthony Faulkes. London: 1980. Pp. 51–61.

Vǫluspá: see *Poetic Edda*

Ynglinga saga
Íslenzk fornrit, 26. Ed. Bjarni Aðalbjarnarson. Reykjavík: 1979. Pp. 9–83.

TRANSLATION

Snorri Sturluson. *Heimskringla: History of the Kings of Norway by Snorri Sturluson*. Transl. Lee M. Hollander. Austin: 2005. Pp. 6–50.

Þorleifs þáttr jarlsskálds
Íslenzk fornrit, 9. Ed. Jónas Kristjánsson. Reykjavík: 1956. Pp. 215–29.

TRANSLATION

"The Tale of Thorleif, the Earl's Poet." Transl. Judith Jesch. In vol. 1 of *The Complete Sagas of Icelanders*. Reykjavík: 1997. Pp. 362–69.

þorsteins þáttr uxafóts
Íslenzk fornrit, 13. Ed. Þórhallur Vilmundarson and Bjarni Vilhjálmsson. Reykjavík: 1991. Pp. 341–70.

TRANSLATION

"The Tale of Thorstein Bull's-Leg." Transl. George Clark. In vol. 4 of *The Complete Sagas of Icelanders*. Reykjavík: 1997. Pp. 340–54.

Secondary Sources

Ahola, Joonas. 2014. *Outlawry in the Icelandic Family Sagas*. PhD diss., University of Helsinki.

Almgren, Oscar. 1903. "Ett guldmynt från en Gotländsk graf." In *Studier tillägnade Oscar Montelius, 1903 af lärjungar*. Stockholm. Pp. 89–98.

Ármann Jakobsson. 2011. "Vampires and Watchmen: Categorizing the Mediaeval Icelandic Undead." *Journal of English and Germanic Philology* 110: 281–300.

Baert, Barbara, Anita Traninger, and Catrien Santing, eds. 2013. *Disembodied Heads in Medieval and Early Modern Culture*. Intersections, 28. Leiden.

Brix, Hans. 1943. "Oldtidens og Middelalderens Litteratur i Danmark." In *Litteraturhistoria. A. Danmark, Finland och Sverige*. Ed. Sigurður Nordal. Nordisk Kultur, 8A. Stockholm. Pp. 3–63.

Bugge, Sophus. 1881–1889. *Studier over de nordiske Gude- og Heltesagns Oprindelse*. Christiania.

The Catholic Encyclopedia: An International Work of Reference. 2003. New York. Orig. pub. 1917. http://www.newadvent.org/cathen/ (accessed on October 23, 2011).

Chadwick, Nora K. 1946. "Norse Ghosts (A Study in the *Draugr* and the *Haugbúi*)." *Folklore* 57: 50–65, 106–27.

Clarke, D. E. Martin. 1923. *The Hávamál, with Selections from Other Poems of the Edda, Illustrating the Wisdom of the North in Heathen Times*. Cambridge.

Cleasby, Richard, and Gudbrand Vigfusson, eds. 1982. *An Icelandic-English Dictionary*. 2nd ed. With a supplement by Sir William A. Craigie. Oxford.

Cohen, Esther. 2013. "The Meaning of the Head in High Medieval Culture." In Baert, Traninger, and Santing 2013: 59–76.

Davidson, H. R. Ellis. 1943. *The Road to Hel: A Study of the Conception of the Dead in Old Norse Literature*. Cambridge.

———. 1988. *Myths and Symbols in Pagan Europe: Early Scandinavian and Celtic Religions*. Manchester.

Davidson, H. R. Ellis, and Peter Fisher. 1980. *Saxo Grammaticus: The History of the Danes*. Vol. 2: *Commentary*. Cambridge.

Egeler, Matthias. 2013. *Celtic Influences in Germanic Religion: A Survey*. Münchner nordistische Studien, 15. Munich.

Falk, Hjalmar. 1924. *Odensheite*. Skrifter utg. av Videnskabsselskapet i Kristiania. 2, Historisk-filosofisk klasse 1924, 10. Christiania.

Fritzner, Johan. 1973. *Ordbok over Det gamle norske Sprog*. 4th rev. ed. Oslo.

Fuglesang, Signe Horn. 1989. "Viking and Medieval Amulets in Scandinavia." *Fornvännen* 84: 15–27.

Gardeła, Leszek, and Kamil Kajkowski, eds. 2013. *Motyw głowy w dawnych kulturach w perspektywie porównawczej/The Head Motif in Past Societies in a Comparative Perspective*. International Interdisciplinary Meetings "Motifs through the Ages", 1. Bytów.

Grabka, Gregory. 1953. "Christian Viaticum: A Study of Its Cultural Background." *Traditio* 9: 1–43.

Gräslund, Anne-Sofie. 1965–1966. "Charonsmynt i vikingatida gravar?" *Tor* 11: 168–97.

Grinsell, Levi V. 1957. "The Ferryman and His Fee: A Study in Ethnology, Archaeology, and Tradition." *Folklore* 68 (1): 257–69.

Gunnell, Terry. 2012. "Waking the Dead: Folk Legends Concerning Magicians and Walking Corpses in Iceland." In *News from Other Worlds: Studies in Nordic Folklore, Mythology and Culture in Honor of John F. Lindow*. Ed. Merrill Kaplan and Timothy R. Tangherlini. Occasional Monograph Series (Wildcat Canyon Advanced Seminars), 1. Berkeley. Pp. 235–66.

Halvorsen, Eyvind Fjeld. 1982. "Mimir el. *Mímr*." In *Kulturhistorisk leksikon for nordisk middelalder fra vikingetid til reformasjonstid*. Ed. Johannes Brøndsted et al., 11: 629–30. Copenhagen.

Harris, Joseph. 1985. "Eddic Poetry." In *Old Norse-Icelandic Literature: A Critical Guide*. Ed. Carol Clover and John Lindow. Islandica, 45. Ithaca. Pp. 68–156.

Holst, M. K., J. Heinemeier, et al. Forthcoming. "Direct Evidence of a Large North European Roman Time Martial Event and Post Battle Corpse Manipulation." *Proceedings of the National Academy of Sciences*.

Jacobsson, Bengt. 2002. *Pestbacken: En begravningsplats för pestoffer från åren 1710 och 1711, Blekinge, Olofströms kommun, Jämshögs socken, Holje 5:68 och 5:69*. Rapport/UV Syd, 2002: 15. Lund.

Jespersen, Poul Helveg. 1938. "Sneglen i digtning, tale og folketro." *Danske Studier* 1938: 147–64.

Kanerva, Kirsi. 2011. "The Role of the Dead in Medieval Iceland: A Case Study of *Eyrbyggja Saga*." *Collegium Medievale* 24: 23–49.

———. 2013. "Rituals for the Restless Dead: The Authority of the Deceased in Medieval Iceland." In *Authorities in the Middle Ages: Influence, Legitimacy, and Power in Medieval Society*. Ed. Sini Kangas, Mia Korpiola, and Tuija Ainonen. Fundamentals of Medieval and Early Modern Culture, 12. Berlin. Pp. 201–23.

Kieckhefer, Richard. 1990. *Magic in the Middle Ages*. Cambridge.

———. 1997. *Forbidden Rites: A Necromancer's Manual of the Fifteenth Century*. University Park, PA.

Klare, Hans-Joachim. 1933–1934. "Die Toten in der altnordischen Literatur." *Acta Philologica Scandinavica* 8: 1–56.

Kragerud, Alv. 1981. "De mytologiske spørsmål i Fåvnesmål." *Arkiv för nordisk filologi* 96: 9–48.

Kroeber, Alfred L., and Lila M. O'Neale. 1926. *Archaeological Explorations in Peru*. Field Museum of Natural History. Anthropology Memoirs 2: 1–4. Chicago.

Larsson, Lars-Olof. 1975. *Den helige Sigfrid: I kult, legend och verklighet*. Växjö.

Lindow, John. 1983. *Scandinavian Mythology: A Bibliography*. Garland Reference Library of the Humanities, 394. New York.

———. 2001. *Handbook of Norse Mythology*. Handbooks of World Mythology. Santa Barbara, CA.

Lobell, Jarrett A. 2012. "The Bog Army." *Archaeology* 65 (6): 14.

Lucas, Gavin, and Thomas McGovern. 2007. "Bloody Slaughter: Ritual Decapitation and Display at the Viking Settlement of Hofstaðir, Iceland." *European Journal of Archaeology* 10 (1): 7–30.

Lundén, Tryggve. 1967. "Medeltidens religiösa litteratur." In *Ny illustrerad svensk litteraturhistoria*. 2nd rev. ed. Ed. E. N. Tigerstedt and Erik Hjalma Linder. Stockholm. Pp. 122–222.

McKinnell, John. 2007. "Wisdom from the Dead: The *Ljóðatal* section of *Hávamál*." *Medium Aevum* 76 (1): 85–115.

Mitchell, Stephen A. 2007. "*Skírnismál* and Nordic Charm Magic." In *Reflections on Old Norse Myths*. Ed. Pernille Hermann, Jens Peter Schjødt, and Rasmus Tranum Kristensen. Viking and Medieval Scandinavia Studies, 1. Turnhout. Pp. 75–94.

———. 2008a. "Spirituality and Alchemy in *Den vises sten* (1379)." In *Lärdomber oc skämptan: Medieval Swedish Literature Reconsidered*. Ed. Massimiliano Bampi and Fulvio Ferrari. Svenska Fornskrift-Sällskapets Samlingar Serie, 3. Smärre texter och undersökningar, 5. Uppsala. Pp. 97–108.

———. 2008b. "The n-Rune and Nordic Charms." In *"Vi ska alla vara välkomna!" Nordiska studier tillägnade Kristinn Jóhannesson*. Ed. Auður G. Magnúsdóttir et al. Göteborg. Pp. 219–29.

———. 2009. "The Supernatural and the *fornaldarsögur*: The Case of *Ketils saga hœngs*." In *Fornaldarsagaerne: Myter og virkelighed: Studier i de oldislandske fornaldarsögur Norðurlanda*. ed. Agneta Ney, Ármann Jakobsson, and Annette Lassen, 281–98. Copenhagen.

———. 2011. *Witchcraft and Magic in the Nordic Middle Ages*. Philadelphia.

Museum Skanderborg. 2013. "Alken Enge—The Mass Grave at Lake Mossø." http://www.skanderborgmuseum.dk/Alken_Enge-English_version-1070.aspx (accessed on July 13, 2014)

Nedkvitne, Arnved. 2003. *Møtet med døden i norrøn middelalder: En mentalitetshistorisk studie*. 2nd ed. Oslo.

Nordberg, Andreas. 2004. *Krigarna i Odins sal: Dödsförestallningar och krigarkult i fornnordisk religion*. PhD diss., Stockholm University. 2nd ed. Orig. pub. 2003.

Ohlmarks, Åke. 1936. "Totenerweckungen in Eddaliedern." *Arkiv för nordisk filologi* 52: 264–97.

Patton, Kimberley C. 2009. *Religion of the Gods: Ritual, Paradox, and Reflexivity*. Oxford.

Persson, Charlotte Price. 2014. "Barbarisk fund: Vores forfædre bar ligrester på kæppe." *Videnskab dk*: July 30. http://videnskab.dk/kultur-samfund/barbarisk-fund-vores-forfaedre-bar-ligrester-pa-kaeppe (accessed on August 1, 2014).

Pipping, Rolf. 1928. *Oden i galgen*. Studier i nordisk filologi, 18: 2. Skrifter utgivna av Svenska litteratursällskapet i Finland, 197. Helsinki.

Price, Neil. Forthcoming. *Odin's Whisper: Death and the Vikings*. London.

Rosén, Helge Ossian. 1918. *Om dödsrike och dödsbruk i fornnordisk religion*. Lund.

Rydberg, Viktor. 1886. *Undersökningar i germanisk mythologi*. Stockholm.

Schjødt, Jens Peter. 2008. *Initiation between Two Worlds: Structure and Symbolism in Pre-Christian Scandinavian Religion*. The Viking Collection, 17. Odense.

Schmid, Toni. 1931. *Den helige Sigfrid*. Lund.

Science Nordic. 2012. "An Entire Army Sacrificed in a Bog." http://sciencenordic.com/printpdf/1490 (accessed on August 1, 2014)

von See, Klaus et al., eds. 1997-. *Kommentar zu den Liedern der Edda*. Heidelberg.

Sigurður Nordal. 1927. *Völuspá = Vølvens spådom*. Transl. Hans Albrectsen. Copenhagen.

Simek, Rudolf. 1993. *Dictionary of Northern Mythology*. Cambridge.

Simpson, Jacqueline. 1963–64. "Mímir: Two Myths or One?" *Saga-Book* 16 (1): 41–53.

Shetelig, Haakon. 1908. "Færgepengen. Spor av en græsk gravskik i Norge." In *Sproglige og historiske afhandlinger viede Sophus Bugges minde*. Ed. Magnus Olsen. Christiania. Pp. 1–7.

Spiegel, Gabrielle M. 1983. "The Cult of St. Denis and Capetian Kingship." In *Saints and Their Cults: Studies in Religious Sociology, Folklore, and History*. Ed. Stephen Wilson. Cambridge. Pp. 141–68.

Stevens, Susan T. 1991. "Charon's Obol and Other Coins in Ancient Funerary Practice." *Phoenix* 45 (3): 215–29.

Stjerna, Knut. 1912. *Essays on Questions Connected with the Old English Poem of Beowulf*. Transl. John R. Clark Hall. Viking Club Extra Series, 3. Coventry.

Ström, Folke. 1947. *Den döendes makt och Odin i trädet*. Göteborgs hogskolas årsskrift, 53: 1. Göteborg.

Sundqvist, Olof. 2009. "The Hanging, the Nine Nights and the 'Precious Knowledge' in *Hávamál* 138–145: The Cultic Context." In *Analecta Septentrionalia: Beiträge zur nordgermanischen Kultur- und Literaturgeschichte*. Ed. Wilhelm Heizmann et al. Ergänzungsbände zum Reallexikon der germanischen Altertumskunde, 65. Berlin. Pp. 649–68.

———. 2010. "Om hängningen, de nio nätterna och den dyrköpta kunskapen i *Hávamál* 138–145—den kultiska kontexten." *Scripta Islandica* 61: 68–96.

Thompson, Stith, ed. 1966. *Motif-Index of Folk-Literature: A Classification of Narrative Elements in Folktales, Ballads, Myths, Fables, Mediaeval Romances, Exempla, Fabliaux, Jest-Books and Local Legends.* Rev. ed. Bloomington.

Tolley, Clive. 2009. *Shamanism in Norse Myth and Magic.* Folklore Fellows Communications, 296. Helsinki.

Tracy, Larissa, and Jeff Massey, eds. 2012. *Heads Will Roll: Decapitation in the Medieval and Early Modern Imagination.* Medieval and Renaissance Authors and Texts, 7. Leiden.

Vésteinn Ólason. 2003. "The Un/Grateful Dead—From Baldr to Bægifótr." In *Old Norse Myths, Literature and Society.* Ed. Margaret Clunies-Ross. The Viking Collection. Studies in Northern Civilization, 14. Odense. Pp. 153–71.

de Vries, Jan. 1956–57. *Altgermanische Religionsgeschichte.* 2 vols. 2nd rev. ed. Grundriss der germanischen Philologie, 12. Berlin.

Wolff, Samuel R. 2002. "Mortuary Practices in the Persian Period of the Levant." *Near Eastern Archaeology* (special issue, *The Archaeology of Death*) 65 (2): 131–37.

Zoëga, Geir T. 1975. *A Concise Dictionary of Old Icelandic.* Oxford.

Vermin Gone Bad in Medieval Scandinavian, Persian, and Irish Traditions

Joseph Falaky Nagy
Harvard University

Abstract: The tales in medieval Scandinavian literature centered on the legendary entrepreneur Ragnarr loðbrók, his wives, and his sons famously feature several serpentine motifs. The narrative construct of a family literally and metaphorically bound together by dragon-like creatures under the control of a daughter, wife, or mother is also to be found in Iranian and Irish storytelling tradition. The parallels point to a genetic mythological relationship among these (in other respects) disparate stories, whose deep-seated affinity cannot be explained on the basis of intercultural borrowing.

Introduction

The cycle of stories about Ragnarr loðbrók and his sons is one of the most celebrated and written-about narratives in medieval Scandinavian tradition. Told in multiform versions in Saxo's *Gesta Danorum* (History of the Danes), the Icelandic *Ragnars saga loðbrókar*, a *þáttr* about Ragnarr's sons, and a Faroese ballad, *Ragnars kvæði*,[1] this narrative complex employs many of the elements that call for analysis in terms of mythology: a serpent equipped with a story of how he came to be a monster; a strong-willed woman who determines the destinies of the man who marries her and his sons, the latter including characters whose distinctive physical features signify unusual powers; the conquest of territories and the founding of royal dynasties; and memorable heroic as well as ignominious deaths.

---

[1] McTurk 1991: 53–61 and especially Rowe 2012 provide inventories of the sources for surviving texts about and references to Ragnarr and his family, including historical figures of the ninth century who perhaps loom in the background of this story cycle, and to whom the traditional or "mythological" features of this cycle became attached.

In an article published in 1941, the American scholar of traditional narrative Alexander Krappe noted the appearance of a distinctive story pattern in this Ragnarr material, as well as in an episode from the medieval Persian compendium of myth and legend, the *Shahnameh* (Book of Kings) attributed to Ferdowsi, and also in a bizarre back-story tucked away in an Early Modern Irish prose text featuring heroes from the so-called Fenian cycle, *Tóruigheacht Dhiarmada agus Ghráinne* (Pursuit of Diarmaid and Gráinne), or TDG, as we shall refer to it henceforth. Krappe observed that all three sources, as well as various other Old- and New-World traditional narratives cited in his article, feature a worm or small serpent that, nurtured by a female (usually), grows to monstrous size and becomes a ravenous dragonlike creature, so threatening as virtually to invite a hero to come and slay it. Krappe's thesis is that the story originated in the Middle East and migrated to Scandinavia, carried by a well-traveled Viking, and thence to Ireland, via the substantial Scandinavian presence on the island in the late first and early second millennium CE (Krappe 1941).

In what follows, I will expand on Krappe's foray among the Persian, Scandinavian, and Irish texts to show that there are possibly even more important parallels and connections to be found among the stories than what Krappe outlined.[2] While the links in the chain of transmission he proposed are credible, the multiformity of the shared story-elements we will be examining from three very different (sets of) sources suggests that these elements underwent parallel processes of adaptation in these different narrative traditions over an extended period of time. I would argue that in the three instances to be discussed, and no doubt in other instances that deserve discussion in the future, this widely disseminated story pattern centered on a worm or serpent (or even a maggot) that "goes bad" under female auspices is in fact part of a more extensive pattern—inherited, I suspect, from the Indo-European heritage of myth, the mother-lode from which all three traditions in question, scholarship has repeatedly shown, derived much of their story-lore.

In addition to a worm, each of our tales features the following elements or motifs that together constitute a narrative pattern deeply embedded in the tale's structure:

- The woman who protects the worm and indulges its increasingly noisome habits is a powerful figure with control over more than just the destiny of the worm. In fact, she is the controlling force of the story itself. Scholars of medieval Scandinavian literature have detected this

---

[2] See also Nagy 2015. Important data and observations concerning "bosom serpents," narrative kindred of the anguine creatures examined here, are now to be found in Ermacora, Labanti, and Marcon 2016.

motif and followed its ramifications in the Ragnarr material,[3] particularly in regard to the character of Kráka/Áslaug/Randalín, but we shall see that this story-device is equally noticeable in our *comparanda* from beyond Scandinavia.

- The magnification of the worm's impact, helpful or harmful, is inextricably bound up with the relationship between a parent and a child. Moreover, the consequences of what the worm does, or what is done to it, redound throughout the life of the main human figure in the story (whether "hero" or "villain") and even extend into the next generation. Here again, there has been scholarly appreciation of the importance of intergenerational (dis)continuity in the Ragnarr cycle, especially in light of the dynastic and genealogical origin legends it accommodates, but the motif is to be found in the Irish and Persian narrative material as well.

- The worm and sometimes the characters who become involved with it play "hide and seek" in the course of the story, concealing and yet also revealing themselves in pivotal situations. The intentional or unintentional act of perceiving what or who is hidden can upset the distribution of power between the seer and the seen.

- The character who benefits from the results of the worm's "going bad", sometimes the hero who has to slay the monster-worm in order to achieve his goal, exhibits an entrepreneurial, mercantile, or even devious side to his narrative persona, which runs counter to a martial-heroic ethos.

The following are sketches of the salient details of the three narratives. I will begin with the Irish, not because it deserves primacy of place in this investigation but because it is where this Celticist first encountered the story pattern we are attempting to elucidate.

The Irish Tradition

The late medieval author of TDG, our main literary source for a tale that lived on into Irish and Scottish oral tradition of recent times, could not resist the temptation to repeatedly sidetrack his reader/listener with stories that delve into the past of his characters and expand upon the background of the main tale that TDG tells. Preserved in a manuscript written in 1651, the earliest surviving version of this text lacks a conclusion, but the authorial interest in

---

[3]   E.g., McTurk 2007 and Larrington 2011.

back-stories, which almost pushes the text into the category of frame tale, is amply on display.[4] The core narrative of TDG centers on Diarmaid ua Duibhne, the "star" of the aging hero Fionn mac Cumhaill's war-band, and what happens to him after he is honor bound by Fionn's young bride, the headstrong Gráinne (daughter of Cormac, the high-king of Ireland), to elope with her.[5]

The particular narrative excursion in which we find our serpentine pattern is actually a prequel to a prequel. It is a strange account that to my knowledge is told nowhere else in extant Irish literature. The story unfolds as follows:

Fionn, humiliated by Gráinne's having left him on their wedding night to run away with the most valuable member of his team, furiously pursues the couple, sometimes sending forth others to conduct the vengeful pursuit on his behalf. Among these is a pair of brothers, seeking not only to make peace with Fionn, whom their father had helped to slay, but also to join Fionn's band of heroes, the *fian*. Fionn imposes upon them as the condition for their acceptance into the band that they fetch either Diarmaid's head *or* a handful of berries from a magical rowan tree guarded by a one-eyed giant. The brothers encounter Diarmaid and declare their intent. He explains to the rookie warriors that they are between a rock and a hard place. Not only would it be impossible for such newcomers to the heroic arena to overcome him, but they would also be incapable of overcoming the giant guarding the tree. Diarmaid, in addition to telling the brothers the story of why the rowan tree has a monstrous guardian, also points out to his would-be opponents that this is not the first time Fionn has deviously drawn those whom he perceives to be his enemies into what most likely will turn out to be a suicide mission. Diarmaid recounts a comparable situation from the past, back when he was still a trusted member of Fionn's retinue.

A warrior named Conán, the son of the Liath Luachra, yet another mortal enemy of Fionn's deceased father, comes to Fionn seeking reconciliation. The price dictated, in this case, is for Conán to bring Fionn a head of the multi-headed, overgrown "worm" (the word used is *cnuimh*, a variant of the more common *cruimh*) which used to dwell in the head of Cian, son of Oilill Ólum and his wife Sadhbh. (This Oilill, or Ailill, is said in earlier texts to have been a king of the province of Munster, but in TDG he is not specifically so described.)

---

[4]   The edition/translation relied upon here is TDG I, with occasional reference to TDG II, a different edition. On the textual history of TDG, see Breatnach 2012.

[5]   For a discussion of the text and an account of the long-lived tradition about this particular love-triangle, see Ó Cathasaigh 2014. Lawrence Eson contextualizes another strand of the medieval Fionn cycle, wherein he leaves behind the unhappy union with Gráinne and engages in a much more successful relationship with Gráinne's sister, Ailbe (Eson 2014).

Diarmaid, at this point in his narration, inserts the story explaining how Cian came to have a worm in his head—quoting *verbatim*, he claims, from the account that Oisín, the son of Fionn, gave to Conán at the time.

Approaching a branch full of sloes, the pregnant Sadhbh, Oilill's wife, riding with her husband in his chariot, is overwhelmed by a craving for the berries. Wishing to satisfy her, Oilill shakes the branch, and she thus obtains her fill of the fruit. Later, when their child is born (named Cian), a protuberance is found on his forehead that grows as he matures. Embarrassed by his deformity, the mature Cian swaddles his head so that the bump will be less noticeable. When he is in need of barbering, Cian slays anyone who, undoing the wrapping, shaves him and/or cuts his hair—in order to keep the unseemly growth on his head a secret.

Like King Midas's donkey ears,[6] Cian's deformity and the contents of his bump do not remain hidden forever. Once, when seeking to pay back Sgáthán, a member of Fionn's band of heroes for an insulting lack of hospitality shown to Cian's servant (who has maliciously misrepresented what Sgáthán did and said), Cian invites himself to Sgáthán's home for a shave and a haircut. Not intimidated by the murderous intent of his guest, who is well known for slaying his barbers, Sgáthán not only removes the covering from Cian's head but, insouciantly expressing his curiosity about what lies therein, slashes the now-exposed swelling with his knife. Out jumps a large worm, leaping onto and winding itself tightly around the top of Cian's spear nearby. Reluctant simply to let Sgáthán kill the beast (as Oilill, his father, advises), Cian asks his mother what should be done, since, as he states, the worm (like Cian himself) came from her womb (presumably, as a result of her having eaten the berries). Sadhbh confirms Cian's suspicion that the worm may have an intimate connection with the lifespan of its uterine mate, so that to kill it, she says, may be to harm Cian as well. Hence, the family decides to keep the worm in a box, feeding it to keep it (and by extension Cian) alive.

The worm in time grows too big for the box, and so a house is built for it. It grows a hundred voracious heads, each big enough to swallow an armed man whole. Hearing of this marvel, Cian's foster brother, the son of the king who raised Cian,[7] comes for a visit, seeking to view the monster. As he does so,

---

[6] The tale type represented by the Midas legend (ATU 782) is mentioned by Krappe as one of the likely sources for elements of the story of the furtive Cian (1941: 329). Máirtín Ó Briain presents the instances of and variations on "Midas and the Donkey's Ears" in Irish tradition, medieval and modern (Ó Briain 1985).

[7] In TDG II it is Cian's royal foster father himself who comes for a visit, wishing to see the beast, and is attacked (p. 130).

the worm takes note (or takes offense?),[8] lunges, and savagely tears off one of the foster brother's legs. Consequently, all the women and lesser members of the household, who presumably had been tending to the creature, flee in panic from the worm's house. This turning-point incident makes it clear to everyone that the creature engendered by Sadhbh's craving has become an unmanageable monster. The insult and injury done to Cian's royal kinsman prove too much even for Cian's mother, who now agrees with her husband and son that the worm must be killed. But how? Turning to a deceitful though sometimes unsuccessful ploy practiced in Celtic (and Norse) storytelling tradition against enemies too fearsome to be confronted directly,[9] Cian's people set the house of the worm on fire, hoping to burn the monster to death. Defeating their expectations with a leap even more spectacular than that with which he erupted out of Cian's head, the worm escapes from the flames and lands far away near a cave in which it subsequently lurks—a lair that even the monster-slaying Fionn and his men are loath to approach, for fear of the hard-to-kill worm.

Oisín's story (as relayed by Diarmaid) does not dissuade the courageous Conán from accepting Fionn's challenge to confront the worm. He in fact succeeds in killing it (as Diarmaid narrates, picking up where Oisín's narrative leaves off), although the feat is accomplished with Diarmaid's special spear, loaned by its owner to Conán.[10] Unfortunately, returning to Fionn with one of the heads of the monster as a trophy of his triumph, the worm-slayer and his plea for reconciliation are still rejected by the stubborn Fionn, who demands even more compensation. This tense moment is interrupted by the approach of a deer, which Fionn and Conán set out to pursue. (Oisín prevents the rest of the *fían* from joining them.) After they return, with Conán carrying the spoils of their successful hunt, Fionn "níor iarr Fionn éraic ar bith ar Conán ó sin a leith [...] Ni fheadamar féin in dá aimhdheóin ro bhean Conán síth d'Fhionn an lá sin" (TDG I p. 64) (did not ask any other compensation from that afterwards [...] We do not know whether it was [against Fionn's will] that Conán gained peace from Fionn that day (TDG I p. 65)).[11]

---

[8] The looking definitely goes both ways: "Mar táinic don bhaile do chuaidh d'fhéachain na cnuimhe ós a cionn, 7 mar do airigh an chnumh é tuc sidhe neimhneach neamh-eglach fair" (And when he [that is, the foster brother] went to see the worm from above, and when the worm noticed him it gave a deadly fearless swoop on him (TDG I pp. 62–64)).

[9] For comparable instances, see "The Iron House, the Men in Bags, and the Severed Head," in Sims-Williams 2011: 262–86 (esp. pp. 262–77).

[10] No other weapon could have slain the monster, Diarmaid proudly claims (TDG II p. 133).

[11] In an older Fenian text, the early-thirteenth-century *Acallam na Senórach* (Dialogue of the Ancients), we learn, according to a worm-less account of the story of Conán's acceptance into Fionn's band, that Conán ambushed Fionn when he was alone, and forced him to accept an offer to make peace—the only time, we are told, that Fionn was ever coerced into coming to terms with an enemy (*Acallam na Senórach* pp. 101–2). On this account, see Nagy 2014.

Whether Diarmaid, having told this story, would have been able to dissuade the brothers from pursuing their quest with the *exemplum* of Conán (perhaps not the best case to cite, since it ends in success for *that* seeker), we will never know for certain. His lover Gráinne, overhearing the conversation between Diarmaid and the young seekers, inquires about the rowan tree from which they are supposed to obtain fruit. Once she hears the story Diarmaid retells about the tree and its guardian (information the brothers, and the audience of TDG, already have), Gráinne, announcing her pregnancy in the story for the first time, insists that she must have some of the berries too—a craving that her man must satisfy, just as Oilill satisfied Sadhbh's craving. Hence, the alternative mission assigned to the brothers, to fetch the fruit of the special rowan tree, has become Diarmaid's task, and those who came seeking to fight with Diarmaid can now rely upon him to do the heavy lifting. After he slays the tree-guardian, there are plenty of berries for everyone. Diarmaid instructs the brothers, now his veritable protégés, to return to Fionn with the fruit and with the false story that they themselves slew the giant. Diarmaid and Gráinne, meanwhile, take shelter in the top of the tree, where the berries are sweetest. Fionn, upon receiving the berries from the brothers, detects the scent of Diarmaid on the fruit and deduces who actually performed the valiant feat. He sets out for the rowan tree himself, bringing the story closer to the climactic encounter between the betrayed husband and his wife's reluctant lover hiding in the tree.

The Persian Tradition

The following is a summary of Ferdowsi's account of the Irish invertebrate's less nasty but equally troublesome distant cousin (*Shahnameh* pp. 544–53).[12] We recall that, according to Krappe, the *Shahnameh* (older than the other texts we are considering) presents us with what may be the most direct surviving descendant of the prototype of the worm story he hypothesizes to have taken shape in the Middle East.

The daughter of an insignificant poor man named Haftvād (Having Seven Sons) finds a worm in an apple she had started to eat at the beginning of the task of spinning her daily portion of cotton. Cinderella-like in relation to her father, who presumably is interested only in his sons after whom he is named, the girl

---

[12]   Alireza Shahbazi examines the legendary figure of Haftvād (Shahbazi 2002), while Kinga Márkus-Takeshita offers a folkloristic analysis of the story, paying special attention to the figure of the supernaturally-aided spinner, comparable to the heroine of the folktale type "Rapunzel" (ATU 310) (Márkus-Takeshita 2001).

My heartfelt thanks go to Dr. Elizabeth Thornton, my colleague in the GE 30 "Neverending Stories" UCLA cluster course, for having introduced me to the stories of Haftvād and Zahhak in her lectures to the class on Persian mythology.

invokes the worm as her good-luck charm to help her to be as industrious and productive as possible. The worm fulfills her wish, and, keeping the creature in her spindle-case and feeding it daily with pieces of the apple, the (unnamed) girl becomes the source of great wealth for her father and brothers. With the riches he wins through his daughter's industry (which in turn is predicated on the worm), Haftvād hires soldiers and has an impregnable fortress built for himself, his family, and the vermian "pet" on a mountaintop. His growing worm-based power starts to threaten even the monarch of the land where Haftvād dwells, the Persian king Ardeshir. In his home on high, Haftvād leaves the task of caring for the worm to his daughter, who found it in the first place, as well as to the other females in the household, while the increasingly omnivorous worm grows to be as big as an elephant.

Ardeshir, thwarted in his military attempts to suppress Haftvād's insurgency, turns to deceit, knowing that eliminating the worm is the only way he can keep his throne. Stooping to the degradation of disguising himself and some trusted companions as merchants, the king gains entrance into the worm-fort and asks to see the wondrous creature that he has heard resides there. Allowed into the worm's presence, and slyly plying the guards with a surfeit of wine, Ardeshir and company are free to kill the worm by "feeding" it molten metal. With Haftvād's good-luck charm eliminated, Ardeshir returns to being the unchallenged sovereign of his realm.

The Old Norse Tradition

In linking together the stories we are considering in this essay, Krappe, who added Cian's internalized worm to the narrative mix, was following the findings of an earlier comparative folklorist, Felix Liebrecht, who had noticed the parallel between the Persian *nouveau riche* despot's luck-bringing *kerm* "worm" featured in Ferdowsi's *Shahnameh* and the serpent(s) slain by the young Ragnarr (Liebrecht 1862). It is to his story that we now turn, relying on *Ragnars saga loðbrókar*.

Ragnarr, the son of the king of Denmark, wins a wife and a fortune in gold after slaying a snake grown monstrously large under the care of Þóra, the daughter of a wealthy man. The latter had given the girl a serpent (*lyng-ormr* "heather-snake", *ormr* being cognate with Irish *cnuimh/cruimh*, Persian *kerm*, and English *worm*) as a token of his paternal affection. (The creature is still small and very pretty.) Þóra, in her own dwelling built specially for her by her father, places the creature on top of some gold in a box. The pile of precious metal subsequently increases in mystical sympathy with the pampered snake, which gradually outgrows the box and even the girl's private quarters, encircling it and becoming an unfriendly, ravenous nuisance.

The father offers the double reward of his daughter and the gold to anyone who can kill the monster. As in the Persian and Irish analogs, cleverness and concealment are required in the encounter with this wormlike serpent-turned-beast, nestled around the girl's bower. Applying a combination of pitch and sand to his pants and cape, Ragnarr invents a way to make his clothes resistant to the flood of venomous blood that erupts after he kills the snake. He also thereby wins the nickname *loðbrók* "Shaggy Pants".

Many years after his youthful triumph, and long after the death of Þóra, the slaying of whose out-of-control pet launched his heroic career, other deadly serpents, both metaphorical and literal, slither into the last chapters of Ragnarr's life. He decides to invade England in order to win fame as impressive and lasting as that of his sons, who are noted for their raiding far and wide. Against the advice of his second wife Randalín (earlier known, we shall see, as Áslaug/Kráka), Ragnarr orders the building of two titanic merchant ships (*kneirr*)[13] in which to convey his invading force, instead of relying upon more conventional (and smaller) battle-ready craft. Seemingly, Ragnarr's plan is to hide his intentions, and his men, by approaching the island on what he refers to poetically as his "snakes of the sea" (*Ragnars saga* p. 236).[14] The ships, however, are wrecked on the English coastline, and the invasion proves a failure. The captured Ragnarr is thrown by the king of England into a snake-pit, where he dies from poisonous bites after his captors remove the magical talisman-shirt given to him by his wife, Randalín, who had made it out of (her own?) hair.

As the arc of Ragnarr's career unfolds, climaxing grimly in the snake-pit, the shadow of the monster-worm falls upon the next wave of family members to rise in prominence in the saga—in particular upon the character whom some consider the main protagonist of the story, namely, the woman who succeeds Þóra at Ragnarr's side. In what cannot be considered a coincidence, this, his second wife, is the daughter of the celebrated dragon-slayer Sigurðr, a girl who, hidden in a harp specially built by her foster-father to hide her and her family's treasure, is rescued from danger by the foster-father, only to fall *incognita* into the hands of a churlish couple. After murdering her foster-father, this ugly pair finds the treasure and the girl in the harp. The wife, Gríma, names the child

---

[13] "Ok þat skildu menn, at þat váru knerrir tveir svá miklir, at engir höfðu slíkir verit gervir á Norðrlöndum" (*Ragnars saga* ch. 15) (Men saw that these were so great that their like had never been made in the Northlands (*Ragnars saga* p. 235)).

[14] "Mars sviðr ófni" (*Ragnars saga* ch.15).

Kráka (Crow) after her own mother, shaves the girl's head and smears it with tar, and makes her wear a hood (making her even more crowlike), so as to sustain the fiction that she is their daughter.[15] Despite this anti-beauty treatment and the cruel exploitation the Cinderella-like orphan experiences at the hands of her pseudo-parents, her radiant beauty persists and cannot remain hidden. When some of the men on a Viking expedition led by Ragnarr (who by now has succeeded his father on the Danish throne) are sent ashore to cook for the crew, they encounter an unhooded, dazzling Kráka in her foster home, after she has washed herself and her hair (which has grown back) in anticipation of meeting the visitors from the ship. They ask her to prepare the dough for them to bake,[16] but they do a terrible job of baking and cooking, on account of being so distracted by the most beautiful girl they have ever seen. The widowed Ragnarr, intrigued by his men's report about Kráka, flirtatiously invites her to visit him at his ship, but with various riddling conditions attached, including that she is only to come if she can be neither naked nor clothed. The clever and willing girl's solution is to come in a fish-net, with her golden hair let down so as to cover her body.[17] The spectacular sight has the desired effect, and Ragnarr takes her back to his Danish home.

On their wedding night, Ragnarr ignores the girl's intuition that intercourse, as appropriate as it might be under the circumstances, would have bad results, and so she conceives and gives birth to a child, Ívarr, who is nicknamed

---

[15] The imposter-mother's comment to her skeptical husband, suggesting that a girl so beautiful *could* have been her daughter—"Má vera, at menn trúi því, at ek hafa mjök væn verit, þá er ek var ung" (*Ragnars saga* ch. 1) (It may be that people would believe that I was much fairer when I was young)—not only humanizes Gríma (as pointed out in Mitchell 1991: 109) but also resonates with the "intergenerational (dis)continuity" motif, which, as mentioned above, underlies all three of the stories in consideration here.

[16] Does the association of Kráka with dough foreshadow her giving birth to a boneless son? It also echoes a key episode in the *Völsunga saga*, with which *Ragnars saga* is closely associated in both its transmission history and narrative content, where Kráka/Áslaug's uncle Sinfjötli is put to the test by his uncle/father (Kráka/Áslaug's grandfather) Sigmundr. Having been given dough to knead that, unbeknownst to the young man, hides a poisonous snake, the nearly oblivious Sinfjötli blends the latter into the former, without any ill effect, and thus wins acceptance from Sigmundr (*Völsunga saga* ch. 7).

[17] The fashion statement is remotely akin to that made by the huge talking *trémaðr* "tree-man", found in latter days, according to the final chapter of the saga—a monument erected by the sons of Loðbrókr (or Loðbróka), and (given that it can speak) the last surviving member of this band of heroes. The "man" describes himself as covered in moss and yet naked: "Ok mosa vaxinn [...] hlýr hvárki mér / hold né klæði" (*Ragnars saga* ch. 20) (I am covered in moss [...] neither flesh nor clothes cover me). It is also relevant in this connection that McTurk's controversial interpretation, according to which Ragnarr's epithet was originally the name of a goddess, would render it "woman with luxuriant hair" or "grass-clad woman" (McTurk 2007: 58–59). There is more on the symbolism of Kráka/Áslaug's hair in the saga in Larrington 2012 (see esp. 262n49).

beinlauss (boneless), missing (the use of his) legs, like a serpent.[18] Later on in their life together, when Ragnarr is about to take another wife, thinking that Kráka is merely a person of lowly origins, the latter reveals that she is the daughter of Sigurðr and Brynhild, and that her real name, given to her by her parents, is Áslaug. She proves her pedigree, and deters Ragnarr from remarrying, by giving birth to a boy (Sigurðr) who has the image of a serpent in his eye. Even when she herself becomes a mother, however, Áslaug seems more devoted to Ragnarr's sons by Þóra than to her own. When two of Þóra's sons are slain by the Swedes, it is Áslaug who incites her own sons to avenge the deaths of their half-brothers, and she assumes the Valkyrie nature of her mother by taking part in the revenge expedition herself, even changing her name (to Randalín) to mark the transformation.

After the death of Ragnarr, his sons plan to attack England and slay the English king in retaliation—except for Ívarr, who holds back and does not participate in his brothers' expedition, which ends in defeat. As was the case with his father when, faced with the *lyngormr* Ragnarr had devised a "shaggy" means of insulating himself from poison and when, planning to invade England, he built his oversized "serpent" ships, Ívarr diverges from the more predictable, confrontational path of behavior and resorts to a more subtle form of attack. This carries its own risks, as we saw when Ragnarr's deceptive vessels went awry. But, entering into seemingly friendly negotiations with King Ella of England, not only does Ívarr succeed in tricking the English king out of a good deal of land, but he craftily lures away enough of Ella's men so that the other sons of Ragnarr, back for a revenge-match, can now have their fill of bloody retribution.

Ívarr's devious strategy for defeating Ella, we should note, is not a necessity dictated by his being *beinlauss*. In an earlier episode, when the sons of Ragnarr take their revenge on the Swedes in the wake of the death of Þóra's sons, it is Ívarr, hoisted on high by his men, who leads the Danes into battle, shooting arrows at the bellowing cow that was the Swedish super-weapon, and finally ordering his own body to be used as a projectile to kill it. Ívarr, the saga tells us, is as light as a child when thrown, but weighs murderously heavy upon the cow when he falls.[19] This remarkably passive-aggressive behavior on the battlefield aligns with the

---

[18] Also, Ívarr, as we shall see, is gifted with cunning reminiscent of the worldly intelligence biblically attributed to snakes (Matt. 10: 16).

[19] "Ok er hún kemr at þeim, biðr hann kasta sér at henni, ok verðr þeim hann svá léttr sem þeir kasti barni litlu, því at þeir váru eigi allnær kúnni, þá er þeir köstuðu honum. Ok þá kom hann á hrygg kúnni Síbilju, ok varð hann þá svá þungr sem bjarg eitt felli á hana, ok hvert bein brotnar í henni, ok fær hún af því bana" (*Ragnars saga* ch. 12) (and when she charged towards them, he ordered that he be cast at her, and he became as light as a little child when they threw him, because they weren't very close to the cow. But when he landed on Síbilja the cow he became as heavy as a boulder, and every bone in her body broke, and from that she got her death).

equally effective fighting style of (H)ubba, another son of Ragnarr (though not mentioned in *Ragnars saga*), who, according to a twelfth-century English source, could destroy an army simply by being lifted up by his men and looking balefully at the enemy force (Rowe 2012: 92; Thomson 1977: 41–42).[20]

A Comparison of "worms"

By now, the reader has perhaps had the opportunity to see the workings of the four narrative elements outlined at the beginning of our traversal of these three stories. The following chart sets out what we have so far:

Controlling Female	Generational (Dis)continuity	Serpentine Hide-and-Seek	Entrepreneurial/ Devious Protagonist
TDG: Sadhbh (Cian's mother) protects the newly emerged worm	Cian's relationship with his protective mother, and his parents' ambivalence about the worm "sibling"	Cian hides his bump; The monster-worm hides in a cave	Conán strikes a shady deal with Fionn, and with Diarmaid for the spear
Shahnameh: Haftvād's daughter nurtures the worm	Haftvād is named after his sons; his daughter loyally creates wealth for her father	The worm is hidden in an apple, in a spindle-case, and finally in an inaccessible fortress	Ardeshir gains access to the monster-worm by disguising himself as a merchant
Ragnars saga: Þóra nurtures the snake; Randalín nurtures snake-like sons	Ragnarr competes with his overachieving sons; Randalín helps to avenge the deaths of Ragnarr's sons	At first the snake lives in a box; as a child, Randalín, the mother-to-be of snakelike heroes, is hidden in a harp and later is forced to disguise herself	Ragnarr launches a secret attack (unsuccessfully) against the English in his snakelike ships; in revenge, his son Ívarr tricks and outmaneuvers the English king

[20] Compare the "moral victory" won by Ragnarr's son, the defiant Eirekr, against his Swedish captors. Refusing their offer of the king's daughter in marriage, he instead requests and receives his choice of the means of his death: climbing up onto the Swedes' spears, which have been fixed in the ground, and impaling himself upon them (*Ragnars saga* ch. 10).

A few additional observations and clarifications are still in order. In the TDG episode, Sadhbh is the controlling female figure, who nurtures the worm both inside her own womb and beyond it in the wider world. Her motherliness and concern for her children—even to the extent that, in one case, she favors a beloved foster child over her own children—are noted elsewhere in the medieval Irish literary tradition.[21] Even though her primary concern is the impact anything harmful done to the worm would have on her "real" son, Sadhbh in the TDG episode stands out for the way she treats the other nonhuman creature to issue forth from her body with such fastidious care.

The tale of Cian and his worm begins with Sadhbh's craving for sloes, which leads to a peculiar situation in which Cian parodies the process of gestation by carrying and giving birth to a worm from his head. The worm, like its story (as told by Diarmaid as previously told in his presence by Oisín), is doubly framed: no wonder, then, that there are thematic links between the framed tale and the master framing narrative as it is picked up after the killing of the worm. In the *now* of the main tale it is Gráinne who, we learn for the first time, is pregnant and, suffering from pica, starts to yearn for berries. On the other "side" of the framed tale, both of the stories framing it present a problem that resonates with the issues of relation and responsibility haunting the parents in the frame tale, Oilill and Sadhbh, as well as Cian—a quandary that also comes to the fore in the latter's obligation to his foster relative who is injured by Cian's verminal "twin". That is, both Conán, in the story Diarmaid tells, and the young men to whom he tells the story seek an answer to the difficult question, "To what extent are children's lives determined by the deeds of their parents?" The answers might share ground with the solution sought by the characters in the Cian story, struggling with the problem of a paradoxical "nonrelative relative", the worm that grows dangerously out of control.

The "hide and seek" motif runs through the Cian episode from beginning to end. First concealed among the sloes, then in Sadhbh's womb, and finally in Cian's head, the worm makes no move on its own to reveal itself. When released by Sgáthán with a slash of his knife, the creature, instead of escaping, pathetically clings to Cian's spear—more conspicuous than ever, but also insisting on his symbiotic connection with his "host". Arguably, when he attacks Cian's kinsman, the worm does so *because he is being looked at*, an act that the creature,

---

[21] *Cath Maige Mucrama* p. 60; *Scéla Moshaulum* p. 82. In these episodes from two different texts (both earlier than TDG), Sadhbh warns her foster son Lughaidh Mac Con about approaching his foster-father, her husband Oilill, who has a poisonous tooth and no love for Lughaidh. When they greet each other, Oilill bites Lughaidh on the cheek, which subsequently melts—a sign of his impending doom. Here, Oilill behaves as viciously as the monster-worm that lashes out at Cian's foster brother or father. In the *Acallam*, Sadhbh is said to have died of grief over the death of Lughaidh (p. 33).

like many animals in the real world, considers an act of provocation. Even in its spectacular leap out of the burning house, the creature, having been left with no choice but to abandon the home where it had been appreciated and protected, seeks not to show itself or to confront anyone, but only to find shelter in a cave, in an area that the worm (or his reputation) makes sure is never visited, even by Fionn and his brave company. There is little sense of Conán's being locked in fierce combat with the worm, or of its savagely defending its lair. From what the text tells (or doesn't tell) us, the feat consists merely of Conán spotting the worm, his shooting Diarmaid's infallible spear into the cave, and the weapon fatally finding its target.[22]

The "entrepreneurial" motif is less developed in the Cian story TDG tells than in the other stories we are considering. True, Sgáthán brings about an end to the vicious cycle Cian has brought upon those unfortunate enough to be his barbers, and Conán, thanks to Diarmaid, goes about slaying the monster in a fool-proof manner. More relevant in this regard are Cian's so easily taking offense at the (false) report of Sgáthán's having withheld hospitality from Cian's servant, and the murderous jealousy Cian feels toward Sgáthán and the supposed recipient (Fionn) of the hospitality withheld from Cian's representative. There is no indication in the story as told in TDG that the presence of the worm brings any good fortune or wealth to Cian and his family. At best, keeping the worm alive keeps Cian alive as well, although the text does not tell us whatever finally happened to Cian—did he die simultaneously with the worm or not? Still, Cian's small-mindedness, his insecurity and fear of others, point to an avaricious personality of a kind we can see most clearly in the figure of Haftvād in the *Shahnameh* episode.

Just as Haftvād, who with the wealth his daughter and the worm supply can buy himself a mighty army and kingdom, presents the most explicit example of the antiheroic entrepreneur in our ensemble of stories, so his (unnamed) daughter showcases how intimate the relationship can be between woman and worm. No less shy than Cian's creature, the girl's wiggly good-luck charm commutes from apple (in which she found it, and from which she derives its food, initially) to spindle-case, and finally to a hidden fortress high in the mountains. Whatever benefit she derives from her relationship with the worm seems to be little more than the satisfaction of having contributed spectacularly to the family's welfare. Moreover, the girl fades away from the story in proportion to

---

[22] Did worm-kind have the last laugh on Conán, as it did on Ragnarr? In the *Acallam* we learn that Conán ended up living apart from the *fian* in a dwelling concealed by the surrounding high land (compare the secluded mountain fortress Haftvād builds for his worm), and that he died not in combat (as a member of Fionn's *fian* should), but in bed, destroyed by a poisonous worm (*cruimh neime*) that somehow found its way into his head (pp. 100–102; see Nagy 2014).

the growth of what was once a rather cute pet. The relative insignificance of her character and of her role in the family's decision-making brings out by contrast the strong bond between father and sons. The former is actually named after his male offspring ("Seven Sons"), who form the core of the "corporation" Haftvād builds with his wealth. With the fall of the father, his sons disappear as well.

His ultimate failure notwithstanding, the poor man turned tyrannical magnate—as insatiable as the worm that brought him his luck becomes (but that could so easily be fooled into consuming molten metal)—does leave his mark on the hero who defeats him and deprives him of his source of wealth and power. For the only way the king Ardeshir can protect his throne, and the only way he can gain access to the secreted worm and thereby aright his own increasingly dire situation, is by assuming the guise of a *merchant*. Ragnarr transports his army to England in merchant vessels, and his son Ívarr bargains with Ella and the English nobles he wins over to his side like a canny trader, but it is in the *Shahnameh* that the "entrepreneurial" and out-of-character element manifests itself in the actions of an individual most clearly. A king in a strictly hierarchical society such as that of medieval Persia should not be lowering himself to the level to which the desperate Ardeshir sinks—but this is what dealing with the overgrown worm and the social disruption it occasions entails.

The story of Ragnarr presents us with a remarkable fungibility among the four motifs I have adumbrated in our three narratives. Lines of descent hold firm in the story as told in the saga, and there is both intra- and inter-generational continuity, extending as far as the seemingly indomitable *trémaðr* "tree-man" (see note 17 above). This continuity is made possible, however, by the repeated demonstrations of the alarming ease with which serpent-slayers in the world the story conjures can pass on serpentine traits to their descendants, serpent-like humans can be heroes, and women can both raise serpents and give birth to heroes.

The central players in this fluid world of possibilities all initially play hide and seek, from the orphan in the harp, to the girl deprived of her beauty and rendered a "Kráka", the snake in the box, the overdressed hero seeking to protect himself from snake poison, and the no-longer-concealed, distractingly beautiful girl, who later is both covered and revealed by her abundant hair. All this hiding-and-revealing bespeaks a fluidity of identity, a characteristic most flamboyantly exemplified by the name-changing figure of Kráka/Áslaug/Randalín. Perhaps it is why the saga leaves out any reference to her death, leaving us with the impression that she lives as long as or even outlives her sons. In this respect, as in many others, she stands in stark contrast to Ragnarr, whose death comes well before the end of the text, once his attempt to compete with a new generation in adventure and deeds of conquest ends in failure. As soon as the hero is deprived of the "shaggy" hair-shirt given him by Randalín, an item of clothing that both harks back to his *loðbrók* days and serves as a reminder of what he has gained by taking her as his wife, Ragnarr is exposed to the attacks of a new generation of serpents in a pit from which he cannot escape. It is undoubtedly a venerable heroic circumstance in which to find oneself, reminiscent of King Gunnar's fate in *Völsunga saga* (ch. 37), but this "downward" and "backward" nightmare of immobilization and vulnerability, where serpents are poisonous nemeses, is the opposite of the shifting, flexible, and "upward" future *Ragnars saga* envisions, in which serpent-sons (and their mother) will prevail.

Works Cited

Primary Sources

Acallam Na Senórach
Acallamh na Senórach. Ed. Whitley Stokes. *Irische Texte* 4/1. Leipzig: 1900.

Cath Maige Mucrama
Cath Maige Mucrama/The Battle of Mag Mucrama. Ed and transl. Máirín O Daly. Irish Texts Society, 50. Dublin: 1975. Pp. 38–63.

Gesta Danorum

Translation
Saxo Grammaticus: The History of the Danes: Books 1–9. Ed. Hilda Ellis Davidson and transl. Peter Fisher. Cambridge: 1996.

Ragnars Kvæði
"Ragnars kvæði." In vol. 1 of *Føroya kvaeði, corpus carminum Faeroensium a Sv. Grundtvig et J. Bloch comparatum.* Ed. N. Djurhuus and C. Matras. Copenhagen: 1951–1963. Pp. 215–43.

Ragnars Saga Loðbrókar Ok Sona Hans
Ragnars saga loðbrókar ok sona hans. In vol. 1 of *Fornaldarsögur Norðurlanda.* Ed. Guðni Jónsson and Bjarni Vilhjálmsson. Reykjavík: 1943. Pp. 219–85.

Translation
The Saga of the Volsungs, The Saga of Ragnar Lodbrok, together with The Lay of Kraka. Transl. Margaret Schlauch. New York: 1930.

Scéla Moshaulum
"Scéla Moshaulum." In *Cath Maige Mucrama/The Battle of Mag Mucrama.* Ed and transl. Máirín O Daly. Irish Texts Society, 50. Dublin: 1975. Pp. 74–87.

Shahnameh

Translation

Ferdowsi, Abolqasem. *Shahnameh. The Persian Book of Kings*. Transl. Dick Davis. New York: 2006.

Tóruigheacht Dhiarmada Agus Ghráinne (TDG) I

Tóruigheacht Dhiarmada agus Ghráinne/The Pursuit of Diarmaid and Gráinne. Ed. and transl. Nessa Ní Shéaghdha. Irish Texts Society, 48. Dublin: 1967.

Tóruigheacht Dhiarmada Agus Ghráinne (TDG) II

Toruigheacht Dhiarmuda agus Ghrainne, or, The Pursuit after Diarmuid O'Duibhne, and Grainne. Ed. and transl. Standish Hayes O'Grady. Transactions of the Ossianic Society, 3. Dublin: 1857.

Völsunga Saga

Völsunga saga. In vol. 1 of *Fornaldarsögur Norðurlanda*. Ed. Guðni Jónsson and Bjarni Vilhjálmsson. Reykjavík: 1943. Pp. 107–5.

Translation See Ragnars Saga Loðbrókar

Þáttr Af Ragnars Sonum

Þáttr af Ragnars sonum. In vol. 1 of *Fornaldarsögur Norðurlanda*. Ed. Guðni Jónsson and Bjarni Vilhjálmsson. Reykjavík: 1943.

Secondary Sources

ATU = Uther, Hans-Jörg. 2004. *The Types of International Folktales: A Classification and Bibliography, Based on the System of Antti Aarne and Stith Thompson*. 3 vols. Folklore Fellows Communications, 284–86. Helsinki.

Breatnach, Caoimhín. 2012. "The Transmission and Text of *Tóruigheacht Dhiarmada agus Ghráinne*: A Re-Appraisal." In *The Gaelic Finn Tradition*. Ed. Sheila Arbuthnot and Geraldine Parsons. Dublin. Pp. 139–50.

Ermacora, Davide, Roberto Labanti and Andrea Marcon. 2016. "Towards a Critical Anthology of Pre-Modern Bosom Serpent Folklore." *Folklore* 127: 286–304.

Eson, Lawrence. 2014. "Riddling and Wooing in the Medieval Irish Text *Tochmarc Ailbe*." *Études Celtiques* 40: 101–14.

Krappe, Alexander H. 1941. "Sur un episode de la Saga de Ragnar Lodbrók." *Acta Scandinavica Philologica* 15: 326–38.

Larrington, Carolyne. 2011. "Þóra and Áslaug in *Ragnars saga loðbrókar*: Women, Dragons and Destiny." In *Making History: Essays on the* Fornaldarsögur. Ed. Martin Arnold and Alison Finlay. London. Pp. 53–68.

———. 2012. "*Völsunga saga, Ragnars saga* and Romance in Old Norse: Revisiting Relationships." In *The Legendary Sagas: Origins and Development*. Ed. Annette Lassen, Agneta Ney, and Ármann Jakobsson. Reykjavík. Pp. 251–70.

Liebrecht, Felix. 1862. "Die Ragnar Lodbroksage in Persien." *Orient und Occident* 1: 561–67.

Márkus-Takeshita, Kinga. 2001. "From Iranian Myth to Folk Narrative: The Legend of the Dragon-Slayer and the Spinning Maiden in the Persian Book of the Kings." *Asian Folklore Studies* 60: 203–14.

McTurk, Rory. 1991. *Studies in* Ragnars Saga Loðbrókar *and its Major Scandinavian Analogues*. Medium Aevum Monographs, New Series, 15. Oxford.

———. 2007. "Male or Female Initiation? The Strange Case of *Ragnars saga*." In *Reflections on Old Norse Myths*. Ed. Pernille Hermann, Jens Peter Schjødt, and Rasmus Tranum Kristensen. Turnhout. Pp. 53–73.

Mitchell, Stephen A. 1991. *Heroic Sagas and Ballads*. Ithaca, NY.

Nagy, Joseph Falaky. 2014. "Death by Pillow." In *Rhetoric and Reality in Medieval Celtic Literature: Studies in Honor of Daniel F. Melia*. Ed. Georgia Henley and Paul Russell, with Joseph F. Eska. CSANA Yearbook 11–12. Hamilton, NY. Pp. 128–36.

———. 2015. "The 'Conquerer Worm' in Irish and Persian Literature." In *Erin and Iran*. Ed. Houchang Chehabi and Grace Neville. Boston/Washington, D.C. Pp. 3–13.

Ó Briain, Máirtín. 1985. "Cluasa Capaill ar An Rí: AT 782 i dTraidisiún na hÉireann" ["Ears of a Horse on the King: AT 782 in the Tradition of Ireland," with English-language summary]. *Béaloideas* 53: 11–74.

Ó Cathasaigh, Tomás. 2014. "The Pursuit of Diarmaid and Gráinne." In *Coire Sois: The Cauldron of Knowledge: A Companion to Early Irish Saga*, by Tomás Ó Cathasaigh and ed. Matthieu Boyd. Notre Dame. Pp. 466–83.

Rowe, Elizabeth A. 2012. *Vikings in the West: The Legend of Ragnarr Loðbrók and His Sons*. Studia Medievalia Septentrionalia, 18. Vienna.

Shahbazi, Alireza S. 2002. "Haftvād." *Encyclopædia Iranica*. http://www.iranica-online.org/articles/haftvad-haftwad (accessed on May 18, 2014).

Sims-Williams, P. 2011. *Irish Influence on Medieval Welsh Literature*. Oxford.

Thomson, R. M., ed. 1977. "Geoffrey of Wells, *De infantia sancti Edmundi* (BHL 2393)." *Analecta Bollandiana* 95: 25–42.

Baldr and Iraj
Murdered and Avenged

Emily Lyle
University of Edinburgh

Abstract: Comparing the Old Norse myth about Baldr with the Persian Iraj story, this essay deals with methodological considerations about comparativism and structural models as heuristic tools for reconstructing ancient traditions. The essay points to common aspects of the narratives focusing on familial relationships among the gods, which are analyzed by using a two-eras model (involving old gods and young gods) focusing on murder, revenge and avengers.

Introduction

This article treats the death of Baldr as related by Snorri and Saxo and the death of Iraj as told in the *Shahnameh* (The Book of Kings) by Ferdowsi of ca. 1000 CE. The Baldr story is mainly recounted in Snorri's *Gylfaginning* 49 (pp. 48–49) and Saxo's *Gesta Danorum* Book 3 (1.69–79) and has been the subject of an illuminating study by John Lindow, *Murder and Vengeance among the Gods: Baldr in Scandinavian Mythology* (1997). The Iraj story occurs near the beginning of the Persian epic history, in the reign of the sixth king, Feraydun (Davis 2007: 33–62). The common narrative features which form a basis for comparison are:

- A murder of a half-brother by two other brothers in conjunction who make complementary contributions to the act.

- The inhibition of immediate revenge by the presence of a kinship tie.

- A revenge killing by an avenger who was not yet conceived at the time of the murder.

The two stories also share the mythic context of a family of gods.

The hypothesis underlying a study of this kind is that it is possible to make fruitful comparisons between Old Norse and Iranian mythic narratives when an appropriate methodology is brought to bear. It was apparently the absence of an effective methodology that led to the shunning for a time of broad comparative study at the Indo-European level by many scholars in Old Norse studies as well as in other areas where it might reasonably have been undertaken. I have attempted to open a way to reenter the field in my book *Ten Gods: A New Approach to Defining the Mythological Structures of the Indo-Europeans* (Lyle 2012a).[1] I argue here that greater coherence can be expected of a posited early form of myth than of the splintered end results of millennia of transmission in changing environments, and that the coherence is related to the connection between myth and the organization of society. On the other hand, I also demonstrate that the end results are capable of carrying information derived from a remote past and that comparison can help to bring it to light.

The comparison being undertaken is of the genetic type in which the compared materials are ultimately derived from a common source. In the linguistic sphere, illumination was only possible when the Indo-European field was considered as a whole. In some place and at some time there was a common language, or cluster of closely related languages, from which most of the languages of Europe and, of course, other languages, including Sanskrit, were derived (Mallory and Adams 2006).[2] The ur-language can be studied synchronically in a hypothetical way and the diachronic developments that led to the historically known languages can be explored.

It seems obvious that this approach could be of value in comparative mythology as well as in comparative linguistics. Within the Indo-European field, the question can be posed: "How can we know the nature of the mythologies that come to us through written records without hypothesizing the nature of the common ground from which they were derived?" Does anyone seriously think that the gods entered the equation within the historical period? It is only if this position is being defended that it makes sense to ignore the wider context that would potentially enable us to supplement the information from the relatively recent times from which direct records are available.

When Martin West surveyed myth at the Indo-European level, he deliberately excluded the structural component exemplified by the functional theory

---

[1] In relation to the ten gods of the title, I may add that Christopher Abram names as major divine figures the ten Old Norse gods that I propose for this set, plus Hǫðr and Heimdallr (Abram 2011: 61). I see Hǫðr as a hypostasis of Þórr and not as a separate figure (Lyle 2012a: 82). For a suggested comparative context for Heimdallr (whom I do not treat), see Prior 2012.

[2] For a recently proposed location of the Indo-European homeland in the area of present-day Romania and Ukraine, see Axel Kristinsson 2012.

of Georges Dumézil that can be seen as one possible modeling device (West 2007: 4). The Dumézilian concept of a functional triad of the sacred, physical force, and fertility (Littleton 1982) has to be applied with discrimination since this triad is likely to be only a part of a larger structure that incorporates other triads besides the one stressed by Dumézil (Lyle 2006, 2012b). Modeling need not be confined to the well-known functional sequence, however, and this method used in a more general way is likely to prove a valuable conceptual tool as we extend the bounds of our enquiry.

The Heuristic Value of Modeling

A model can be a useful aid to perception, as recently argued by Jens Peter Schjødt (2013a: 37–39, 2013b: 9–10). It can also serve as an intermediary, when both A and B have perceptible similarities to the model C, while a claim of a direct similarity between A and B would be unconvincing.

A model is a means for sorting out information from background noise. We necessarily come to any body of material with built-in expectations of what is relevant. Researchers may simply assume that what is relevant is already known and, when the assumption is shared by scholars in a field, it may take on the force of authority and shut down lines of exploration. A model is overt and does away with the possibility of undeclared presuppositions, in so far as these relate to the model. A model is also what has been called an "external memory device" (Donald 1991: 274, 296–97; Lyle 2012a: 10). It has an objective existence and can be explored both by the originator and by other enquirers.

A model, however, is not reality. A model may be especially valuable when it approaches reality but its usefulness is not confined to this. That is to say that a scholar is free to operate with a model without any commitment to its truth value. A model is a heuristic device.

A model and a metaphor have much in common. In introducing the value of using models in the mythological context, Jens Peter Schjødt has employed the metaphor of a jigsaw that we are trying to put together when we find ourselves in possession of a jumble of pieces. He writes:

> Now, in order to do anything with these pieces we have to have an idea of what the picture could have been like. Part of this idea will come from the pieces themselves, but it is a necessary prerequisite that we have an idea of the structure of the picture. The blue will probably belong to the sky, the green to the grass and the trees, there may be pieces with parts of persons that must belong together with other parts of persons, and so on. Because of that idea we do not have to assemble every piece

with every other piece: the possibilities can be delimited to those that seem to be part of the same motif. (Schjødt 2013a: 37)

A valuable model to apply in the Indo-European context is the division by eras between the old and the young gods which can be seen as corresponding to a culturally defined division at the human level between the living and the dead. The two-era scheme has a simple outline that can be filled out in a similar way to the "blue sky, above" and "green grass, below" scheme, but with the components "old gods/the dead, above" and "young gods/the living, below".

The Indo-European Two-Eras Model and the Old Norse and Iranian Murder-and-Revenge Protagonists

The human capacity for using models is not just of value for modern scholarship, but would have been employed in the past to build up the imaginative structures containing the gods. The basis of a two-era system of gods would have been the human experience of living in one generation (era 2) but having a memory of a limited number of earlier generations (era 1). This is the temporal field that Jan Assmann has referred to as that of communicative memory and that I have called the memory capsule (Assmann 1992: 56; Lyle 2012c; see also Erll 2011: 29). The evidence seems good that a conceptual structure with four generations was emphasized among the Indo-Europeans in prehistory. This is the Common Celtic grouping, which corresponds to the Irish *derbfine*, as well as the Greek *angkhisteia* and the Indian *sapiṇḍa* (Charles-Edwards 1993: 55, 187, 213–14, 471–72; Foxhall 1995: 134; Dumont 1980; Lyle 2012a: 40, 2013). In the Indian case, it is explicit that only the last generation contains the living. The sacrificer in this generation makes offerings to his ancestors in the three previous generations. Michael Witzel in his recent study of myth has independently seen the relevance of the four-generation block at both the human and the divine levels (Witzel 2012: 64, 425–27, 576n24).

In the Old Norse context, there was certainly awareness of schemes with a limited number of ancestors, although the number of past generations counted in this way varied and could be as many as five (Laidoner 2015: 52–53, 104; Brink 2012: 103–6). To capture something of the flavor of the proposed Proto-Indo-European four-generation series in this context, we can turn to the case of Auðr hin djúpúðga (Auðr the Deep-Minded) at the time of Iceland's settlement (Laidoner 2015: 155–60; Jesch 1991: 80–83, 194–95). Auðr's great-grandson Þórðr gellir, when he was about to enter into manhood, went to the place where she was commemorated, so establishing a connection with the first-settler foremother to whom he was linked through his father and grandfather (*Landnámabók* 97; Laidoner 2015: 159). This specific case can be shown as in Table 1.

Eras	Generations
Prior generations	Auðr hin djúpúðga
	Þorsteinn rauða
	Óláfr feilan
Youngest generation	Þórðr gellir

Table 1. Auðr hin djúpúðga and representatives of
three following generations.

The scheme in Table 1 can be generalized to one in which the predecessors are all defined as deceased and are referred to as ancestors (Table 2).

Eras	Generations
Ancestors	foremother
	grandfather
	father
The living	male ego

Table 2. An apical ancestress and three following generations,
divided into eras of the living and the dead.

It is a human model like this that I argue gave rise to a two-era scheme of the gods, as shown in Table 3.

Eras	Generations
Old gods	Generation of primal being
	Generation 2
	Generation 3
Young gods	Generation 4

Table 3. The posited eras and generations among the Indo-European gods
in prehistory.

Turning now to the Iranian *Shahnameh*, where the gods are reflected in epic, we find that it is structured in terms of succession, and that the two eras among the gods can be posited to relate to the first six reigns.

Eras	Regnal Series	Years of Reign	Kings
Old gods	1	30	Kayumars
	2	40	Hushang
	3	30	Tahmures
Young gods	4	700	Jamshid
	5	1000	Zahhak (usurper)
	6	500	Feraydun

Table 4. The first six kings in the regnal series of the *Shahnameh*.

The first three kings (equated with the old gods) are quite briefly treated and have relatively short reigns assigned to them while the next three are treated more fully and have impossibly long reigns in human terms (Robinson 2001: 11–18, 153). As young gods, in terms of the model, these three belong to a single generation and, in the narrative, despite the great extent of time, this is also true of the kings, for Zahhak and Feraydun marry the two sisters of Jamshid. Salm, Tur, and Iraj, the sons of Feraydun, are best understood in terms of the model as belonging to this generation also, with the authority of Feraydun over them being that of king, not father. Jamshid (whose name means King Jam) corresponds linguistically to the Indian Yama.

Eras	Generations
Old gods	Kayumars
	Hushang
	Tahmures
Young gods	Jamshid, Zahhak, Feraydun, Salm, Tur, Iraj

Table 5. The succession sequence related to four generations and two divine eras.

As regards the eras in the Old Norse context, the major young gods are of the same generation and so conform to the model. Members of a following generation are also known, and of course their position should be considered, but initially it seems that we can take the major gods as a guide; doing so requires no modification in the number of generations in the case of the young gods. On the other hand, there is a missing generation in the era of the old gods since the three old gods born from the primal being are presented as of the same generation (*Gylfaginning* 5–7). They are shown in Table 6 along with the three young gods who feature in the murder story.

Eras	Generations
Old gods	Bestla
	Óðinn, Vé, Vili
Young gods	Baldr, Loki, Hǫðr

Table 6. The Old Norse murder triad shown in relation to the two eras.

The linking among the generations has a base in a birth series but, since the Indo-European divine system is centered on kingship, the transfer between one generation and the next is also a matter of succession. We can therefore look for the linkages in one or both of the domains of human-style birth from a female,[3] or of royal succession.

Clearly succession is dominant in the Iranian case and totally absent in the Old Norse one. Since succession can be traced elsewhere in the Indo-European area (Lyle 2012a), we can understand the absence in Old Norse as being related to the exceptionally dominant place of Óðinn who just *is* king in the stories we have, without having any need to replace a predecessor or to fear the coming of a successor. The whole mythic pattern associated with royalty is liable to have been affected by this, and we can expect to find truncated, skewed, or lost narratives. One apparently truncated story occurs in *Ynglinga saga* in the episode where Vé and Vílir/Vili sleep with Óðinn's wife Frigg (*Ynglinga saga* 3). Lindow comments:

> According to *Ynglinga saga*, ch. 3, when Odin is away, Frigg is possessed by his two brothers Vili and Vé and is then returned to Odin like some kind of street-walker upon his return [...] Basing his insult on this episode, which he goes on to mention, Loki tells her in *Lokasenna* 26 that she has ever been *vergiorn* (eager for a man). (Perhaps, however, she was simply filling the role of consort of the chief god[s]). (Lindow 1997: 50)

This multiple union of Frigg and three gods does not result in offspring whereas comparable mythological stories of a female lying with three males concern the begetting of the young king (Bek-Pedersen 2006: 332; Lyle 2012a: 59–68, 77).[4] Although this completion of the narrative is not included in the corpus, the

---

[3] This is by way of contrast with the earlier male pseudo-procreation (Clunies Ross 1994: 1.158, 185–86).

[4] The most striking case adduced in these studies is the begetting of the cosmologically significant Irish royal figure, Lugaid of the Red Stripes, by the three fathers whom he resembles in the three parts of his body divided by the red lines round his neck and waist (Lyle 2012a: 62–64).

most likely young-king figure, Þórr, shorn of royal attributes, is given a compensatory cosmic birth as son of a primal being, the Earth.

Feud as a Binding Motif in the Scandinavian Context

The interesting point that emerges from the present study is that there is a third strand besides birth and succession through which the sequence of generation-periods can be expressed—that of feud. The generation-periods are tied together through the negative reciprocity of murder and revenge. When succession is preceded by killing, feud can be seen as the shadow side of the regnal sequence. In Saxo, both Balderus and Høtherus have claims to the kingship, and Høtherus becomes undisputed king after he kills Balderus.

Generally, human feuding is carried out between family groups. A significant difference when we look at feud among the gods is that the population is extremely limited; therefore, revenge has to be taken within the confines of a single family. However, the implication of the feud motif is that there are two branches within the family of the gods that are opposed to each other. After the murder of Baldr/Balderus, his father Óðinn/Othinus takes steps to bring about the killing of the murderer (Hǫðr/Høtherus) by a killer named Váli or Bous. This aligns the gods or god-descendants in two opposed camps over three generations or quasi-generations. I say quasi-generations since Óðinn/Othinus is the biological father of Váli or Bous as well as of Baldr/Balderus and Hǫðr/Høtherus but, as the latter two are adult before the birth of the avenger, they can be regarded as being of a different social generation (see Tables 7 and 8).

Snorri's murder-and-revenge myth, centered on Baldr and Váli, and Saxo's Latin account of Balderus and Bous both come from the early part of the thirteenth century CE, but the myth, with other protagonists in the roles, can be taken back to the first half of the ninth century through a runic inscription on the Rök Stone in eastern Gautland in Sweden. This exceptionally elaborate inscription alludes to Óðinn (under the name of Kinsman) arranging that Þórr will avenge the killing of Vilinn by the *iatun* (enemy or monster). The allusion includes the point that the sacrifice of a woman leads to the birth of the avenger and this is in keeping with the motif found in the later form which speaks of the rape of Rindr/Rinda. I give the key parts of the inscription:[5]

[Riddle 1] hvaR Inguld/inga vaRi guldinn at kvanaR husli?

---

5   I follow Harris (2010) but with some modifications, giving 'Riddle' and 'Solutions' instead of 'Question' and 'Answers', and replacing 'the descendants of Ing-Vald' by 'the Inguldings', 'for' (in Riddle 2) by 'in compensation for' and 'Thor' by 'Þórr'.

[Riddle 2] [h]vaim se burinn nið/R drængi?

[Solutions] Vilinn es þat + knua knatt/i iatun [...] Þor / ol nirøðR / sefi via vari.

([Riddle 1] Who among the Inguldings was compensated for through the sacrifice of a woman?

[Riddle 2] To whom was a son born in compensation for a gallant young man?

[Solutions] Vilinn it is, whom the enemy slew [...] At ninety, the Kinsman, respecter of shrines, engendered Þórr. (Harris 2010: 93))

The short solutions to the riddles are: 1. Vilinn, and 2. Óðinn. The explanations of the solutions tell the story. Vilinn, slain by the enemy, was compensated for through the suffering of a woman [Vrindr]. A son was born to the Kinsman [Óðinn] who, at the age of ninety, engendered Þórr in compensation for Vilinn.

	Allied	Opposed
Father	Kinsman aged 90	
Victim and murderer	Vilinn	enemy
Avenger	Þórr	

Table 7. The oppositions in the Rök stone runic inscription.

In Saxo, Høtherus and Balderus were at war but Balderus was not killed in battle. When Høtherus was walking alone he unexpectedly met Balderus and struck him in the side with his sword, wounding him so that Balderus died a few days later. Saxo then tells how Othinus finds out how the revenge can be accomplished through his engendering of a son on Rinda, whereupon Othinus rapes her and she gives birth to Bous (*Gesta Danorum* 3, 3, 5; 3, 3, 6 – 4, 8; 3, 4, 13–15). In the cognate story from Iceland, Óðinn obtains Rindr through sorcery (*Skáldskaparmál* pp. 68, 133) and engenders the predestined killer, Váli (*Baldrs draumar* st. 7–11). In Saxo, it is Høtherus's counsellor Gevarus who suggests the murder weapon, while in Snorri, it is Loki. In both cases the weapon is the only tool that can penetrate Balderus/Baldr's invulnerability.[6]

---

[6] Dumézil comments: "Il y a, dans l'*Edda* en prose, le conseil de Loki et l'acte de Hoðr, il y a conjointement, chez Saxo, a) le conseil de Gevarus qui donne le moyen de tuer Balderus, b) l'acte formel d'Høtherus tuant Balderus" (Dumézil 1986: 108–9) (There are in the *Prose Edda*, the advice of Loki and the act of Hǫðr, there are taken together, in Saxo, a) the advice of Gevarus which provides the means of killing Balderus, b) the formal act of killing Balderus.)

	Allied	Opposed
Father	Óðinn/Othinus	
Victim and murderers	Baldr/Balderus	Loki or Gevarus, Hoðr/Høtherus
Avenger	Váli or Bous	

Table 8. The oppositions in Snorri and Saxo.

Feud is also a binding motif in the Iranian context, but the *Shahnameh* narratives will be introduced before the oppositions are presented.

The Deaths of Iraj and Jamshid

As will be seen, discussion of the death of Iraj should probably not be considered in isolation from that of the death of Jamshid, but the murder-and-revenge story of Iraj is treated first.

The following outline covers the points in the story of Iraj's murder that are comparable to the story of Baldr.[7] The demon-king Zahhak, who has magical powers, has usurped the throne and has had his predecessor, Jamshid, put to death. He holds in his harem the two sisters of Jamshid, Shahrnaz and Arnavat. After conquering Zahhak, Feraydun marries them, and has three sons, the older two, Salm and Tur, by Shahrnaz and the youngest, Iraj, by Arnavat.

I have divided the summary into two parts to bring out the distinction between the separate motifs of distribution and murder, which will be discussed below.

The distribution

Feraydun tests his sons by turning himself into a dragon and observing their reactions. The oldest, Salm, flees; the second, Tur, is impetuously brave; and the youngest, Iraj, chooses "the middle way between earth and fire" and is brave without rashness. After this Feraydun divides the world into three parts and makes Salm King of the Western Lands and Tur King of Turan and China. Finally, he makes Iraj Lord of Persia and gives him his crown (*Shahnameh* pp. 33-36).

---

[7] I use the translation of the *Shahnameh* by Dick Davis (2007). Full discussion of the main protagonists may be found under Aždahā, Ferēdūn, Iraj, and Jamšid in Yarshater (3: 181–205, 9: 531–33, 13: 200–2, 14: 501–28).

The murder

> Salm is dissatisfied and sends a message to Tur saying that the throne of Persia should have come to Salm as the oldest, or to Tur, if Salm is set aside. He says that they have been wronged by their father's decision to favor the youngest. When Tur receives the message, he leaps up in rage and says that they should not hesitate to act. Iraj wishes for reconciliation and arrives with a few companions for a meeting with his brothers. That night Salm and Tur decide to murder him. The next day, when they are alone together, Iraj tells his brothers that he does not value the kingship and is prepared to abdicate. Tur is angered, snatches up the golden throne he is sitting on, and strikes him on the head. Iraj asks him "How can you long to spill your brother's blood and torment our father's heart with such a crime?" and begs him to desist, but Tur draws his dagger and kills him. He cuts off his head and sends it to Feraydun. Feraydun curses the two unjust brothers and, addressing himself to God as lord of justice, says, "I ask only that I be given a little time, my lord, until I see a child from Iraj's seed, who will bind on his belt for vengeance." Feraydun is happy to find that Mah-Afarid in Iraj's harem is pregnant, "hoping that her child would be a means to vengeance for his son's death." Mah-Afarid, however, gives birth to a daughter called Canopus and, when she grows up, Feraydun marries her to his nephew Pashang. Canopus gives birth to a fine boy who is called Manuchehr. The two unjust brothers pretend to seek Feraydun's favor and try to lure Manuchehr into visiting them but Feraydun is not deceived and says they will only see Manuchehr at the head of an army seeking vengeance "for his grandfather's death." Feraydun adds: "Previously, we did not seek vengeance for [Iraj] for we did not think the times were propitious; it would not have been suitable for me to fight against my two sons." Manuchehr kills Tur in battle, cuts off his head, and sends it to Feraydun. In a later battle, Salm flees for the safety of a castle but Manuchehr pursues and kills him, and sends his head to Feraydun. Manuchehr is enthroned and crowned, but Feraydun spends the rest of his life grieving for his sons (*Shahnameh* pp. 36-62).

So far as I am aware, the Baldr and Iraj stories have not previously been explored as mythic parallels. The murder-and-revenge theme in relation to

Salm, Tur, and Iraj seems to have been masked by the theme of the distribution of territories, which was studied extensively by Georges Dumézil (1973: 9–20, esp. 13–14, 1971: 251–64, esp. 257–58, 1968: 586–88). It can be argued that the distribution is attached primarily to the three characters named while the murder-and-revenge story is a secondary development that has been displaced onto them from the figures who appear in the king list: Jamshid as victim and Zahhak and Feraydun as perpetrators. The revenge motif is found only in the Iraj story but the resolution is the same in both cases. Manuchehr is the successor of Fereydun in the king list and is the avenger of Iraj. The oppositions as expressed in the Iraj story are presented in Table 9.

	Allied	Opposed
Father	Feraydun	
Victim and murderers	Iraj	Salm, Tur
Avenger/Successor	Manuchehr	

Table 9. The Iraj story murder-and-revenge protagonists.

We have two ways to explore the story. We can see it simply as told of Salm, Tur, and Iraj, as actually present in the epic and as shown in Table 9, or we can see it, more speculatively but probably more fundamentally, as displaced from the Jamshid sequence. There is a narrative weakness in the Iraj story which points to the probability of adaptation. The brothers kill Iraj because they covet his kingship and yet Salm and Tur continue to reign in their own realms in the West and East, with neither taking over the vacant throne of Iraj. The motivation of grasping royal power, on the other hand, is strongly present in the main king series when Zahhak usurps the kingdom and then has the former king, Jamshid, put to death, and when Feraydun takes over the kingdom and has Zahhak bound. If we take it that the murder was primarily that of Jamshid we can sketch out the process of revision in the following way.

In the initial, hypothesized, story Jamshid becomes king but his rule is contested by Feraydun who, with the help of the magician Zahhak, kills him and succeeds to the throne, as shown in Table 10. It is supposed that it was found inappropriate to present the heroic Feraydun as the murderer of his predecessor and that the story was converted to one where Zahhak alone was responsible for the death of Jamshid and became a usurper who was later removed from the throne by Feraydun. This would have made the theme of long-delayed revenge redundant here, but the story material was too good to throw away and it was conflated with the story of distribution which was already present as an independent entity.

	Allied	Opposed
Father	Tahmures	
Victim and murderers	Jamshid	Zahhak, Feraydun
Avenger/Successor	Manuchehr	

Table 10. The reconstructed *Shahnameh* murder-and-revenge protagonists.

There is no trace remaining of Feraydun's guilt in the *Shahnameh* but his hypothesized murder of Jamshid does appear to relate to the murder motif involving royal pairs in other Indo-European contexts, notably the murder of Remus by Romulus. The Indo-European royal pair may or may not be treated as twins, and they are certainly to be distinguished from the divine twins who appear in the Roman context as Castor and Pollux (Ward 1968: 6–7). There is an ambiguity about who has the right to be king, which comes out in various ways in different Indo-European stories (Lyle 1990: 105–18), and it is worth dwelling on this since the parallel element in Saxo has not hitherto been pointed out in this connection. In the Roman case, the twins and their supporters separate and watch for the appearance of augural birds in order to determine which of them has the right to be king (Livy 1, 6, 4–7, 3). Remus sees birds first, but there are only six of them and, when Romulus sees birds later, there are twelve. Clearly, a case could be made for either of the contestants on the grounds of priority or greater number. Similarly, in Saxo (3, 3,1–2, 1.73–74) Høtherus and Balderus both have claims to the kingship of Denmark and are "hungry for sovereignty". When Høtherus arrived, "The Danish people came out to meet him and appointed him their king" but later, when Høtherus was absent, Balderus "gained the speedy acquiescence of the Danes to all his demands for royal honour". Saxo stresses the ambivalence, commenting: "Such was the wavering determination of our forbears". Although both the claimants arguably had good cases, the matter was only settled by the brute act of killing one of the contenders, both here and in the Roman example.

The Fettering of Loki and Zahhak

The death of Baldr/Balderus was the result of a throw or thrust by Hǫðr/ Høtherus, but was there a single murderer or a pair? John Lindow, although deciding to leave Loki's role intact in his discussion of the texts, refers to this as a long-standing question in the scholarship (1997: 68):

> Since both *Baldrs draumar* and *Vǫluspá* mention only Hǫðr as the slayer
> of Baldr and leave Loki's connection to the deed unclear, there has

naturally arisen a huge debate as to the "original" presence or absence of Loki in the myth.

We can usefully refer to the last revision of Dumézil's book on Loki, where he argues for the two-murderer scheme (1986: 102–22), and also to a recent comment on the subject by Joseph Harris, who finds the one-murderer scheme the more likely at an early stage in the story's life (2010: 98). It is clearly still a live issue. If the Iranian parallel is accepted, it supports the view that the two-murderer scheme is primary.

After Baldr's death, Hǫðr is killed but Loki is fettered (*Gylfaginning* 50–51). These various fates could be regarded as an execution and very lengthy prison sentence. Hǫðr's "crime" is simply the killing of Baldr but Loki's fettering is ascribed to more than a single cause (Lindow 1997: 163), and it could be seen as the containment of a more generalized evil, of which Baldr's murder was but one manifestation.

Treating Loki a good many years ago, Anna-Birgitta Rooth refers to "a myth of the fettered monster, a cosmological myth of the Enemy of the World who is to be released at the End of the World". She adds: "The models for the Old Norse myth are found both in biblical and Christian Mediaeval tradition as well as in the Classical myth of Prometheus with which the Scandinavian myth is closely related" (Rooth 1961: 185). Elsewhere, she notes similarly that the "*fettered* giant or devil thus is found both in Classical and Christian tradition," but at this point she adds: "It is however an interesting fact that also in Mohammedan tradition we encounter the motif of the bound Ḍaḥḥāk and his release at the end of the world" (Rooth 1961: 84–85). This is Zahhak of the *Shahnameh*.

Rooth's reference is to page 327 of A. J. Carnoy's contribution, *Iranian Mythology*, in the Mythologies of the World series (1917). Here Carnoy refers to the end of the world "when Ḍaḥḥāk (Azhi Dahāka), fettered by Farīdūn on Mount Damāvand, will be released by the powers of evil, who will rally for the last struggle against good". A few pages earlier, Carnoy had described the exploit of Feraydun's capture of the dragon-king Zahhak and continues: "He conveyed the captive to Mount Damāvand, where he fettered him in a narrow gorge and studded him with heavy nails, leaving him to hang, bound by his hands, to a crag, so that his anguish might endure" (Carnoy 1917: 323; cf. Davis 2007: 27). Carnoy then sums up the reign of Feraydun, which he has dealt with in terms of the *Shahnameh*, and includes references to the Pahlavi *Dinkard* and *Bundahis* passages from the ninth century CE (*Dinkard* VIII, xiii, st. 9; *Bundahis* xxxi, st. 9–11).

Tradition knows little of Farīdūn outside of his healing power and his victory over the dragon. Nevertheless the *Dīnkart* mentions the division of his kingdom between his sons Salm, Tūr, and Īraj; and the *Būndahish* explains that the two former killed the latter, as well as his posterity, with the exception of a daughter who was concealed by Farīdūn and who bore the hero Manushcithra, or Minūcihr, the successor of Farīdūn. The legends concerning these princes thus date back to a fairly ancient period, although it is doubtful whether they had the amplitude and the character which they assume in Firdausī's epic. These stories are not mythical, but merely epic. (Carnoy 1917: 323)

The last statement may give us pause. If there is one thing that has emerged as a consensus on myth in the century since Carnoy was writing, it is that epics may contain myths and that stories about human heroes may reflect the actions of the gods. Jaan Puhvel, appositely, applies this insight to the *Shahnameh* in a chapter on "Epic Iran" (Puhvel 1987: 117–25, esp. 118–20).

As regards the position of Zahhak, approaching the matter through the Iraj murder and its postulated displacement, I arrived at the view that Zahhak was the counsellor who joined with Fereydun in the murder of Jamshid, and so found him to correspond to Loki in relation to the murder without any reference to their parallel fates. If this view is accepted, the tie between Loki and Zahhak, already made by Rooth in 1961, will be very much strengthened: Loki/Zahhak aids the killer of Baldr/Jamshid and is fettered to a rock.

The Specially Begotten Avenger as First King

In both the Baldr/Balderus and Iraj cases, the avenger is not yet conceived when the killing takes place and, in both, the father of the murdered man takes a hand in the process of revenge. In the first case, the victim's father discovers that the avenger has to be born of a specific woman/giantess and begets him with her. In the second case, he finds the woman who is pregnant by the murdered man and cares for her in the hope that she will bear a son who will carry out the revenge. When she bears a daughter, he cares for the daughter until she conceives and bears the avenger.

The reign of Manuchehr does not fall in the part of the *Shahnameh* that has been equated here with the eras of the gods but immediately follows it. It seems that the story of revenge carries over from the eras of the gods into the era of humans and covers the transition to the human institution of royal succession with Manuchehr in the position of first human king. Bous (in Saxo) dies of his wounds the day after he avenges the murder, while the Norse Váli simply does not become king; there is thus no succession in this revenge story in the Old Norse context.

However, it can be suggested that the succession of the specially begotten son has survived as a narrative detached from the revenge story. When we take the aspect of the Óðinn/Othinus and Rindr/Rinda story that runs "god lies with giantess," we find that conception takes place and birth follows and that the outcome is the avenger. In the "god lies with giantess" story of Freyr and Gerðr in the eddic poem *Skírnismál*, the outcome, according to *Ynglinga saga*, is the first king, Fjǫlnir (*Ynglinga saga*, ch. 10–11; Finlay and Faulkes 2011: 14–15). The parallel reinforces the idea that birth is an important part of the *Skírnismál* story (though not narrated in the poem), as argued by Gro Steinsland, who finds in this narrative "the outlines of a mythical pattern that concerns the ideology of kingship" that stresses the contribution of the mother (Steinsland 2012: 228).[8] She points out also that, after Óðinn's union with the giantess Skaði, their son, Sæmingr, becomes the first of the Hlaðajarl line of earls in Norway. This case is found in the *Háleygjatal* of Eyvindr skáldaspillir Finnsson, composed ca. 985 CE, with the relevant verse (st. 2) quoted by Snorri in *Ynglinga saga* (ch. 8).[9] It seems as if we may have in these god-and-giantess stories the two facets of a motif of the engendering of a king-avenger.

In the Old Norse materials as well as in the Indo-European ones more generally, the gods do not go on proliferating indefinitely, and the interest turns to the human kings who are their descendants. It seems that the avenger in the generation after that of the gods fundamentally belongs in the human category, and that the murder-and-revenge motif negotiates this crucial transition.

Fjǫlnir, the son of Freyr and Gerðr, was said to be the first king at Uppsala and members of the Svea line of kings there could be called the descendants of Freyr (Sundqvist 2000: 39, 152–55). This raises the question of how a mortal could inherit from a god. If we take the Iranian parallel as guide, it seems that the first king could be the avenger of the death of a god—but we can ask how that revenge could be accomplished. The killing of the murderer is straightforward if it is placed in the historical context as it is in Saxo; a man is killed. On the other hand, Hǫðr is a god in Snorri but is put to death; a god is killed. What does it mean to kill a god, who is an immortal? Clearly the death of Baldr (and of Yama) is cosmologically significant and is a tremendous event. This seems to be the exceptional case when a god really dies. The killing of the murderer is not highly charged in this way. Possibly we should invoke the idea of compensation found in the Rök carving. I have found no statement to this effect, but perhaps the story ran that the last god in a genealogical reckoning yielded the throne to the first human in compensation for the murder.

---

[8] I have discussed elsewhere the possible importance of the mother of the avenger understood as the primal goddess (Lyle 2012a: 85–86).

[9] For discussion of the context, see Poole 2007: 154–55, 161–66 and Abram 2011: 127–34.

Conclusion

When stories are attached to the gods, it can be expected that they would have been in some sort of structured relationship. This is not to say that stories, once the bonds of the original sequences were loosened, did not take off on their own and become elaborate, largely independent units that generate their own interest. Compared narratives from different branches of Indo-European tradition can sometimes display a revealing lack of connection that highlights the extent of diachronic change.

What can we learn from the present comparison that might inform the study of Old Norse mythology? It reinforces the view that two males were responsible for the death of the Baldr figure, one as counsellor and one as actor. It reinforces the idea that the avenger has to be specially conceived and introduces the idea that this special conception is followed by the birth of a son who would be king as well as avenger. That point can lead to a reinterpretation within the Old Norse material that would allow the convergence of the birth of an avenger (from a giantess) and the birth of a founder king (from a giantess).

In the stories considered, comparison becomes especially rewarding when we allow for two possible major shifts: the rise to dominance of one of the old gods (Óðinn) in the Old Norse context, and the purification from guilt of the young king-god (Feraydun). The Old Norse and Iranian strands of narrative offer supplements to each other and it seems feasible, by taking them together, to advance our understanding of a key sequence of Indo-European myth.

In the Old Norse context, it is the feud motif, with murder and revenge, that ties the generations together. The theme of feud has allowed the survival of a sequence (formerly one of succession), otherwise lost in the Old Norse context through the increase in the power of Óðinn relative to the other gods.

The two-era model enables us to focus on potentially relevant connections. As indicated by Schjødt in the quotation above, an advantage of the use of modeling is that it directs attention to a specific, limited area where comparison is likely to be valuable. I argue that the default position should be that connections are present between Old Norse stories and cult on the one hand and Indo-European myth on the other. It remains for these connections to be widely and deeply explored in the critical climate that has been established through the detailed study of sources in recent decades of scholarship.

Works Cited

Primary Sources

Baldrs draumar: see *Poetic Edda*

Bundahis
Bundahis. In *Pahlavi Texts* 1: *The Bundahis, Bahman Yast, and Shâyast Lâ-Shâyast*. Transl. E. W. West. Sacred Books of the East, 5. Oxford: 1880. Pp. 3–151.

Dinkard
Dinkard. In *Pahlavi Texts* 4: *Contents of the Nasks*. Transl. E. W. West. Sacred Books of the East, 37. Oxford: 1892. Pp. 3–398, 406–17.

Eyvindr skáldapillir Finnsson: see *Háleygjatal*

Gesta Danorum
Saxo Grammaticus. *Gesta Danorum: Danmarkshistorien*. Ed. Karsten Friis-Jensen and transl. [into Danish] Peter Zeeberg. Copenhagen: 2005.

TRANSLATION
Saxo Grammaticus. *The History of the Danes: Books 1-9*. Ed. Hilda Ellis Davidson and transl. Peter Fisher. Cambridge: 1996.

Gylfaginning: see *Prose Edda*

Háleygjatal
Eyvindr skáldapillir Finnsson. "Háleygjatal." Ed. and transl. Russell Poole. In vol. 1 of *Skaldic Poetry of the Scandinavian Middle Ages: Poetry of the Kings' Sagas 1: From Mythical Times to c. 1035*. Ed. Diana Whaley. Turnhout: 2012. Pp. 195–213.

Heimskringla
Íslenzk fornrit, 26–28. Ed. Bjarni Aðalbjarnarson. Reykjavík: 1941.

TRANSLATION
Snorri Sturluson. *Heimskringla*. Transl. Alison Finlay and Anthony Faulkes. London: 2011.

Landnámabók
Íslenzk fornrit, 1. Ed. Jakob Benediktsson. Reykjavík: 1986. Pp. 29-397.

TRANSLATION
The Book of Settlements: Landnámabók. Transl. Hermann Pálsson and Paul Edwards. Winnipeg: 1972.

Livy

Livy. *History of Rome: Books 1-2.* Transl. B. O. Foster. Loeb Classical Library, 114. London & Cambridge, MA: 1919.

Lokasenna: see *Poetic Edda*

Poetic Edda

Eddukvæði I-II. Ed. Jónas Kristjánsson and Vésteinn Ólason. Reykjavik: 2014.

TRANSLATION

The Poetic Edda. Transl. Carolyne Larrington. Oxford World's Classics. Oxford: 2008.

Prose Edda

Snorri Sturluson. *Edda Snorra Sturlusonar: Udgivet efter håndskrifterne.* Ed. Finnur Jónsson. Copenhagen: 1931.

TRANSLATION

Snorri Sturluson. *Edda.* Transl. Anthony Faulkes. London: 1987.

Shahnameh

Ferdowsi, Abolqasem. *Shahnameh.* 12 vols. Ed. Jalal Khāleghi Motlag. Bibliotheca Persica. New York: 1988–2009.

TRANSLATION

Ferdowsi, Abolqasem. *Shahnameh: The Persian Book of Kings.* Transl. Dick Davis. London: 2007.

Skaldskaparmal: see *Prose Edda*

Skírnismál: see *Poetic Edda*

Ynglinga Saga: see *Heimskringla*

Secondary Sources

Abram, Christopher. 2011. *Myths of the Pagan North: The Gods of the Norsemen.* London & New York.

Assmann, Jan. 1992. *Das kulturelle Gedächtnis: Schrift, Erinnerung und politische Identität in frühen Hochkulturen.* Munich.

Axel Kristinsson. 2012. "Indo-European Expansion Cycles." *Journal of Indo-European Studies* 40: 365–433.

Bek-Pedersen, Karen. 2006. "Interpretations of *Ynglingasaga* and the *Mabinogi*: Some Norse-Celtic Correspondences." In *Old Norse Religion in Long-Term*

Perspectives: Origins, Changes and Interactions. Ed. Anders Andrén, Kristina Jennbert, and Catharina Raudvere. Vägar till Midgård, 8. Lund. Pp. 331–35.

Brink, Stefan. 2012. "Law and Legal Customs in Viking Age Scandinavia." In *The Scandinavians from the Vendel Period to the Tenth Century: An Ethnographic Perspective*. Ed. Judith Jesch. Woodbridge. Pp. 87–117.

Carnoy, Albert J. 1917. *Iranian Mythology*. The Mythology of All Races, 6. Boston.

Charles-Edwards, T. M. 1993. *Early Irish and Welsh Kinship*. Oxford.

Clunies Ross, Margaret. 1994. *Prolonged Echoes: Old Norse Myths in Medieval Northern Society*. 2 vols. Odense.

Davis 2007. See *Shahnameh.*

Donald, Merlin. 1991. *Origins of the Modern Mind: Three Stages in the Evolution of Culture and Cognition*. Cambridge, MA.

Dumézil, Georges. 1968. *Mythe et Épopée* 1. Paris.

———. 1971. *Mythe et Épopée* 2. Paris.

———. 1973. *The Destiny of a King*. Transl. Alf Hiltebeitel. Chicago & London.

———. 1986. *Loki*. Rev. ed. Paris.

Dumont, Louis. 1980. "La dette vis-à-vis des créanciers et la catégorie de sapiṇḍa." *Puruṣārtha: sciences sociales en Asie du sud* 4: 15–37.

Erll, Astrid. 2011. *Memory in Culture*. Transl. Sarah B. Young. Basingstoke.

Foxhall, Lin. 1995. "Monumental Ambitions: The Significance of Posterity in Greece." In *Time, Tradition and Society in Greek Archaeology*. Ed. Nigel Spencer. London. Pp. 132–49.

Harris, Joseph. 2010. "Varin's Philosophy and the Rök Stone's Mythology of Death." In *New Perspectives on Myth: Proceedings of the Second Annual Conference of the International Association for Comparative Mythology, Ravenstein the Netherlands, 19–21 August, 2008*. Ed. Wim M. J. van Binsbergen and Eric Venbrux. Haarlem. Pp. 91–105.

Jesch, Judith. 1991. *Women in the Viking Age*. Woodbridge.

Laidoner, Triin. 2015. *Ancestors, their Worship and the Elite in Viking Age and Early Medieval Scandinavia*. PhD diss., University of Aberdeen.

Lindow, John. 1997. *Murder and Vengeance among the Gods: Baldr in Scandinavian Mythology*. Folklore Fellows Communications, 262. Helsinki.

Littleton, C. Scott. 1982. *The New Comparative Mythology: An Anthropological Assessment of the Work of Georges Dumézil*. 3rd ed. Berkeley.

Lyle, Emily. 1990. *Archaic Cosmos: Polarity, Space and Time*. Edinburgh.

———. 2006. "The Importance of the Prehistory of Indo-European Structures for Indo-European Studies." *Journal of Indo-European Studies* 34: 99–110.

———. 2012a. *Ten Gods: A New Approach to Defining the Mythological Structures of the Indo-Europeans*. Newcastle-upon-Tyne.

———. 2012b. "Entering the Chimeraland of Indo-European Reconstruction." *Retrospective Methods Network Newsletter* December: 6–10.

———. 2012c. "Stepping Stones through Time." *Oral Tradition* 27 (1): 161–70.

———. 2013. "Defining the Religion that Lay behind the Self-Colonization of Europe." In *Critical Reflections on Indigenous Religions*. Ed. James L. Cox. Farnham & Burlington, VT. Pp. 93–101.

Mallory, J. P., and D. Q. Adams. 2006. *The Oxford Introduction to Proto-Indo-European and the Proto-Indo-European World*. New York.

Poole, Russell. 2007. "Myth and Ritual in the *Háleygjatal* of Eyvindr skáldaspillir." In *Learning and Understanding in the Old Norse World: Essays in Honour of Margaret Clunies Ross*. Ed. Judy Quinn, Kate Heslop and Tarrin Wills. Turnhout. Pp. 153–76.

Prior, Daniel. 2012. "Integral or Incidental? Indo-European Mythic Fragments in Inner Asia." Paper presented at *The Steppes: Crucible of Eurasia*, Miami University Art Museum, Oxford, Ohio, Nov. 30–Dec. 1. http://muamgrassroutes.wordpress.com/symposium2012/ Accessed on 04/04/2016.

Puhvel, Jaan. 1987. *Comparative Mythology*. Baltimore.

Robinson, B. W. 2001. *The Persian Book of Kings: An Epitome of the Shahnama of Firdawsi*. Richmond.

Rooth, Anna Birgitta. 1961. *Loki in Scandinavian Mythology*. Skrifter utgivna av Kungl. Humanistiska Vetenskapssamfundet i Lund, 61. Lund.

Schjødt, Jens Peter. 2013a. "Reflections on Some Problems in Dealing with Indigenous Religions of the Past: The Case of Pre-Christian Scandinavian Religion." In *Critical Reflections on Indigenous Religions*. Ed. James L Cox. Farnham & Burlington, VT. Pp. 29–47.

———. 2013b. "The Notions of Model, Discourse, and Semantic Center as Tools for the (Re)Construction of Old Norse Religion." *Retrospective Methods Network Newsletter* May: 6–15.

Steinsland Gro. 2012. "Rulers as Offspring of Gods and Giantesses: On the Mythology of Pagan Norse Rulership." In *The Viking World*. Ed. Stefan Brink in collaboration with Neil Price. London. Pp. 227–30.

Sundqvist, Olof. 2000. *Freyr's Offspring: Rulers and Religion in Ancient Svea Society*. Uppsala.

Ward, Donald J. 1968. *The Divine Twins: An Indo-European Myth in Germanic Tradition*. Berkeley and Los Angeles.

West, M. L. 2007. *Indo-European Poetry and Myth*. Oxford.

Witzel, E. J. Michael. 2012. *The Origins of the World's Mythologies*. New York.

Yarshater, Ehsan. 1986–. *Encyclopædia Iranica*. New York. http://www.iranicaonline.org. Accessed on 05/30/2016.

Ymir in India, China—and Beyond

Michael Witzel
Harvard University

Abstract: In examining the Old Norse mythological creation story about Ymir, that is, the creation of the world from the body of a primordial giant, from a broadly comparative perspective, this essay refers to a variety of creation myths, some from Indo-European and some from Chinese and Polynesian mythologies, and argues that a "Laurasian myth" entailed the origin of the world from a pre-existing giant, a myth, the author contends, with roots in Stone Age hunting cultures.

Introduction

In this paper, I partially employ the new theory of historical *and* comparative mythology that leads to increasingly earlier reconstructions of mythological systems, as laid out in my recent book, *The Origins of the World's Mythologies* (2012). My premise is that earlier forms of myths, especially those of Eurasia and the Americas, can be compared and successfully reconstructed, resulting in a unique story line from the beginning of the world to its end. Here I will use as an example of this theory the myths of Ymir, Puruṣa and Pangu.

The myth about a primordial giant forms part of the creation myths, or as we should rather say, in non-Judaeo-Christian terms: *emergence* myths. That of the giant is found from Iceland to Southern China and beyond. It stands somewhat apart among the more common myths of a primordial Nothing, Chaos, Darkness or Water. As such, it can perhaps lay claim to what Dumézil called a *bizarrerie*, a feature that does not make much sense in the narrative in which it is found, but as it turns out, goes back to a much older layer of myths.

In this myth, the primordial giant was in existence before the world emerged: he was somehow killed and carved up, and his various body parts became the origin of heaven and earth and even of humans.

The well-known prototype is the Germanic Ymir, who is slain, and from his skull heaven is made; from his bones, the mountains; and so on. In the parallel version of Old India, it is *puruṣa* (man) from whose body the various parts of heaven and earth are created, including humans (Ṛgveda 10.90). In Old China, there is the quite similar myth of Pangu (P'an ku), which seems to derive, not from the Han people of Northern China but from the Austric populations in what is now Southern China. [1]

Prima facie, the three major myths referred to, those of Pangu, Puruṣa and Ymir, have no connection with each other, as they are located in very distant regions and at various equally distant time periods: the Chinese case is attested in the last few centuries BCE, the Indian one is found in a text composed a few hundred years earlier (around 1000 BCE), and the Icelandic one more than 2000 years later, while many thousand miles separate their respective places of origin.

Puruṣa

The oldest version of the Puruṣa myth is found in the Ṛgveda, the first preserved text of India. It is the poetic composition in archaic Sanskrit (Vedic) of traditional bards following the convention of the Indo-Iranian, and even Indo-European, poetic language and style. These bards roamed the northwestern Indian subcontinent and Afghanistan, while composing traditional hymns praising the deities. They expected a gift from the local chieftains ("kings") for their recitations, which often included praise of the ancestors of the local magnate.

> When the primordial Puruṣa (man) is carved up[2] (Ṛgveda 10.90.7), the gods, the Sādhyas,[3] and the Ṛṣis (seers, poets) offered him (Puruṣa) for themselves [...]

---

[1] *Austric* refers to a large language family that includes Austroasiatic in India, S.W. China and S.E. Asia as well as Austronesian that spread out of Taiwan to the Philippines, Indonesia, Madagascar and to all of Polynesia. For the Chinese myth, see Aston [1896] 1972: 33n2; Mathieu 1989. Recently, a Chinese version of a continuous creation myth has been published: Hu Chongjun, (2002; cf. *China Daily*, Wednesday, April 3, 2002, p. 9). This looks like an artificial compilation, intended to provide China with a "creation myth", which it is lacking; we only have fragments, adapted to the rationalistic, Euhemeristic Confucian tradition. On the oldest Chinese myths, cf. David Hawkes, quoted in Barrett 1995: 72 f.: "to arrive at some archetypal Ur-myth is a waste of time. The Eocene Age of myth is unknowable [...] as we work backwards [...] we find an even greater number of groups and [...] diversity". However, for methods to address this welcome diversity, see Witzel 2012: §2.3, and cf. Birrell 1993: 18, 22, for reconstructing older forms of Chinese myths. For major sources of Chinese myth, see Yang and An 2005: 4 ff.

[2] Cf. the discussion by Baumann 1986: 144 ff.

[3] A rather vague, little mentioned group of deities, apparently the ancestors of the current gods; see Kuiper 1978, appendix.

11. When they portioned out Puruṣa, in how many parts did they fashion him? What are his mouth, arms, thighs, and feet called?

12. His mouth was the Brahmin, his arms were fashioned (into) the nobleman (Rājanya), his thighs were the Vaiśya,[4] from his feet the Śūdra (serf) was born.

13. The moon has been born from his mind, the sun was born from his eye; from his mouth was born Indra and Agni,[5] and from his breath the wind.

14. From his navel there was the intermediate space (atmosphere), from his head developed heaven, from his feet the earth, from his ears the cardinal directions. Thus they fashioned the worlds.

16. With sacrifice the gods offered to sacrifice. These were the first forms (of sacrifice). (RV 10.90.7 ff.; my translation)

Ymir

In Old Norse mythology, as recorded in the Poetic Edda and the *Prose Edda* in the 13th century,[6] there was chaos at the time of the beginning of the world, "a yawning abyss" (*gap var ginnunga; Vǫluspá* 3). Then the sea was created; as were Niflheim, the land of clouds and fogs in the North, and Muspelheim, the southern land of fire. Through the contact of ice from the north and the warm breezes from the South, a first being, the primordial giant Ymir, was created.[7]

The *Prose Edda* offers an extensive version, highlights of which include:

Svá sem segir í Vǫluspá: Ár var alda [...] gap var ginnunga, en gras ekki [...] Svá sem kalt stóð af Niflheimi ok allir hlutir grimmir, svá var allt þat, er vissi námunda Múspelli heitt ok ljóst, en Ginnungagap var svá hlætt sem lopt vindlaust. Ok þá er mœttisk hrímin ok blær hitans svá at bráðnaði ok draup, ok af þeim kvikudropum kviknaði með krapti þess er til sendi hitann, ok varð manns líkandi, ok var sá nefndr Ymir [...] Hann er illr ok allir hans ættmenn. Þá kǫllum vér hrímþursa.

---

4 Derived from *viś* "the people". The tripartite division reflects the Indo-European social set-up, see Benveniste 1969: 65–79; and many works by G. Dumézil, beginning in 1934, such as 1939, 1959.
5 Two of the most prominent Vedic deities.
6 For a discussion of Germanic myths about creation, see Puhvel 1987: 219.
7 Who was to be dismembered like the Indian *puruṣa*.

(As it says in Voluspa: It was at the beginning of time [...] The mighty gap was, but no growth [...] Just as from Niflheim there arose coldness and all things grim, so what was facing Muspell was hot and bright, but Ginnungagap was as mild as a windless sky. And where the rime and the blowing of the warmth met so that it thawed and dripped, there was a quickening from these flowing drops and due to the power of the source of the heat it became the form of a man, and he was given the name of Ymir [...] He was evil and all his descendants. We call them frost-giants.)

Næst var þat, þá er hrímit draup, at þar varð af kýr sú er Auðhumla hét, en fjórar mjólkár runnu ór spenum hennar, ok fœddi hon Ymi [...] Hon sleikði hrímsteinana [...] þriðja dag var þar allr maðr. Sá er nefndr Búri [...] Synir Bors drápu Ymi jǫtun.

(The next thing when rime dripped was that that there came into being from it a cow called Audhumla, and four rivers of milk flowed from its teats, and it fed Ymir [...] It licked the rime-stones [...] the third day a complete man was there. His name was Buri. He begot a son called Bor [...] Bor's sons killed the giant Ymir.)

En er hann fell, þá hljóp svá mikit blóð ór sárum hans at með því drektu þeir allri ætt hrímþursa, nema einn komst undan með sínu hýski. Þann kalla jǫtnar Bergelmi.

(And when he fell, so much blood flowed from his wounds that with it they drowned all the race of the frost-giants, except that one escaped with his household. Giants call him Bergelmir.)

Þeir tóku Ymi ok fluttu í mitt Ginnungagap ok gerðu af honum jǫrðina, af blóði hans sæinn ok vǫtnin. Jǫrðin var ger af holdinu, en bjǫrgin af beinunum. Grjót ok urðir gerðu þeir af tǫnnum ok jǫxlum ok af þeim beinum, er brotin váru.

(They [Bor's sons] took Ymir and transported him to the middle of Ginnungagap, and out of him made the earth, out of his blood the sea and the lakes. The earth was made of the flesh and the rocks of the bones, stone and scree they made out of the teeth and molars and of the bones that had been broken.)

Tóku þeir ok haus hans ok gerðu þar af himin ok settu hann upp yfir jǫrðina með fjórum skautum.

(They also took his skull and made out of it the sky and set it up over the earth with four points.)

Þá tóku þeir síur ok gneista þá er lausir fóru ok kastat hafði ór Múspellsheimi, ok settu á miðjan Ginnungahimin bæði ofan ok neðan til at lýsa himin ok jǫrð.

(Then they took the molten particles and sparks that were flying uncontrolled and had shot out of the world of Muspell and set them in the middle of the firmament of the sky both above and below to illuminate heaven and earth.)

Þeir tóku ok heila hans ok kǫstuðu í lopt ok gerðu af skýin.

(They also took his brains and threw them into the sky and made out of them the clouds.)[8]

Vǫluspá 3–4, 19 in the Poetic Edda has this shorter version:

3 Ár var alda,   þar er Ymir bygði,
   vara sandr né sær né svalar unnir;
   iorð fannz æva   né upphiminn,
   gap var ginnunga en gras hvergi.

   (Early in time Ymir made his settlement,
   there was no sand nor sea nor cool waves;
   earth was nowhere nor the sky above,
   a void of yawning chaos, grass was there nowhere.)

4 Áðr Burs synir   bioðum um ypþo,
   þeir er miðgarð   mœran scópo;
   sól skein sunnan á salar steina,
   þá var grund gróin grœnum lauki.

   (before the sons of Bor brought up the land-surface,[9]
   those who shaped glorious Midgard;[10]
   the sun shone from the south on the stone-hall,
   then the ground was grown over with green leek.)

---

[8] Faulkes 1995: 9–11; *Snorra edda* pp. 9–11.
[9] *Burs synir* (literally, "Burr's sons") refers to the gods, Óðinn, Vili, and Vé.
[10] The earth of human beings, other than Ásgarðr (Asgard), of the gods, and the world of the giants.

19   Ask veit ec standa, heitir Yggdrasill,
        hár baðmr, ausinn hvítaauri;
        þaðan koma dǫggvar,   þærs í dala falla,
        stendr æ yfir, grœnn   Urðar brunni.

(An ash I know that stands, Yggdrasill[11] it's called,
a tall tree, drenched with shining loam;
from there come the dews which fall in the valley,
green, it stands over Urd's well.)[12]

The myth of carving up Ymir also occurs elsewhere in the Poetic Edda, in *Grímnismál* 40:

40   Ór Ymis holdi   var iorð of skǫpuð,
         en ór sveita sær,
        biorg ór beinum,   baðmr ór hári,
         en ór hausi himinn.

(From Ymir's flesh the earth was created,
and from his blood, the sea,
mountains from the bones, trees from this hair,
and from his skull, the sky.)[13]

The corresponding Old Indian hymn from the Ṛgveda (10.90), quoted above, often reads like a translation of the Norse text, or vice versa. Their close correspondence opens up the possibility that this is an old, Indo-European idea.[14] This is strengthened by the closely related Old Norse myth of the god, Óðinn (Odin), who hung himself on the tree Yggdrasill for nine[15] days and nights as

---

[11] Literally, "Óðinn's (Odin's) horse"; Óðinn hung himself in its branches for nine days to receive universal wisdom; cf. below.

[12] Transl. Larrington 2014; cf. Orchard 2011. *Urðar brunnr* (Urd's well) is said by Snorri to lie under one of the three roots of Yggdrasill, but as Old Norse *urðr* means "fate", *Urðar brunnr* can also be translated as "the well of fate". *Urðr*, one of the three norns, is almost always mentioned in association with the well.

[13] Larrington 2014: 4 ff.; Orchard 2011: 57.; cf. Witzel 2012: 109n28. Linguistically, Ymir = Old Indian (Vedic) Yama, the brother of Manu, ancestor of all humans; see Witzel 2012: 119, n. 115; cf. Thompson 1993: Motifs A961.4. Mountains spring from scattered parts of slain giant serpent's body, India; A961.5. Mountains (cliffs) from bones of killed giant, Iceland.

[14] For the description of the "canonical creature" visible in this myth, in sorcery (Merseburg sorcery stanzas, Atharvaveda, etc.) and also elsewhere, see Watkins 1995. For the Indo-European narrative structure of the sorcery stanzas, see Thieme 1971: 202–12: a mythological narration or poem is followed by the actual spell; details in Witzel 1987.

[15] Nine is the typical number of North Asian shamanism, although some have compared Óðinn's self-sacrifice with that of Christ, which was well known in Iceland by then.

an offering *by himself to himself*. This again has a Vedic parallel, in that "the gods offered the sacrifice with the sacrifice" (RV 1.164.50, cf. 10.90.16, above).[16]

Descent of Ymir/Yama

A short excursus should be added here: in Norse myth, Ymir is one of the primordial beings, and the father of the giants (*Prose Edda*) and contemporaneous with Óðinn and his brothers, thus deities of the current era.

The ancestry of Ymir's linguistic counterpart in India and Iran, Yama/Yima, however differs. Indo-Iranian **Yama* means "twin" and indeed he has a twin sister, Yamī. In the Ṛgveda, Yamī tries to seduce Yima to produce children, but he refuses. In Iran, however, brother-sister incest (*Avestan, xvaētuuadaθa*) was sanctioned and common down to the Arab conquest in 650 CE. In India, thus, early humans had to be created in another fashion.

Another brother of Yama, Manu, became the ancestor of humans (just as Tacitus' Mannus is for the western Germanic tribes). As no other female but his sister Yamī was around then, Manu had to fashion his wife out of clarified butter (*ghee*). As the myth says, when she walks you still can see butter in her footsteps. Subsequently, Yama becomes the king of the netherworld and departed humans, while his Iranian counterpart, Yima, is killed (sawn into two!) by his brother Spitiiura.

Here we notice the typical repositioning of certain mythological persons up and down on the family tree: Manu and Yama are descendants of the sun deity, Vivasvant (Mārtāṇḍa), belonging to the 4th ("Olympian") generation of gods, while Ymir has an undetermined, earlier and independent origin, while interacting with one god of the current generation of deities, Óðinn, before the emergence of humans (from Askr and Embla).[17]

Nuristani and Mediterranean Reminiscences

There are a number of local South Asian reminiscences of this myth, for example, in Nuristan (Kafiristan) in Northeastern Afghanistan and in neighboring Kashmir.[18]

---

[16] For other Indo-European parallels (Russian, Greek, etc.), see Lincoln 1986: 1 ff.

[17] Tree origin would be another one of Dumézil's "bizarreries". The origin of humans from trees is otherwise very rare and mostly restricted to the "southern" (*Gondwana*) mythologies of sub-Saharan Africa (Baumann 1936) and Sahul Land (New Guinea-Australia); see Witzel 2012: 335 f.

[18] Thompson 1993: Motifs A642.1. Primeval woman cut in pieces: houses, etc., made from her body, India; A1724.1; A1724.1. Animals from body of slain person, India; however, note A969.1. Mountain from buried giant, India; A1716.1. cf. also the initial section of the Finnish Kalevala (Witzel 2004).

In Kashmir, a giant Rākṣasa demon was killed, and an embankment was built from his remnants on the Vitastā (Jhelum) River using his leg and knee.[19] It is called *setu* "dam", the modern Suth area at Srinagar (see Witzel 2012: 476n108).

The Nuristani (Kafiri) myth is more elaborate than the brief references from medieval Kashmir.

> A demon (Espereg-era) brings sun and moon into his house. The god Mandi changes into a boy, and eventually he breaks the door. He puts the Sun on his right shoulder, the Moon on his left, and rides out of the house. The dark world becomes bright. Espereg-era follows them, but Mandi cuts off all his seven heads, drags him to the right side of the valley and covers him up.[20]

In Rome, the mythical founder figure Romulus' kills his brother Remus < Proto-Indo-European *Yemo-s, representing the Indian Yama and Old Iranian Yima.[21] Like Remus, Yima is killed by his brother Spitiiura.[22]

In the Hebrew Bible, the myth of Cain and Abel may be compared, though occurring in a different context, that of offerings to Jehovah. Abel was a shepherd, Cain a farmer; Jehovah preferred the animal sacrifice, hence Cain killed his rival brother Abel (Genesis 4).

A similar contest is seen between Jacob and Esau (Genesis 25). Esau was a skillful hunter, while Jacob "dwelt in tents", apparently as a herder. Once, coming home rather hungry, Esau asked Jacob to feed him but the latter agreed only if Esau handed him his birthright as firstborn, which was what occurred.

A similar myth is found in Japan, however, again without the lethal outcome of the clash between Cain and Abel. The contest between the divine elder Ho-wori and the younger Ho-deri (Kojiki 1.42) does not lead to killing.[23] Their father, the primordial deity Ninigi, gave Ho-deri a magic hook for fishing and his brother Ho-wori a magic bow for hunting. Ho-deri became jealous of Ho-wori's success in hunting and proposed to exchange the paternal gifts, which was done. Both were unsuccessful in their new pursuits and Ho-wori even lost the magic hook. When Ho-deri asked his hook to be returned, it could not be found. The angry Ho-deri threatened to kill his brother. Ho-wori fled to the ocean deity's palace

---

[19] See Stein, *Rājataraṅgiṇī* 3.336–58, cf. 1.159, for Yakṣa dikes.

[20] See Witzel 2004, based on accounts of G. Buddruss (field work 1955–1956, 2002) and Jettmar (1986).

[21] See Dumézil 1995: 289 ff.; Puhvel 1987: 287–89.

[22] Apparently Yama and Yima had committed some evil action. Yama became the Lord of the Netherworld and the dead and Yima that of a similar underworld palace (Vara).

[23] Philippi 1968: 148 compares the tale to others in Indonesia, the Marshall Islands, and the American Pacific Northwest.

under the sea, married his daughter, got the hook back and then returned home, where Ho-deri attacked him; however, Ho-wori finally forgave him.

One may also compare the ancient Mesopotamian creation of man from mud and blood. According to the *Enuma Elish*, the gods decided that one of them, Kingu, was to be killed so that humans could be created. Marduk killed Kingu, mixed his blood with clay and formed the first humans. Like Yima and Yama, Kingu then lived in the Netherworld.[24]

Pangu

The myth of a primordial giant is also found in what is now Southern China, from where it has entered the standard Old Chinese texts (late first millennium BCE). It thus originally was not a Han but an Austric or Austro-Thai myth.[25] The primordial giant Pangu was cut up in a fashion similar to Ymir and Puruṣa.[26]

The first version quoted here has close similarities with the Tahiti myth of Ta'aroa (see below), which is not surprising, given that both the Austro-Thai and Austronesian language families originated in what is now Southern China.

1. First there was the great cosmic egg.[27] Inside the egg was Chaos, and floating in Chaos was P'an ku, the undeveloped, the divine embryo. And P'an ku burst out of the egg [...] with an adze in his hand with which he fashioned the world [...] He chiseled the land and sky apart. He pulled up the mountains on the earth and dug the valleys deep, and made courses for the rivers. High above ride the sun and moon and stars in the sky where P'an ku placed them; below roll the four seas [...][28]

2. The world was never finished until P'an ku died [...] [F]rom his skull was shaped the dome of the sky, and from his flesh was formed the soil of the fields; from his bones came the rocks, from his blood the rivers and seas; from his hair came all vegetation. His breath was the wind; his voice made thunder; his right eye became the moon, his

---

[24] Jacobsen 1976: 181.

[25] Austro-Tai is a hypothetical S.E. Asian language family that, other than Austric (see above n. 2), includes Austronesian and the Tai-Kadai languages (such as Thai, Shan, etc.). Benedict 1990 even wants to include (what at best can be called a substrate of) Japanese. For the myth see Mathieu 1989.

[26] See Münke 1976: 254 f.; Yang and An 2005: 75, 176 ff.

[27] Note another translation of a similar text dating from the third century CE, taken from San Wu li chi ("Three kings and five emperors") by Hsü Chen, in Mair 1998: 14; cf. Yang and An 2005: 65.

[28] Note the concept of four real oceans, situated in the four cardinal directions; all four could, of course, not have been known at the time of the composition of this myth. Cf. the "eastern, western, and northern(!) sea" in landlocked Vedic India (Atharvaveda 11.5.6).

left eye the sun.[29] From his saliva or sweat came rain. And from the vermin which covered his body came forth mankind.[30]

Austronesian Polynesia

Far away from the Indo-Europeans and China, the Polynesians—a seafaring Austric people whose ancestors, ultimately, had emerged from Southern China around 4000 BCE[31] —speak of primordial emptiness and darkness. In the Maori version (New Zealand), negation or nothingness (*kore*) gives birth to chaos or darkness (*po*), and this, to *rangi* (heaven or sky).[32]

Another version, involving the primordial deity, Io,[33] has the following account:

> Io dwelt within the breathing space of immensity.
> The Universe was in darkness, with water everywhere.
> There was no glimmer of dawn, no clearness, no light.
> And he began by saying these words—
> That he might cease remaining inactive:
> "Darkness become a light-possessing darkness".
> And at once light appeared [...][34]
> Then (he) looked to the waters which compassed him about,
>   and spake a fourth time, saying:
> "The waters of *Tai-kama*, be ye separate.

---

[29] Note that Pangu's left eye became the sun, and his right eye, the moon. (One would expect the opposite as the right side / hand is usually preferred). In Japan, too, the sun deity originated from the left eye of Izanagi; cf. Naumann 1988: 65.

[30] Sproul 1991: 201–2 (retold from Mackenzie 1925: 260 f., 247 f.); for a similar text by Hsü Cheng, *Wu yün li-nien chi* ("A chronicle of five cycles of time"), see Mair 1998: 15. Cf. also Mathieu 1989 for similar versions from the *Yiwen leiju* and *Yishi*, both referring back to the *Sanwu liji* of the third century BCE.

[31] For connections between Indian myths and those of Austric and some East Asian populations, see Sergent 1997: 369–96; for a brief linguistic overview of these areas, including putative homelands, see van Driem 2006.

[32] See Tregear 1969: 391. Note that the Pueblo-area myth of the Zuni Amerindians is quite similar, also as regards the separation of Father Heaven and Mother Earth; see Eliade 1992: 130 ff.

[33] Io as primordial deity has been controversially discussed, see J. Z. Smith 1982 who believes that Io has been invented at the end of the nineteenth century under missionary influence; however, it is typical that esoteric deities are known only to small groups of priests. (Note early Japan for the primordial pair Kamurogi/Kamuromi that appears not even in the official, imperial Kojiki myths but only in some archaic Shintō prayers). Cf. the discussion in Witzel 2012: 126–27; 131n213.

[34] Cf. the Biblical and Maya myths, but note the old poetical style of this passage which excludes missionary influences. Stress on various types of darkness is also found in Maori myths; see Witzel 2012: 109 ff.

Heaven be formed". Then the sky became suspended.

"Bring forth thou *Tupua-horo-nuku*".

And at once the moving earth lay stretched abroad.[35]

In still another version, the Tahiti creator god is Ta'aroa (Maori *Tangaroa, Takaroa*; Hawai'ian *Kanaloa*).[36]

> Ta'aroa [...] was his own parent, having no father or mother [...] Ta'aroa sat in his shell (*pa'a*) in darkness (*te po*) for [...] ages [...] The shell was like an egg revolving in endless space, with no sky, no land, no sea, no moons, no sun, no stars. All was darkness [...]

> But at last Ta'aroa [...] caused a crack [...] Then he slipped out and stood upon his shell [...] he took his new shell for the great foundation of the world, [...] And the shell [...] that he opened first, became his house, the dome of the god's sky, [...] enclosing the world (*ao*) then forming [...]

Related are the (Austric) Borneo and Filipino myths of the origin of animals from different parts of the body of a slain giant.[37]

In Japan, whose ancient myths (in the Kojiki, Nihon Shoki) mostly relate to those of the neighboring steppe areas of Asia, dismemberment is not a feature of primordial creation, but it occurs after the violent death of the primordial goddess Izanami. She was severely burned while giving birth to the fire god Hi.no yagi-haya-wo.no kami (Kojiki 1.7).[38] From her dead body were created the eight thunders.[39] Her consort, Izanagi, then killed the fire god and from

---

[35] Translation from Sproul 1991: 345, quoting Hare Hongi's *A Maori Cosmology*. Hare Hongi was a prominent Maori priest at the turn of the 20th century (accused by Z. J. Smith of myth forgery; see above n. 33).

[36] This version was reliably recorded twice between 1848 and 1922; Eliade 1992: 88; cf. Sproul 1991: 249 ff.

[37] Thompson 1993: Motif A1716.1. Animals from different parts of body of slain giant. Giant person, cow, ox, etc., Borneo, Philippines: Dixon 177.

[38] In the Veda, Mātariśvan "swelling inside the mother", is a secret name of the fire deity, Agni. Note that Agni is born three times: in heaven, on earth (in ritual), and in the waters, Ṛgveda 3.20.11, 10.45.1; (sometimes he also is found *garbho rodasyoḥ*, "in the earth"). There are several fire gods in Japan: the one mentioned above and then others born from the decaying body of Izanami. The first fire god is killed by Izanagi in revenge for burning her (cf. Agni's repeated death, explained in Vedic texts as burning up in ritual). Izanami's burn injuries and subsequent death could then reflect the ritual production of fire by drilling it (as is still done at important Shintō and Vedic rituals).

[39] This is somewhat reminiscent, as Japanese mythologists have pointed out, of the myth of Hainuwele, "Coconut branch", (in Ceram, New Guinea); cf. Eliade 1992: 18. This myth has been studied in detail by Jensen 1979, no. 11 sqq, 1948: 113 f.: Hainuwele had grown from a coconut tree, furthered by the blood from the wound of a man, and quickly grew into a woman; she was killed by local people during the great *maro* festival (cf. Campbell 1989: II.1: 70 ff.) and buried in

his blood various deities were created. This constitutes a general trend that is continued by the creation of many other deities from the various polluted parts of the dress and body of Izanagi, at the great purification carried out upon his return from the Netherworld where he went, Orpheus-like, to meet his departed wife Izanami.

Differing, however, from the other Eurasian myths, the various parts of Izanami's or Izanagi's body do not become parts of the universe. In fact, most of the constituent parts of the universe, in particular, all the islands of Japan, as well as many deities of the sea, the waters and rivers, the wind, the mountains, the plains, the land, and so on, had already been born by Izanami.

Connections between India and South China?

The Puruṣa myth of old India clearly has Indo-European connections in Iceland and Anatolia (see below) and some other reminiscences,[40] however, the Sino-Indian connection may have been reinforced in India by a corridor linking Austric myths in Southwestern China and Northern India, between Yunnan and Assam. There are some indications of an old link between the two areas,[41] long before the rather difficultly passed "southern Silk Road" (from Yunnan to Assam) was established.

Indeed, both areas share a number of myths such as that of the turtle supporting the earth, or the origin of certain types of human beings (Ṛṣi Vātaraśana) from a gourd, found only in the late Vedic Taittirīya Āraṇyaka 2; or epic heroes and Chinese "emperors" who have been born from gourds (or eggs, as also with the Munda people of Eastern India).[42]

It is interesting to note that such similarities, except for Puruṣa/Pangu, are *not* found in the oldest Indian texts but first come up only in a late layer of the Vedas, and subsequently in Epic and Puranic texts: they "bubble" up from the local substrate and get officially accepted only after many centuries.

The similarity between Southern Chinese (Austric) and Indian myths may have been due to an old substrate underlying the myths of both areas.[43]

While this is an interesting line of speculation that would have to be substantiated by future research, I must leave it at that here.

---

pieces; from her several graves grew various plants, especially tubers. Her arms were made into a gate: all men who could pass through it remained human; those who could not, became various animals or spirits.

[40] Cf. also above on Rome (Remus).

[41] See Sergent 1997.

[42] Cf. also Sergent 1997. For more on the gourd origins of Mahābhārata heroes see Berger 1959.

[43] Cf. Sergent 1997, Witzel 2012: 230.

Hittite and East Asian Tales of Rocks

The hypothetical Austric/South Chinese connections of Indian myth are, however, balanced by another version of the tale of the primordial giant that is found in Hittite, and thus Indo-European texts of roughly the same time as the Ṛgveda, actually a few hundred years before its composition. Yet, as so much in Hittite myth and ritual, the tale goes back to previous Hatti and Hurrite texts.[44]

The Hittite myth is a somewhat aberrant version in which Ullikummi stands on a primordial giant of stone, Upelluri.[45] It may be compared to the Austronesian story (Taiwan, Polynesia) of a preexisting rock,[46] from which humans frequently emerge.

In Japan, the large rock pillar at Shingu (Kii Peninsula), now representing the primordial god Izanagi, is worshipped rather than the deities in the adjacent Shintō shrine.[47]

Note also that in Chinese myth, Yü, the first king of the early Hsia dynasty, was born from his father, Kun, who had turned into stone. This occurred after his execution by the High God, because he had stolen the magic "swelling mold", by which one could build dams to stem the primordial flood (covering Northern China). Yü was born when his father's belly was cut open after three years.[48] Similarly, Ch'i, the son of this legendary first Hsia king, was also born from a rock: his mother, Tu Shan, had changed into a rock when she was frightened by her husband, Kun, who had changed into a bear.[49]

Conclusion

Hypothetical connections between Southwest China and North India apart, we have widely scattered evidence of the myth of a primordial giant, whether it

---

[44] The Hatti were a pre-existing local population in the Hittite realm, from which the Hittites took over many myths and rituals: some of them are transmitted in Hatti language in Hittite documents. The Hurrites originally stemmed from the Caucasus area, and are related to the Urartu people; they became the southern neighbors of the Hittites in Northern Syria/Iraq and influenced them as well.

[45] Colarusso 2006: 32; Gurney 1976: 192; Haas 1982; Puhvel 1987: 25 f.

[46] Personal observation in Austronesian T'aitung, Taiwan 2005. See Thompson 1993, Motif A644. Universe from pre-existing rocks. Originally rocks are assumed, and everything is made from them. Samoa: Dixon 17.

[47] Personal observation, February 1990. On the other side of the valley there is another rock, with a vulva-like cavity; it represents Izanagi's wife, Izanami.

[48] Chang 1983: 10, and Bodde 1961: 399.

[49] Chang 1983: 10. Note the role of the bear as ultimate ancestor in Korean myth, at the mythical time of c. 2500 BCE, described in *Samguk Yusa*.

was locally conceived as made of stone (Anatolia/Caucasus) or emerging from chaos (Ymir, Puruṣa) or from a primordial egg (Polynesia/China).

Taking all the evidence together and tracing it back to the area of origin of the populations and languages involved, we get:

- Indo-European area (Ymir, Puruṣa): steppe belt, probably in the Pontic area north of the Black Sea, c. 3000–4000 BCE[50]

- Anatolia and Hurrite: neighboring Caucasus area c. 2000 BCE

- Chinese: with southern non-Han minorities, attested only in the later 1st millennium BCE

- Southeast Asia/Polynesia: emerging from Taiwan and neighboring (non-Han) mainland China, c. 4000 BCE.

In sum, we have two old foci that are distant from each other by thousands of miles and a few thousand years: one in the western steppe/Caucasus belt and one in what is now South China. The two are not directly connected (forgetting about Heine-Geldern's great Pontic migration),[51] and must go back to a much older pre-horticultural origin, in short, to a Paleolithic pattern.

In sum, there is fairly widespread evidence for an archaic Eurasian myth that entailed the origin of the world from a preexisting giant, sometimes made of stone. The carving up of the primordial giant may represent a very old stage of (Laurasian) mythology,[52] going back to the times of Stone Age hunters.[53] The giant would then be a reflection of the hunted or killed animals that were carved up in a similar way, one that could be seen until recently in the Northern European (Saami), North Asian, and Ainu bear sacrifice.[54] The bones of such animals must not be cut or cracked and were preserved intact (like Þórr's [Thor's] ram) as to allow their rebirth (in heaven or in this world).[55]

---

[50] See now D. Anthony and D. Ringe 2015.

[51] Heine-Geldern 1951.

[52] For the terms, see above and Witzel 2012: 4–5, and *passim*.

[53] There even is a slight chance that the myth may already have been a Neanderthal one (if they had speech, as it seems possible now): bear offerings, head separated, are widely found (though some have been explained as accidental, due to flooding in caves); for illustrations, see Campbell 1988: I.1: 54 ff. Also, a Stone Age bear figure, with head still attached, has been found at Montespan (Campbell 1988: I.1: 62), as well as a bear skull, clearly in an early Homo Sapiens context, on an "altar" in the undisturbed Chauvet Cave (Southwest France) that is to be dated at 32,000 years ago.

[54] See the pictorial evidence in Campbell 1988: I.2: 152 ff.; cf. Ōbayashi and Klaproth 1966 for Sakhalin Island.

[55] For the Vedic customs, see Witzel 1987; cf. the tale of Þórr's ram whose body is reconstituted from his bones, and similarly the role of *astuuant* (bone having [life]) in Zoroastrian texts (Avesta). Note also the Achaemenid-period rebirth of humans from their graves referred to in the Hebrew Bible (Daniel 12.2). See further Thompson 1993, Motifs A1724.1. Animals from body of slain

While the Germanic and Vedic myths of Ymir and Puruṣa may thus go back to Proto-Indo-European mythology,[56] the Austric, Austronesian, Polynesian, and Hittite versions represent other traditions.

These myths were, however, no longer told by ancient hunters and gatherers, but by members of the subsequent food-producing societies.[57] In sum, they are reminiscences of a much earlier stage of culture—and of mythology. Thus, they are fairly isolated and "bizarre" in the respective mythologies of the Indo-Europeans and East Asians.

Works Cited

Primary Sources

Grímnismál: see *Poetic Edda*

Poetic Edda
Edda: Die Lieder des Codex regius nebst verwandten Denkmälern. 5th rev. ed. Ed. Gustav Neckel and Hans Kuhn. Germanische Bibliothek. Heidelberg: 1983.

TRANSLATION
The Poetic Edda. Transl. Carolyne Larrington. 2nd ed. Oxford World's Classics. Oxford: 2014.

Snorra Edda
Snorri Sturluson. *Edda. Prologue and Gylfaginning.* 2nd ed. Ed. Anthony Faulkes. London: 2005.

TRANSLATION
Snorri Sturluson. *Edda.* Transl. Anthony Faulkes. London: 1995.

Vǫluspá: see *Poetic Edda*

---

person, India; A2001. Insects from body of slain monster; A2611.3. Coconut tree from head of slain monster; E610. Reincarnation as animal; E613.0.5. Severed heads of monster become birds. In general, for animal killing in hunting and later societies, see Burkert 1983 [1972], 2001.

[56] Thompson 1993: Motifs A642. Universe from body of slain giant. Ymir; see A621.1. Iceland; A831.2. Earth from giant's body (Ymir [cf. A614.1]), Iceland, India.

[57] Being older than food producing societies, however, they do *not* represent archaic horticultural/agricultural mythology (going back some 8–10,000 years), such as seen in the Melanesian Hainuwele myth; see Hatt 1951; Jensen 1968; cf. Lincoln 1986: 173n1.

Secondary Sources

Anthony, David, and Don Ringe. 2015. "The Indo-European Homeland from Linguistic and Archaeological Perspectives." *Annual Review of Linguistics* 1: 199–219. http://www.annualreviews.org/journal/linguistics. (last accessed February 21, 2016)

Aston, William G. 1972. *Nihongi: Chronicles of Japan from the Earliest Times to A.D. 697*. Rutland. Orig. pub. 1896.

Barrett, T. H. 1995. "Comparison and Chinese Mythology." *Cosmos* 11: 69–78.

Baumann, Hermann. 1986. *Das doppelte Geschlecht*. Berlin. Orig. pub. 1955.

Benedict, Paul K. 1990. *Japanese/Austro-Tai*. Ann Arbor.

Benveniste, Emile. 1969. *Le vocabulaire des institutions indo-européennes. 1. Economie, parenté, société*. Paris.

Berger, Hermann. 1959. "Deutung einiger alter Stammesnamen der Bhil aus der vorarischen Mythologie des Epos und der Purāṇa." *Wiener Zeitschrift zur Kunde Süd- und Ostasiens* 3: 34–82.

Birrell, Anne. 1993. *Chinese Mythology: An Introduction*. Baltimore.

Bodde, Derk. 1961. "Myths of Ancient China." In *Mythologies of the Ancient World*. Ed. Samuel N. Kramer. New York. Pp. 367-408.

Burkert, Walter. 1983. *Homo Necans. Structure and History in Greek Mythology and Ritual*. Berkeley. Orig. pub. 1972.

———. 2001. "Shamans, Caves, and the Master of Animals." In *Shamans through Time: 500 Years on the Path to Knowledge*. Ed. J. Narby and F. Huxley. London. Pp. 223-26.

Campbell, Joseph. 1988. *The Way of the Seeded Earth. Part 2. Mythologies of the Primitive Planters: The Northern Americas*. New York.

———. 1989. *The Way of the Seeded Earth. Part 3. Mythologies of the Primitive Planters: The Middle and Southern Americas*. New York.

Chang, Kwang-chih. 1983. *Art, Myth and Ritual. The Path to Political Authority in Ancient China*. Cambridge, MA.

Colarusso, John. 2006. "The Functions Revisited. A Nart God of War and Three Nart Heroes." *Journal of Indo-European Studies* 34: 27–54.

Dixon, Roland. 1964. *Oceanic Mythology*. Ed. Louis Herbert Gray and George Foot Moore. The Mythology of All Races, 9. New York. Orig. pub. 1916–1932.

Dumézil, Georges. 1934. *Ouranos-Váruṇa*. Paris.

———. 1939. *Mythes et dieux des Germains: Essai d'interprétation comparative*. Paris. Repr. 1959. *Les dieux des Germains: Essai sur la formation de la religion scandinave*. Paris.

———. 1995. *Mythe et Epopée*. 3 vols. Paris. Orig. pub. 1968–1973.

Eliade, Mircea. 1977. *From Primitives to Zen.* New York. [= *Essential Sacred Writings from around the World.* San Francisco: 1992].

Gurney, Oliver R. 1976. *The Hittites.* Harmondsworth. Orig pub. 1952.

Haas, Volkert. 1982. *Hethitische Berggötter und hurritische Steindämonen: Riten, Kulte und Mythen: eine Einführung in die altkleinasiatischen religiösen Vorstellungen.* Mainz.

————. 1994. "Das Pferd in der hethitischen religiösen Überlieferung." In *Die Indogermanen und das Pferd. Festschrift für Bernfried Schlerath. Akten des Internationalen interdisziplinären Kolloquiums, Freie Universität Berlin, 1.-3. Juli 1992.* Ed. B. Hänsel et al. Budapest. Pp. 77–90.

Hatt, Gudmund. 1951. "The Corn Mother in America and Indonesia." *Anthropos* 46: 853–914.

Heine-Geldern, Robert. 1951. "Das Tocharerproblem und die pontische Wanderung." *Saeculum* 2: 225–55.

Hu, Chongjun. 2002. *The Story of Darkness* [in Chinese]. Wuhan.

Jacobsen, Thorkild. 1976. *The Treasures of Darkness: A History of Mesopotamian Religion.* New Haven.

Jensen, Adolf E. 1939. *Hainuwele.* Frankfurt [Engl. trans. New York, 1978].

————. 1948. *Die drei Ströme.* Leipzig.

Kuiper, F. B. J. 1978. *Varuṇa and Vidūṣaka: On the Origin of the Sanskrit Drama.* Amsterdam.

Lincoln, Bruce. 1986. *Myth, Cosmos, and Society.* Cambridge, MA.

Mackenzie, Donald A. 1925. *Myths of China and Japan.* London.

Mair, Victor. 1998. *The Bronze Age and Early Iron Age Peoples of Eastern Central Asia.* 2 vols. Ed. Victor Mair. Journal of Indo-European Studies Monograph, 26. Washington & Philadephia.

Mathieu, R. 1989. *Anthologie des mythes et légendes de la Chine ancienne.* Paris.

Münke, Wolfgang. 1976. *Die klassische chinesische Mythologie.* Stuttgart.

Naumann. Nelly. 1988. *Die einheimische Religion Japans. Teil 1. Bis zum Ende der Heian-Zeit.* Leiden.

Ōbayashi, T., and H.-J. R. Klaproth. 1966. "Das Bärenfest der Oroken auf Sachalin." *Zeitschrift für Ethnologie* 91: 211–36.

Orchard, Andrew. 2011. *The Elder Edda. A Book of Viking Lore. Translated with Introduction and Notes by Andy Orchard.* London.

Patton, Kimberley C. 2009. *Religion of the Gods: Ritual, Paradox, and Reflexivity.* Oxford.

Philippi, Donald L. 1968. *Kojiki. Translated with an Introduction and Notes.* Tokyo.

Puhvel, Jan. 1987. *Comparative Mythology.* Baltimore.

Sergent, Bernard. 1997. *Genèse de l'Inde.* Paris.

Smith, Jonathan Z. 1982. *Imagining Religion: From Babylon to Jonestown.* Chicago.

Sproul, Barbara C. 1991. *Primal Myths: Creation Myths around the World*. San Francisco.

Stein, M. Aurel. 1900. *Kalhaṇa's Rājataraṅgiṇī*. Westminster.

Thieme, Paul. 1971. *Kleine Schriften*. Wiesbaden.

Thompson, Stith. 1932–1936. *Motif-Index of Folk-Literature: A Classification of Narrative Elements in Folktales, Ballads, Myths, Fables, Mediaeval Romances, Exempla, Fabliaux, Jest-Books and Local Legends*. Bloomington, IN. [2nd ed. 1966; computer file, Blomington: Indiana University Press/Clayton: InteLex corp. 1993].

Tregear, Edward. 1969. *The Maori-Polynesian Comparative Dictionary*. Oosterhout. Orig. pub. 1891.

van Driem, George. 2006. "The Prehistory of Tibeto-Burmese in the Light of Emergent Population Genetic Studies." *Mother Tongue* 11: 160–211.

Watkins, Calvert. 1995. *How to Kill a Dragon: Aspects of Indo-European Poetics*. New York.

Witzel, Michael. 1987. "The Case of the Shattered Head." In *Festschrift für W. Rau, Studien zur Indologie und Iranistik 13/14*. Reinbek. Pp. 363–415.

———. 2004. "The Ṛgvedic Religious System and its Central Asian and Hindukush Antecedents." In *The Vedas: Texts, Language and Ritual*. Ed. A. Griffiths and J. E. M. Houben. Groningen. Pp. 581–636.

———. 2012. *The Origins of the World's Mythologies*. New York.

Yang, Lihui, and Deming An, with J. A. Turner. 2005. *Handbook of Chinese Mythology*. Santa Barbara.

Index

CPSIA information can be obtained
at www.ICGtesting.com
Printed in the USA
JSHW070920260223
38183JS00002B/2